EMMA
GOLDMAN
IN
EXILE

Alice Wexler

EMMA GOLDMAN IN EXILE

From the
Russian Revolution
to the
Spanish Civil War

BEACON PRESS

Boston

Beacon Press
25 Beacon Street
Boston, Massachusetts 02108

Beacon Press books
are published under the auspices of
the Unitarian Universalist Association of Congregations.

Selections from the following volumes have been
reprinted by permission of the publishers:
Anna Akhmatova, *A Poem without Words,* trans.
Carl R. Proffer with Assya Humesky (Ann Arbor:
Ardis Publishers, 1973); Roque Dalton,
Clandestinos/Clandestine Poems (San Francisco:
Solidarity Educational Publications, 1986).

89 90 91 92 93 94 95 96   2 3 4 5 6 7 8

Text design by Molly Renda

Library of Congress Cataloging-in-Publication Data
Wexler, Alice
Emma Goldman in exile : from the Russian Revolution to the Spanish
Civil War / Alice Wexler.
p. cm.
Includes index.
ISBN 0-8070-7004-1
1. Goldman, Emma, 1869–1940. 2. Anarchists—United States—
Biography. I. Title.
HX843.7.G65W49 1989
335'.83'0924—dc19
[B]   88-43317

for my father

Milton Wexler

The white nights pass over you.
But the happy words "at home"
Are not known to anyone now,
Everyone is looking in someone else's window.
Some in Tashkent, some in New York,
And the bitter air of exile
Is like a poisoned wine.

—Anna Akhmatova

Contents

List of Illustrations.   xi

Acknowledgments.   xiii

Introduction.   1

PART ONE: Ruptures

1 The Sailing of the *Buford*.   9

2 Stranger in a Strange Land.   21

3 Russia as (M)other.   57

4 Anti-Soviet Campaigns.   92

5 Hearts in Unison with Mine.   114

PART TWO: Recoveries

6 Writing a Life.   131

7 My Hungry Heart.   157

PART THREE: Beginnings and Endings

8 The Death of Alexander Berkman.   181

9 Spain and the World.   196

10 Last Exile.   234

Abbreviations.   247

Notes.   249

Index.   291

List of Illustrations

Illustrations follow page 176

Emma Goldman and Alexander Berkman

Flyer for Emma Goldman lecture

Mollie Steimer

Emma Goldman in St. Tropez

Alexander Berkman and Rudolf Rocker

Alexander Berkman and Emmy Eckstein

Max Nettlau

Emma Goldman arriving at Penn Station

Emma Goldman with Stella Ballantine

Emma Goldman at the City Club, Rochester, New York

Emma Goldman's "home" in Toronto

Emma Goldman, Senya Flechine, Modest Stein ("Fedya"), and Alexander Berkman

Emma Goldman with comrades of the CNT-FAI, Albalate de Cinca, Aragon, Spain

Emma Goldman visiting an agricultural collective, Spain 1936

Anniversary of the Russian Revolution, November 1936, in Barcelona

Acknowledgments

Many comrades and relatives of Emma Goldman, and also their children, have generously shared memories and sketched an anarchist geography of the world as she knew it in the 1920s and 1930s. Over the years, Federico Arcos sent me a virtual library of important anarchist materials, including papers from his personal archives. Ahrne Thorne, last editor of the *Fraye Arbeter Stimme,* illuminated many strands of anarchist tradition with his wit and wisdom. I also wish to thank Pura Arcos, Arturo Bortolotti, Sam and Esther Dolgoff, Eva Langbord, Arthur Lehning, Clara Larson, Dan and Bertha Malmed, Vernon Richards, Fermin and Dorothy Rocker, and Paula Thorne for their invaluable assistance. Hilda Adel, Charles Glasser, Jim Huggon, Albert Meltzer, William Mendelsohn, Mollie Steimer, and Clara and Sidney Solomon also offered aid and information.

Many of these people I met through Paul Avrich, whose assistance I deeply appreciate. Richard Drinnon has offered support and encouragement from the beginning of my work on Goldman. Martha Ackelsberg, Arch Getty, Douglas Little, and Irwin Wall generously helped negotiate the European contexts of Goldman's life and read parts of a very long manuscript. José Peirats patiently answered questions about Spain, as did Kenneth Barkin about Germany. Sandra Schickele and Sarah Stage offered incisive readings of the entire manuscript in various stages and helped shape my thinking about Goldman in other ways as well. Carole Fabricant and Brian Finney raised important questions about Goldman's use of the autobiographical genre. Robert d'Attillio, Georg Gugelberger, Harry Lawton, Blaine McKinley, and Jeff Schneider helped with information and translations. Conversations with Rise Axelrod, Steven Axelrod, Michael Balter, Jane Burbank, Marc Cooper, Dorothy Gallagher, Herb Pardes, Karen Rosenberg, Robert Rosenstone, David Schickele, Ada Schmidt, Kay Trimberger, Nancy Wexler, Milton Wexler, and members of the UCLA Women's History Teaching Workshop also influenced my thinking. A fellowship and a summer stipend from the National Endowment for the Humanities supported part of the research and writing. A dialogue with Helena Mueller, begun in Amsterdam and carried on in letters between Riverside and Rio de Janeiro, continues in this book.

Many librarians and archivists have steered me through Emma Goldman's papers, and have granted permission to quote from their collections. At the International Institute of Social History in Amsterdam, Heiner Becker, himself a historian and scholar of anarchism, tracked documents from the vast archives of the Institute and from his personal collection. His insights and arguments have been critical to this work as were those of Rudolph de Jong, also a scholar and historian, who shared his knowledge of Spanish anarchism. Mieke Yzermans helped with photographs and with many other things; her assistance and hospitality, as well as that of Thea Duijker and Kees Rodenberg turned work into pleasure. I am grateful also to Jaap Kloosterman, Maria Hunink, and W. H. van der Linden for their help. I wish to thank Dorothy Swanson and Mary Allison at the Tamiment Library of New York University; Edward Weber of the Labadie Collection, University of Michigan Library; Hilda Kukk at the Hoover Institution, Stanford University; Patricia King and Eva Moseley at the Schlesinger Library, Radcliffe College; J. Dane Hartgrove at the National Archives; David Wigdor at the Library of Congress; the staffs of the Rare Books and Manuscripts Division, New York Public Library, Astor, Lenox and Tilden Foundations; the Yivo Institute of Jewish Research; the Princeton University Library; the Yale University Library; the Houghton Library at Harvard University and the Harry Ransom Humanities Research Center at the University of Texas, Austin. Librarians at the Tomás Rivera Library of the University of California, Riverside, have been unfailingly helpful; I especially wish to thank Renate Gugelberger, Ruth Halman, Nancy Huling, Judy Lee, and the staff at the Inter-Library Loan Department for their patience and assistance. Ian Ballantine, Emma Goldman's literary executor, graciously gave permission to quote from her papers and manuscripts. Carl Baldwin kindly gave permission to quote from the papers of Roger Baldwin. I am grateful also to Carol Inglis Spicer for permission to quote Agnes Inglis.

A younger generation of anarchists has also influenced this work. In September of 1984 I attended a memorable International Anarchist Gathering in Venice, where over three thousand anarchists and anarchist sympathizers came together from all over the world. The Venice event was organized by the Centro Studi Libertari in Milan, whose leading spirits, Rossella di Leo and Amadeo Bertolo, I had the pleasure of meeting, along with Paolo Finzi and Aurora Failla, and others associated with *Revista A* and *Voluntá*. The following year in Montreal, at a conference of the Anarchos Institute, I also had the good fortune to spend time with Murray Bookchin, Marsha Hewitt, and Dimitri Roussopoulos. I am grateful to all of these people for showing me the vitality of contemporary anarchism and for illuminating the links between the concerns of the older anarchists such as Goldman and radical social movements today. Their arguments have been important to this work, even if they may not agree with my conclusions.

I wish to thank my agent, Frances Goldin, for her warm support and penetrating recommendations. I am also grateful to Wendy Strothman, my editor at Beacon, for her trenchant suggestions and enthusiasm for this project, and to Pam Pokorney, Tom Fischer, and Sharon Yamamoto for their imaginative, incisive input at various stages of this book.

One hundred years ago, Emma Goldman stepped off the Weehawken ferry into a new world of anarchy and love. That city at the edge of the Hudson River also entered my horizons when I met John Ganim, who has indelibly shaped my life ever since. To him I owe my greatest debt, for showing me the view from Weehawken and the worlds that lie far beyond its borders.

Introduction

This book is about the last twenty years of the American anarchist Emma Goldman, who was deported from the United States to Russia at the height of the Red Scare of 1919. For nearly thirty years, she had taunted conservative Americans with her outspoken attacks on government, big business, and war. On her freewheeling coast-to-coast lecture tours she defended everything from free speech to free love, from the rights of striking workers to the rights of homosexuals. Her name became a household word, synonymous with everything subversive and demonic, but also symbolic of the "new woman" and of the radical labor movement that blossomed in the years before World War I. To the public she was America's arch revolutionary, both frightening and fascinating. She flaunted her lovers, talked back to the police, smoked in public, and marched off to prison carrying James Joyce's *Portrait of the Artist* under her arm. The young intellectuals adored her, bohemian artists flocked to her lectures, rebellious women worshipped her, and radical workers considered her their god, though she never joined a union or anything larger than her own small group. She helped raise the social consciousness of thousands of people even if most of them never became anarchists.

This image of Emma Goldman as "the most dangerous woman in America" is central to what has become almost a cult of personality surrounding her since the early 1970s. Many plays have celebrated the drama of her life, an opera portrays her as a latter-day Judith, university courses study her politics, and health centers, magazines, and anarchist groups adopt her name. T-shirts emblazoned with her portrait insist on the importance of dancing in the revolution, and feminists march in brigades under her name. She emerges as a character in E. L. Doctorow's novel *Ragtime,* and in Warren Beatty's movie *Reds,* while the avant-garde filmmaker Yvonne Rainer, daughter of anarchists, quotes her throughout her film

Journeys from Berlin/1971. Her unpublished writings are suddenly in print.[1]

In part, this fascination with Goldman reflects a general upsurge of interest in anarchism since the sixties, with the emergence of a student New Left that was antiauthoritarian and antihierarchical, opposed to the Old Left's bureaucracy and rigidities. In the civil rights movement, the struggle to end the war in Vietnam, and later in the antinuclear and women's movements, libertarian ideas found a new hearing, most dramatically during the revolutionary May Days of 1968 when all of Paris marched in the streets, many of them under the black flag of anarchy. And then Emma Goldman had questioned the authority of men over women, in the anarchist movement as well as outside it. Today she still seems "a woman of the future," as the writer Meridel LeSueur characterized her.

But this image of Goldman is incomplete, for it is based mainly on her career in America before 1920, the period that has attracted the greatest attention. In some respects the most dramatic years of her life were yet to come. After she left the United States in 1919, she was allowed to return only once, for a visit. Yet she continued to make herself heard. For, with her talent for controversy, she again addressed the most pressing issues of her time—the Russian Revolution and Bolshevik regime. As the historian Eric Hobsbawm has written, "the danger of 'Bolshevism' dominates not only the history of the years immediately following the Russian Revolution of 1917, but the entire history of the world since that date."[2] "Bolshevism" also dominated Emma Goldman's life, not only during her years in Soviet Russia, but later on, in England and especially in Spain during the years of the Spanish civil war.

Although Goldman expressed attitudes representative of the international anarchist movement as a whole, her access to the Western mainstream press and her wide contacts outside the movement, especially in America, gave her an influence not shared by her comrades. She went to Russia, moreover, at a critical moment when that country was not yet accessible to the West and news reporting about the revolution was, in the words of Walter Lippmann, "nothing short of a disaster."[3] Her words, therefore, carried considerable authority. She has generally been praised as an early anti-Stalinist for her critique of Soviet Russia's "totalitarianism" in the 1920s. The view presented here is considerably different: that in arguing against one "Bolshevik myth," Emma Goldman helped shape another; in short, that she contributed to the emergence of an anti-

Communist consensus of which the anarchists—and she herself—would become tragic victims.

This book, then, is partly about the origins of anti-Communism in America. It is about how one woman's shattering crisis of identity intersected with a pivotal moment in the history of an epoch, in a dramatic confluence of the personal and the political. It is about the ways in which images of Soviet Russia—and later of revolutionary Spain—were transmitted to the world outside those countries. It is also about the anarchist movement in the years between the two world wars, when anarchism achieved its worst defeat but also its most sublime, if temporary, triumph: the alternative society built up by the Spanish anarchists amid the flames of civil war.

Yet Goldman's significance and interest for us extend beyond the causes to which she devoted her life. As a political exile, she endured dislocations and losses which made her experience emblematic of an entire era. As a single, older woman, she suffered the loneliness and sexual sorrow shared by many women of her generation. She managed, moreover, in her vast outpouring of letters and other writings, to make herself accessible to us as few women in public life, and surely no other women anarchists, have attempted. To use Sartre's term, she made herself "transparent," so that we may see in the conflicting crosscurrents of her character the marks of a history that is also our own.

To understand Goldman's encounter with Soviet Russia, it is essential to grasp the long tradition of hostility between anarchists and Marxists that formed the background to her experience there. Anarchists had been at odds with Marxists even before the First International in the 1860s was torn apart by battles between Michael Bakunin and Karl Marx. Theirs was, in part, a family quarrel, for both anarchists and Marxists proposed to foment revolutions that would overthrow the capitalist order and institute a new socialist society without domination or exploitation. They differed on how to make the revolution, on what that revolution would look like the day after the barricades came down, and, more abstractly, on the basic nature of society and history. While Marxists fought capitalism as the main enemy of the working class, anarchists identified the state, whether capitalist or socialist, as the principal enemy. Instead of capturing the state on behalf of the workers, as Marx proposed, they sought to destroy the state, since only then could the authentic social forms of the people emerge. Opposed to all forms of centralized control, they urged decentralization and local control, with decision making from the bottom up. Beyond the state, the anarchists questioned all forms of authority as expressed in the church, the army, and the patriarchal family, developing alternative institutions such as libertarian schools to help educate people for freedom. Instead of organizing political parties and electing officials to office, they formed small groups or joined large labor organizations in order to infuse them with antiparliamentary, direct action ideals. Anarcho-syndicalists saw the revolutionary labor union as the kernel of the new society, while anarchist communists, followers of Peter Kropotkin, put more emphasis on communes and collectives. Yet Michael Bakunin spoke for them all when he succinctly summed up their effort to synthesize socialism and liberalism: "Liberty without socialism is privilege, injustice; socialism without liberty is slavery and brutality."[4]

At the heart of Emma Goldman's anarchism, however, and that of many other Jewish immigrant anarchists in America, was a powerful ethical vision. Her anarchism was as much a vision of a new moral consciousness, an ideal of tolerance toward difference, as a commitment to fight against capitalism and the state. During her life in America, Goldman achieved her influence as much for her criticism of conventional values, particularly sexual values, as for her defense of labor and the Left. She thought of herself as an educator as well as an agitator and, like many anarchists, placed great emphasis on education by promoting libertarian schools, selling anarchist literature, and always urging her listeners to read, study, and think for themselves: to question received wisdom, even that of the anarchists.

It is one of the many ironies of Emma Goldman's life that the historical record of her career in America is so thin while her quieter years in exile are documented by mountains of letters. In exile, she depended on letters to maintain contact with hundreds of people, including even her closest friend, Alexander Berkman, from whom she was often separated. Those letters and Goldman's other writings draw a portrait of the world viewed from a very particular and, in some ways, problematical angle. Though she thought of herself as a destroyer of fictions, she too was a mythmaker whose most powerful myth turned out to be herself. Yet with all her self-deception, she remains a powerful and compelling figure, who still moves us with her courage and her loneliness. In exile, she seemed to personify the uprootedness of an entire generation of political refugees, yet in an emotional sense she had always been an exile, searching all her life for a home she had never known. That quest acquired a special urgency during the years following her deportation and came to form the central thread of her existence, shaping her fictions and her truths, her limitations and her legacy.

PART ONE

Ruptures

1

The Sailing of the *Buford*

Freedom is always and exclusively freedom for
the one who thinks differently.

—Rosa Luxemburg

New York, Ellis Island. December 20, 1919, late Saturday night. Two hundred forty-nine immigrant radicals imprisoned on the island, including three women, prepared to enter their bunks for the night. For weeks they had been arriving by train, on "Red Specials," from Cleveland, Philadelphia, Buffalo, Baltimore, from as far away as Detroit and Seattle. They were steelworkers from Youngstown and from Pittsburgh, miners from West Virginia, editors of radical newspapers, and lecturers as well as manual laborers. They were Russians, Ukrainians, Letts, Lithuanians, and Tartars, some who had been in the United States for over a decade. The two most famous anarchists among them, Emma Goldman and Alexander Berkman, had lived in the country for over thirty years. Many of the group were members of the anarcho-syndicalist Union of Russian Workers. They had committed no crime except that of disbelief in government.[1] Many had been arrested at their workbenches, held incommunicado, and denied counsel or a chance to contact families and collect belongings. All had been ordered deported by administrative decision of the Labor Department under the provisions of the 1918 Immigration Act, which made anarchist convictions or membership in an anarchist organization deportable offenses. Some had been promised a few days' notice before they must sail, for an unknown destination. Others had been promised release on bail. In the prevailing atmosphere of antiradical hysteria that followed in the wake of World War I and the Russian Revolution, such promises remained empty. The government had targeted foreign-born radicals in its crusade against the Left and against a newly militant labor movement. Strikes against low wages and poor working conditions were blamed on "Bolshevik" subversion in an effort to discredit legitimate labor protest. After championing a European war for freedom and democracy, leading Americans lauded the repression of radicals. General Leonard Wood, a hero of the War of 1898 and a former military governor of Cuba, advised, "They should be put on a ship of stone with sails of lead and their first stopping place should be Hell."[2]

In public, Emma Goldman claimed that she was proud to be selected for the honor of deportation. Privately, however, she worried considerably about leaving the country she had come to regard as her home. Daughter of a Jewish shopkeeping family of declining fortunes, she had arrived in New York in 1885 at the age of sixteen, with memories of an unhappy youth in Lithuania, East Prussia, and Russia. She had been radicalized by the harsh conditions of the industrial sweatshops where she worked in Rochester, and later by the trial and conviction of the Chicago anarchists, falsely convicted of inspiring a bombing at Haymarket Square. Briefly married to a fellow immigrant, Jacob Kersner, she left her husband and also her parents in Rochester (where they had joined her from St. Petersburg), and fled to New York City where she joined the circle around the German-American Johann Most, the flamboyant editor of an anarchist weekly, *Die Freiheit*. Under Most's tutelage, she soon gained national fame as a witty, courageous speaker, moving quickly out of the radical immigrant subculture in which anarchism had an important place. In the late 1890s she began her sensational coast-to-coast annual lecture tours, speaking both in German and English on a broad range of controversial issues outside the conventional arsenal of the anarchist propagandist: free love, birth control, homosexual rights, parent-child relations, the "tragedy" of women's emancipation, and the radical ideas of the modern European drama. Her defense of labor and support for the strikes and free speech fights of the Industrial Workers of the World—the IWW or Wobblies—awakened the admiration of the radical workers. Her sexual radicalism, controversial even among anarchists, influenced many early twentieth-century feminists who championed her as a feminist heroine, despite her outspoken criticism of the suffrage movement.

From the start, she was an unorthodox figure. Attracted early to the communist anarchism of Peter Kropotkin, she never shared Kropotkin's unwavering faith in the revolutionary potential of the masses. She combined his ideal of a libertarian society organized into communes and collectives with a strong Nietzschean individualism, and she often took a dim view of "the ordinary man." She was less interested in drawing up plans for a future society than in criticizing the evils of the existing one, especially its social and sexual taboos. During her last years in America, Goldman wooed the young intellectuals, and was courted by them, although few became anarchists. She was never an original thinker, but in two books, *Anarchism and Other Essays,* published in 1911, and *The Social Significance of the Modern Drama,* which appeared in 1914, she summed up her ideas on politics, art, and sex with her characteristic boldness. Her lively monthly magazine, *Mother Earth,* which she published for twelve years, also suggests the broad range of her commitments.

In fact, Goldman greatly enjoyed the drama and adventure of her life on the road, with all its obstacles and emergencies: "The more opposition I encountered, the more I was in my element and the more caustic I became with my opponents," she wrote later in her autobiography. She was frequently denied access to halls, often harassed at hotels, routinely arrested, and falsely accused of fomenting acts of violence (including the assassination of President McKinley in 1901). She served three extended prison terms, the first a year in Blackwell's Island Penitentiary in 1893 for allegedly inciting a riot during a New York City hunger demonstration, though no riot ever occurred. Later, she served two weeks for disseminating illegal birth control information from the lecture platform, and she served nearly two years in the Missouri State Penitentiary for opposing the draft during World War I.

Many Americans considered her a terrorist. As a young woman of twenty-two, she aided her lover, Alexander Berkman, in his attempt to assassinate steel magnate Henry Clay Frick during the Homestead Steel strike of 1892. The disastrous aftermath of that failed attempt—which Berkman had intended as an act of revolutionary suicide to rouse the masses to protest—turned her away from such acts forever: the workers had not risen, the strike was broken, and Berkman's act deepened divisions among the already fragmented anarchists. Goldman never again participated in any similar attempt although, partly out of loyalty to Berkman, she often defended those who did. But his *attentat* and fourteen-year imprisonment became the leitmotif of her life, and the eighteenth of each month—the day of his release—an occasion for celebrating their friendship, which continued to deepen over the years.

However, at the age of thirty-nine, she met her "Great, Grand Passion," an uninhibited hobo-turned-physician from Chicago, one Ben L. Reitman, who was ten years younger than she and strained her commitment to free love with his compulsive unfaithfulness and promiscuity.

Reitman drew her sexually as no other man had, and taught her the meaning of an erotic love more intense than any she had ever imagined. As her "manager," moreover, he proved a talented public relations man who greatly enlarged her audiences with his flair for advertising and promotion. Yet not even her nine-year obsession with Reitman, which ended when he left her to marry another woman, weakened her fierce devotion to Berkman who, in any case, had turned to other younger lovers when he emerged from prison in 1906. Berkman and Goldman had continued working together: he had edited *Mother Earth,* which she published, and they had collaborated in many campaigns, including legal defense for a host of imprisoned radicals. He remained Goldman's best editor and critic, while she offered him her energy and camaraderie and, at times, her financial support. For Emma, loyalty to Berkman, her beloved "Sasha," was almost a religion, and possibly the deepest emotion of her life.

The turbulent years of World War I proved the most exhilarating of the decade. With the outbreak of hostilities in 1914, Goldman and Berkman stepped up their antimilitarist campaign. In the spring of 1917, when the United States declared war on Germany, they organized a No-Conscription League, offering counseling to draft resisters and continuing their outspoken opposition to the war. They were arrested together for their antidraft protests in June of 1917. Subsequently they were tried together for violating the Selective Service Act of 1917, charged with having formed a "conspiracy" to induce young men not to register for the draft. They appealed their conviction to the Supreme Court, and while awaiting the court's decision, Emma, who was out on bail, literally saved Berkman's life: she mobilized a defense campaign against his extradition to San Francisco, where he was wanted on (false) charges of inspiring the Preparedness Day bombing of 1916. Her efforts proved successful. However, their appeal to the Supreme Court failed, and each was sent to separate prisons—she to Jefferson City in Missouri, he to Atlanta, Georgia. While they were still in prison, Washington began deportation proceedings under the terms of the 1918 Immigration Act. Berkman made no effort to fight these proceedings, particularly since rumor had it that the deportees would be sent to Russia. But Goldman, who claimed American citizenship through her marriage to Jacob Kersner, a naturalized immigrant, initially planned to fight the order. In the end, however, her loyalty to Berkman and desire not to be separated from him took precedence, and she withdrew her Supreme Court appeal. Even now, on Ellis Island, as she contemplated her departure from America, she found some consolation in the thought that at least the two of them would remain together.

It was past midnight when Goldman sat down to write her last letters of farewell. She felt "terribly empty," she confided to Eleanor Fitzgerald, Berkman's lover and her own close friend, "as if my insides were pulled out of me."[3] Though the government had long pursued her with a special animus, even Goldman had not expected to be expelled "for opinion's sake," especially not at the age of fifty, when she had lived over half her life in the United States. As she dashed off a few more notes, she heard guards march down the corridor, keys rattling as they entered the cells and ordered all deportees to prepare for departure. After packing her bags, Emma was led, along with the other deportees, into a large, bare, glaringly lit room on the second floor, south wing, of the main immigration building. Some sat on old tin trunks or suitcases, surrounded by bundles, hands under chins, elbows on knees; a few tried to read books; others leafed through tattered copies of newspapers. Groups talked anxiously in Russian. Here and there a man strummed a battered banjo or guitar or mandolin, seeking solace in the melancholy strains of Russian peasant songs. Alexander Berkman, pale and drawn, sat apart from the others, coat off, in a black tie and khaki shirt and pants. Beads of perspiration shone on his forehead as he struggled to tie up packages for the coming journey. Emma, carrying her typewriter, had dressed entirely in black, as if in mourning.[4]

Outside, Ellis Island was dark and still, except for several bright searchlights playing on the building, enhancing the atmosphere of surveillance and suspicion. The entry station for immigrants to America, Ellis Island now acquired a sinister new symbolism as the port of exit for deportees, with the record-setting, freezing weather offering an appropriately cold setting for the events to come. No relatives had been told when the ship would sail, and no wives were permitted on the island that Saturday, though many had petitioned the Justice Department to join their husbands and would later suffer severe hardship as the "*Buford* widows." At about 2:00 A.M., coast guard cutters departed from the Battery heading toward Ellis Island, carrying congressmen who had come up from Washington to witness the sailing, along with Commissioner of Immigration Anthony Caminetti, William J. Flynn, director of the Justice Department's Bureau of Investigation, and other federal agents and detectives. The group included twenty-four-year-old J. Edgar Hoover, the head of the department's Radical Division who had played an instrumental role in engineering Goldman's deportation. As the cutters approached Ellis Island, the *Buford,* an old army transport used during the Spanish-American War and World War I, slipped from its berth at Pier 4 in South Brooklyn and moved west and north through drifting ice to an anchorage point just off Fort Wadsworth, at the upper end of Gravesend Bay and the easternmost tip of Staten Island, just below the present-day Verrazzano Bridge.

Toward 3:00 A.M., the doors of the Immigration Building opened, and a squad of federal agents marched outside into the snowy yard. The deportees followed, walking in single file, shivering with cold and tension. With federal agents and detectives in two lines on either side of them, the three women boarded a waiting Immigration Department tender, where soldiers with fixed bayonets awaited them, with "scores of cruel eyes staring us in the face."[5] A reporter from the *New York American* noted Goldman's bravado as she announced her pride at being deported as a political agitator to Russia and predicted her triumphant return, yet he observed too her "solemn face" as she entered the launch. She said later she felt as if she were reenacting a scene from a Russian novel, a cruel parody of the long sea voyage that symbolized her ultimate fantasy of freedom.

The men filed on after the women. All the deportees carried bundles, including books. Most were silent. A few quietly wept. Aboard the launch, some of the men crowded into the cabin where the women were seated, but most were forced to remain above on the open deck lashed by a freezing wind that swept across the water. Some had torn shoes and no overcoats. Behind them, shrouded in heavy mist, rose the lighted skyline of Manhattan, menacing and sinister in the winter darkness. A reporter, moved in spite of himself by the sadness and solemnity of the scene, observed that Ethel Bernstein and Dora Lipkin, the other women deportees, were "bravely silent under the ordeal." He offered a poignant glimpse of Bernstein sitting in the dark cabin of the launch, watching it slipping away from its mooring, shaking her head and whispering, "Goodbye, America," as she buried her face in her hands. Later, Emma recalled looking up at a clock inside the cabin as the tender backed out and headed south through the Narrows toward Gravesend Bay and the anchorage of the *Buford;* it was 4:20 A.M.[6]

In less than an hour, the army tender had made its way down the Bay past the Statue of Liberty—dark except for a single light in the torch— and reached the *Buford,* where it was made fast to the larger ship that loomed above it. A gangplank was lowered, and a lower deck port swung open. Soldiers and immigration officers took their places on both sides of the gangplank. As the transfer began, the huge black hulk of the Cunard liner *Saxonia* approached through the mist, lights blazing from her portholes, and her passengers, most of them newly arriving immigrants, crowded on deck to greet the New World. As their ship ploughed past the *Buford,* they cheered, not knowing the grotesque meaning of the scene that passed before them.

The transfer to the *Buford* proceeded quickly, in silence. Just before six, as the first light of dawn broke through the mist above Bay Ridge, the last deportees filed across to the *Buford.* Reporters watching from a coast guard cutter could see them silhouetted for a moment against the cold gray light. The gangplank lifted, and within minutes, the big troopship, ghostly in the early morning mist, turned south, sliding down the harbor toward the open sea. Slowly the *Buford* vanished behind Sandy Hook, heading out toward the gale-tossed Atlantic.

The sailing of the *Buford* had been carefully staged to stir up public support for draconian legislation designed to limit admissible dissent. Wartime censorship in effect on Ellis Island—though the war had long been over—and secrecy surrounding the precise time of departure heightened the aura of mystery and suspense. The *Buford* was intended as the first of a long series of "Soviet Arks." The departure was orchestrated to dramatize the government's determination to quell labor and radical militance by branding it "foreign." For days the press had been full of front-page articles about the imminent sailing of the "Red Ark," with special emphasis on the welcome departure of Goldman and Berkman, the two famous radicals with the "star quality" J. Edgar Hoover had been anxious to secure for the performance. If anyone still doubted the legitimacy of the deportations, the Justice Department released a report on the day the *Buford* sailed that claimed to show Goldman's involvement "directly or indirectly" with "nearly a score" of killings and assassinations.[7] The aggressive military presence aboard the *Buford* added to the dramatic effect—besides the crewmen armed with revolvers, the ship boasted a stiff detachment of marines who, at first, were "silent and sullen; strict orders not to talk to us," as Berkman noted dryly in his diary.[8]

Goldman, herself a master of political theater, understood very well the dramatic significance of this performance, playing her own role with great aplomb. In the thirty-two-page pamphlet she and Berkman wrote on Ellis

Island, *Deportation: Its Meaning and Menace,* they described how anti-German wartime propaganda was now being directed against radicals and "Bolsheviks" for the purpose of quelling labor militance. The pamphlet presciently asserted that "the fortunes of labor in America are at stake," and warned that laws and statutes restricting free speech and press for radicals would eventually serve the government as weapons against labor generally. They especially berated the liberal and radical intellectuals who had been seduced by the Wilson administration into supporting his crusade for war and the repression of civil liberties, and they appended a list of quotations from famous Americans, including Thoreau, Emerson, Lincoln, and Jefferson, which would be liable under the current criminal syndicalism laws.[9]

Understanding the purposes of the deportation did not make it easier to bear. Once aboard ship, an exhausted Goldman immediately fell asleep in her bunk, remaining there until roused late in the afternoon. Upon awakening, the deportees found themselves in a large floating prison, constantly reminded of their status as dangerous subversives. The men especially suffered severe physical discomfort. They were crowded into three steerage cabins designed for half their number, where sea water constantly flooded the floor and the toilets were inadequate, the food bad, and the bunks cramped. Many became ill. Yet they quickly developed a strong camaraderie that helped ease the anxiety of the trip and kept morale relatively high. They shared clothing, demanded and received exercise on deck, engaged their guards in long talks about anarchism and war, put two of their own men into the bakery, and soon were able to do as they pleased below deck. They negotiated for the return, to wives and children, of money left in the United States. "In spite of the great anxiety regarding our destination," Berkman wrote, "there is much laughter and joking in our cabin." He himself was busy day and night, having been elected "commissar" by his fellows. Not only his fellow deportees but also the men in charge of the soldiers and crew sought him out to negotiate disputes.[10]

The three women deportees enjoyed considerably better physical accommodations than the men. They shared a cramped but clean, dry cabin. They ate at their own table in the dining room with the ship's officers. Berkman noted that the French chef even prepared special dishes for the seasick Ethel and Dora. The women also befriended their guards, who "hung around our cabin all the time, eager to ask questions," and were solicitous in a way that Emma found very touching. But most of the day the three were locked into their small cabin and were prohibited from fraternizing with the men, a gratuitous act of cruelty that was perhaps the most frustrating and demoralizing part of the entire ordeal. Unlike Berkman, Emma found herself with nothing to do but write letters, worry, and care for her two frightened young companions who were seasick for most of the trip. They were allowed on deck only a few hours a day. Emma alone was permitted to see Berkman, and that only for about twenty minutes every few days under the eyes of a guard, though they did manage to smuggle daily notes to each other through the good offices of a friendly crew member. "They looked forlorn, those 'dangerous enemies of the United States,'" Berkman noted after a visit.[11]

At moments, Emma managed a certain detachment, as if she were watching events happening to someone else. She appreciated the high drama of this "weird and strange journey." But much of the time she worried. She worried about the unseaworthiness of the *Buford* and the danger of hitting mines in the North Sea. She worried about the dangers of falling into the hands of anti-Bolshevik Finns or White Russians on their arrival in Russia, since they were traveling to a country at war, where the Bolsheviks controlled only part of the territory. There had been much talk about their being sent to Siberia, where they would face the armies of the counterrevolutionary Admiral A. V. Kolchak. Most of all, she worried about how she and Berkman would survive in Russia. "I could never in my life work within the confines of the State, Bolshevist or otherwise," she confided to her beloved niece, Stella Ballantine. "Lecturing and writing is out of the question for a year at least." And writing articles was always an uncertain, ill-paying proposition. "It isn't as if S[asha] and I were twenty," she wrote frankly. "We cannot do the things of the past or live that life at our age." If things were "normal" in Russia and they could carry on their usual work, it would be different, she reflected. "But under the present conditions we'll be terribly handicapped."[12]

Such anxieties were ironic for one who had always longed to join a revolutionary struggle and had championed the October revolution of 1917. Yet they expressed Goldman's realistic appraisal of a situation that she knew, even before her arrival there, did not favor the free-lance agitation around which she had built her career in America. Although she continued to defend the Bolsheviks, by the spring of 1918, she had begun to change her arguments. By early 1919, she acknowledged that indeed the Bolsheviks were establishing a centralized, bureaucratic dictatorship.[13] Already she anticipated a time in the future when she too would oppose them. Still, in opposition to many other anarchists who had already turned against the regime, she argued that as long as the Bolsheviks were fighting a war against foreign and domestic counterrevolutionary armies, the anarchists should defend them. As she actually prepared to enter Russia, however, she found herself considering more realistically, and more apprehensively, the prospects of living in this centralized "dictatorship of the proletariat." For she and Berkman came not as tourists who could always leave, but as prospective residents who must make a new home, and as anarchists who opposed all states, capitalist or socialist. Now the criticisms of many of her comrades in America, whose early opposition to the Bolsheviks she had violently attacked, began to appear more convincing.

Goldman's apprehension mounted as they approached Europe. "The English coast looked so cold and forbidding to me," she wrote Stella Ballantine, "but then the whole world looks that way to me. We who call the world our own are like Ahasuerus, wanted nowhere." [14] As they approached Russia, Goldman's thoughts turned increasingly toward America. She inquired of her lawyer whether she might (re)gain her citizenship by marrying an American citizen. She asked Stella to inquire about the chances of living and publishing an English-language anarchist paper in Mexico. "If I fail in my plans to return," she told Stella, "I will go to Mexico and do the work from there." [15] For the present, she wrote, she was thinking only of one thing: how to continue her work for America.

Achingly homesick, Emma wrote long, emotional letters to Stella. With the loss of Ben Reitman in her intimate life, Emma had elevated her niece to the position of confidante, representative, and manager, a position that Stella, a young mother with two small children, sometimes found overwhelming. "Darling, precious," Emma wrote from the *Buford*, "you don't know how hard the thought is of not being able to see you again soon . . . I embrace you all. . . . Good night again. E." [16]

On January 6, 1920, the *Buford* arrived at Kiel Canal, near Hamburg, where it anchored in a lock and remained two days for repairs. The ship came so close to the German shore that those on board could see ruined villas, houses, and meadows and even perceive a terrible stillness, which they interpreted as a sign of the hunger wrought by the wartime Allied blockade. No one was allowed ashore or even on deck, for fear they would jump overboard and escape. In this setting, small signs of solidarity loomed large. Emma was thrilled when German repairmen working on a barge below her porthole responded to a note she threw down to them by giving three cheers for the political deportees from America and the "Soziale Revolution." [17]

Later, as the *Buford* approached the Baltic, tension aboard the ship mounted. The deportees feared striking ice or unexploded mines. Moreover, their destination was still uncertain. All feared falling into the hands of the Whites, and rumors fed their fears. Finland, which some of the deportees had heard named as a possible destination, was a dangerous place for "Reds." All were exhausted from the prolonged journey and "nearly crazy" with the worry and uncertainty.

On January 16, at 4:25 P.M. the *Buford* docked at Hangö, Finland. The next afternoon, the deportees disembarked, amid expressions of warm concern by the crew, some of whom had become quite attached to their prisoners. Joined now by several reporters, including John Clayton of the *Chicago Tribune,* the deportees entered a Finnish train where they were locked into unheated compartments with little food or water, and with hostile soldiers posted at every door. Now they began a nightmarish journey toward the Russian border, across snow-bound terrain, passing by railroad stations where armed sentries stood on the alert. Emma's two female companions were ill, the guards stole most of the food provided for the deportees from the *Buford,* and no one was allowed off the train.

Around noon on January 19, near the Russo-Finnish border (a few miles north of Vyborg), the train halted. The Finns wanted the deportees to cross immediately into Russia, but they refused; word had not yet been received from Petrograd in answer to their cables, and they feared, with good reason, that if the Soviet border guards were not informed of their identity, they would mistake the "Americans" for invading Finns and shoot. Berkman was chosen to walk to the border, accompanied by a Finnish officer, a soldier, and an interpreter. Several journalists trailed behind. In a heavy snowfall, the group set out, wading through deep drifts in the sparse forest at the border, just west of a ruined railroad bridge. After fifteen minutes they reached the creek that marked the boundary between the two countries. Berkman shouted in Russian across the frozen creek, explaining their mission to the impassive Soviet guards, who finally shouted back that a three-person committee of greeting, including S. Zorin of the Petrograd section of the Communist party and Madame Andreyeva, the wife of Maxim Gorki, had arrived from Petrograd to welcome them. [18] Sleighs were secured and arrangements made to transport the deportees with their luggage across the frontier. As the snow continued to fall, the deportees crossed the ice into "Matushka Rossiya," while a Soviet military band played the "Internationale" and Russian civilians cheered in welcome.

Later, John Clayton described a tearful Emma Goldman turning to him as she crossed the border and declaring emotionally, "This is the greatest day in my life. I once found political freedom in America. Now the doors are closed there to free thinkers, and the enemies of capitalism find once more sanctuary in Russia."[19] The Irish-American journalist Griffin Barry reported that Goldman compared her feelings on entering Soviet Russia to those of the ancient Jews entering the Inner Temple of Jerusalem. Yet Barry also recorded a more somber reflection, which hinted at complications to come. The anarchists among us, Goldman warned, were opposed to Bolshevism "unless freedom is preserved for the individual to do what he likes with his own body and mind so long as it does not involve others to their harm." Goldman affirmed that she would not accept a paid post under the Soviet government, but would offer her services as a trained nurse at the front, "without remuneration."[20]

At the railway station in the nearby village of Belo-Ostrov, the deportees were greeted with more music and speeches. In a bitterly cold dark hall, dimly lit by a few candles on a platform, they attended their first meeting on Soviet soil. The flickering light, the pale, madonna-like faces of the Russian women, framed by black nurses' hoods, gave the entire event a mystical, religious aura.[21] Berkman spoke briefly in English. Emma Goldman said a few words in Russian. Once again they boarded a train for the trip to Petrograd, the city that had once, long ago, been their home.

2

Stranger in a Strange Land

Will the frost never lose its grip
or the wind lay its whips aside?
—Alexander Blok

Shipped out of the United States as a pariah, Emma Goldman was greeted warmly in Petrograd. As revolutionists of international stature, she and Berkman were invited to stay at the first house of the Petrograd Soviet, formerly the elegant Hotel Astoria, where high-ranking Soviet officials lived.[1] She felt grateful for the hospitality shown her and moved by the extraordinary dedication of the people she and Berkman met, including their host Zorin, who had lived in America and spoke fluent English. But she was not prepared for the devastation all around her. She remembered the Russian capital romantically from her adolescence as a place full of life and gaiety, of secret reading circles and "revolutionary mysteries of which no one dared to speak." Now, imperial Petersburg had been transformed into wartime Petrograd, a ghastly, ghostly metropolis of cold, hunger, hatred, and endurance. Its streets were dirty and deserted, shops closed and shuttered, windows barred, and its population shrunk from nearly a million to five hundred thousand, decimated by war, disease, and hunger as industrial workers fled to their native villages in search of food. The great Nevsky Prospekt, once alive with Gogolian crowds, now crossed an abandoned silent city. An occasional exhausted pedestrian dragged a loaded sleigh through the snowy streets. Here and there the remains of barricades—piles of sand bags—bore witness to the recent defeat of the counterrevolutionary general, N. N. Yudenich, on the outskirts of the city.

The devastation of Petrograd mirrored that of the country, ravaged by six years of war and revolution. The revolution of 1917 had emerged out of the ashes of World War I, a war that had left an immense legacy of destruction. In March of 1918, the Treaty of Brest-Litovsk had taken Russia out of the war but at a terrible cost, for it had ceded to Germany much of the country's most productive agricultural and mining regions in the Ukraine. In the summer of 1918, civil war erupted. Counterrevolutionary White armies converged on Petrograd and Moscow from the Ukraine, Siberia, the Caucasus, the Baltic regions, and Poland, aided by British, French, Czech, Japanese, and American expeditionary forces. The Bolsheviks, their power ever more precarious, were forced to fight along a vast five-thousand-mile front, exhausting desperately needed resources in the endless military campaigns.

As the civil war dragged on, the euphoria of October was almost forgotten. Industrial production practically ceased. Fuel supplies plummeted. Railway transport was virtually destroyed. The Allied military blockade of Russian ports cut off desperately needed trade from abroad, so that vital imports such as soap, medicine, food, and industrial parts were unavailable. Millions of vagrant children roamed the emptied cities and the countryside, homeless and orphaned, psychologically as well as physically traumatized. The vast Russian peasantry, whom the revolution had made individual landowners, found that their grain and other produce could not buy machinery or manufactured goods, since none were produced. Workers' control of industry, widely instituted in 1917 in response to deepening economic chaos and the attempts of capitalists to shut down factories, proved unable to cope with the disorganization of the war. Women especially felt the brunt of the war. While the revolutionary Family Code of 1918 remained on the books, mandating equal pay for equal work, civil and legal equality for women, easy access to divorce and other dramatic changes, the resources for implementing the law were increasingly scarce. Facilities for prenatal and child care for working women, established in the early days of the revolution, were closed. Not only the gains of 1917, but of an entire half-century vanished. As the historian Moshe Lewin put it, "It was as if most of the fruits of social and economic development Russia experienced since 1861 were wiped out and its culture, spiritual and political, had retreated to some earlier primitive stage difficult to define or date." [2]

In an effort to stave off total economic collapse, the regime in the summer of 1918 introduced the draconian policies known as "War Communism." These policies meant, in essence, requisitioning agricultural produce in the countryside and strictly rationing supplies, including food, in the cities. War Communism halted the democratic, egalitarian thrust of the early stages of the revolution, moving instead toward increasingly centralized control of industry, compulsory labor for all, a return to one-man management in the factories, and growing differentials in pay for various classes of workers. War Communism also meant a policy of terror against counterrevolutionists, a flexible category easily stretched to include hungry workers selling goods on the black market, and members of other left-wing parties. Indeed, as the Bolsheviks grew more isolated, with peasant revolts erupting in the countryside and worker demoralization spreading in the cities, they stepped up terror against rival revolutionary parties, including the anarchists and Left Socialist Revolutionaries, who had reverted to the terrorist practices of their earlier days. Highly controversial within the Bolshevik party, War Communism undoubtedly saved the cities from starvation and even yielded certain gains (e.g., in providing jobs and social benefits to previously unemployed women). Yet in relying on compulsion and allotting broad powers to the Cheka, or secret police, War Communism led to massive abuses. It alienated broad sectors of both the peasantry and the industrial working class, who saw their early gains steadily eroded.

Despite her shock at the ravaged condition of Petrograd in early 1920, Emma Goldman found much to praise in the first weeks of her stay in Russia, especially the revolutionary spirit of the people, which was not dampened by starvation and cold. She marveled at how the Russians, fed on half a pound of bread a day, on watery soup and kasha, could enthusiastically shiver through a six-hour performance of *Othello,* listen with rapture to the famous tenor Chaliapin in the opera *Russalka,* attend a reading by Maxim Gorki of the work of the playwright Andreyev, "and do a thousand other amazing and extraordinary things, which would exhaust the vitality of almost any other nation even normally fed." She delighted in the theater, especially the old Moscow Art Theater of Konstantin Stanislavsky, and the "wonderful" art galleries, which remained open even if unheated.[3] Indeed, the arts flourished, aided by an enlightened Commissar of Culture, the poet and playwright Anatoly Lunacharsky, and by the initial enthusiasm of the avant-garde artists, who saw analogies between the social revolution and their own aesthetic experiments. Futurists, Constructivists, and Cubo-Suprematists—Vladimir Tatlin, Lyubov Popova, Alexander Rodchenko, and Vsevolod Meyerhold to name just a few—continued the revolution in painting, sculpture, architecture, photography, film, graphics, and especially theater, which had begun before the war. Poets recited new work in the literary cafes, painters designed agit-trains to bring the message of the revolution to the countryside, actors performed people's theater in factories and villages, and filmmakers documented daily life in avant-garde newsreels. Proletkult, a workers' arts organization formed before the revolution, promoted efforts to create a new proletarian culture experimental in form as well as content. For a few years, Soviet Russia dominated the international avant-garde, while the institutions of traditional Russian culture were opened to a broad public, with peasants and workers flocking to palaces and museums and to the ballet, theater, and opera, previously accessible only to the wealthy.[4]

Goldman lauded these efforts, but at the same time her letters to Stella Ballantine indicated her uncertainty and ambivalence. In a long emotional letter to Stella, written late in January 1920—a letter that may not have reached its destination after it was intercepted by the U.S. Military Intelligence Office at Helsinki, in Finland—Emma poured out her enthusiasm, homesickness, excitement, and uneasiness, hinting at disturbing "extraordinary events" for which they had not yet found an answer. Goldman did not identify these events, but she probably referred to the execution by the Cheka of some five hundred alleged counterrevolutionists in Petrograd and Moscow shortly before her arrival, on the eve of a decree abolishing capital punishment.[5]

Petrograd, Jan. 28th, 1920

Darling. We are here ten days, but the impressions crowded in, make our presence in Russia seem 6 months. My head is in a whirl, my heart full to the bursting point. There are a million things I would like to write you about, but I can't do it now. Even if we had come to a normal Russia it would have been difficult for us to act just ourselves. But Russia is herself in such an abnormal state, that we are completely uprooted. It will take us months to find our bearings, to know where we might fit in and the work we might do. Russia is marvelous, yet painfully confused. We are torn in a hundred directions. We can join now, and may never be able to do so. We are just adrift. We are sure only of one thing, until we have grasped the raison d'etre for many extraordinary events we will not be able to work within the Soviet regime or even with our own comrades. We're like babies in a wilderness. For the first time in our lives we can find no way out of the tangle. I can say no more, dearest. But you will understand. *All is only for you* and *the very few immediate friends.* . . .

Life for us here will be extremely difficult. You see, we can accept no support from the Soviet Government until we can render some service. And we can not consistently do that, until we have learned to understand and absorb what now seems to us conflicting. On the other hand, it is well-nigh impossible to live here outside the Soviet regime. Things are terribly scarce and still more terrible in price. . . . There is one way out, that is to get money from home in gold. Its value is ten times as much as that of paper. . . . You see then that unless we can get gold from time to time we will not be able to live in Russia at all, in view of the fact that we must retain our independence if we are to decide without fear or favor whether we can work within the Soviet regime. . . .

We're going to Moscow in about ten days, but will return to Petrograd to live. This is the revolutionary workers' centre, while Moscow is the seat of the government, needless to say, we prefer to be far distant from Moscow. . . . Of the leading men in Petrograd we've met only two so far, Zinoviev [head of the Executive Committee of the Third International] and S. Zorin . . . the latter has devoted much of his time to us. He is a most lovable personality. In fact, they all are, and so earnest and dedicated. All work themselves to death—they are starved and exhausted. But their spirit is beyond belief. And yet we may not be able to work with them. The situation is such that we are now going through the deepest spiritual conflict in our lives. . . . We both feel very, very lonely so far. . . . It is 2:30 A.M. now and I am numb with cold. We're lodged in the famous Astoria hotel—now called the Soviet house— several hundred Soviet officials live here. Nothing has remained of the old splendour, except the spacious rooms and the high ceilings, which make the cold more acute. I sit in my warm robe with blankets over my feet and we have steam and electric light. Most of the workers haven't even that. You can imagine how they suffer. . . . But the spirit of the Revolution burns like a magic flame. It is truly miraculous. . . .

Beloved mine, I long for you with all the intensity of my being. I'd give ten years of my life to be able to look in upon you, hold you close, to see our own beloved baby. No such red cheeks and shiny eyes as Ian's here. No such well-fed precious bodies. Yet pale and frail as the children are, they too are consumed by the divine spirit which has imbued the Russian people and made them invincible against the whole world. . . . It all seems a dream, yet it is vividly real. Darling, darling, I wish I could write even one millionth part of what is going on within me . . . more than ever I agree with Ibsen that it is the struggle for rather than the attainment of the ideal, which alone makes life rich and full. The ideal achieved means the ideal fettered—crushed. . . .

Everybody here is very kind to us, especially the Zorins . . . without him we'd have been utterly lost. We're that pretty much anyway. But even the Zorins are removed from us in many ways—we have no one of our own. I mean in ideas of thought. I really don't know what I would have done here all alone. . . . We both miss you dearie. Yet I haven't it in my heart to urge you to come. It isn't only because of the dreadful poverty—it is the extreme difference of viewpoint on life in general and our ideas—in particular. We're in a strange world altogether. . . .[6]

By the end of February 1920, both Emma Goldman and Alexander Berkman confessed to feeling "very lonesome and forlorn here." They were both finding it difficult to acclimate themselves to this country wracked by war and disorganization, one which they had left more than thirty years earlier.[7] Berkman adjusted somewhat more easily, but even he felt disoriented and confused. "Life seems a puzzle, and those who think they can solve it are happy mortals indeed," he wrote wistfully to Eleanor Fitzgerald, or Fitzi, "I was one of their numbers, once upon a time, millions of years ago." Emma's feeling of dislocation and loss was even stronger. "I cannot tell you in words how torn away I feel from all that was dear and precious to me during a lifetime," she wrote Stella. The lack of communication with America tormented her. "Forgive me this time," she added, "I do not feel equal to writing anything today."[8]

Soon after her arrival in Russia, Goldman met with a number of Bolshevik leaders in order to clarify her understanding of the Russian scene, and also to find work for herself. Sometime in March she met Alexandra Kollontai, the only woman on the Central Committee of the ruling Communist party and the head of its semiautonomous women's section, Zhenotdel. The daughter of an aristocratic family, Kollontai had long been one of the leaders of the Russian socialist feminist movement and, like Goldman, a sharp critic of bourgeois feminism. As the first Commissar of Public Welfare, and later head of the Zhenotdel, Kollontai worked to raise the political consciousness of Russian women and train them for leadership in the party and the state. Organized as a network of female Communists and nonparty volunteers, the Zhenotdel set up training centers, reading cabins, literacy classes, and family counseling centers all over Russia. Despite inadequate funding and ambivalent party support, it achieved impressive progress, drafting protective legislation and also acting as an affirmative action agency and grievance committee for women workers. By the mid-twenties, the Zhenotdel counted half a million activists in its ranks.[9] Kollontai also stood alone among the Bolsheviks in acknowledging sexuality as a valid concern for revolutionaries. In her 1908 book, *The Social Basis of the Woman Question*, she had argued along lines similar to Goldman that the liberation of women meant freeing them from their emotional and sexual dependence on men, which in turn required restructuring the family. But despite similarities in their thinking about women, Goldman found Kollontai cold and unsympathetic. She wrote later that she had been "unpleasantly affected" by what she considered Kollontai's "rather superficial" attitude toward the "dull sides" of the regime.[10]

She reacted more positively to Anatoly Lunacharsky, who worked hard to maintain a policy of openness in the arts despite the initial hostility of nearly all the established artists and intellectuals to the new regime, and despite criticism from leftist artists for his tolerance. Emma liked Lunacharsky, whom she later described as kind and gracious and eager to learn of experimental educational ideas and methods. She was less impressed with Zlata Lilina Ionovna, then head of the schools subdepartment of the Petrograd Educational Department (and the wife of Zinoviev), who struck her as prim and dogmatic, "a frail woman with a hard face, the typical New England schoolma'am of fifty years ago."[11] The school system had been hard hit during the early months of the revolution by a massive strike of teachers, nearly all of whom opposed the Bolsheviks. By early spring of 1918, however, most had returned to work, and the number of schools increased rapidly until the end of the civil war, when state funding for education was drastically cut. Though she was appalled by the antiquated educational ideas that prevailed, including the practice of sequestering delinquent children as "moral defectives," Goldman nonetheless admired Soviet efforts on behalf of children, carried out in the face of a paralyzing state bureaucracy.

Lenin himself granted an interview to Goldman and Berkman, but Emma found him inscrutable and strange; "a shrewd Asiatic," as she wrote later, whose approach to people was "purely utilitarian." She was also disappointed by Maxim Gorki, the pro-Soviet writer whose work she had praised in her book *The Social Significance of the Modern Drama*. Her meetings with him left her "depressed."[12] Only Angelica Balabanoff, secretary of the Third International and a former militant in the Italian Socialist movement, won Goldman's admiration and sympathy, perhaps because she too had begun to entertain doubts about the Bolsheviks and would leave Russia within a few years. Balabanoff's warmth, helpfulness and kindness toward her at this difficult moment moved Emma greatly, so much so that at their first meeting, in February or March of 1920, she confided in Balabanoff her growing distress. Balabanoff recalled in her 1938 memoir, *My Life as a Rebel,* that, at the time of this visit, Emma had not yet lost faith in the "real leaders" of the revolution and was eager to work for it, but "much of the initial enthusiasm with which she entered the workers' Republic had already been chilled." When they began to speak, "Emma suddenly broke down and wept. It was in this fit of weeping that she poured forth all her shock and disillusionment, her bitterness at the injustices she had witnessed, the others of which she had heard." Executions, secret police, persecution of honest revolutionists—"Was it for this the Revolution had been fought?" she asked. Balabanoff replied that "external conditions, life itself, rather than theory, had dictated the course of the Revolution." Emma was not persuaded, but she was impressed by Balabanoff's refusal to blame everything on the Allied blockade and the intervention—"the usual excuses"—and Balabanoff's personal warmth and sympathy offered some comfort.[13]

As she had hoped, Emma received offers of work from nearly all the Soviet officials she met. Kollontai invited her to work with Russian women; both Lilina and Lunacharsky offered her work in the Department of Education; Lenin evidently welcomed her proposal to form a society of Russian Friends of American Freedom, though he insisted the society operate under the auspices of the Third International, a condition that she rejected.[14] As she reported to Stella in May of 1920, she and Berkman had all sorts of offers of work, but Emma particularly still felt she needed to become more informed, to travel, and to "get close to the Russian people."[15]

Throughout the spring of 1920, feeling more like a tourist than a revolutionist, she continued to explore the streets, markets, factories, hospitals, schools, theaters, art galleries, and museums in Petrograd and Moscow, sometimes with Sasha, but more often without him, since he had been recruited as a translator for some visiting journalists (including Griffin Barry, foreign correspondent for the liberal *London Daily Herald*) and later for the British Trade Union Mission, work that often separated the two. According to her later accounts, on the request of S. Zorin, she helped renovate some shabby hotels to be used as living quarters for a thousand Russian immigrant deportees expected momentarily from America. But after a month of frustrating effort, she learned that the arrivals were Russian war prisoners from Germany; the hotels were locked and sealed for possible future deportees; the work had been in vain. A short time later, Zorin asked her and Berkman to supervise the transformation of expropriated villas on the Kameniy Ostrov, villas once belonging to the Russian nobility, into vacation homes for Petrograd workers. Emma again found herself thwarted by disorganization, the meddling of scores of commissars, and the resentment of workers—mostly convicts and military deserters—whose hunger, exhaustion, and apathy undercut all her efforts. Berkman, refusing to evict bedraggled bourgeois residents from the confiscated neighboring buildings in the district, was dismissed from the project. Emma quit in disgust two weeks later.

In the midst of these struggles to find herself, Goldman began meeting the Russian anarchists, who presented a far more negative picture of the regime than she had heard so far. Although individual anarchists were involved with the nineteenth-century Narodniks, a consciously anarchist movement had emerged relatively recently in Russia around the time of the 1905 revolution and reviving again during the February 1917 upheaval, when militants began to engage in systematic agitation. Active especially among the industrial workers of Petrograd and in the cities of the Ukraine, the Russian anarchists nonetheless exercised a very limited influence. Throughout 1917, most militants had sided with the Bolsheviks as fellow revolutionists, supporting Bolshevik calls for workers' control of industry, peasant takeovers of the land, and the transfer of power from parliament to the soviets—all essentially anarchist demands. Indeed Lenin's 1918 pamphlet, *State and Revolution,* seemed to some almost an anarchist manifesto, despite the call for a transitional government. "So long as the state exists there is no freedom," Lenin wrote. "When there is freedom, there will be no states." Individual anarchists had also played important roles in the October revolution, in the factory committees, in the trade unions and schools, in the Red Army and the navy and among the Red Guards, and even as heads of government bureaus. "Sovietsky" anarchists, such as Goldman's comrade from New York, William Shatov, continued to work with the Bolsheviks in important state positions, during the civil war and after.[16]

For other anarchists, however, the growing centralization of the regime, the establishment of a political police, or Cheka, with vast powers, and especially the humiliating March 1918 Brest-Litovsk Treaty with Germany, inspired a growing opposition. The anti-Soviet anarchists opposed the regime, first in an escalating barrage of anti-Soviet criticism in the anarchist press, and, by the spring of 1918, with acts of terrorism, particularly "expropriations" or "ex's"—the robbing of banks or seizing of mansions in order to collect funds for the movement. To carry out these ex's, the Moscow anarchists organized "Black Guards" armed with pistols, rifles, and grenades. Numbering at least several thousand men, the casually organized Black Guards offered cover to criminal and counterrevolutionary elements whose actions deepened anarchist conflicts with the regime. In 1918, a small but militant anti-Bolshevik anarchist underground also emerged, which linked the armed groups of the capital with groups in the south.[17]

In response to these anarchist attacks and to pressure from foreign diplomats—including the American representative Raymond Robbins, whose car had been confiscated by an anarchist group—the Bolsheviks decided to act. In early April of 1918, some 5,000 troops of the Red Army and the Cheka surrounded buildings in Moscow occupied by the Black Guards and opened fire. The siege lasted through the night, killing or wounding forty anarchists. Another five or six hundred were arrested, though one quarter were immediately released. This action initiated a long but inconsistent campaign against the anarchists, who were branded as "bandits" or "criminal elements." While most anarchists confined their opposition to words, some militants continued their violent protests, engaging in ex's and attempting assassinations of government officials. They sometimes worked together with Left Socialist Revolutionaries who, by the summer of 1918, had also returned to the terrorist practices inherited from their predecessors, the Narodniks.

The outbreak of civil war in the summer of 1918, with its heightened counterrevolutionary dangers, persuaded many anarchists to give some level of support to the regime. Throughout the civil war period, most Russian anarchists remained ambivalent, siding with the Bolsheviks against the counterrevolutionaries, but opposing the consolidation of power by the Communist party. Sporadic anarchist terrorism continued, most spectacularly in September 1919, shortly before Goldman's arrival in Russia, when anarchists and Left Socialist Revolutionaries threw a bomb into the headquarters of the Moscow Committee of the Communist party, killing twelve members and wounding fifty-five. Many anarchists were arrested, imprisoned, and exiled in consequence, their access to paper for publication denied, their centers raided and sealed. Still, the policy of the regime remained inconsistent: arrested anarchists were periodically released; centers closed down one week were opened the next. As late as 1927, the anarchist bookshop in central Moscow, on Tverskaya Street opposite the university, remained open, and some anarchist books were still published each year. A museum dedicated to Peter Kropotkin remained open until 1938.[18]

The regime demonstrated its inconsistency most brutally toward the peasant anarchist leader Nestor Makhno—a sort of Ukrainian Emiliano Zapata—whose partisan bands, made up mostly of poor peasants, helped defeat various counterrevolutionary armies in the south while also attempting to institute an anarchist revolution in the countryside. In the early spring of 1920, after having decisively thwarted the White armies of Petlura and Denikin in the Ukraine, Makhno and his guerrilla troops found themselves outlawed—many of them arrested and shot—for refusing to fight under Red Army command against invading Polish troops. Their refusal was motivated by the fear that to leave the regions they controlled would simply open them to Bolshevik conquest. In the fall of 1920, Makhno once again agreed to a truce with the Bolsheviks to fight against the White general P. N. Wrangel. But that truce too abruptly ended in November when Wrangel no longer posed a threat. The Bolsheviks again denounced the Makhnovists as counterrevolutionaries and arrested other anarchists en masse. Pursued by the Bolsheviks for the next six months, Makhno escaped into Rumania in August of 1921, eventually making his way to Paris, where he died in 1935. Although the Makhno movement was not, strictly speaking, anarchist, it was a popular insurgency that implemented libertarian forms of social organization in the territory it occupied. Within the limits imposed by the war, the Makhnovists organized free agricultural communes and established nonparty peasant soviets. They instituted free speech and press, a voluntary army, and schools imbued with anarchist educational ideas. Ironically, most of the leading Russian anarchists, particularly the intellectuals, remained apart from the Makhno movement in the Ukraine, which they regarded as insufficiently anarchist or excessively military. According to the historian of the movement, Peter Arshinov, who also participated in it, the Russian anarchists failed to recognize that this was the movement they had been anticipating for many years; instead they "remained in their circles and slept through a mass movement of paramount importance."[19]

Though she had come to Russia as an anarchist, Emma Goldman approached her comrades cautiously. She hesitated to draw conclusions in a situation so complex, and she repeatedly complained in her letters home about foreign visitors who presumed to judge Russia after a few weeks in Moscow. She admitted after nearly ten months that even she and Berkman, who knew the language and had traveled widely, still did not understand many things.[20] In the beginning she accorded the arguments of her comrade Bill Shatov a certain validity, accepting the possibility that the evils all around her—terror, bureaucracy and inefficiency, the starvation of some and the privileges of others—resulted mainly from the civil war and the blockade. She seems to have been skeptical at first of the more outspokenly critical Russian anarchists whom she met. She may well have shared the reactions of Berkman, who noted in his diary in April of 1920, "There is no An. movement in Petr. or Moscow. A few good comrades here & there, but really no movement worthy of the name. . . . Not much enthusiasm, no outstanding directing figure among them. It all depresses me terribly."[21]

By the time Emma visited Peter Kropotkin, she had evidently begun to find the anarchist critics more convincing. Emma, Sasha, and George Lansbury, editor of the pro-Soviet Labourite paper, the *London Daily Herald,* made the pilgrimage to Dmitrov sometime in March of 1920. Following long years of exile in England, Kropotkin had returned to Russia after the February 1917 revolution, only to find himself increasingly angered by the authoritarian directions the regime was taking. He expressed his criticism to Lenin personally, and in several public letters he protested against both the Bolshevik practice of taking hostages and the interference of the state with the peasant cooperatives. At the time Emma went to see him, he was an old man in ill health, living practically in internal exile with his wife Sophie in the provincial village of Dmitrov, forty miles north of Moscow, where he gardened, played the piano, painted in watercolors, involved himself with the local cooperative, and worked on his last book, *Ethics.*

This was not Goldman's first meeting with Kropotkin, for she had known him since 1895 and visited him a number of times thereafter. Their relationship was friendly, but evidently rather formal, and Emma had always taken a certain pride in challenging Kropotkin's thinking, especially his conventional views about women and sex. Now, however, she went to him almost as a disciple. In their conversations, Emma reported later, Kropotkin argued that independent trade unions, free soviets, and peasant cooperatives offered the best hope for reviving the revolution in which he continued to have faith. He laid out a theory of Bolshevism as a conspiracy against the revolution, which Emma would essentially adopt as her own. "We have always pointed out the effects of Marxism in action," Emma quoted him as saying. "Why be surprised now?"[22] When Kropotkin died in February 1921, his funeral in Moscow became a demonstration of protest against the deepening authoritarianism of the regime, and, for Emma, a moment of profound mourning, not only for Kropotkin, but for the revolution, which she felt had been buried with him.[23]

By late spring of 1920, as the political situation worsened, Goldman still had not found congenial work. After a lull in the civil war, fighting resumed in the south as counterrevolutionary Polish armies smashed into the Ukraine, and the White general Wrangel began a new campaign in the Crimea. Industrial production continued to decline, famine again threatened the cities, the work force continued to disappear into the countryside in search of bread. Trotsky attempted to address the crisis. At a January 1920 meeting of trade union leaders, and later at the Ninth Party Congress in March 1920, Trotsky had tried unsuccessfully to push through a proposal for the militarization of labor; that is, he proposed to apply to the exhausted civilian labor force the harsh discipline and coercion he had used to whip together the powerful Red Army. His plan was rejected, but the assignment of demobilized military units to civilian labor—the so-called labor armies—was accepted so long as an army was needed for military tasks. Moreover, trade unions were to employ "severe labour discipline from below upwards," combined in practice with various material and moral incentives aimed at increasing productivity.[24]

In this alarming setting, Goldman tried hard to avoid any criticism that might aid the counterrevolutionaries. Her letters home were full of pleas to "read between the lines" and allusions to her inability to write. She sent cryptic assurances that certain trusted acquaintances, returning to New York from Russia—including the journalist John Clayton—would clarify her "vagueness."[25] She had some suspicion that she was being watched by Soviet authorities, and apparently she was, according to Marguerite Harrison, an Associated Press correspondent who lived next door to Berkman at the Hotel Kheritonensky in Moscow.[26] Berkman struck up an acquaintance with the intrepid Harrison, intrigued by her stories about difficulties with the Cheka. What he did not know was that Harrison was also a highly esteemed spy for United States Military Intelligence. Since Soviet authorities were evidently aware of her identity, Berkman's relations with her may have complicated his and Goldman's relations with the regime.[27]

On her return to America in 1921, Harrison published a book, *Marooned in Moscow,* describing the two "American" anarchists as people who "commanded almost universal respect on account of their personal character and attainments." Berkman appeared to Harrison as "one of the gentlest, most courteous and kindliest individuals it has ever been my pleasure to meet." Harrison liked Goldman too, praising her honesty, "good nature and a delightfully refreshing sense of humor . . . mixed with a keen intelligence, considerable shrewdness and great executive ability."[28] Although Emma never mentioned Harrison in her writing on Russia, the two women were evidently fairly well acquainted, for Harrison described Goldman astutely in her book, offering a poignant glimpse of Emma in the early period of her Russian sojourn:

> The feeling of being a round peg in a square hole wore on her energetic temperament. She hated her enforced idleness, but she was absolutely unwilling to go into any sort of work where she would be directly or indirectly supporting Communist policies. She spoke Russian very poorly and she was desperately and humanly homesick for America. I do not believe for one instant that Emma is any the less a sincere anarchist for her experience in Russia, but I believe that she is a much better American. I am not sure even that she is in her heart of hearts not convinced that it is not such a simple thing to bring about a social revolution and that it would not be well to make haste slowly in the United States. I greatly enjoyed listening to her apt criticisms of leading personages, whose weak spots she picked out unerringly, and her efficient scorn of the loose business methods and administrative incapacity of the Russians.[29]

It is almost certain that Harrison was the "confidential source" who kept Goldman and Berkman under U.S. government surveillance. Washington officials, especially J. Edgar Hoover, had lost none of their preoccupation with the two anarchists and had them watched throughout their sojourn in Russia.[30] Their letters were regularly intercepted at the Central Intelligence Police Office in Helsinki and transmitted via the State Department to Hoover at the Department of Justice. Hoover, in turn, "carefully noted" their contents and decided which ones could be forwarded to their addresses. On at least one occasion, letters from Berkman were deemed "undeliverable."[31] Both Emma and Sasha repeatedly complained that their letters did not arrive in America. They suspected Soviet interference, but the breakdown of the mail system in wartime Russia and U.S. interference seemed the more likely reasons. Whatever the causes, the consequences were painful. "E is entirely discouraged about the matter of mail," Berkman wrote Eleanor Fitzgerald in May of 1920. "It is a pity to look at her. She feels terrible about the complete isolation from all those dear to her." As of May 1920, they had received one letter from Stella and none from Fitzi.[32]

Unfortunately, the letter from Stella, which arrived in May, contained sad news. Emma's beloved older half-sister, Helena, who had been more like a mother to Emma than her real mother, had died in February. Emma was "quite crushed," Berkman reported to Fitzi. Her grief was deepened by a guilty sense of having failed her sister at her moment of greatest need. "I cannot get used to the loss of our beloved Helena," Emma wrote back. The death of this sister crystallized for Emma the many recent losses of her life—loss of country, of her work, and of a whole support network of friends and comrades. In subsequent letters to her niece, Emma apologized for her inability to write. Her mind was too much in turmoil, she explained; she wondered if she would ever be able to speak or write again.[33]

John Clayton, the correspondent for the *Chicago Tribune* who had reported Goldman's entry into Russia in January, offered another telling glimpse of Emma's state of mind in the early summer of 1920. Clayton found himself in a peculiar position at this time. His early articles on the Russian Revolution were so anti-Bolshevik that he had been barred on occasion from entering the country; nevertheless, the U.S. State Department considered him a "Bolshevik sympathizer" and kept him under surveillance. In May 1920, he showed up in Petrograd, where he spent a week with Emma and Sasha. He had "brought with him the spirit of fellowship, so scarce in struggling Russia now," Emma reported to her niece. "We enjoyed him very much."[34]

In an article he wrote for the *Chicago Tribune* that was widely printed in other newspapers, Clayton quoted Emma as saying that Russian Bolshevism was "rotten" and tyrannical. "But it is what we should have expected," she had said. "We always knew the Marxian theory was impossible, a breeder of tyranny. We blinded ourselves to its faults because we believed it might accomplish something." After four months, wrote Clayton, Goldman had concluded that there was "no health in it." Bolshevism had "taken away even the little freedom man has under individual capitalism and has made him entirely subject to the aims of a bureaucracy, excusing its tyranny on the ground it is all done for the welfare of the worker." Clayton reported that Emma kept a little American flag stuck up on her bureau and that she longed for America. "For I love America," she had said, "as I love no other land." [35]

Emma had not intended her remarks to Clayton for publication. She was embarrassed to see her outspoken statements against the Bolsheviks in print. Yet her warnings to Stella Ballantine not to believe what she read in the newspapers suggest she was aware that the American press reveled in reports about her disillusionment; that the *New York Times,* for example, regularly printed squibs about her alleged change of heart, while gloating editorially that "it does add a bitter vividness to our conception of the horrors of the dictated proletariat to think that even she finds them intolerable." [36] But however prematurely published, Clayton's report of her views is consistent with her own later accounts. Goldman's rejoinder, published in *The Nation* and in the *Liberator,* charging that Clayton's article was "an absolute falsification, full of lying insinuations," was unfair. Ironically, while *The Nation* defended Goldman against reports that she had turned anti-Soviet, her own defense, also published in *The Nation,* was ambiguous and evasive, noting that she was "with the Russian revolution, with the Russian people," while avoiding any mention of the Bolsheviks. Even to Stella she wrote, "I have undying faith in the Russian people, whatever faith I may have lost in other directions." [37] The Clayton episode lingered in Emma's memory. Years later, in her autobiography, she used it as an example of journalistic unreliability, although in this case it was her version that was unreliable. [38]

In any event, in the early summer of 1920, Goldman was considering two promising arenas of activity. One was the Board of Health, which was doing "wonderful work," she wrote to Stella. They had asked her to join them, and she was seriously considering the prospect. [39] In fact, she and Berkman had all sorts of offers, she noted, and were still considering how they could do the greatest good yet remain true to their ideals. In the end, Emma decided not to work with the Board of Health, since it would tie her to Petrograd and she wished to see more of the Russian countryside. [40] Instead both she and Berkman accepted an offer to work with the Petrograd Museum of the Revolution, a relatively "nonpartisan" institution that was organizing an expedition to southern Russia, primarily through the Ukraine, to collect documents and materials bearing on Russian revolutionary movements, including those of 1917. Why Emma felt that joining the museum, which was a state-run institution, compromised her principles less than, say, working for the Board of Health or the Education

Department, remains unclear. More likely, the museum work appealed to her because it opened the possibility of travel and offered relative autonomy. The project—"to collect dead material amidst the raging life of Russia"—appeared to Emma and Sasha as rather academic at first. But finally, feeling that all other possible work was unacceptable and eager to see more of the country and the people, they decided to join.

While fighting continued in parts of the Ukraine, the museum personnel in Petrograd prepared for the journey. As treasurer, housekeeper, and cook of the expedition (Berkman was chairman), Goldman helped outfit a museum railway car, spending a memorable afternoon rummaging in the basements of the czar's Winter Palace for imperial china to use on the journey. The museum car had six small compartments, which the group organized into sleeping rooms, an office, kitchen, and dining room. Besides the two "Americans," the staff included a secretary, Alexandra Shakol, who turned out to be an anarchist; a young Communist student from the university in Petrograd, assigned to visit local party institutions; and a Russian couple, "experts" on revolutionary documents. At their first stop, in Moscow, where the train was delayed several weeks in July, they picked up another passenger, Henry Alsberg, who became Emma's good friend and sympathetic critic. Alsberg was an easy-going, congenial bachelor of forty from New York with a law degree from Columbia University. He had given up potential careers in law and academia in favor of more adventurous pursuits, first as secretary to the U.S. ambassador in Turkey, and later as foreign correspondent for *The Nation,* the *New York World,* and the *London Daily Herald.* Alsberg had also been involved with Jewish relief work in Turkey and Palestine, and had become an ardent Zionist.[41] In 1921, he would turn critic of the Soviet regime for reasons similar to those of Goldman.[42] Inspired partly by his friendship with Goldman and Berkman, he would help organize the controversial International Committee for Political Prisoners to agitate on behalf of Soviet prisoners and exiles. But while he traveled with Goldman and Berkman, Alsberg remained friendly to the regime and wrote intelligent, sympathetic reports that appeared in *The Nation* in the summer and fall of 1920.[43] Later he would serve as director of the Federal Writers' Project under the New Deal.

After many delays, on July 30, 1920, the museum train began its laborious crawl south from Moscow, toward the oak and beech forests and the black soils of the Ukraine. As Emma recalled it later, the nightmarish scenes along the railroad tracks seemed a metaphor for the ruin of all Russia: "Broken cars dotted the landscape, disabled engines lay along the route and frequently the tracks were torn up." Railroad stations were packed with people, many of them sick and dying, frantically struggling for a foothold on a train. Emma often felt uncomfortable viewing such scenes from the relative comfort of the museum railroad car. Still, as they stopped in Ukrainian cities and towns such as Kharkov, Poltava, Fastov, Kiev, and Odessa—places few travelers from the West reached while the civil war was still raging—they had extraordinary opportunities to meet and talk with Communists, Zionists, Left Socialist Revolutionaries, Bundists, anarchists, writers, prisoners, doctors, shopkeepers, peasants, and workers in the streets, markets, and even a prison.

Despite the chaotic travel conditions, the work assumed a certain regularity. In each city, Emma and Sasha would orient themselves by visiting the local government headquarters, the Ispolkom or Executive Committee of the soviet, or, if the Bolsheviks had not been in control long enough to organize a soviet, the Revkom or Revolutionary Committee. After this initial visit, Emma would usually visit the Departments of Education, of Social Welfare, and of Workers' and Peasants' Inspection to see what documents she could assemble. At the same time, she and Sasha also sought out anarchists and other non-Communists and anti-Communists, the "tabooed part of the population," as she admitted frankly in her autobiography.

Numerous ironies characterized this three-month expedition. Although Goldman and Berkman undertook it partly in order to "get close to the Russian people," the Ukraine was not typically Russian. The region had a distinct cultural tradition, with a history of tense relations with the Russian "center" as well as with neighboring Lithuania and Poland. Ukrainian nationalism had emerged in the latter part of the nineteenth century. It had strong support among the intelligentsia in university cities such as Kharkov and Kiev, where a distinctly Ukrainian literature, in the Ukrainian language, had flowered, partly in response to the growing immigration of Russian workers into southern cities. Still, this nationalism was not a definite political movement. Its supporters included liberal and radical professionals and intellectuals as well as conservative landowners. As Emma and Sasha quickly learned, conflicts between Russians and Ukrainians occurred within the Communist party as well as outside it.

Economically, too, the Ukraine differed from other regions in its greater wealth: it supplied much of Russia's grain and sugar, as well as coal and iron ore from the Donetz Basin. These resources made it the most fiercely contested region of the country. Germans and Austrians occupied it first in the spring of 1918, following the Treaty of Brest-Litovsk. Subsequently, the White armies of General A. I. Denikin, the Ukrainian nationalist troops of S. Petlura, the partisan anarchist bands of Nestor Makhno, the Polish army, and the Red Army all battled for control. Between 1918 and 1921, the Ukraine was virtually an independent region, with successive warring governments headed by Germans, liberal Ukrainians, conservative Ukrainians, White Russians, Poles, and finally Communists.

Complicating this situation was the presence in the Ukraine, mainly in the cities, of perhaps two million Jews, whose middle-class occupations as merchants, tradesmen, or agents for the landowners made them vulnerable targets for economic resentment and pogroms. Although they formed a tiny minority in the Ukraine, only about 5 percent of the population, Jews made up about 22 percent of the urban middle class, with many Jewish doctors and lawyers as well as small shopkeepers and craftsmen. Kiev, Poltava, and Odessa were important centers of Jewish cultural life. All had strong Zionist movements, with many Hebrew schools and publishing houses and highly organized Jewish communal institutions, which the Bolsheviks alternately closed down or tried to take over. In the history of Russian Jews, the years of the civil war were particularly horrific: it has been estimated that as many as sixty thousand Jews in the Ukraine were murdered between 1917 and 1920, victims of pogroms instigated under the fiercely anti-Semitic regimes of Denikin, Petlura, and the Poles. Only with the establishment of Soviet power committed to halting pogroms did the massacres cease.

Goldman soon became familiar with the special history of the Ukraine, including its ambivalent relations with Russia. Yet her position as member of the museum put her in a role that was particularly ironic for an anarchist. An ardent proponent of local control and self-governance, she now found herself acting as agent for the "center," defending Russian interests against those of the Ukrainians. She was often impatient with the efforts of Ukrainian officials to retain materials for local use. In Kharkov, capital of the Ukraine, for example, the chairman of the Department of Education, a "cordial and competent man," decided, after promising to provide documents, that he wished to keep educational materials for a Ukrainian museum. Emma was "indignant at the miserable deception practiced upon us by a man in high Communist position. Surely Ukraina has the right to have its own museum, but why this petty fraud which caused the Expedition to lose so much valuable time." In Kiev, Emma spoke, by her own account, in the rather bullying voice of the center, applying what she jokingly called "the American amulet"—presenting herself as an American rather than a Russian—to persuade reluctant local officials to give up their materials. "Are you willing that it become known in America that you prefer to have valuable historical material rot away in Kiev rather than give it to the Petrograd Museum, which is sure to become a world centre for the study of the Russian Revolution and where Ukraina is to have such an important part?" she would ask. The threat usually worked.[44]

Although the Ukraine was predominantly a rural region, the museum expedition spent most of its time in the cities. Goldman seems to have had relatively little contact with peasants, whom she viewed mainly from the windows of the museum train. When she did talk with them, she was understandably put off by the anti-Semitism prevalent in the region. In fact, she wrote Stella, she found "every Ukrainian saturated with anti-Semitic feelings," which the Soviet government rigidly held in check. In *My Disillusionment,* she described an encounter with a Ukrainian peasant that summed up her feelings of scorn and disgust. This man had refused to drive her and Berkman through a dark forest at night to a nearby train station without the protection of two armed Jewish militiamen. "The peasant, a true Ukrainian, would not have hesitated a moment to beat and rob Jews in a pogrom," she noted caustically, "yet he felt secure in the protection of Jews against the possible attack of his own co-religionists."[45]

Goldman spent more of her time in the Ukraine with professional people and members of the middle-class intelligentsia. Apart from certain Soviet officials, some of whom were former workers, she spoke by her own account mainly with doctors, teachers, engineers, writers, and "literary men." These were the people whose homes she visited, whose gatherings she attended, whose dilemmas she understood. In Poltava, for example, she met the famous Ukrainian writer Vladimir Korolenko, a moderate critic of the new regime, and also his daughter, a teacher, whose home was "an oasis in the desert of Communist thought and feeling." In Odessa, she spent an afternoon with the great Hebrew poet Hayyim Nahman Bialik, just before he left for Israel. In Kiev she spent an evening with "the best elements of the local Jewish intelligentsia."[46]

Many of the intellectuals whom Goldman and Berkman met in the Ukraine were Jews, including Bundists, Zionist-Socialists, and also anarchists, with whom they discussed anti-Semitism, the recent wave of pogroms, and inconsistent Bolshevik policies toward Jewish cultural endeavors. In these discussions, Emma and Sasha's identity as "Americans" enhanced their welcome, for the Jews they met were eager to hear of the

"New World" and to convey messages to relatives there. This was especially true in the town of Fastov, site of a devastating pogrom in September of 1919 in which some sixteen hundred Jews had been slaughtered. Goldman was shocked by the women of Fastov, most of whom had been repeatedly raped and forced to witness the murder of male relatives. "When I was in America I did not believe in the Jewish question removed from the whole social question," Goldman admitted later on her return to Petrograd. "But since we visited some of the pogrom regions I have come to see that there is a Jewish question, especially in the Ukraine." Goldman now argued that the effort of the Soviet government to hold anti-Semitism "rigidly in check" was reason enough for American Jews to demand the diplomatic recognition of Russia. She continued to praise the efforts of the regime "to hold the hatred of the Jews in check," even though "many Communists themselves are anti-Semitic." [47]

This encounter with Russian Jewry moved Goldman unexpectedly, for she later wrote Stella that of all the suffering she had witnessed in Russia, that of the pogrom victims left the deepest impression. [48] She had always felt proud of her Jewish heritage, which she believed was the source of her own tenacity and perseverance. For all her outspoken attacks on religion, she never criticized Judaism quite as bitterly as she did Christianity, and she admired Jewish cultural institutions, such as the Kulturliga in the Ukraine, which sponsored art studios and schools. She had long been sensitive to anti-Semitism, criticizing Ben Reitman, for example (who was Jewish) for his occasional anti-Semitic remarks and on one occasion inquiring anxiously of a comrade about Bakunin's alleged anti-Semitism. [49] Although Goldman had always kept her distance from the Yiddish-speaking Jewish immigrant anarchists in America, whom she found timid and parochial, she counted many of her warmest supporters among them.

Still, like many of the assimilated Jewish radicals and revolutionaries of her generation on both sides of the Atlantic, her identification as a Jew was secular and cultural rather than religious. She continued to see Jewish emancipation as inextricably linked with larger movements of social revolution, and was unmoved by the appeals of Zionism, which she believed would resurrect all the ills of the state. She remained wary of the anti-Bolshevik attitude of the Ukrainian Jews, since she recognized that they were, for the most part, petit bourgeois rather than working-class. Quick to criticize anti-Semitism, Goldman was also quick to criticize Jews who in her view failed to protest against oppression. With the rise of Adolf Hitler in Germany in the thirties, this ambivalence would again come to the fore, as she alternately attacked Nazism and accused the German Jews of passivity and subservience. Her exposure to the suffering of the Jews in the Ukraine, and the success of the Bolsheviks in halting the pogroms did not, finally, change her views toward the regime, or encourage her to press for recognition.

Goldman continued to react cautiously to the anarchists whom she met on this journey. The Ukraine was an important center of anarchist activity and the home of the Nabat Confederation, one of the largest anarchist organizations in Russia, forming an umbrella for a host of smaller groups throughout the region. Although recently organized, Nabat conducted active propaganda on behalf of anarchist ideas and ran an anarchist bookstore in Kharkov.[50] Goldman and Berkman met with members of the Nabat Confederation before the mass arrests of anarchists and Makhnovists in November of 1920, but Emma reported later that, although her comrades had urged her to help, or at least inform European and American anarchists of the situation in Russia, she did not feel free to do so; her own views were still too unclear.[51] She also remained uncertain in her attitude toward the Makhnovists, again outlawed and pursued by the Bolsheviks. Nestor Makhno sent his wife, Galina, as an emissary to the two Americans while they were in Kiev, inviting them to a clandestine meeting. But they decided the venture entailed too many risks to other members of the museum expedition. The meeting did not take place.

Emma and Sasha arrived back in Petrograd in late October of 1920. The trip had been extremely interesting, Sasha reported to Fitzi, successful from a historical point of view, and "mentally profitable for ourselves." They had collected valuable material of all sorts—printed matter, proclamations, pamphlets, banners, posters, weapons, stamps, money—relating to revolutionary movements as far back as the early nineteenth-century Decembrists. They had also amassed data on various counterrevolutionary movements, on the secret police archives of the czars, and on pogroms against the Jews.[52] Within a few weeks, Emma and Sasha departed again on a second, shorter lap of their collecting expedition. This time they traveled north, to Archangel, a city only recently evacuated by British and American occupying troops in collaboration with the White forces of General Yudenich. Instead of chaos, sabotage, and bitter hatred of the intelligentsia and bourgeoisie, they found organization, tolerance toward former enemies, and friendliness toward the "center." Emma reported later that she had found all doors open to her, thanks to the cordial attitude of the chairman of the Archangel Ispolkom, "a pleasant type of Communist, not at all officious or stern." She visited several schools, art studios, and a local theater. She was impressed, not only with the warmth and cooperative spirit which prevailed, but also with the efficiency of all the local Soviet institutions, including food distribution, the source of so much corruption elsewhere. "There was no sabotage," she wrote later, "the various bureaus worked in good order, and the general spirit was sincere and progressive." [53]

Goldman might reasonably have considered Archangel as an encouraging example of Soviet potential, but her experience there failed to raise her hopes. She returned to Petrograd in late December more lost and bitter than before. That winter of 1920 to 1921 was one of the most brutal on record. Temperatures hovered below freezing for months on end. Darkness shrouded the cities, which lacked fuel for heat and light. A deathlike pall hung over Petrograd and Moscow. Inside the great abandoned apartments of Petrograd, people crowded into one room around a stove, tearing up floorboards and burning whole libraries for fuel. A few swallows of oatmeal or rotting horsemeat constituted a meal. "A lump of sugar would be divided into tiny fragments among a family and a single mouthful taken out of turn would start angry scenes," reported Victor Serge in his *Memoirs of a Revolutionary.*[54] Children and old people died by the thousands. Although the blockade had ended the previous November, medicines and soap remained scarce; cholera, typhoid, influenza, and especially typhus, carried everywhere by lice, raged out of control. The years of war and extreme deprivation left many Russians with a sense of acute shell shock. "Never before in history, perhaps, did so many people suddenly feel conscious of having what they regarded as the solid ground suddenly crumble and disappear from beneath their feet." [55]

Living among Soviet officials and supplied with American gold, which they had brought with them and which visitors apparently continued to bring over, Emma and Sasha were shielded from the worst effects of the famine and cold. Yet witnessing the ghastly suffering around her, Goldman felt overcome by a sense of futility, frustrated at her inability to "take root" and find a way of participating in an independent, nonpartisan capacity. The museum work did not qualify, in her eyes, for it was not exactly the most burning need of the day; she did it simply to keep at work. "I have never felt more useless," Emma confided to Stella. More than ever, Emma was tormented by the irony that she, who had always longed "to be in the thick of the revolution," should find herself so completely at sea. If only they had come during the October days, it would have been different, she speculated. "Perhaps it is conditioned in life that each should play only one part in the revolutionary process. I don't know, I only know that I never longed so much to give out of myself to the revolution and never found myself so utterly unable to give." [56]

During the next several months Goldman returned often to this theme, lamenting over and over to Stella how paralyzed she felt, and how unable she was to take part in the overwhelming events all around her, even in those capacities such as nursing, where her skills were in great demand, or in areas such as women's emancipation, which had previously commanded her attention. Her depression stermmed partly from her unhappiness with the directions the Soviet regime was taking, and a feeling that all her values had been shattered. As Henry Alsberg later wrote, "Her belief in human rights, in honor, in mercy, in individual liberty, and even in efficiency, which latter she learned to know in America, excluded her from participation in this hell's kitchen of revolution. Speaking Russian, and famous as a revolutionary leader, she naturally became the haven to which all the unhappiness and misery of the disillusioned came for sympathy. And yet except in a few individual instances, she found herself unable to give help, or even counsel." She became increasingly aloof from the ruling powers until finally she withdrew altogether from any connection with public activity. As Alsberg concluded, "She was an outsider, one who had come too late." [57]

But Goldman's depression, with its attendant self-absorption and loss of energy and interest, was also, by her own admission, a result of her loneliness and homesickness; it was the cumulative effect of a series of losses that had robbed her of all her emotional supports. Beginning with her release from the Missouri State Penitentiary (where she had been imprisioned for her antidraft activities) in September 1919, she had gone from one maelstrom into another, with no time to readjust to life outside of prison, or to prepare herself psychologically for departure. Deportation meant a violent rupture with a whole network she had built up over many years, the severing of vital personal connections. Suddenly, at the age of fifty, Emma was left on her own, in a psychological sense, with Berkman as her only emotional anchor.

Now in this state of mourning, Emma filled her letters with inquiries about America, expressions of anxiety about loved ones far away, and laments about her "hunger of the spirit which longs to help and relieve and is yet unable to take root." [58] She repeatedly complained to Stella and Fitzi that they failed to understand her "spiritual travail." Yet her letters were uncharacteristically cryptic, partly because of her desire not to provide ammunition for counterrevolutionaries and her fear that her criticism might redound badly for her Russian comrades. Until she had arrived at definite conclusions, she chose not to explain. "Believe me dearest," she wrote Stella at the end of November 1920, "I suffer as much as you and F[itzi] from our enforced silence, but until I have solved in my own mind what should or should not be I can not write the things which disturb our minds and souls, things which have brought us the deepest travail of our lives." [59]

But Goldman also found herself literally unable to speak. "Every time I begin to write my heart sinks," she explained. "A thousand things crowd in upon me demanding expression." Unless she wrote when mail from home had just arrived, "while my spirit is still aflame," she could not write at all. "The amount one wants to say and the utter impossibility of saying it adequately paralyzes me." [60] Emma compared herself to the blind, deaf, and dumb Helen Keller, whose autobiography she had read en route to Archangel. But even she was struck by the irony that, in returning to the land of her youth, to the revolution for which she had longed, she felt like "a stranger in a strange land." "Oneself no longer exists in the terrible struggle and turmoil of the world," she lamented. She lived only for letters from home, and longed for expressions of warmth and solidarity, which she found painfully lacking in war-torn Russia. "It is so cold and dissolute [sic] in R," she wrote plaintively in the spring of 1921. "War and four years of suffering have made everybody so self-centered." [61]

Back in Petrograd in February of 1921, Emma and Sasha now found themselves witnesses to a dramatic turning point in the history of the regime. Hunger, first in Moscow, then in Petrograd, triggered an escalating series of strikes. To an exhausted, starving, demoralized population, the lack of food capped a wide range of grievances that had accumulated over seven years of bitter foreign and civil war. In Petrograd, the strikers demanded changes that would put an end to the most onerous policies of War Communism: substitution of a tax for the hated grain requisitions; removal of roadblocks so city dwellers could seek food in the countryside; permission to barter personal possessions for food; an increase in the food ration. As the strike movement spread, political demands appeared. Strikers urged the restoration of basic civil and political rights, including free speech and press, the disbanding of labor armies, and freedom for socialist political prisoners. [62]

The Petrograd Soviet and the Cheka responded with force. They arrested strikers, moved military forces into the city, blamed the protests on

White Guards and their alleged Menshevik and Socialist Revolutionary (SR) allies. But the government also made some concessions that, within the limits of available supplies, met the demands of the strikers. They distributed additional rations, removed roadblocks, and released soldiers who had been assigned to labor duty. By the beginning of March, the protests had ceased.

By this time, however, the strikes in Petrograd had stirred similar unrest among the sailors of the Kronstadt naval base, located on an island some twenty miles west of the city in the Gulf of Finland. These sailors, with their tradition of militancy and rebellion, had played an active part in the October revolution. They had also continued to provide crucial support for the Bolsheviks throughout the civil war. At the same time, they had come to resent the increasingly authoritarian voice of the party. Periodically they voiced their demands for freely elected soviets, a return to the democratic military practices of 1917, and an end to commissars and "military specialists" with authority over the sailors' elected representatives. In late February, the sailors supplemented these demands with calls for increased rations of food and warm clothing. They also supported the widespread protests against requisitions and roadblocks. With tensions building swiftly, the sailors elected a Revolutionary Committee to negotiate with the authorities in Petrograd, while holding the local Communist authorities under arrest.

From the Hotel Astoria in Petrograd, Emma and Sasha followed these events with growing excitement and apprehension. They were elated by the "splendid solidarity" of the Kronstadt sailors with the striking workers of Petrograd, and they strongly supported their demands. Indeed, Emma briefly considered going to Kronstadt to experience for herself this revival of the spirit of October, but wisely decided against it, recognizing that her presence there would lend ammunition to Bolshevik claims about outside agitators. Instead, she and Sasha met nightly with other anarchist comrades, including several *Buford* deportees and with Victor Serge, a former anarchist and later a Trotskyist, who was then working with the regime. Because of the strong anarchist or "anarcho-populist" spirit of the sailors, the group felt that Goldman and Berkman especially might be able to exercise a restraining influence over the sailors, as well as among the Petrograd officials with whom Berkman, at least, still maintained cordial relations.

As the Kronstadt conflict escalated, Emma decided the moment had come to act. On the night of March 5, she, Sasha, and two other comrades drew up an offer of mediation, addressed to Zinoviev as president of the

Petrograd Soviet. They proposed to organize a Committee of Five, which would include Goldman and Berkman, to go to Kronstadt to settle the dispute peacefully. "Cold and hunger have produced dissatisfaction," they wrote, "and the absence of any opportunity for discussion and criticism is forcing the workers and sailors to air their grievances in the open." Any resort to force of arms would only do incalculable harm and aid the international forces of reaction. "Comrades Bolsheviki, bethink yourselves before it is too late. Do not play with fire. You are about to make a most serious and decisive step." [63]

The appeal went unanswered, but it may have had some effect, for the next day, March 6, the Petrograd Soviet telegraphed the Revolutionary Committee in Kronstadt, proposing that a delegation from the Soviet, of party and nonparty members, visit Kronstadt to explore the situation. By this time, however, the sailors had come to distrust too deeply the Petrograd officials who had arrested their wives and children. They rejected the offer, demanding instead a delegation of "true non-party members," with a maximum of 15 percent Communists. With this offer, repudiated by the Petrograd Soviet, all efforts at negotiation ceased.

On March 7, the military assault began. Soviet troops fired on Kronstadt intermittently for the next eleven days. From her room at the Astoria, Emma listened to the bombardment, overcome with grief and anger, not only at the authorities who had ordered the attack, but also at the intellectuals, Communist and non-Communist, whose failure to protest haunted her as well. Later Emma angrily accused these intellectuals of cowardice, a "spineless acquiescence," but her analysis was unfair, for some of the "Communists" to whom she alluded, such as Victor Serge, had acted on painful conviction rather than cowardice. As Serge explained it in his *Memoirs,* they had decided, "after many hesitations and with unutterable anguish," that it was necessary to declare themselves on the side of the party, even while acknowledging the justice of the Kronstadt sailors' demands and the symbolism of Kronstadt as "the beginning of a fresh, liberating revolution for popular democracy." The country was absolutely exhausted, there were no reserves, and the best members of the party had been decimated by the civil war. The counterrevolutionary forces could come back to life in a few weeks. "If the Bolshevik dictatorship fell," he wrote, "it was only a short step to chaos, and through chaos to a peasant rising, the massacre of the Communists, the return of the émigrés, and in the end, through sheer force of events, another dictatorship, this time antiproletarian." [64]

As the historian Paul Avrich has shown, the uprising was indisputably a spontaneous popular protest sparked by hunger, cold, and the desire to renew the democratic promises of October. It was not a deliberately planned counterrevolutionary plot, as government propaganda alleged. Yet White émigré organizations in Paris and elsewhere were clearly prepared to use the uprising for their own counterrevolutionary purposes. The anxieties of the regime over the possibilities of a White resurgence were by no means unfounded.[65] Kronstadt, writes Avrich, presents a situation "in which the historian can sympathize with the rebels and still concede that the Bolsheviks were justified in subduing them."[66] When the bombardment finally ceased on March 18, some six hundred Kronstadt sailors were dead, with over one thousand wounded and perhaps two thousand taken prisoner, of whom several hundred were later shot or sent into exile. Most of the dead, however, had fought against Kronstadt on the Soviet side, with an estimated total of ten thousand wounded and killed.[67]

Kronstadt dealt a further blow to the Russian anarchists. Militants were again arrested in various cities, dismissed from jobs, imprisoned, and sent to labor camps. Anarchist centers in Petrograd and Moscow were "sealed" by the Cheka and all publishing activities forced to stop, although some centers were later reopened and limited activity allowed to resume. Emma and Sasha signed their names to a strong protest issued by three Russian anarcho-syndicalist groups condemning the arrests and harsh treatment of anarchist prisoners (some of whom were not released until late in the summer after a hunger strike and intervention from foreign delegates to the Red Trade Union International).

Kronstadt represented a defeat for the anarchists in another way as well, for it interrupted the fruitful self-criticism that they had begun. "I, for my part, feel that An. & the An. have failed to work out concrete forms of action, even of thought, to apply to actual revolution & the revolutionary period bound to follow it, as is now the case in R.," Berkman wrote in December of 1920. "Many vital problems find no adequate answer in our books & theories. Result—the tragedy of the An. in the midst of the revolution & unable to find their place or activity." It was not enough, he wrote, for anarchists to oppose the dictatorship of the proletariat. "Have we anything to offer in its place? How would we manage things? What would we, as An., advise in this or that urgent moment at the time of revolut. upheaval? And how would we carry on the work of rebuilding?"[68] Just before Kronstadt, on March 2, 1921, when he was still expressing optimism about the regime, Berkman had noted the inapplicability of certain anarchist tenets and tactics. "There are some basic questions that need revision—or at least clarification," he wrote. "We must clearly define our position on the dictatorship, our proposed method of conducting the revolution, our program industrial & agrarian the day after the barricades. These & many other questions must receive our immediate attention. And the An. movement, as such, has so far not said its word on these vital matters, except taking a negative attitude on some of them." Berkman felt that anarchists "must profit by the great lessons of the Rev. & revise, where necessary, our foundations even, not to speak of our methods and tactics."[69]

After Kronstadt, however, such considerations yielded to more immediately pressing issues. By April 1921, both Berkman and Goldman had evidently decided that, as anarchists, they had no future in Soviet Russia. As Emma wrote, "More and more we have come to the conclusion we can do nothing here. And as we can not keep up a life of inactivity much longer we have decided to leave."[70] Anarchist agitation was out of the question. Further, outside of some form of state employment, there was almost no way Emma could earn a living much less use her talents as a speaker. On this point Goldman's discomfort was personal as well as political, for, as a lifelong free lance, she considered salaried employment of any kind unacceptable. She was irritated by Stella Ballantine's suggestions that she seek a diplomatic post abroad. "How do you suppose one can keep one's integrity while pledging oneself to any kind of an agreement?" she wrote Stella. "One must keep such a pledge, mustn't one? And how is one to do it without feeling under obligation? Dearest, dearest, don't you know that one cannot remain true to oneself if one binds oneself?"[71]

Berkman evidently remained uncertain and conflicted about the regime for several months more.[72] Not until July did Emma really indicate that Sasha had come to share her frank hostility toward the Bolsheviks, and that she felt less alone. "It is not so hard now since S has at least come to see things in their proper light," she wrote Stella early that month. "But it was bitter hard to go it all alone in the face of so many overwhelming events." As she put it years later in her memoirs, it was a relief not to have to "choke back my thoughts and emotions before the one human being who had shared my life, my ideals, and my labours through our common lot of thirty-two years."[73] Several more months elapsed, however, before Emma and Sasha finally applied for permission to leave at the end of October or early November. During this time, they watched the signs of economic recovery introduced by the New Economic Policy (NEP) in the spring of 1921. Initiated in response to the catastrophic state of the economy at the end of the civil war, and to the demands particularly of peasants for an end to the hated system of forced grain requisitions, the NEP represented a program of economic liberalization and political tightening. A tax was substituted for the requisitions, peasants were allowed to sell surplus on the free market, and barriers to trade between the cities and countryside were removed. Some nationalized enterprises were returned to private hands and the cooperatives were revived. Rather than a forced race toward socialism, which meant breaking the peasantry in an effort to supply the capital for rapid industrialization, Russia under NEP would travel a more moderate road, accepting the necessity for a mixed economy, both capitalist and socialist—or "state capitalism" as Lenin called it—until a more substantial level of industrial development was reached.[74]

Moderation in economics did not translate into political liberalization, however. The Tenth Party Congress that introduced NEP also approved Lenin's famous "ban on factions," which prohibited organized opposition within the party. The Workers' Opposition, a group within the party that argued for greater autonomy and more power for trade unions in economic planning, was effectively silenced, though not without heated debate. The only two opposition parties still active, the Mensheviks and the Left SRs, would soon find themselves completely swept from the scene. Dissent and even opposition—most notably the Trotskyist Left Opposition—were still possible for several years, but only within the ruling party, the sole arena for any remaining political dialogue. It was no longer possible to question publicly the legitimacy of the one-party dictatorship, which civil war had made increasingly authoritarian. Still, a considerable degree of nonpolitical freedom remained. Economically, intellectually, and culturally, Russia under the New Economic Policy would become a relatively pluralistic society.[75]

Such "nonpolitical freedom" did not satisfy Goldman and Berkman. Eager to leave Petrograd on account of its painful associations with Kronstadt, they moved to Moscow into a two-room apartment in the Leontevsky Prospekt, which was vacated by Kropotkin's widow and her daughter. For the first time since they had arrived, the two exiles lived like ordinary nonparty Russians, although they were shielded from the worst hardships by their American dollars. But they were determined not to receive privileges from the regime. They evidently severed, with considerable regret, their connections with the Petrograd Museum of the Revolution, partly in order to organize a new Kropotkin Museum to be established in Dmitrov, but possibly also because a commissar from

Moscow had been appointed to oversee the Petrograd operation: a condition the two anarchists could not accept.[76] Emma lived a desultory life. She spent much of her time shopping for food in the markets, now well-supplied as a result of NEP, and cooking for a few anarchist comrades who gathered at their place. Unable to engage in public activity, Emma, who had always been an excellent cook, found some solace in being able to feed others, even if she was unable to offer help on a wider scale.

The summer of 1921, the occasion of the founding congress of the Red Trade Union International, or Profintern, marked another turning point in the history of anarchist relations with the Bolsheviks. Despite their campaigns against the anarchists in Russia, the Bolsheviks had been eager to woo foreign anarcho-syndicalist organizations into the new Third International, or Comintern, and away from the Socialist Second International. In the eyes of the Soviet leaders, the anarcho-syndicalists were revolutionaries, not reformists, and were still desirable allies. Nearly all the syndicalist organizations of Europe had sent delegates to the first congress of the Third International in the summer of 1920. But the Third International was essentially an organization of political parties, while the anarcho-syndicalist organizations were antiparliamentary trade union federations. The Comintern decided to create a separate international alliance of revolutionary trade unions. By the summer of 1921, when the founding congress of the new Trade Union International was held, discontent had mounted among the foreign anarcho-syndicalist delegates on account of the conditions laid down by the Russians as requirements for membership in the new organization, such as cooperation with local Communist parties. Leading militants had begun to speak out against the Bolsheviks in the anarchist press abroad, including Rudolf Rocker, whose influential pamphlet, *Die Bankrotte des russischen Staatskommunismus*, had been published in Berlin earlier that year.[77]

It was in this atmosphere of deepening tensions between anarcho-syndicalists and Bolsheviks that the founding congress of the Red Trade Union International took place in the summer of 1921. Goldman and Berkman were not delegates, since they did not belong to any anarchist or anarcho-syndicalist organization. But as leading figures in the German, Italian, Spanish, French, and Swedish movements arrived in the Russian capital, Emma and Sasha found themselves playing host, as they had the summer before, to comrades whose disillusionment had not yet crystallized, including such figures as Gaston Leval, one of the early critics of the Bolsheviks and author of an important work on the anarchist collectives during the Spanish Revolution, and Augustine Souchy, a German anarcho-syndicalist with whom Goldman would later work during the Spanish civil war. Anarcho-syndicalists everywhere were debating whether to affiliate with the Red Trade Union International, which meant accepting Moscow's model and dominance. While some opted to join the Communists, most followed a path of disillusionment similar to that of Goldman and Berkman; on returning from Moscow, they would urge anarcho-syndicalist federations in their home countries against affiliation. Later they would draw up plans for a new syndicalist international, which would be organized in December of 1922.

It is unclear whether Goldman and Berkman may have influenced the delegates who came to Moscow at this time, as Victor Serge suggested in his memoirs.[78] Certainly they were in a position to do so, since they spoke Russian, had remained much longer in Russia than most foreign delegates, had traveled widely and were closer to leading figures in the government than most of their comrades from abroad. On the other hand, the conditions demanded by Moscow for membership in the Profintern sufficed to alienate many anarcho-syndicalists, for whom independence from all party ties remained a basic tenet. Moreover, the persecution of the Russian anarchists, dramatized that summer by a hunger strike of anarchist prisoners arrested at the time of Kronstadt, further dampened the enthusiasm of the visitors.[79]

Goldman seems to have been most disturbed that summer by the reverential attitude of the American delegates toward the Bolsheviks and their aloofness from herself and Berkman. She found it painful to be ignored by former friends such as Big Bill Haywood of the Industrial Workers of the World, the radical journalist Mary Heaton Vorse, the organizer Ella Reeves Bloor, and Robert Minor, whose ascerbic cartoons had once graced the covers of *Mother Earth*. "The city swarms with Americans," Emma wrote Stella in October of 1921, "but we see no one. Most of the Americans are people I never would have turned the corner to meet while at home. Much less would I want to meet them here. And the few so-called friends have got 'religion' so bad, they would without hesitation hang everyone who has not grown blind, deaf and dumb as they." She was hurt by the readiness of former friends to repudiate her, even if she was equally ready to castigate all sympathizers with the regime as "cowards," "dupes," and "dilettantes."[80] She did not attend the various congresses that met in Moscow during the summer of 1921 (including an International Congress of Communist Women), except for an occasional meeting of the Red Trade Union International. But for the most part she remained a spectator.

She did, however, meet the American journalist, Agnes Smedley, who was covering the Women's Congress for the *Liberator*. The two women would later become friends in Berlin, where Smedley worked on behalf of the independence of India. They shared confidences about men, love, loneliness, and other intimate matters. Smedley admired Goldman and contrasted her own spiritual isolation with what she considered as Emma's gift for mingling easily with people. "You are wise and sane. But I am lonely and insane," she once wrote. Emma too cared for Smedley. She was hurt years later when the younger woman broke off relations with her after becoming convinced that the Communists held out the only hope for change in impoverished Third World countries such as China. "I knew to meet your friends or you would lead to nothing whatever but bitterness," Smedley would write to her in 1934, on the eve of sailing for China. "I do not want to think of you with bitterness, and I think you prefer not to think of me so." [81]

Despite her pleasure in contacts with Smedley and her efforts to secure the release of her great heroine, Maria Spiridonova, a leader of the Left Socialist Revolutionaries whom she had met the summer before, Emma remained depressed and withdrawn. When several years of drought upset agricultural planning in the Volga district and led in the summer of 1921 to a catastrophic famine—an estimated twenty-two million people were affected, and perhaps five million perished—she considered joining the relief effort, where her nursing and organizing skills would have been valuable. Indeed, the situation was so dire that the Soviet regime mobilized many non-Communists, and even organized a nonparty All-Russian Committee for Aid to the Hungry, though this committee was soon disbanded and several bourgeois members arrested. [82] The United States also organized an American Relief Administration to distribute aid to the stricken regions. But even in this devastating emergency, Emma found herself paralyzed, unable to act. She wrote Stella later that she would have loved to help in the famine district but could not because she was unable to do so in a nonpartisan manner. Emma saw the relief campaign as merely another cynical ploy of the regime to exploit widespread sympathy for the famine victims, and even to profit from it. The famine was being used, she argued, "as an excuse for most of those who are making capital out of it. The famine stricken will be the last to benefit, or will benefit only very little. For the rest, the famine is another link in the chain of enslavement by pity. Perhaps if I would not see through it all I might be able to work with the relief people. For my own peace of mind I wish I would not see. As it is I can not hitch up with them. I simply can not." [83]

In her plaintive laments to Stella, Emma tried to explain her failure to join the relief effort by emphasizing the strength of her scruples, but she seemed not entirely convinced herself. Later, in her autobiographical account of this period, she would characteristically shift the blame for her inactivity onto the regime, writing that the offers of help that she and "other Left elements" made to the government were declined. At the same time, Emma acknowledged that "the workers of Russia and the majority of the non-Communist population" carried out superhuman relief efforts, and that the intelligentsia—doctors, nurses, distributors of supplies—performed "miracles." [84]

By this time, however, Emma's letters from Russia were mostly taken up with laments about her failure to "take root" and with a deep visceral homesickness that nothing could ease. Even applying for a passport required more energy than she could muster. By late October 1921, she and Sasha still had not attempted to leave. Emma assured Stella that she was not losing her strength or will: "I only feel paralysed, temporarily overwhelmed by the deep tragedy of R." Not only Goldman and Berkman, but many other Russian anarchists as well now turned their thoughts toward leaving the country, especially after the shooting, in late September, of ten leading militants, including the poet, Lev Cherny, and a woman, Fanya Baron, whom Emma had known in America. [85] Indeed, these executions had shocked many Communists, according to Goldman, and the scandal eventually led the regime to release and deport a number of remaining anarchist prisoners.

Even so, Goldman was considering alternatives if they should have to remain in Russia for the winter. They would probably work again with the Petrograd Museum of the Revolution, or she could "grow rich" on nursing and giving private lessons in English. "Fine spiritual occupation for people who all their lives longed to be a part in the Revolution, isn't it?" she exclaimed bitterly. "However, it is better to earn one's living and retain one's spirit than to lose one's self-respect and be engaged in some public work. . . ." [86]

Thanks to the intervention of Angelica Balabanoff, Emma, Sasha, and a third comrade, the Russian Alexander Shapiro, secured Soviet passports and Latvian visas sometime in late November. Emma appears in her passport photograph in a heavy coat and woolen scarf, her hair hidden under a soft hat, her eyes staring into the camera with an uncharacteristic gaze of resignation and weariness. She looks frozen emotionally as well as physically, as she contemplates a future she cannot yet imagine. The departure was part of a larger exodus of anarchists whom the regime had decided to deport. For all their frustrations, neither Emma nor Sasha were overjoyed at the prospect of leaving. "Somehow news of these passports did not gladden me as one might think," Berkman noted in his diary, "and I don't know if I am more glad than sad at leaving this poor suffering country and all these lovable people and all the friends we have made in almost two years." [87]

For Emma, their departure marked the end of a lifelong romance with Russia. In what may have been her last letter to her niece from that country, she returned to the theme of her own suffering and guilt. "It was excruciating to go through the last two years," she wrote.

But you need not think it will be easy to go away. All my life I fed on the wonderful spirit of Russia, all my life I longed to see it free. Then to have found it prostrate, kicked into the gutter, attacked on all sides, enduring tortures Dante's Inferno did not contain. Above all, stabbed to the heart by its own friends. And then not to be able to help even a little bit. Yes, that was the hardest to bear, for never in all my life did I long to help, to be of service, to give out of my overflowing heart to the people of Russia. But it was impossible. So if we go, we will have given nothing. . . . [88]

Actually, Goldman's work as a member of the Petrograd Museum expedition added valuable materials to the archives of the revolution. For all their discomfiture in Russia, Emma and Sasha still impressed others as cooperative and generous. Angelica Balabanoff later observed that, despite their disillusionment and disorientation, "they cheerfully went on working without complaints or recriminations," and rarely asked for help. [89] But historical research did not rank high among Emma Goldman's priorities, and she worried now about her ability to accomplish anything worthwhile in any other country. "Will I be able to give anything in other lands? I am not deceived. I know only too well how rooted I have become. I know how little I could do now in America which seems to have gone mad with reaction. Yet I feel that I belong there and nowhere else. However, I must try other shores, get away from the nightmare, look at the tremendous panorama of Russia at a distance. That is necessary if one is not to judge too objectively."[90] Her slip of the typewriter here is revealing, for in her later writing about Russia she would move steadily away from her earlier, more "objective" recognition of the immense complexity of the Russian scene to a simpler perspective. In her search for "some outstanding feature in the blurred picture," she would increasingly pin all evils on a clearly identifiable source—"the political machine."

As Emma Goldman, Alexander Berkman, and Alexander Shapiro crossed the border into Latvia in early December of 1921, Emma was filled with bitter thoughts—of the destruction of the Russian anarchist movement, of her own "uselessness," of the immense suffering she had witnessed. She was filled with sadness for the loss of a great vision that had sustained her all her life. "Ah dearest girl," she had written her Ann Arbor friend Agnes Inglis a few months before, "how we used to dream of the wonderful things to come true in Russia. But like all dreams there is an awakening. . . ."[91] Only by writing, by bearing witness to what she had seen, could she hope to work through her grief and anger.[92] Upon that project rested all her hopes.

3

Russia as (M)other

This about telling the truth is all very well if there
were only one side to it. Unfortunately there is
nothing more complicated than the truth. . . .

—Emma Goldman, 1938

For all her claims about the "failure" of the Bolshevik regime, there is little question that Emma Goldman experienced her two years in Russia as a personal defeat. Despite many opportunities, she had found herself unable, for psychological as well as political reasons, to participate actively in the constructive work of the revolution. She had also lost a powerful ideal—the beacon of an idealized Russian revolutionary movement—which she had cherished since her adolescent years in St. Petersburg. Later Goldman would explain her withdrawal and anger in Russia as the result of her revulsion against the authoritarian directions the regime was taking. But her sense of paralysis also reflected a deep depression, a mourning for her lost life in America. It is likely that the shrillness of her later anti-Communist tirades owed something to her need to justify and explain to herself the paralysis she had suffered. By portraying the Bolshevik regime of 1920–21 as essentially evil, she could also explain her own withdrawal as a principled refusal to participate in the government's crimes. Her longing to return to capitalist America appeared more understandable in light of the grotesque alternative that, in her eyes, Bolshevik Russia presented.

Goldman's anger toward Russia may also have had other sources, for it contrasted dramatically with her apparent lack of anger at the United States, the country that had deported her. Indeed it is possible that her disillusionment with that country was even more painful than her disillusionment in Russia, since she had lived there much longer and all her family was there. It was as if she were unable to acknowledge fully the cruel injustices that had been done to her—and to many other immigrant radicals—by the U.S. government, since to do so would have left her feeling utterly abandoned and alone. As a way of protecting her attachment to America, and also to keep open the possibility that she might one day return, she may unconsciously have displaced her anger onto Russia, which then became the symbol of her double disillusionment.

In any event, throughout the period of her sojourn in Russia, and after she had left, Goldman seemed unconcerned with possible American interference with her actions. She routinely blamed her difficulties—with mail, passports, and visas—on Soviet meddling, though she had reason, given her prior experience, to suspect American involvement as well. In any event, she expected trouble from the Russians after she and Berkman crossed the border into Latvia (with minimal inspection by Russian border officials), for she was convinced that Soviet authorities had allowed them to leave in order to demonstrate to the world their tolerance toward anarchists; persecution would continue outside Soviet borders.[1] She was unaware that the United States kept her and Berkman under surveillance, directly intervening with foreign governments to monitor their movements. Indeed, the volume of correspondence and memoranda pertaining to their movements that U.S. officials exchanged on both sides of the Atlantic suggests a veritable obsession. Within five days of their arrival in Riga on December 5, 1921, the American commissioner in Riga had wired the U.S. secretary of state in Washington, informing him of their arrival and reported plan to proceed to the United States. "Am investigating carefully and will keep Department informed," he wrote, suggesting the importance of this case to Washington.[2]

The following week, Washington alerted American embassies in all the major European capitals—Berlin, Paris, London, Rome, the Hague, Christiania, Stockholm, Warsaw—advising them of Emma Goldman's possible efforts to secure a visa for the United States and asking to be kept informed of her movements. Her photograph, taken at her deportation, was circulated to the embassies, along with those of Alexander Berkman and Alexander Shapiro. Members of the American legations made inquiries of the local secret police, picking up stories, part fact, part fiction, which were circulated among the Departments of State, Justice and Labor. Washington was concerned mainly to prevent Goldman from reentering the United States, but the surveillance carried out in Europe—which included monitoring the mail of her comrades and associates—could not have helped her efforts to secure entry into other countries.[3]

It was true that Goldman wished to return to the United States. As soon as she left Russia, she contacted her lawyer in New York, Harry Weinberger, asking him to "write me with perfect frankness about my chance of returning to America." "It is no use deceiving myself and others by saying I will feel at home and be able to take root anywhere out of America," she admitted. She wanted to know if there was any sense in pressing the claim to U.S. citizenship (through her marriage to Jacob Kersner in 1886) and "any good going through with the marriage farce. I mean any good for a deported woman to attach herself to an American gentleman?" Emma joked to Weinberger that she had not yet "found the unfortunate one who will sacrifice himself for a 'good cause.' Still I mean to be prepared."[4]

Weinberger could not offer much encouragement. He advised her of the conservative mood in America and suggested she not press the issue for the time being. Meanwhile, arriving in Riga, the three anarchists went to stay in the apartment of a friend from Petrograd who was now an employee of the Soviet Embassy in Riga. Using this apartment as their headquarters—it was located, ironically, in the same building as the embassy—they made the rounds of the consulates; "some nuisance," as Berkman quipped, trying to secure visas for Germany where an international anarchist congress was scheduled for late December. They also applied for the necessary transit visas through Sweden, Lithuania, and Estonia. At the same time, anticipating possible difficulties, they asked comrades in Czechoslovakia, France, England, and Austria to try for visas in these countries. The uncertainty and anxiety of waiting tormented all of them, so that they even began planning a possible clandestine departure for Berlin.

Expecting the worst, Emma was not surprised when a promised visa to Germany was denied. She was convinced that "a Bolshevik Chekist" in Riga had engineered the denial by notifying the German consul in that city that she and Berkman and Shapiro were "dangerous Bolsheviks" on a secret mission for the government. Emma's evidence came partly from Rudolf Rocker in Berlin who, on her behalf, had approached the uncle of the German consul in Riga, a prominent Social Democrat, who assured Rocker that the visas would be granted. But after much delay the consul in Riga denied them, explaining later to his uncle that machinations from Moscow had caused the difficulty.[5]

That a Bolshevik official in Riga would reveal the identity of agents on a secret government mission seems implausible at best; certainly anyone traveling from Soviet Russia came under suspicion in anti-Bolshevik Latvia, without the necessity of machinations from Moscow. As Goldman put it to Stella, traveling with a Soviet passport was like being afflicted with leprosy.[6] Moreover, Emma changed the story in her memoirs, writing that the Chekist had warned the German consul that they "were dangerous conspirators on a secret mission to the Anarchist Congress in Berlin."[7]

In any case, within two weeks, comrades in Stockholm managed to secure visas for Sweden. The three anarchists departed Riga December 22, on the afternoon train for Reval (Tallinin), Estonia, en route to Stockholm. They were arrested by Latvian secret police a few stations down the line and brought back to Riga, where their belongings were seized and examined, and they were thrown into jail for a week. In his letter informing the State Department of these events, the American commissioner in Riga made clear his complicity with the Latvian secret police, who had turned over to him the material seized from the arrested parties. "The object of the action of the Latvian secret police in removing them from the train," he explained in a classified memorandum, "was to afford their agents an opportunity to search the baggage, personal effects etc., and to examine all of their papers and documents, which of course could not be done while they were housed in [the same building as] the Bolshevik consulate." The commissioner added that "all of the papers and documents found in the possession of these three parties came into my hands for a few hours." During this period, the commissioner had made copies "of those which it was thought would be of interest to the [State] Department," including Berkman's diary for September through December 1921, and his extensive address book, which he and Emma shared. All of these, including personal letters, were sent to the State Department, which circulated copies to the Bureau of Investigation, the Department of Labor, and even the Post Office Department. Many of Goldman's former associates in America were already under surveillance, but the list seized at Riga provided the Bureau of Investigation with additional names and information, which they lost no time in pursuing. Even European comrades, such as Albert Jensen in Stockholm, were subsequently spied on, their mail examined, and their associates reported to the State Department in Washington.[8]

These actions of the zealous American commissioner in Riga were not unusual: the year before, he had also mistaken Henry Alsberg for a Bolshevik agent. Alsberg in fact blamed the commissioner for Emma's arrest as well. Emma, however, was unshakably convinced the Russians lay behind her difficulties, taking the incident as further evidence of Bolshevik depravity and "Jesuitism," a view with which her Latvian captors concurred.[9] Released with apologies on December 30, the three anarchists finally departed for Reval, where they boarded a steamer for Stockholm. Here too, the American consul had been warned of their imminent arrival. He now took over the surveillance process, reporting dutifully to Washington on the activities and plans of the travelers.

Emma relaxed a little on her arrival in Stockholm. Sweden had an active anarcho-syndicalist movement, with daily and weekly papers where she could make her views known. She felt glad to be among comrades. Still, the relief was short-lived and their situation tense. The visas granted to Goldman, Berkman, and Shapiro were good only for two weeks. Information from comrades in Vienna, Paris, London, and Prague was not encouraging. Austria demanded a pledge that the anarchists refrain from participating in the movement there, a pledge Emma could not bring herself to sign. England, under a Tory government, flatly refused, despite petitions from Bertrand Russell and others on her behalf.[10] However, Czechoslovakia did grant a visa, which held out the possibility of also securing a transit visa through Germany. Once in Berlin, they could try for an extension.

Waiting once again to hear from Berlin, Emma found the delays almost unbearable. Her anxiety grew as days dragged into weeks, then months. The three anarchists remained in Sweden on sufferance, pledged to remain quiet and uninvolved in Swedish anarchist activity, although they did give interviews to the Swedish press. They could not extend their Swedish visas indefinitely, and if no other country allowed them entry, deportation to Russia remained a frightening possibility. By mid-February, two months after their departure from Russia, Emma was beginning to despair. "Our people simply do not realize what it means to be cast out from the whole world," she wrote a comrade, "the feeling of being absolutely adrift, it is the worst I have ever experienced, and I have known some hardships in my time."[11]

Desperate and lonely, Emma found solace in the companionship of a young Swedish sailor, Artur Svensson—Arthur Swenson to Emma—who had once been a Wobbly during a sojourn in the United States. Because he could speak English, Svensson acted as guide and translator for the three exiles in their dealings with Swedish authorities. Hungry for warmth and tenderness, Emma welcomed his admiration for her. A romance blossomed. Putting aside the twenty-two-year difference in their ages—she was fifty-two, he was thirty—Emma gave herself up to her infatuation for this youth, "the one comforting association of my dismal sojourn in Stockholm." [12]

In this setting of uncertainty and anxiety, Emma Goldman and Alexander Berkman began to speak and write about Russia in the anarchist press. Berkman wrote a series of polemical pamphlets which were published in Berlin by the anarchist publishing house, Der Syndikalist. [13] The London monthly, *Freedom,* also began, in January 1922, to print a series of their letters and articles condemning what they called "the most revolting Asiatic form of a war of extermination," and "Asiatic barbarism." The prisons of Russia were "densely populated," they wrote, with Left SRs, Maximalists, anarchists, anarcho-syndicalists, Universalists, and members of the Workers Opposition, all "true revolutionists and most of them enthusiastic participants in the November Revolution of 1917." [14] Goldman and Berkman made no attempt to estimate the numbers of revolutionists actually in prison or exile or how these compared with other countries—these were soon to become controversial issues. But they called on comrades outside of Russia to protest the antianarchist policies of the Soviets and asked for money to help the victims. Russia was far from being a "Workers' and Peasants' Republic," they wrote. "The workers and peasants have no more influence on the Bolshevik Government than they have on the Government of any other country." [15]

By early 1922, the anarchist and anarcho-syndicalist movements outside of Russia had developed a generally hostile relationship with the Soviet regime, which was increasingly viewed within the movement as a dictatorship *over* the proletariat by a new class of rulers. Still, first-hand accounts of Soviet Russia by comrades who had actually been in that country were few, and Emma Goldman and Alexander Berkman could speak with a special authority as respected Russian-speaking militants who had spent two years, not two weeks, in Russia.

Moreover, articles in the anarchist press were for Goldman only a beginning. From the start, she wanted to address an American audience— "the American public"—not the "foreign elements" or the few readers of anarchist weeklies. [16] She remembered, from the period prior to her deportation, how inaccurate and unreliable U.S. press coverage of the Russian revolution had been, even in supposedly reputable papers such as the *New York Times.* Indeed, coverage in that paper, according to journalist Walter

Lippman, had been "nothing short of a disaster," with "news" distorted by a fiercely anti-Bolshevik editorial policy, which substituted wish fulfillment for fact. At a critical historical moment, wrote Lippman, the American people "could not secure the minimum of necessary information on a supremely important event." [17] Goldman had carefully followed American press coverage of the revolution while still in prison and therefore attached great importance to the project of publicizing her and Berkman's views for an American audience. How to reach this audience, and for what purpose, became a point of dissension between Goldman, Berkman, and Shapiro, particularly when the *New York World* offered to publish a series of articles about Goldman's disillusionment in Russia (this was how the offer was stated).

Emma had an ambivalent, long-standing relation with Joseph Pulitzer's *World,* the mass-circulation, Democratic daily which, from the 1890s, had alternately courted Goldman, publishing her own statements, and violently attacked all anarchists. At the time of her deportation, the *World* expressed no regrets. Even while she was still in Russia, however, Goldman had contemplated the possibility of writing for the *World.* Now, the paper offered to pay three hundred dollars in gold for each of a series of five or six articles, which the editors promised to print as delivered.

Emma was torn. On the one hand, articles in the *World* would reach a wide audience. The money she would receive could relieve her own financial straits, as well as aid other émigrés and exiles. On the other hand, anti-Communist articles published in a capitalist paper like the *World* would arouse mistrust in the labor movement and the Left, since they would appear to be attacks on the revolution and on socialism generally, rather than on the Bolshevik version of it. As Emma put it, "It is bound to leave a stigma to my name . . . in time, even serious people will get the impression that I was with the bourgeoisie, not merely against the Bolsheviki but against the Revolution." She recalled ruefully her own criticism, in 1917, of Catherine Breshkovskaya for voicing anti-Bolshevik views under conservative auspices in the United States. Emma worried now that she was proposing to do the same thing. Berkman and Shapiro, adamantly opposed to publication in the *World,* urged her to offer the series to the anarchist press, which could turn them into a pamphlet. [18]

Although Emma admitted the validity of their objections, she felt, with good reason, that pamphlets would reach a limited audience. She wanted a liberal or radical paper or magazine—oddly enough, she thought even a conservative magazine would do, because "it makes a more serious and solid impression"—to accept her articles instead. Publication in the *Nation*, the *New Republic*, the *Freeman*, or the *Call* would at least put her views in a liberal context. She urged Stella Ballantine, acting as her agent in New York, to try them all. But Stella reported to Emma that the liberal and radical press would not accept articles attacking the Bolsheviks. In Stockholm, Emma had no way to verify Stella's report or how hard she had worked to secure publication. Certainly the *Nation* and the *New Republic*, both strongly pro-Soviet, had also published sharp criticism of the regime. But Emma believed that no liberal publication would accept her work. "I am so confused and unhappy," she admitted to Stella late in January. "Frankly, I don't know what to do." [19]

She decided to poll other comrades—Max Nettlau in Vienna, Rudolf Rocker in Berlin, Harry Kelly in New York, Errico Malatesta in Italy—all of whom urged her to go ahead with the *World* offer, though as Emma recognized, the European comrades were not familiar with American journalistic practice and could not have grasped the full implications of the decision. Berkman and Shapiro remained adamantly opposed. So did the International Anarchist Aid Federation in New York, which represented fifteen predominantly foreign-language groups (Russian, Yiddish, Italian, and Spanish as well as English) in the United States. Federation members, alarmed by news of Goldman's intentions, offered to print thousands of pamphlets and warned Emma that her anti-Soviet reports in a capitalist paper like the *World* would seriously damage their own efforts to reach radical workers. [20]

This reasonable suggestion infuriated Goldman. She fired off a long tirade dismissing the importance of foreign-language agitation in America and accusing her comrades of the Anarchist Aid Federation (an organization she said she had never heard of) of acting as fanatically as Bolsheviks in ignoring the individual for the sake of the cause. She insisted that the capitalist press had more influence on the Bolsheviks than the radical press, and that her thirty-two years in the movement had not impressed her with the efficiency of anarchist groups in publicizing critical issues. She was determined to proceed with publication. [21]

Emma's reply suggests how angry and abandoned she felt at that moment. Her letter to the New York Federation was full of bitter comments about how ill-used and neglected she had been by her comrades the previous two years. Once again, her anger seems misplaced, directed against other anarchists instead of against those in America responsible for her deportation and exile. Moreover, a large number of those attracted to the

American Communist parties were in fact immigrants whom the anarchists proposed to address. The "American public" Goldman wanted to reach was more likely the liberal intelligentsia, which had formed an important part of her audience in the years prior to her deportation. Ironically, these people—readers and writers of the *Nation* and the *New Republic*, for example—were among the few sane voices calling for normalizing relations with Russia and opposing the Red Scare mentality that lingered throughout the 1920s.

After many hesitations, Emma decided to accept the *World* offer, on the condition that the anarchist press would be able to reprint the articles.[22] She quickly completed the series, which she had begun sending to Stella in January of 1922, instructing her niece to give them all to the *World*. Before the first installment appeared on March 26, the paper noted that announcement of the articles had already stirred up "hot dispute," a "widespread storm of discussion," "unprecedented interest." " 'Now We Will Get Truth about Soviet Russia,' Trend of Most Comment," promised the *World*. This newspaper, which had once roundly denounced Goldman, now paid tribute to her "brilliant mind and political understanding," noting that of all travelers to Russia, she was perhaps "best qualified to see and judge the effect of the Bolshevist revolution there."[23]

The ten front-page articles, under predictably sensational headlines ("Russian Revolution A Failure, Says Miss Goldman, and Slain by the Bolsheviki Themselves"; "Her Body Dying Under Torture, Spirit of Maria Spiridonova Still Flames for her Russia"; "Miss Goldman Heard But One Happy Child's Laugh in Russia"), addressed such topics as peasant discontent, the "Red Terror" of the Cheka, Russian children, and trade unions, and included portraits of the outlawed Left Socialist Revolutionary leader Spiridonova and of Peter Kropotkin. Throughout the articles, Goldman attempted to distinguish between the popular Russian revolution from below, which she defended, and the October seizure of power by the Bolsheviks and subsequent creation of a bureaucratic, authoritarian state, which she opposed. She argued against the Bolsheviks because, in her view, they had halted the revolution rather than carrying it forward. Instead of moving toward socialism, they were returning the country to a new form of capitalism—"state capitalism," as Lenin called it—while continuing, indeed intensifying, the repressive power of the state. Instead of moving toward a stateless society—the famous "withering away of the state"—the Bolsheviks were creating a Leviathan state far more stultifying and dangerous than any government before them.

At the center of Goldman's libertarian analysis was a point that echoed the earlier critiques of the Bolsheviks by Kropotkin, by Rosa Luxemburg, and by Alexandra Kollontai, whose 1921 pamphlet on "The Workers' Opposition" Goldman had read.[24] "If a revolution is to survive in the face of opposition and obstacles," Goldman wrote, "it is of the utmost importance that the light of the revolution be held high before the people; that they should at all times be close to the living, throbbing pulse of the revolution. In other words, it is necessary that the masses should continuously feel that the revolution is of their own making, that they are actively participating in the difficult task of building the new life."[25] According to Goldman, instead of widening mass participation, the Bolsheviks had steadily encroached on the liberties of the masses, until the party had come to monopolize all power. A vast state bureaucracy, cumbersome and inefficient, crushed any possibilities for independent initiative. Oppositionists, including dissenters within the ruling Communist party, were increasingly silenced. The Cheka—or GPU as the political police was now called—had become virtually a state within a state, arresting, shooting, imprisoning, exiling, and deporting people with impunity. Under the regime of War Communism, peasant cooperatives had been largely converted into state organs of distribution, with peasants subject to forcible grain seizures by brutal bureaucrats who did not hesitate to shoot or beat recalcitrant *muziks*. Trade unions had become creatures of the state, lacking any autonomy, as were the soviets, where elections were manipulated to ensure party dominance. Vast numbers of starving, war-orphaned children roamed the streets or were herded into prison-like colonies or schools for "defectives" while resources were concentrated in a few "show schools" to impress visitors; the rest of the schools were miserable institutions where corrupt attendants were not above grabbing the bulk of food or other goods for themselves.

Goldman left no doubt that she considered the Marxist politics of the Bolsheviks ultimately responsible for Russia's "collapse." Eschewing distinctions between Marxism and Leninism—though she focused her critique on Leninist policies—she denounced "the Marxian policies of the Bolsheviks" as "the tactics first extolled as indispensable to the life of the revolution only to be discarded as harmful after they had wrought misery, distrust and antagonism"; these "were the factors that slowly undermined the faith of the people in the revolution." And again, "It is their Marxism that has determined their policies and methods. The very means they have employed have destroyed the realization of their end."[26]

Still, with all her criticisms, Goldman saw possibilities for change. She acknowledged, albeit reluctantly, commendable social achievements of the Bolsheviks, such as the abolition of child labor, the eight-hour work-day, and massive educational efforts for children. "It is true," she wrote, "that the Bolsheviki have attempted their utmost in regard to the child and education. It is also true that if they have failed to minister to the needs of the children of Russia, the fault is much more that of the enemies of the Russian Revolution than theirs. Intervention and the blockade have fallen heaviest upon the frail shoulders of innocent children and the sick." [27] Al-though its members were all Bolsheviks, all Marxists, the Workers' Op-position movement appeared to her as an authentic, democratic voice of the rank and file. They were silenced in the spring of 1921 under the ban against factions, but, as Emma acknowledged implicitly, their presence indicated the potential for dissenting democratic voices within the Com-munist party. Indeed, the resurrection of capitalism in Russia under the NEP meant that labor resistance was bound to reemerge, this time less amenable to party manipulation. "Is it that the anarcho-syndicalist star is rising in the East?" she concluded. [28]

Predictably, although Goldman had condemned the Bolsheviks for being too conservative and for reviving capitalism, the *World* editorials pounced on her articles to make a different point, arguing that "the revolu-tion, so badly needed and accomplished at such cost, had been made worse than useless by the attempt to apply Marxian principles to a people who didn't want them." Blurring her attempt to distinguish between the revolution and the regime, the *World* concluded that the Bolsheviks had "alienated the Russian people from the revolution and filled them with ha-tred for everything emanating from it." Goldman's failure to call for West-ern recognition of the Soviet regime (as she did privately in letters) left the impression that she opposed such recognition—then being debated in the U.S. Senate—and that she favored efforts to overthrow the Bolsheviks, though she later denied that this was the case. In any event, the articles stood as a portrait of a Russia devastated and enslaved by the attempt to apply "Marxian principles to a people who didn't want them." [29]

A few days before the first articles appeared, Goldman received word that she, Berkman, and Shapiro would be permitted entry to Berlin and could remain there four weeks. The pressure to leave Sweden had intensified, for the Social Democratic prime minister, Karl Branting, responding to pres-sure from conservatives, had informed them they would have to depart by April 19. Final permission to enter Germany arrived on April 21. On

April 23, Goldman left for Berlin, alone this time, since "the two Alexanders," thoroughly frustrated by the uncertainty, had left clandestinely for Germany where they were eventually able to secure temporary residency permits. Emma too succeeded in securing permission to remain until the end of May, a period later extended at two-month intervals.[30]

On entering Germany, Emma found herself in a world at once familiar and alien. As she wrote in her memoirs, German was "my mother tongue. Whatever schooling I had received was in that country, and my early influences were German." She was welcomed by the leading figures of the German anarcho-syndicalist organization, the Freie Arbeiter Union Deutschlands, or FAUD, including her friends Rudolf and Millie Rocker. In Berlin a large enclave of Russian revolutionary émigrés—anarchists, Mensheviks, Socialist Revolutionaries, Zionist-Socialists—shared her anti-Soviet convictions. Conditions in postwar Germany were favorable for émigré publishing of all persuasions, while the German anarcho-syndicalists had their own press, Der Syndikalist, which published a variety of books and periodicals. Here was a community she clearly could join.

On the other hand, Germany was the one country where a significant Communist party had emerged and where a Communist-led uprising had already taken place. Here Russian Bolshevik leaders had anticipated the next Soviet-style revolution. Even when that expectation proved illusory, they anxiously sought a friendly neighbor in the West. And defeated, postwar Germany, strategically located between East and West, sharing with Russia a common pariah status among nations and immense problems of postwar reconstruction, had strong reasons for seeking reconciliation with the Soviet regime. The Treaty of Rapallo, signed in April of 1922, marked an important step toward normalizing relations between the two countries. Berlin, moreover, was a kind of crossroads between Russia and the West, with many Soviet artists, writers, businessmen, and diplomats coming and going. Left German intellectuals were attracted by the Russian avantgarde. Although the ruling German Social Democrats despised the Communists, they restrained overt criticism of the Bolsheviks as part of a policy aimed at furthering trade and military relations.

Still, Germany felt like a safe haven to Emma, the first she had experienced in two years. It was as if a tremendous tidal wave of anxiety pursuing her during the previous months had suddenly caught her as she reached shore. "I don't know what got into me when I struck Germany," she wrote a friend. "A few days after my arrival in this city I felt a creeping lethargy take hold of me." She felt "physically exhausted and mentally absolutely paralyzed."[31] The hostile American reaction to her articles in the *World,* not only in the Communist press but in the anarchist press as well, added to her unhappiness. She claimed she was used to being "excommunicated" and later wrote to her comrade in Vienna, Max Nettlau, that she had never paid the slightest attention to such criticisms. "So let them howl away," she exclaimed.[32] But the charges hurt; that some papers, such as the socialist *Call* and the *Nation,* defended her critique as that of a consistent anarchist helped only a little. A visit from Stella, and her young son Ian seemed only to make things worse.

Emma was eager for her young Swedish lover to arrive. Because of passport irregularities, Swenson had not left with Emma for Berlin but planned to join her a month after her departure. During their month apart, "Arthur" wrote Emma adoring, fulsome, childlike letters assuring her that "before I met you I did not live" and signed "your loving infant" or "your sunbeam."[33] Arthur Swenson's admiration for Emma appears to have been genuine. Possibly he was briefly swept up in the epic of Emma Goldman. But his cloying letters suggest that he may not have been above using Goldman as a means of getting out of Sweden or even of returning to the United States. He did not hesitate to ask her for money, which she gave him willingly—too willingly, perhaps. Once again, as she had with Ben Reitman years before, she appears to have been caught up in a love affair with a much younger man who was overwhelmed by her neediness, and who alternated between effusive expressions of devotion and abrupt withdrawal.

Arthur arrived late in May, traveling on a false passport (as an associate of Goldman's, he too was spied on by the U.S. authorities in Stockholm) and moving into the flat Emma shared for a time with Berkman and with Fitzi, who had come for an extended visit. Emma and Arthur lived together as lovers for several months, but the ardor he had shown her in Stockholm had vanished. Emma wrote later that she had sensed the difference at once. "I long for the sun and you give me black clouds, I hold out my hands for something which you can not, or will not give," she wrote, using images reminiscent of her appeals to Reitman.[34] This time, however, Emma was not so willing to continue in a relationship that made her miserable. Ironically, this great speaker often preferred to write out her deepest feelings, rather than express them aloud in a face-to-face encounter. Now, she wrote several poignant letters that were accusing and conciliatory, pleading and yet proud, all at the same time. Though she still wanted to "help him grow finer," help him find himself, she could not continue to put up with his "face hardened," she wrote, "and your voice raised in anger." Perhaps too Emma suspected that he was taking advantage of her generosity. "Dear, dear Arthur," she began her last, long letter to him, "when one's life depends upon a surgical operation it is folly to postpone the painful process. One's condition only grows worse and worse and brings one to death's door. For months I have seen with absolute clarity that my peace of mind and soul and my very life depends upon our separation. But I have gone on postponing the painful operation until I can bear it no longer."

Wondering now if he had ever really loved her, or if "it was not self-deception on your part," Goldman insisted that she did not blame him, for "my brain sees, even if my heart refuses to submit to the verdict of my mind. You are thirty and I am fifty-two. . . . How then can it be your fault?" But she lashed out angrily at the "cruel injustice which grants to the man the right to ask and receive love from one much younger than himself and does not grant the same right to the woman. . . . Every day one sees decrepit men of more than 52 with girls of twenty," she observed bitterly, perhaps thinking of Berkman and his much younger women. But it was different with older women and young men, for "even the most advanced people can not reconcile themselves to the love of a man of thirty for one much older than he. You certainly could not, you have a very decided prejudice against what you so often call 'old people.'" Emma admitted that even friendship, at this point, would not satisfy her "so long as I am obsessed by a wild longing for you." Now Goldman asked Arthur to "go away," expressing the hope that he would not go "in anger or hate and that I have not lost all your faith in my friendship." She was not angry, not embittered, she insisted, denying feelings that were all too evident, "only unspeakably sad that I have lost a rare and precious thing, the love you had once for me. I must find the strength to face this great loss. Be big, dear Arthur, try to understand. Do not rush away in madness. Let us separate in the same beautiful spirit as one separates from something dead, something one has loved and cherished." She was, she assured him, "your friend whom you can always call upon, I will never fail you."[35] Arthur agreed to move out of the apartment. According to her autobiography, he had already fallen in love with her secretary. The two young people acknowledged their feeling for each other and later left, together, for America.

Emma, lonelier than ever, tried to pull herself together to face what seemed the empty horizon of her life. Sometime over the summer, she moved to a spacious four-room flat on the Soorstrasse in Berlin's Charlottenburg district, formerly a high-income residential neighborhood in the southwestern part of the city, which in the 1920s became almost a Russian suburb, since most of the émigrés lived here. Fortified with American dollars Stella sent her that insulated her from the effects of the inflation—she could even afford a maid to do her shopping and cleaning—Goldman began to write her book on Russia.[36] She had been considering the project for some time, but she undertook it now at the suggestion, according to her own account, of Clinton Brainard, president of Harper and Brothers, whom Emma met in Berlin through the publisher Albert Boni, and Clifton Swope, of the *World.* Brainard offered to syndicate the material in the American press, and then to publish it as a book. Eager for the widest possible exposure for her views, Emma accepted the offer.

She found the book immensely difficult to write. Her doubts and uncertainties, added to her general depression, made writing it a "torture." In addition, although she was writing a personal, eyewitness account, in fact, as she admitted to Max Nettlau, she had had to rely "a good deal" on the interpretations of others for her understanding of events in Russia, since she had arrived there over three years after the revolution had begun.[37] She relied as well on the diary Berkman had kept in Russia and on his translations of documents and pamphlets—to the point that Berkman, who planned to write his own book, felt he was giving away the "meat" of his material. Emma felt no sense of release when the book was completed, nor was she happy with the results. She found the writing pale and colorless, without the power she could command when she was "intensely aroused over something." While checking the manuscript to eliminate errors, she was tempted "to eliminate the whole MSS!" she told Stella. "I am so dissatisfied and unhappy about it."[38]

Within a few months, Emma's distress deepened as a series of untoward events plagued the manuscript's publication. The publisher, Brainard, thought it disappointing, as if it had been written "by a very conservative college professor," and rejected it. Eventually he sold it to another publishing house, Doubleday and Page, which brought it out in November of 1923.[39] When Emma received the book, she was stunned to discover not only that the title had been changed—it was no longer *My Two Years in Russia,* but *My Disillusionment in Russia*—but that nearly half the text was missing. Brainard had evidently sent Doubleday only part of the manuscript, and in order to hurry publication, Doubleday had not sent proofs to Emma, or to her representatives in New York, so the error had gone unnoticed.

Outraged and frantic, she protested vehemently to both publishers, to her lawyer, and even in the press. She was tempted to press legal charges, despite her opposition on principle to such action, in order to compel either Brainard or Doubleday to issue the missing pages. Finally, a generous and relatively affluent New York comrade, Dr. Michael Cohn, agreed to underwrite publication of the missing portion, entitled *My Further Disillusionment in Russia,* which appeared in 1924. Eventually the complete version was published in England in 1925. But the whole episode deepened Emma's feeling, expressed at intervals throughout her life, that all her projects were doomed, and that everything she attempted would inevitably fail.[40]

Still, even before the complete edition appeared, Goldman began to feel more confident about the book. From her earlier feelings of hesitancy, dissatisfaction, and uncertainty, by the middle of 1924 she had come to regard it as "the only authentic book on Russia written by a woman, in fact by anyone outside of Berkman's which no one has yet seen. I know you will not consider that I have acquired an egolomania [*sic*]," she wrote coyly to Weinberger, "Not at all. But I have read most books written on Russia and I know that they are false, every one of them."[41]

By the time Goldman came to writing her book, her vision of Russia had grown darker and more pessimistic. The mixed, sometimes contradictory picture offered in the *World* had begun to coalesce in her mind into a more uniform, more negative whole. Whatever had been ambiguous, contradictory, open-ended, increasingly appeared certain, consistent, closed. Gains, hopeful changes reported in the *World* were glossed over or ignored in the book. The Russian people had gained nothing, she now wrote. "Try as I might I could find nowhere any evidence of benefits received either by the workers or the peasants from the Bolshevik regime."[42] Whereas earlier she had described "a social cataclysm uprooting all life, transvaluing all values—smashing all theories—tearing asunder all preconceived notions," now she described only "a purely physical change," "political scene shifting and institutional rearrangements." Where earlier she conceded that the revolution had not been in vain, now she described it as an unmitigated tragedy.

The reasons for the change were several. First, an anarchist consensus on Russia was beginning to emerge in the movement press in the writings of Kropotkin, Rudolf Rocker, Errico Malatesta, Gaston Leval, Voline, and other influential militants.[43] By the summer of 1922, Goldman could speak with the authority of the movement behind her, not only as an individual. Second, her residence in Weimar Berlin may have deepened her sense of urgency about Russia. For here, where Left intellectuals were enthusiastic about contemporary Russian culture, where German Communists were active, and even anti-Communist Social Democrats wished to normalize relations with the Soviets, it was possible for her to imagine that "Bolshevism" had captured the allegiance of the masses abroad. Most of all, as she recognized herself, her depression over her own anomalous situation colored her outlook, so that everything appeared bleak and futile. As she wrote Nettlau, "Russia has knocked the bottom out of me, I see no hope anywhere, least of all do I see any imminent change anywhere. That and my own personal misery which I have not yet overcome though the object is removed for good and all make my writing seem colorless to me." [44]

Within this bleak setting, then, Goldman set out to write her book, to come to terms with an overwhelming sense of personal failure and political defeat. If she was not the first anarchist to write critically about Russia, she was the first to write historically, narrating her experiences chronologically over a two-year period and weaving together personal and political observations. On the one hand, she planned an "objective" report that would expose "the ghastly delusion" that had been foisted upon the world: the idea that "the Russian workers and peasants as a whole had derived essential social betterment as a result of the Bolshevik regime." On the other hand, she intended to write a more subjective piece, "my personal impressions and reactions, a sort of human document which will portray the desperate struggle I have made to find myself in the chaos and confusion of the Russian tragedy." [45]

My Disillusionment in Russia traced Goldman's travels, geographically and also emotionally, from the moment she set out on the *Buford* in December 1919 to her departure from Russia in December 1921. At the center of the narrative was Goldman's account of her deepening revulsion, both for Bolshevik procedures and personnel, and for official explanations for the catastrophic conditions all around her: explanations that blamed external factors such as the civil war, the Allied intervention, and the blockade. She told how she gradually came to believe that the inequality, repression, misery, and especially the terror were largely internally and politically caused, an inevitable outcome of Bolshevik ideology. Following Kropotkin's anarchist interpretation, Goldman concluded that "the Russian revolution was a libertarian step defeated by the Bolshevik state." [46]

My Disillusionment offered a compelling portrait of the disorganization, demoralization, exhaustion, and chaos during the final year of the civil war, when popular discontent reached a critical point and the Bolsheviks found themselves increasingly isolated. Especially in her description of traveling through the Ukraine, which occupied nearly one-third of the text, Goldman painted a vivid picture of the reigning panic and chaos in besieged cities such as Kiev and Odessa. She captured the bitter conflicts between Ukrainians and Russians, inside and outside the Communist party, and the frustrations of battling the bureaucracy, drawing on contacts available to few Western visitors to Russia at this time.

Goldman wrote with special insight about the plight of Ukrainian Jews, capturing a wide range of Jewish opinion, from gratitude toward the Bolsheviks for halting the pogroms, to resentment of inconsistent state policies toward Jewish cultural endeavors and even fear that popular identification of hated Russian Communists with Jews would deepen traditional Ukrainian anti-Semitism. She noted the arguments of those, many of them Zionists and Bundists, who termed the Bolsheviks guilty of "silent pogroms" because they closed Jewish hospitals and religious homes and encouraged Yiddish in place of the traditional religious Hebrew. She also described the victims of the devastating Fastov pogrom of 1919 and acknowledged that "the Bolshevik regime was at least free from that worst of all Russian curses, pogroms against the Jews." At the same time, however, she did not accept Jewish criticisms of the new regime without reservations, noting that most of the Russian Jews were bourgeois rather than proletarian and did not speak for the interests of the masses.

She also wrote sympathetically about the old middle-class liberal intelligentsia, many of them Jewish as well, whose attitudes toward the Bolsheviks ranged from ambivalence to hostility. Of particular interest were the accounts of her conversations with Russian anarchists, both the pro-Soviet anarchists and the much larger contingent of anti-Soviet anarchists who argued that the revolution had been betrayed by the Bolsheviks after the October assumption of power. Although she minimized armed anarchist opposition to the regime, omitting discussion of the Black Guards and blaming "Communist treachery and despotism" for acts such as the 1919 bombing by anarchists and Left SRs of Communist party headquarters in Moscow, she did not idealize the Russian movement, and even underestimated the anarchist potential of the Makhno movement, which she described as "purely of a military nature," and therefore "not expressive of the Anarchist spirit."[47] As few Western visitors had access either to the Russian anarchists or to the Ukraine at the height of the civil war, Goldman's account was valuable as one of the earliest to present a first-hand report of these relatively unknown sides of Russia.

As an attempt to evaluate the impact of the Bolshevik regime "upon Russia as a whole," to discover whether "the Russian workers and peasants as a whole had derived essential social betterment as a result of the Bolshevik regime," *My Disillusionment* was less successful. Claiming a broad perspective, in fact the book judged Russia through a narrow lens, offering a highly selective portrait that concentrated on the tiny, disaffected middle class, the intelligentsia in particular, while paying relatively little attention to "the Russian people," who were mostly peasants. It took a highly atypical region, the Ukraine, as emblematic of Russia as a whole. It took the last year of a catastrophic civil war as an example of how Communism, how "Marxism," must inevitably function. It omitted any real economic analysis, explaining all shortages of goods as simple problems of an overcentralized system of distribution while ignoring the underlying problem of disastrously low levels of industrial productivity.

Examples of Goldman's selective use of evidence and her sometimes inconsistent point of view occur throughout the book. Her treatment of labor was characteristic. While the *World* articles had acknowledged some gains for the Russian workers, such as the long fought for eight-hour day, *My Disillusionment* focused almost entirely on their grievances, emphasizing their suffering under the regime of War Communism, and describing the bitterness of hungry workers in a Petrograd flour factory, kept under quasi-military surveillance allegedly on account of flour thefts. The eight-hour day was mentioned now only in passing, while the comment of a worker is made to stand for the attitude of labor generally: " 'Has the Revolution given you nothing?' I asked. 'Ah, the Revolution! but that is no more. Finished,' he said bitterly." Quick to defend the Russian workers against abuses of the government, Goldman was also quick to criticize the workers themselves as lazy and inefficient, offering evidence from her own experience of trying to organize workers' hotels, which cast doubt on her argument for the reestablishment of workers' control within the factories. The book failed to mention the disastrous economic conditions during the early months of the revolution, which the widespread institution of workers' control could not improve.[48] A chapter on trade unions took as representative two highly atypical Moscow unions—the Menshevik printers, one of the oldest and most elite unions and one of the few that had held out in opposition to the regime, and the anarcho-syndicalist bakers, also a notable exception. There was no mention of their party affiliations and no indication that they were unusual in any way.[49]

Although peasants made up the overwhelming majority of the Russian population in 1920, some 85 percent of the people, *My Disillusionment* had little to say about them. When peasants appeared in the narrative, they were described from afar as they crowded onto railroad platforms in the Ukraine or clung to the tops of trains, an enigmatic, paradoxical, alien people, described in generalities: "unsophisticated and primitive, often crude," "unspoiled," "clear about their needs," "possessed of a deep faith in elementary justice and equality," yet capable of violent pogroms. In Goldman's descriptions, they appeared distant and strange, viewed en masse rather than as individuals: "At the stations, while the train waited for an engine, the peasants would gather into groups, form a large circle, and then someone would begin to play the accordion, the bystanders accompanying them with song. It was strange to see these hungry and ragged peasants, huge loads on their backs, standing about entirely forgetful of their environment, pouring their hearts out in folk songs. A peculiar people, these Russians, saint and devil in one, manifesting the highest as well as the most brutal impulses, capable of almost anything but sustained efforts."[50]

Goldman's bias was most evident in her limited account of social and cultural issues in which she had taken a strong interest while in America. Apart from a few references to the discontent of female servants at the Hotel Astoria and the unhealthy conditions for pregnant women workers in a Petrograd tobacco factory, *My Disillusionment* was largely silent on the subject of women. There was no mention of the Zhenotdel, or the Family Code of 1918, or of other Soviet efforts on behalf of women, beyond a brief reference to Kollontai.[51] Similarly, despite Emma's background as a nurse, she did not discuss the considerable achievements of the Health Department in eradicating cholera and smallpox, as well as in instituting improved sanitation in far-flung corners of the country: a surprising omission in light of her praise for the "wonderful work" of this department in a letter from Russia. Nor, despite her commitment to birth control, did she mention the legalization of abortion in 1920, undertaken as an emergency measure in the absence of easily available contraceptives.

Most striking, considering Goldman's commitment to the arts as a vehicle for fostering revolutionary consciousness, she accorded cursory attention to Soviet cultural affairs, describing Russia in 1920 and 1921 as a "cultural desert" in which she found little to praise. The country had become, in her words, simply "the dumping ground for mediocrities in art and culture" who "fit in the narrow groove of the Communist state." This assessment was patently unfair since, as Emma must have known from her own work for the Petrograd Museum, in the early years after the October revolution, party loyalty was not required for state employment in many departments, including the arts, education, and the press.[52] Moreover, it reflected Goldman's hostility to the Russian avant-garde. Though impressed by the open-air mass theater of Meyerhold and the Constructivist decor and emphasis on spectacle of A. Tairov's Kamerny Theater, she preferred the more traditional theaters, such as Stanislavsky's Moscow Art Theater. She disliked the "mechanistic approach" of Proletkult, whose efforts struck her as "barren of ideas or vision," "hopelessly commonplace." The work of Futurists and Constructivists did not interest her. Rather she lamented the absence of "new Ibsens, Tolstoys or Tchekovs to thunder their protest against the new evils." Admitting generous Soviet support for the arts, Goldman found in this support further reason to condemn the regime, since it was not given "so much [for] love of art as the necessity of finding some outlet for the checked and stifled aspirations of the people."[53]

Although Goldman closed the book with her departure from Russia in December of 1921, the narrative essentially ended with a brief account of the Kronstadt tragedy the previous March, omitting discussion of the dramatic changes introduced under the New Economic Policy, other than to note that the markets were now well-supplied. These omissions gave the misleading impression that the requisitioning, rationing, and compulsory labor endemic to War Communism were intrinsic to the politics of Bolshevism, whereas in reality these hated policies, all of them highly controversial, were halted under NEP.[54] At the same time, by dismissing NEP as essentially a return to capitalism, a resurrection of the social conditions that "the great Revolution had come to destroy," Goldman implied that the old evils of capitalism had returned with no significant corresponding benefits. In fact, a significant public sector remained, and NEP Russia emerged as the earliest example of a mixed economy, combining private and nationalized enterprise. By ending the chronological narrative with Kronstadt (with several topical chapters following), Goldman obscured the significant economic, social, and cultural liberalization that began about the same time and continued until late in the decade.[55] Similarly, in her account of the great famine that began in the summer of 1921,

Goldman blamed Soviet errors of agricultural planning, implying that the catastrophic two-year drought that had preceded it was a fiction invented by the regime to cover its own disastrous mistakes. (In the *World* she had acknowledged that the drought had been a central cause of the famine; by the time she wrote her autobiography, she had forgotten completely about the drought, which was nowhere mentioned.) [56]

In the end, she presented a starkly negative picture of a revolution betrayed from within, defeated by a Communist party motivated solely by greed for power. Arguing that a genuine libertarian revolution had taken place, not in October, but over the summer of 1917, as peasants seized the land and workers took control of the factories, she nonetheless concluded that the outcome had been simply superficial "political scene shifting," with revolutionary human and social values subordinated totally to interests of state. The Bolsheviks were simply opportunists who had exploited mass revolutionary sentiment in order to establish a state under their own direction. She described how they had "clothed themselves with the agrarian programme of the Social Revolutionists and the industrial tactics of the Anarchists" in order to ride the wave of popular revolutionary enthusiasm. After assuming power, they had "discarded their false plumes." They gradually sheared the power of the soviets, trade unions, and cooperatives, subordinating them to their own needs, while eliminating rival parties and establishing the "dictatorship of the proletariat," which was, in reality, the dictatorship of the Communist party. As she put it in the Afterword, "the triumph of the State meant the defeat of the Revolution." For her, even more than for other anarchists, Marxist theory had led directly to the Bolshevik state. She insisted that it was "not only Bolshevism that failed, but Marxism itself." It was "Marxism, however modified." It was "the whole Socialist conception of revolution itself." [57]

As a historical account, this description imposes a unity of purpose and program that the Bolsheviks did not in fact possess. It represents the actions of the Bolsheviks outside of any economic or political context. It exaggerates the influence of anarcho-syndicalist ideas. Yet, while Goldman drew a straight line from Marxist theory to "the great Russian debacle," she suggested that "any political party in control of the government" would have yielded similar results, an acknowledgment, perhaps, that policy choices were not, after all, unlimited. [58]

She did not spell out an anarchist alternative to Bolshevism beyond repeating Kropotkin's call for a revival of peasant cooperatives, free soviets, and independent trade unions, although unlike Kropotkin, she placed special emphasis on the role of intellectuals in any future revolution. At the heart of *My Disillusionment,* however, was a profound ethical argument with the Bolsheviks, an emphasis on the need for a revolutionary movement to embody the antiauthoritarian values it aimed to establish. "There is no greater fallacy," she wrote, "than the belief that aims and purposes are one thing, while methods and tactics are another. . . . Psychologically and socially the means necessarily influence and alter the aims." Even the period of actual revolution, the transition stage, must embody as far as possible the values of the future, which Goldman defined as "the sanctity of human life, the dignity of man, the right of every human being to liberty and well-being." "The means used to prepare the future become its cornerstone."

This idea, of course, had been central to Bakunin's polemic against Marx in the 1870s, when Bakunin had insisted that "freedom can be created only by freedom." [59] Yet Goldman doubted now whether such consistency was possible. What she left out of *My Disillusionment in Russia* was her uncertainty about any revolution. "I have not the same faith in the masses and in the efficacy of revolution," she wrote Max Nettlau in December of 1922. "The masses cling too much to their belief in authority. They are too easily swayed by those who know the demagogic gesture, those who flatter them. Above all, those who do their thinking. So I am not quite sure, as I have been, of the immediate results of any fundamental upheaval. And yet I also know that without that upheaval no fundamental change can take place. . . ." [60]

A few years later, in a letter to Berkman who was writing *What Is Communist Anarchism?*, Goldman expressed her reservations more strongly. "The entire old school, Kropotkin, Bakunin, and the rest, had a childish faith in what Peter calls 'the creative spirit of the people,'" she wrote Berkman. "I'll be damned if I can see it. If the people could really create out of themselves, could a thousand Lenins or the rest have put the noose back on the throat of the Russian masses? I don't think so." Goldman urged Berkman "to hold up the mirror of slavish acquiescence and willingness to follow any charlatan who can hoodwink the workers up before your readers, to stress the urgent necessity for the masses to learn how to construct, to rebuild, to do independent work for themselves and the community, without the feel of the master's whip." [61]

Goldman always insisted that this pessimism grew directly out of her experience in Russia and that her two years there had forced her to reconsider all her old values, but this was only partly true. She had long been ambivalent toward the masses, swinging between a Kropotkinite faith and Nietzschean contempt, pushed in one direction or another by dramatic events. The revolutions of 1917 had renewed her faith in the masses, but the subsequent consolidation of the Bolshevik regime, and her own observations during her travels in Russia, sent her back toward her earlier pessimistic view, which was deepened by her sense of possibilities destroyed. What had changed was not so much her assessment of the masses, which remained ambivalent, but her attitude toward revolution, her fear of making the wrong kind of revolution, and her sense that the anarchist revolution was more distant than she had thought.

But Goldman's pessimism was not only political. What made Russia so overwhelming an experience for her was its challenge to her deepest sense of personal identity as well. Having long considered herself a revolutionary, she suddenly found that she had no place in an actual revolution. She felt excluded, defeated, useless, alien in a country whose revolutionary traditions she had long revered. *My Disillusionment* was partly an attempt to come to grips with that discovery by showing that, not she, but the Bolsheviks, had abandoned the cause of revolution, and that by remaining true to her original convictions, she had remained a revolutionary. Her damning portrait of Russia was partly an attempt to explain her own inactivity there. In this sense, then, *My Disillusionment* is a self-portrait as well as a portrait, for in it Russia has become a metaphor for Goldman's sense of betrayal and loss, a mirror of her own interior landscape of desolation.

Emma Goldman has often been praised as a prescient early critic of Soviet totalitarianism, one of the few "who had the perception and courage to criticize the Bolshevik regime." *My Disillusionment* has been touted by scholars as "probably the best analysis by an anarchist of the failure of the Russian revolution." [62] There is no question that the book pointed to disturbing authoritarian directions the new regime was taking. But despite its considerable insights, Goldman's analysis of Russia in 1920 and 1921 seriously distorted a complex reality. Conflating the emergency measures of War Communism with Bolshevism as a whole, Goldman helped lay the foundations for a caricature of Russian history that served interests profoundly hostile to her own.

For Goldman and for nearly all anarchist writers—and many non-anarchists—who followed, Russian history stopped with Kronstadt, or jumped directly, "inevitably," to Stalin. [63] The NEP era of the 1920s—

which has become a focus of renewed interest for those committed to socialist alternatives to Stalinism—was simply nonexistent. Her analysis of an enslaved, brutalized, terrorized country with no breath of freedom greatly exaggerated party control over many domains and denied benefits—for example, to the peasantry—that even she would later acknowledge. In reality, the Soviet 1920s were an era of unprecedented social and cultural freedoms prior to the great reversal of 1928–29, when Stalin assumed power over the party. The peasants were the chief beneficiaries of the new regime but workers too lived better now than they had under the Czars. As Stephen Cohen has written, these years also brought "a remarkable explosion of artistic ferment and creativity in almost every field," with vigorous debates and competing theories in all areas of intellectual endeavor. "Looking back," he writes, "it is clear not only that the Soviet twenties were a 'golden era' in Russian culture, but that NEP culture, like Weimar culture, was a major chapter in the cultural history of the twentieth century, one that created brilliantly, died tragically, but left an enduring influence." [64] Attempting to counter a romanticized image of Soviet Russia that was accepted by a small but vocal minority on the Left, Goldman contributed to a far more enduring Western myth of Bolshevism as a monolithic, unchanging, static tyranny, irrevocably determined by a Marxist ideology that was inherently totalitarian and repressive. [65]

Despite the vicissitudes of its two-part publication, *My Disillusionment in Russia* was favorably received in the mainstream press in England and the United States, where most reviewers interpreted the book as the recantation of a former Communist. H. L. Mencken exaggerated considerably when he quipped that "it was almost as if a Baptist rector from the remote swamps of Georgia had been sent to the Vatican," but he was one of very few reviewers who understood that anarchists had a long history of opposition to Marxism. [66] More typically, the *New York Times* described Goldman as "a disillusioned Bolshevik," noting that she won sympathy if not admiration by the "great retraction" in her preface. [67] The *Springfield Republican* described the book as "a convincing indictment of Bolshevism." [68] The *Times Literary Supplement* (London) praised it as a "sincere and authoritative statement," noting that "no more scathing attack upon the Soviet tyranny and its leaders has been written." [69] The liberal *Nation* and the *New Republic* were more critical, as was Goldman's friend, Henry Alsberg, writing in the *New York Post*. [70] Alsberg disagreed with Emma that a revolution à la Bakunin would have been different, or could have defeated the forces arrayed against it; though Goldman had insisted on the distinction between the "revolution" and the "regime," Alsberg interpreted the book, correctly, as "my disillusionment with revolution." In Alsberg's view, the Bolsheviks during the civil war period had been driven to harsh measures by grim necessity, "the driving need to preserve, not the revolution but the remnants of civilization. . . ." What Goldman had seen struggling for life "was not the revolution but Russia." [71]

Alsberg's review is interesting because he had been close to Goldman in Russia and shared many of her criticisms of the Bolsheviks. More than anyone else, including Berkman, he seems to have been sensitive to her emotional distress there and to her efforts to reconstitute a shattered sense of self. "Deeply shocked by what she saw all around her," he wrote, "so different from what she expected, one feels that Miss Goldman was trying to save her own revolutionary soul by proving that this revolution was a particular instance and not a generalized example." Alsberg, in fact, tended to see Goldman's book as an example of the general tendency of Americans to judge Russia in terms of their own preconceptions. "What you write about the Bolsheviks," he suggested, "depends very largely on what you, yourself, take with you to Moscow when you go there." [72] What Goldman had taken was not only an idealized view of the Russian Revolution, but a complicated personal and political history that included a longstanding hatred of Marxism, and also what one reviewer called "the unconscious Prussian attitude" with which she was raised as a child, that had included a hatred of everything Russian. [73] Despite her sense of identification with Russia, and her eagerness to defend the revolution, she discovered when she arrived there in 1920 how ephemeral this identification really was. She discovered that her Russia had been more a country of the imagination, of books, than of real life. Attached to an idealized notion of "Mother Russia," she was forced now to face the "otherness" of Russia. *My Disillusionment* was a portrait of Russia both as betrayed Mother and as alien Other, a memoir of the author's deep sense of alienation in the land she had long considered her spiritual home.

At the time Goldman began to write about Russia, she imagined herself as a voice in the wilderness, speaking out against "the monstrous delusion," the "popular craze that Bolshevism had become." With little access to the press in England or in America where she hoped to find her audience, she imagined that "Bolshevism" had captured the allegiance of vast numbers of people, and that Soviet or pro-Soviet "salesmen of the revolution" had somehow managed to hypnotize the entire world. This assessment greatly exaggerated the following that the Communists had actually attracted, especially in the United States, where the party counted only about fifteen thousand members in 1923, a number reduced to about seven thousand two years later.[74]

In the early 1920s, the Soviet Union was in fact a pariah nation, politically and diplomatically isolated, the object of almost universal hatred outside of intellectual and leftist circles. As Dorothy Brewster noted in her review in the *Nation,* the "denunciation of Bolshevism" had been "staled by repetition."[75] An article in the *New York Times* in 1919 expressed a prevailing attitude: "Bolshevism means chaos, wholesale murder, the complete destruction of civilization."[76] These images endured through most of the 1920s, engendering a bitter, often bizarre hostility toward Bolshevism, Communism, and Soviet Russia generally. Marguerite Harrison, the American journalist and spy whom Goldman and Berkman had met in Moscow, found on her return to the United States in 1923 that people were disappointed when she could relate no tales of atrocities; indeed, when she lectured on her experiences in Russia, she found herself accused of offering "flagrant radical propaganda," so unwilling were people to hear anything positive about the Soviets. "In those days," she wrote in her memoirs, "few people were willing to admit the possibility that any good could come from the Communist experiment. The United States had been fed on propaganda ever since the beginning of World War I, liberalism was out of fashion, and most Americans had lost the faculty of being able to see both sides of social and political problems." Harrison recalled that she had fought, with little success, to persuade Americans in 1923 "that Bolshevism was not a Jewish plot to wreck Western civilization."[77]

Far away from the Red Scare atmosphere of Harding's America, however, Goldman easily overestimated the extent of pro-Soviet sentiment there. She underestimated the prevailing conservative, nativist atmosphere, in which all dissent and labor protest was vulnerable to charges of "Bolshevism," where Communists had replaced anarchists and Wobblies as symbols of evil in the national imagination. Although American liberals in the conservative 1920s generally took a more favorable view of Russia, few were converts to Communism. They looked rather to Russia as a hopeful bulwark against despair, balancing enthusiasm for Soviet social experiments with uneasiness at Soviet methods. Socialists in America were bitterly anti-Bolshevik: papers such as the *New York Call* and the Jewish *Daily Forward* regularly attacked the Soviet regime. Anti-Communist labor leaders such as Samuel Gompers, president of the American Federation of Labor, vehemently opposed resuming normal diplomatic relations with Russia. The relatively small group of pro-Soviet liberals and radicals in America fought an uphill battle just to secure a rational dialogue about Russia; there were no official diplomatic relations between Russia and the United States until 1933.

Within the European socialist movement, the war and the October revolution had generated deep divisions, with Communists and social democrats almost as bitterly opposed to each other as to their capitalist enemies.[78] Despite support from Moscow, Western Communist parties remained small and isolated during the 1920s, unsuccessful in their efforts to affiliate with larger left-wing parties (such as the British Labour party). Nor did they capture the leadership of the largest, most powerful labor unions.[79] The British Communist party had only about three thousand members in the early 1920s. Those in the West who admired the Soviet leaders for achievements in Russia and who favored normalizing relations were inclined to emphasize the different conditions prevailing in Europe. The British Labour party, for example, urged a normalization of relations but was by no means uncritical of Russia and was resolutely anti-Communist at home, as Goldman would soon discover; leading socialist intellectuals in Britain, such as Beatrice and Sidney Webb, were still, in the 1920s, fiercely anti-Bolshevik.[80] Only those who formed the small Communist parties in the West actually accepted Bolshevik theories and methods, and even members of these parties often privately criticized Russian practices. According to one historian of Western opinion, "everywhere in the Western world, except on the extreme left, bolshevism and Soviet Russia aroused a moral abhorrence that differed only in degree between countries and parties."[81]

Still, influential sectors of the Left and liberal intelligentsia in Europe and in America defended the Soviet regime as a successful socialist revolution. These were the people Goldman hoped to persuade. Available evidence suggests, however, that she may have had more influence on conservative than on liberal opinion, for it was the conservative, anti-Soviet press—the *New York Times,* the *Chicago Tribune,* the *Times* (London), the *Spectator,* and the *New York Herald Tribune,* for example—that reviewed her favorably, quoted her approvingly, and gave space to her opinions. According to one historian of U.S. opinion toward Russia, her "chronicle of disillusionment delighted antagonists of Soviet Russia and dismayed sympathizers."[82] *My Disillusionment* and also Goldman's articles in the anarchist press were circulated enthusiastically among officials of the State and Justice Departments in Washington as well as within the London U.S. consulate. One official of that consulate gloated, after reading the book, that "it is certainly a cause for some satisfaction to see such an old war horse as Emma Goldman condemn the failure of the Great Experiment."[83]

Although her views attracted special attention because they were hers, as the *New York Times* noted, they were not unique. They were part of a flood of anti-Bolshevik writings. If Goldman offered a critique from the Left, defending the overthrow of private property and offering prescient glimpses of the dilemmas of Soviet Jews, her portrait of an enslaved, prostrate, terrorized Russia merely confirmed the prevailing image.[84] An astute reporter for the *Times* summed it up neatly when describing the British reaction to Goldman's views: Goldman condemned Soviet Russia, not because it was too revolutionary, but because it was not revolutionary enough. However, "the conservative mind in England discounts all that. It merely grasps the fact that here is 'one of them' admitting that Bolshevism is wrong."[85] Goldman's emotional polemics lent themselves to misappropriation by both the Right and the Left. Calling Bolshevism "the greatest delusion the world has suffered since Christianity was thrust upon mankind" did not inspire rational debate.[86] What was clear, however, was her assault on "Marxism, however modified," and on "the whole Socialist conception of revolution itself." That argument, rather than the anarchist alternatives, received extensive and respectful attention in the mainstream press.

Once she sent off the Russian manuscript in December of 1922, Emma Goldman once again faced the dilemma of how to become active. Being outside the movement, outside any public activity, deepened her anxiety and restlessness, yet she feared anarchist agitation in Berlin would endanger her position there. In the tumultuous political atmosphere of Weimar Berlin, she felt her inactivity as a kind of imprisonment. She was glad when her niece, Stella Ballantine, returned to Berlin in the spring of 1923 and stayed through the summer. Yet Stella was suffering from a serious eye ailment, which caused Goldman much worry. And then Emma's mother died in July in Rochester, deepening her sense of loss.

Goldman found some solace among several German anarchists with whom she developed close friendships. She grew deeply attached to Rudolf Rocker, a German Gentile who, in the years before World War I, had become a leader among the Yiddish-speaking Jewish immigrants of London's East End where Emma had first met him. His companion, Millie Witcop, was of Russian-Jewish origins. As editor of the Yiddish *Arbeter Fraint* (*Worker's Friend*) and leader in the labor struggles of the Jewish garment workers, Rocker was a greatly loved and admired figure who helped catalyze a lively anarchist movement in the slums of East London. Interned in England during World War I, he later returned to Germany where he became active in the FAUD. Like Emma, Rocker was a gifted speaker, propagandist, and historian, the author of several influential books on anarchism, including an autobiography and a biography of Johann Most. He was also a man of great personal warmth whose convivial charm attracted many friends. Like many in the movement, Emma grew to love and trust both Rockers, confiding in them as she did with few comrades. Inclined to treat her American comrades abruptly, letting them know she did not consider them serious radicals, Goldman approached her European comrades with more respect; she especially adored Rocker, and years later, she would turn to him as the one man in the movement whose opinion she really valued.

Other Berlin friends included Mollie Steimer and her companion, Senya Flechine, who had arrived from Russia late in 1923. Steimer was twenty-six, and shared Emma's outspokenness and strength of conviction. As a Russian-Jewish immigrant in New York, she had been one of the defendants in the famous Abrams free-speech case and had been sentenced to fifteen years in prison for a leaflet opposing United States intervention in Russia. Deported to Russia in 1921, she had come up against Soviet authorities as well, and after several arrests and imprisonments for her anarchist activities, she was expelled from that country too.[87] Emma had followed the Abrams case in the press, and she admired the courage of the youthful defendants, but she met Mollie only briefly in New York in 1919, shortly before her own deportation. In exile, the two became close, almost like mother and daughter. Emma often referred to Mollie and Senya as her "children," and Senya Flechine, also Russian-born, had in fact worked in the *Mother Earth* office in New York for a time before returning to Russia in 1917. Emma found their presence in Berlin comforting, though she was often irritated by what she considered Mollie's rigidity and fanaticism, and she tried on occasion to get her to relax. "Never mind the movement and your principles, Mollie dearest," she once advised, "enjoy life for a while. That will make you more worth[while] to the movement later on."[88] Although devoted to each other, there were tensions and political differences between Emma and the more doctrinaire Mollie—less so with Senya—that would grow sharp in years to come. Yet theirs was a relationship of considerable intimacy. In times of depression, each found much solace in the company of the other. To Mollie, who died in 1980 in Mexico, Emma remained almost a sacred figure, whose memory she continued to reverence until the end of her life.

But by early 1923, not even the presence of these friends could alleviate Goldman's unhappiness in Berlin, or her sense of uselessness and futility. Certainly she lived more comfortably than most of the anarchist émigrés, since she had funds from America—which she generously shared with others. And Berlin at that moment was becoming a major center of the international avant-garde, with new developments particularly in the German theater, which would soon make Berlin the experimental theater capital of the world. Politically and culturally, postwar Germany, rebuilding itself out of the ashes, seemed to many the key to the future. The Russian writer Ilya Ehrenburg recalled that "in those days the entire world was watching Berlin. Some with dread, some with hope: in that city the fate of Europe for the next decades was being decided." [89] But Emma Goldman found Berlin empty of possibilities. Writing, the occupation of many émigrés, was too solitary to satisfy her. In her eyes, the city was stifling, the theater had "deteriorated beyond belief," the people were dull, the arts uninteresting. "In two years I have not met one solitary interesting German," she wrote Frank Harris in the spring of 1924, exaggerating to add urgency to her pleas for help with a British visa. "As far as any cultural life or companionship is concerned," she exclaimed, "I might as well live in the desert." [90]

To make matters worse, Goldman's relationship with Alexander Berkman deteriorated to a point where Emma feared a lasting rupture. Though she helped him while he wrote his book, *The Bolshevik Myth*, the collaboration exacerbated tensions between them. Her use of his Russian diary for her own book clearly angered him, and if he did not confront her about it directly, he withdrew and confided his feelings to others with uncharacteristic bitterness. [91] Moreover, sometime in 1922 or 1923, he had met Emmy Eckstein, a lively and spirited young German-Jewish woman who would become his companion for the rest of his life. The two had met on the terrace of a Berlin cafe, when Emmy was in her early twenties and Sasha was fifty-two. Despite Emmy's conservative, middle-class upbringing, they had fallen in love. Her parents disapproved violently and evidently threatened to commit her to a mental institution if she did not end the relationship. Eventually, Emmy had run away from home and gone to live with Berkman in France.[92] Intelligent and warm, with a keen sense of humor, Emmy suffered from fits of jealousy toward Emma and other women friends of Sasha, whose anarchist world remained alien to her. And Emma could not help but feel jealous herself toward this much younger, bourgeois woman who had come to share her former lover's life.

Drifting apart from Berkman, with no compelling activity to claim her energies, Emma felt more bereft and abandoned than ever, viewing her life as a complete "debacle." At moments waves of self-pity overtook her. She found herself thinking often of Leon Malmed, the anarchist delicatessen owner in Albany, New York, who had once proclaimed his love for her and had been a devoted supporter. They had met long before, in 1906, and he had become a devotee, organizing her Albany lectures, selling her magazine, sending funds for her campaigns, scandalizing Albany when he left his wife to accompany Goldman and her lover at the time, Ben Reitman, on their 1915 cross-country lecture tour to California. "Oh Leon, dearest Leon, I am so hungry for some one who knew my life, my work, my devotion to our cause," she wrote plaintively. "Of all the people I long for you most. You really must come over, if only to bring with you a breath of that past. Yes, you must come over, if you really feel the friendship and devotion to me . . . I can not write any more, my heart aches and my spirit cries out in rebellion against the cruel circumstance that has thrown me overboard and made me so utterly useless."[93]

It was almost as if the full force of her losses struck her all over again, for she seemed to go through a renewed mourning for America. She repeatedly queried Weinberger regarding laws applying to the return of deportees and the possibility of marriage to an American citizen which, she now learned, would not ensure her citizenship (after passage of the Citizenship Act of April 1922). Still, in her more practical moods, Emma recognized that she might find an arena of action in the German movement. She could marry a German citizen and acquire citizenship. This possibility had some appeal, particularly since, with the founding of the Syndicalist International (International Workingmen's Association, or IWMA) in December of 1922, as heir to the nineteenth-century Bakuninist association, Berlin was becoming a center for the international anarchist movement.[94] But Goldman, who had always been a "free-lance," preferred to work on her own, outside of any organization, which was difficult here. The absence of women in the German movement may also have discouraged her.

The Frauenbund, in which Millie Rocker was active, was mainly an association of housewives, a sort of women's auxiliary within the FAUD, rather than a militant woman's organization.[95] After serious consideration, Goldman rejected Rudolf Rocker's suggestion that she marry a German citizen.

Despite the risks, Goldman did address some meetings in Germany in 1923 and 1924. But she found the experience excruciating after her six-year absence from the platform. She was so nervous that she worried she might have lost her gift for speaking entirely, although witnesses still recall her charismatic power. Rudolf Rocker's son, Fermin, vividly recalled attending a meeting in Berlin in support of political prisoners in Russia, where his father, no mean speaker himself, was shouted down by Communist hecklers. "Suddenly this small pudgy woman got up on the podium and gave them hell. She let them have it, and they took it. That was really a tour de force," he recalled. "It was her presence, her voice, it was like someone pouring oil on stormy waters. It made an indelible impression."[96] Still, Goldman was not satisfied and disliked the German atmosphere: no response, no spirit, no intense feeling, she complained; the thought of devoting herself to public life in Germany was "paralyzing."[97]

By February of 1924, Goldman decided she could not afford to remain in Germany, for economic as well as psychological reasons. The worst of the postwar inflation had passed, and the mark was recently stabilized. Though shielded from destitution with her American currency, her funds were dwindling, and she was determined to secure some form of income. More important, she did not want to work only within the émigré and exile community, on behalf of imprisoned revolutionists in Russia, as Berkman was now doing, though she aided all his efforts.[98]

England held out the possibility of appealing to broader audiences through public lecturing in a language in which she felt more comfortable. A Labour government had just been elected; she believed it might look more favorably than the previous government on her application for admission. She was also hatching a plan for a book about creative women, which she hoped to research in the British Museum. Although she found no one to advance funds for this project, planning it focused her efforts to gain entry into England. Her friend, the British writer and editor Frank Harris, who was now back in London, encouraged her and offered to act as her sponsor.

Fifteen years older than Goldman, Harris had long been a controversial figure on the London literary scene. He had written several novels, including one about the Haymarket affair, and biographies of writers such as Bernard Shaw and Oscar Wilde, with whom he was also friends. He had also edited a number of magazines, most notably the distinguished London *Saturday Review* and *Pearson's,* in New York. Although Harris and Emma had begun to correspond while she was still in the Missouri State Penitentiary, their friendship had blossomed in Berlin where Harris interviewed her for a glowing portrait, later published in his *Contemporary Portraits.* Their friendship deepened into an affectionate, teasing camaraderie, strengthened by their kinship as sexual outlaws and opponents of censorship. After publishing the first volume of his sexually explicit autobiography, *My Life and Loves,* in 1922, Harris had fought legal battles against the banning of his book on grounds of obscenity. The flamboyant, egotistical writer and the militant anarchist got along famously. "It has been one of the few pleasures of my life in Berlin the meeting with you," he wrote her warmly, "and deeper knowledge of you has only increased my admiration." [99] In his portrait, he called her the greatest woman he had ever met, "among the heroic leaders and guides of humanity forever." [100] Emma, whose morale had sunk to rock-bottom, was pleased and flattered. She teased him about *My Life and Loves,* of which he had sent her the first volume. "Full of devilry, aren't you dear Mr. Harris?" she wrote him coyly. "Still the boy enjoying mischief. You bet I am looking forward to that [second] volume." [101] When she felt depressed and torn with self-doubt, he cheered her with hope. When she complained about her inability to adjust to circumstances, he insisted that she was a great woman precisely because she would not adjust to circumstances. He promised not to lose a minute in working for her English visa, and consoled her about her book with tales of his own prosecution on obscenity charges for *My Life.* "So keep up yr courage; the darkest hour is just before the DAWN!" [102]

Harris was as good as his word. On her behalf, he contacted George Slocombe, an M.P. in the Labour party, George Lansbury, the editor of the liberal *Daily Herald,* whom Emma had met in Russia, and others, all of whom helped push matters forward with the Home Office. Harris himself pledged that Emma would never become dependent on English charity. Although determined to leave Germany, Emma still approached England with serious reservations, for she had never liked England or the English. "I frankly admit that I go to England not out of joy but because I hope to find a footing there," she confessed to Harris in June of 1924, "to be able to earn my living and become active again in some way. The English I have met haven't warmed my heart unless they were Irish like yourself. But England is an English-speaking country and somehow not quite so far away from A. I may be able to find a way of resuming my work for A. left off when I was gagged and kidnapped and rushed out of the country. That is my reason for wanting to make England my home." [103]

Berkman too was skeptical about Emma's proposed move to England; he hated England even more than she, and did not feel optimistic about her "taking root" there. Perhaps more than anyone, he recognized the psychological motives for her need to flee Berlin. "The truth is," he wrote her, "you are trying to get away from yourself, chiefly, and in that England can help you no more than any other place." Berkman also was wary about trying to make a living in the movement; he thought an occupation preferable. [104]

Still, Emma was determined to go ahead. In early August, she left for Paris. The depression and despair that had gripped her since early in her sojourn in Russia gave way to an almost manic elation and energy. She found herself "in a state of mind not unlike that of a released prisoner who after many years of confinement is finally turned loose." She spent hours wandering the streets, sitting in cafes watching the crowds pass, or running up to Sacre Coeur to look out over the city she had always loved. [105] She bombarded Berkman with friendly, affectionate letters ("Don't get too blue dear brave old scout," she wrote him from Paris, "You have already gone through so much and have come out so wonderful in spirit. . . .") Their approaching separation had already helped heal the rift that had opened between them, for they often got along best when physically distant, as Emma would remark ruefully years later. In an English-speaking country, Goldman felt she might again make her life count for something. That thought filled her with new energy and excitement as she crossed the channel toward London.

4

Anti-Soviet Campaigns

From revolutionary Petrograd and postwar Berlin to the cafes of Mont-parnasse and the flats of West Kensington stretched distances not easily traversed. Emma Goldman could not help feeling apprehensive about what awaited her in England. Yet the prospect of speaking from the plat-form again, after seven years of near silence, lifted her spirits consider-ably. She arrived in London on September 23, 1924, full of plans to orga-nize an anti-Soviet campaign. With her keen instinct for the dramatic, she did not immediately announce her intentions. In her autobiography, she explained that she did not wish to interfere with the efforts of the Labour Government to secure diplomatic recognition of Russia, a subject in which she was "vitally interested" because she knew recognition "would remove the halo of martyrdom from the brow of the Communist state."[1] In fact, the government had already recognized Russia months before her arrival; her delay more likely reflected her decision to wait until public attention was less distracted. For, as she soon realized, she had arrived in the midst of a political crisis. On taking power the previous February, the new La-bour Government had moved quickly to grant de jure recognition to Rus-sia and to begin negotiations on czarist debts and resumption of trade. These modest efforts at normalizing relations aroused tremendous opposi-tion, given the general British atmosphere of hostility toward Soviet Rus-sia. The social democratic Labourites found themselves labeled by their critics as "dupes" of the Communists, and soon became the target of Red-baiting in the conservative press.

Actually, most Labourites were hostile toward local Communists, rebuff-ing all efforts of the tiny British Communist party for affiliation. Though Communist leaders gained control of a few small unions, these remained the exception. In a majority of unions, the Communists were steadily si-lenced, thwarted or ousted, and by 1926, violently anti-Communist trade union officials would be in control of the powerful Trade Union Congress, which formed the heart of Labour party strength. Despite its domestic anti-Communism, however, the Labour party, especially its radical wing, the Independent Labour party, had been almost the only voice, apart from the British Communist party and a few other tiny left-wing groups, to oppose British military intervention against the Bolsheviks during the Russian civil war, and to press for normalizing relations. Labour party policy was motivated less by solidarity with the social aims of the Soviet regime, than by pragmatic hopes that expanding trade with Russia might relieve the mounting unemployment and declining wages in Great Britain that followed in the wake of World War I. This moderate policy, however, aroused a kind of anti-Communist hysteria on the part of conservatives. By the end of September, a full-fledged Red Scare was under way. New elections were scheduled for October.[2]

Days before the election, publication of the famous "Zinoviev letter" in the newspapers sealed the fate of the already precarious Labour Government. The letter, allegedly a communication between Comintern officials and the British Communist party regarding plans for Communist infiltration in Great Britain, was later proven a forgery. But the ease with which the conservative press exploited it reflected the obstacles to any British-Soviet understanding. On October 29, barely a month after Goldman's arrival, the Labour government went down to defeat. Soon afterward, all efforts at normalizing diplomatic and trade relations between Britain and Soviet Russia ceased. Anglo-Soviet relations limped along in "the most abysmally bad state" for three years until they were finally broken off altogether late in 1927. They were not resumed until 1930.

A few weeks after the election, Emma's anarchist comrades held a banquet to welcome her to England. By this time, the lively prewar Jewish immigrant anarchist scene of London's East End—the counterpart of New York's Lower East Side—had largely vanished, its members drawn away by the triple attractions of Orthodox Judaism, Zionism, and, to some extent, Communism.[3] Some of the former anarchists had become fairly prosperous people—"alrightniks," according to Emma—united mainly by nostalgia for the militant trade union struggles of earlier years; after meeting them Emma believed she would have no problems in England if she worked primarily with the Jews, but that alternative did not attract her.[4] The anarchist monthly, *Freedom*, still appeared, outspokenly anti-Soviet since the fall of 1920, but it was an isolated paper with few subscribers, kept afloat largely by the dedication of two men, Thomas Keel and W. C. Owen, with little connection to the labor movement or even to a larger circle of supporters. Anarchist groups stumbled along in provincial cities, such as Bristol and Norwich and Glasgow, and among the unemployed miners of South Wales. But the libertarian landscape was one of depression and disarray.[5]

The few remaining anarchists hoped Emma's presence might spur a revival. To everyone's surprise, the small, semiprivate affair they had planned to welcome her blossomed into a large public gathering, as some 250 people turned out on November 12, 1924, a night of pouring rain, for a dinner at the Anderton Hotel. Josiah Wedgwood, a joint vice-chairman and colonial spokesman of the Labour party, presided. The young journalist and novelist Rebecca West spoke in Goldman's honor. West had previously met Emma's niece, Stella Ballantine, in New York, and now generously responded to Goldman's appeal. Bertrand Russell, whom Goldman had met in Moscow in 1920, gave a speech of welcome "anarchistic enough even for me," as Emma later quipped. Havelock Ellis, "new life" advocate Edward Carpenter, the playwright Israel Zangwill, and H. G. Wells, West's lover who had also visited Russia and written critically on his return, sent messages of greeting. As *Freedom* reported wryly, the tone of the evening was heavily Labourite, with Goldman welcomed less as an anarchist than as an exile facing possible deportation under the new Tory government. Emma herself supposed that the audience thought she was coming to England to defend Soviet Russia. She staged her announcement with consummate skill. In his *Autobiography,* Bertrand Russell described the moment. When Emma rose to speak, he wrote, "she was welcomed enthusiastically; but when she sat down, there was dead silence. This was because almost the whole of her speech was against the Bolsheviks."[6]

Having thrown down the gauntlet, Goldman now set out to organize the most controversial campaign of her career. She wished to mobilize protest against the Soviet imprisonment of left-wing dissidents and, at the same time, to arouse public opinion against the Soviet regime. She particularly hoped to recruit Harold Laski, the distinguished political scientist, an influential professor at the London School of Economics and advisor to many Labour party politicians. Armed with a letter of introduction from Roger Baldwin in New York, she contacted Laski, who invited thirty-five prominent Labour and ILP guests for tea on a Sunday afternoon shortly before Christmas. Here she could present her views. As Emma wrote Sasha anxiously the day before, "tomorrow will decide much." She hoped at this gathering to recruit a number of people to form a committee to back her efforts.

Even before the tea, however, Goldman had begun to recognize the ambiguity of her position. "My situation is really a desperate one," she wrote Sasha on December 20. "The tories have taken a stand against the communists, in France they are being hounded, the Pope comes out against them. And here I am doing the same. It is no wonder that everybody refuses to join me. It really means working hand in glove with the reactionaries. On the other hand," she continued grimly, "I know I must go ahead and that our position is of a different nature." [7]

The Laski tea proved a disappointment. Emma blamed it partly on a favorable preliminary report of the British Trade Union Mission to Russia that had appeared in the Sunday morning newspapers. No one present at the tea would join a committee, she reported to Sasha, "if I should use the proposed meeting for a presentation of facts about the Bolshevik regime. Some of them are willing to go on a Defense Committee of the Politicals, if I will speak [only] about the conditions of the politicals." For Goldman, however, the conditions of the political prisoners were an inevitable outcome of the Bolshevik regime, inseparable from its Marxist foundations. To protest the holding of political prisoners without addressing the larger questions of the revolution and the regime seemed like "starting from the tail end." [8]

Goldman's insistence on linking these two issues became the central controversy in her campaign and a major stumbling block to recruiting support. Harold Laski's response was typical. He initially offered to assist a campaign for Russian political prisoners. [9] But talking with Emma persuaded him, along with other Labourites, that she was interested mainly in attacking Bolshevism. He agreed with Bertrand Russell that any effort on behalf of Russian prisoners must not be part of an anti-Bolshevik campaign. "I do not think you would be willing to limit yourself to speaking at your meeting solely upon facts of prison treatment," he wrote her; "I gather that you want to trace it to the inherent nature of Bolshevism. I therefore recommend you hold your meeting under your own and your friends' auspices. I will meanwhile try and get people interested in protesting about the politicals. But I am not hopeful." [10]

Goldman also hoped to recruit Bertrand Russell to her campaign. A long-time socialist who had also written sympathetically of anarchism, Russell had accompanied the British Trade Union delegation to Russia in 1920.

He "loathed the Bolsheviks" almost from the moment he set foot in Russia, for reasons tinged with anti-Semitism and anti-Americanism as well as objections to tyranny. It was, he wrote, "a close tyrannical bureaucracy, with a spy system more elaborate and terrible than the Tsar's, and an aristocracy as insolent and unfeeling, composed of Americanised Jews." [11] Russell's influential critique, *The Practice and Theory of Bolshevism*, published in 1920, set forth his analysis of the "failure" of Bolshevism, arguing that while the violence and repressiveness of the Soviet regime may have been unavoidable, the Russian outcome was not a desirable road to communism and should not be emulated in Britain, where a more gradual, peaceful, and democratic path to socialism was possible.

Russell had responded favorably in 1923 when Emma's friend, the former *Nation* correspondent Henry Alsberg, had approached him about the possibility of an international protest against political persecutions in Russia. [12] He agreed to draft a protest letter that could be circulated to other European intellectuals, couched as an appeal for amnesty from the international socialist movement. (The letter was later circulated in the United States and eventually sent to Moscow.) He also agreed to write a brief endorsement for a collection of letters from Russian political prisoners, which was later published as *Letters from Russian Prisons*. When Harold Laski contacted Russell, however, in December of 1924, following the tea for Goldman, Russell replied that he could not cooperate with her efforts, since he saw no possible alternative to the Bolsheviks on the horizon, and he believed that any protest meeting regarding Russian politicals "must not be held under anti-Bolshevik auspices such as yours." [13]

Goldman decided to pursue the matter with Russell directly in a letter, insisting that no one was attempting to overthrow the Bolsheviks "forcibly," but that "everyone should be interested in bringing enough moral pressure to bear upon the rulers of Russia to change their tactics toward their political opponents." [14] In his reply, which illuminated the opposition of many British socialists and liberals to Goldman's campaign, Russell explained why he had not definitely joined her movement.

I am prepared to sign definite letters of protest to the Soviet Government, or documented statements as to the existing evils; in such cases, I know exactly what I am committing myself to. But I am not prepared to advocate any alternative government in Russia: I am persuaded that the cruelties would be at least as great under any other party. And I do not regard the abolition of all government as a thing which has any chance of being brought about in our lifetimes or during the twentieth century. I am therefore unwilling to be associated with any movement which might seem to imply that a change of government is desirable in Russia. I think ill of the Bolsheviks in many ways, but quite as ill of their opponents. I feel that your movement, even against your wishes, will appear as political opposition to the present Soviet Government; and that being so, I feel that my support must be limited to signing documents such as Alsberg's, which cannot be taken to have any such implication. I am sorry to have failed you, and I hesitated for a long time. But the above view is what, in the end, I felt to be the only possible one for me.[15]

Her failure to recruit Harold Laski or Bertrand Russell disappointed Goldman deeply, especially since she did not perceive her efforts as "political opposition" to the Bolsheviks. Convinced that political persecution was "inherently" and "inevitably" linked with Bolshevism, she found any effort to separate the two issues incomprehensible. She continued to deny her assaults on the Bolsheviks. "Laski's suggestion that I am more interested in attacking Bolshevism than helping the politicals is absolutely unfounded," she protested to Roger Baldwin. "To be sure I consider it of utmost importance to the revolutionary movements of the world to investigate the confusions created by Bolshevism. But I do not have to tell you that my interest in the terrible fate of the politicals is beyond even that of exposing the Bolsheviki. The only thing I fail to see is how one can discuss the conditions of the politicals without discussing the very institution which made political terror inevitable."[16]

Here was the heart of Goldman's dilemma in Britain. By linking repression "inevitably" with Bolshevism, socialism, and all forms of Marxism, she effectively distanced herself from the entire socialist movement in Britain, which had struggled since 1917 against the virulently anti-Bolshevik policies of the government. Her analysis of "inevitable" terror inside Russia in effect denied the possibility of improvement, a deterministic view that conflicted with the voluntarism of her anarchist politics. It allowed no legitimacy to the democratic aims of British socialism, or to the dissident Communists who argued for more democratic practices, inside and outside of Russia. As an anarchist, of course, Goldman in theory abhorred all forms of the state, regarding Bolshevism as one kind of "fanatical governmentalism"; but in practice, she focused her attacks on the evils of the Soviet state while downplaying those of capitalist and colonialist regimes. By couching her concern for Russian political prisoners as an all-out condemnation of the Soviet government, she not only alienated people who shared her concerns, but helped discredit the amnesty campaign by making it into an anti-Communist crusade.

Interestingly, Goldman continued to deny any intention of supporting an overthrow of the Bolshevik regime. She insisted, rather disingenuously, that her anti-Soviet efforts actually favored diplomatic recognition because when other governments realized that the Russian regime was far from revolutionary, they would be more willing to grant recognition. Indeed, Goldman claimed she strongly supported such recognition because it would lessen the appeal of Communism inside and outside of Russia, and also allow other nations to exploit Russia's resources. (In contrast, some British socialists argued that normalizing relations with Russia would favor a relaxation of the internal dictatorship in that country: a view supported by the testimony of those inside Russia, including persecuted dissenters, who urged closer contacts between Russia and the West.)[17] But despite Emma's insistence that her campaign had "no relation whatever with any attempt or desire to overthrow the Bolshevik government," the entire thrust of her argument led toward the conclusion that only the defeat of the Bolsheviks held out real hope of amelioration, since the evils they practiced were "inherent" in their politics.[18]

Given her inability to recruit supporters among the British Labourite intelligentsia, it is puzzling that Goldman failed to pursue contacts with left-wing dissidents such as the feminist Sylvia Pankhurst, whom she visited in February of 1925 and found "intensely interested in Russian affairs and willing to cooperate."[19] Pankhurst had been one of the earliest and most outspoken British defenders of the Bolsheviks and a founder of the British Communist party, which expelled her after a few months for her persistent antiparliamentarianism and lack of "discipline." Subsequently Pankhurst defended the persecuted Workers' Opposition in her paper, the *Dreadnaught,* which continued as a voice of dissident Communists. Prior to Goldman's arrival in England, Pankhurst evidently participated in efforts on behalf of Russian political prisoners. But Emma's visit with her led to no further action, and Goldman did not mention Pankhurst in her memoirs.[20] Nor did Goldman build ties with socialists involved in efforts to mobilize the Socialist Second International on behalf of Soviet political prisoners.[21]

As she grew increasingly isolated, Goldman became more vehement on the subject of Russia. One notes in her letters the hint of paranoia in her allusions to a gigantic conspiracy centered in Moscow, which had somehow "bought" the support, or at least the acquiescence, of the whole world and terrorized the radical intellectuals into submission. Occasionally she acknowledged, privately to Sasha, the ambiguities of her position, but most of the time she blamed the Left for cowardice, opportunism, and inconsistency. Battling her growing feelings of frustration, she insisted on the correctness of her claims. "I am confident that the time is not far off when the very people who today engage in a conspiracy of silence will be forced by the overwhelming facts coming out of Russia to take the position I am taking now," she wrote Ellis in February of 1925. "I console myself that by that time I will have paved the way for a better understanding of the Russian debacle, which might have proven a great social experiment but for the Communist state crushing every attempt of the people toward a new social structure." [22]

Years later, Goldman would insist she had been prophetic, and many people would agree with her as the depredations of Stalinism began to take their toll. Yet it is worth recalling that the Soviet Union in the mid-1920s was not the same as in the mid-1930s; the "overwhelming facts coming out of Russia" in 1935, say, were not the same as those of 1925, or 1921. Emma's claim in 1925 that "the Bolsheviki continue to employ exactly the same methods to-day as they did in . . . 1919, 1920, and 1921," was untrue.[23] Nor was it true, as she would write in 1935, that "fundamentally it has remained exactly the same state, based on the same principle of violence and coercion and using the same methods of terror and compulsion as in the period of 1920–1921." The Stalinist state differed dramatically from that of Russia under the New Economic Policy. Moreover, as Victor Serge once noted in a famous metaphor, the germs of Stalinism may have been present in Bolshevism, but "Bolshevism also contained many other germs—a mass of other germs—" and the transition from Bolshevism to Stalinism was far from "inevitable." Goldman's claim collapsed fifteen years of turbulent Soviet history into a moment outside of time, as if the only reality of the Soviet landscape was "the dreaded sword of Bolshevik terrorism," monopolizing every phase of life.[24]

Despite her frustrations, Goldman managed to make her voice heard on both sides of the Atlantic, especially in the capitalist press which carefully followed her anti-Soviet campaign. The *Times* (London), the *New York Times,* the tabloid *Daily Express* and the *Illustrated London News,* as well as the liberal *Westminster Gazette* and *Time and Tide* covered her activities and quoted her generously. Rebecca West wrote an introduction to the British edition of *My Disillusionment* and helped secure publication in England of both Emma's and Sasha's books on Russia. The Sunday *Times* (London) published selections from Emma's book in a three-part series of articles, and the *New York Times* devoted several respectful half-page spreads to her attacks on the Bolsheviks.[25] Goldman also organized a British Committee for the Defense of Political Prisoners in Russia, which gave her backing, at least on paper, for public protests. Her most successful meeting took place on January 29, 1925, at the South Place Institute. Josiah Wedgwood again presided, while Rebecca West and John Turner attended. Turner was the longtime head of the powerful Shop Assistants' Union and a member of the British Trade Union Delegation, which had visited Russia in late 1924. Emma had known him since 1903, when he visited the United States and was promptly arrested and threatened with deportation under the 1902 antianarchist laws. She had organized a campaign of protest that delayed his deportation long enough for him to deliver a number of well-attended lectures.

Once again, however, Goldman combined her plea for political tolerance with a blistering attack on the Bolsheviks. She claimed that the life of the peasants was worse than before the revolution, even though they now owned land, and that there was no free intercourse between the peasantry and the cities—a portrait that resembled the civil war Russia of 1920 more than Russia under the New Economic Policy in 1925. A resolution drawn up and passed by the assembled crowd, however, was considerably more restrained. The resolution urged the release of all prisoners and exiles "whose sole crime is that they differ politically from the Party now in power." It also took pains to place the protest in a larger libertarian and anticolonial context, stressing that "the Chairman and Emma Goldman have both claimed the right to criticize and condemn political tyranny in Russia today because they have always been opposed to political persecution wherever it occurred—including the Tsarist regime in Russia, the English occupation of Ireland, Egypt or India, or on the part of any other Governments." After the meeting, which was well publicized in the press on both sides of the Atlantic, the resolution was presented to the Soviet representative in London.[26]

Next, Emma went to work on the report of the British Trade Union Delegation. The British delegates of the General Council of the Trade Union Congress had visited Russia for six weeks in November and December of 1924, returning to England to issue a three-hundred-page report. Their findings were measured, but generally positive, expressing optimistic hopes for future possibilities "in respect of popular government, political peace, and social progress." [27] The report vehemently denied that anything like a "reign of terror" prevailed and emphasized the importance of normalizing relations with Russia. While praising achievements in the areas of health, sanitation, education, the arts, prisoner education, agriculture, and trade unionism, the report criticized the absence of a political opposition, the practice of strict censorship, and the existence of political prisoners.

This report infuriated Emma. As she put it later to Roger Baldwin, "not one word in it is actually true." [28] Goldman insisted that, in six weeks, knowing no Russian, accepting the lies of translators and guides, the British delegates were incapable of ascertaining the truth. Even the preliminary report outraged her. It was, she told Baldwin, a "miserable whitewash," and it had ruined whatever support she had roused for her campaign in the previous two months. [29] As she wrote Harold Laski, "Such testimony can have no weight with people who know the country and its language." Emma cited as an example the naive contention of the report that the GPU was comparable to Scotland Yard. [30] She did not mean to impugn the sincerity of the delegation, but, she wrote Laski, "I do mean to charge them with lack of political grasp of the Russian situation, ignorance as to the terrible conditions of the masses, above all excessive partiality to the ruling regime—all of which makes the opinions of the delegation utterly worthless to fair-minded men and women." [31]

Now, in letter after letter to friends and acquaintances, Emma charged the Labour delegates with naïveté, cowardice, corruption, greed, and dishonesty. The Labour press, she claimed, was engaged in "a deliberate campaign of lies" to exonerate Soviet Russia. Every one of the delegates "consciously and deliberately misrepresented the actual situation: some of them for personal reasons; these are men who have been in the T.U. movement all their lives and out of loyalty to the gang submitted to the farcical Report." [32]

These attacks angered even those sympathetic to her position, such as John Turner, who urged her to challenge facts rather than impugn the honesty of the Labour delegates. [33] Goldman took Turner's advice to heart. She decided to write an article and issue a pamphlet that would expose the "lies" of the report. Although she denounced the Bolshevik experiment as "the most colossal failure in history" and insisted the report was based on appearance, not on fact, her criticisms were actually quite modest. Many of her allegations were based on information readily available in the Soviet press, from *Pravda*, for example. They indicated the extent of public criticism inside Russia and the continuing struggle of the regime to address overwhelming problems such as inadequate educational facilities, poor health of children, excesses of the GPU, unemployment, and unhealthful factory conditions. Goldman's most serious criticism of the report concerned its claim that the GPU was comparable to Scotland Yard. "I wonder what the same Delegation would say, if Scotland Yard could arrest, exile and shoot workers for strikes or for their political opinions," she wrote. She also ridiculed the claim that "the humanization of prison-life is a striking feature in Russia," citing appeals from prisoners at various prisons such as the immense Solovetsky Island, where "the spirit of the old asiatic regime was revived."[34]

Goldman trenchantly criticized the report's failure to address obvious issues, such as the practice of administrative exile, the secrecy of the GPU, and lack of rights for the accused. Yet while she might usefully have pointed out limitations, she instead mixed up justified criticism with exaggerated rhetoric, ridicule, and inaccurate information of her own. Many of her allegations were based on émigré sources that Berkman sent her from Berlin. Her "quotes" from *Pravda,* for example, were second hand, as they appeared in a Menshevik paper published in Berlin. Emma herself was unsure if her sources were trustworthy. "I hope they are reliable," she wrote Sasha. She would have liked to credit her source, "but I could not do that as it would have prejudiced the accuracy."[35]

Ultimately, Goldman's argument with the report rested less on questions of fact than of philosophy. In her view, the report's (exaggerated) statement that "in Russia the State is in control not only of the Press, the platform and the political machine, but also of the schools, universities and the creative arts" condemned the Bolshevik experiment as "the most colossal failure in history."[36] She was outraged that people did not believe her claims, that they placed greater trust in the reports of people who neither spoke Russian nor spent much time in Russia. As she found herself increasingly isolated, she grew more insistent that the "lies" about Russia, in the report and the Labour press, were a deliberate campaign of misrepresentation.

Meanwhile, in the late spring of 1925 as Goldman's campaign in England faltered, a related campaign got underway on the other side of the Atlantic, inspired by Goldman's friend, Henry Alsberg. In late 1920 and early 1921, Alsberg had grown increasingly critical of the repression of opposition parties under the Bolsheviks. In a *Nation* article in June 1921, "Russia: Smoked-Glass vs. Rose-Tint," he had argued that that Western radicals were romantic in their views of Russia and urged Western pressure to force a relaxation of the dictatorship.[37] Visiting Berlin in the summer of 1922, Alsberg began gathering lists of imprisoned revolutionists from the émigrés there, including Emma and Sasha. His conversations with them left a deep impression, for he returned to America determined to make the issue of political prisoners a kind of personal mission. He helped raise money for Berkman's Joint Committee, and contributed substantial funds of his own. In 1923, he had contacted Bertrand Russell, who had drafted a protest letter to the regime in Moscow. The letter, couched as an appeal on behalf of the international socialist movement, urged the inauguration of a "new political policy" that would proclaim amnesty "for those Russians whose conflict with the authorities is exclusively political. Such a step would do more than anything else to remove the suspicions of the Soviet regime entertained by many of the most sincere socialists throughout Europe, and would complete the breach with the evil traditions of Tsarism." A modified version of the letter was later circulated in the United States—mainly to liberals associated with the American Civil Liberties Union—and submitted, with American signatures, to Moscow.[38]

By the time Russell had drafted the letter, late in 1923, Alsberg had returned to America, where he proposed to Roger Baldwin that the ACLU take up the campaign. Like Russell, Baldwin responded enthusiastically to Alsberg's proposals. The ACLU was limited by its mandate to addressing domestic issues, he told Alsberg; as an organization it could not undertake work on behalf of Russia. But Baldwin personally wanted to act. In the spring of 1924, he and Alsberg considered the question of how to proceed. Both of them recognized the central difficulty of such a campaign: how to keep it from becoming a forum for anti-Communist and anti-Soviet propaganda.[39] With his legalistic turn of mind, Baldwin now decided that, before undertaking a public effort, they needed hard evidence of persecution that could stand up "in court." He looked forward to a report from Dr. Harry Ward, a liberal Unitarian minister and chairman of the ACLU, who planned a trip to Russia in the summer of 1924 to secure information on civil liberties and political persecution and to gather signatures of European intellectuals for the petition drafted by Russell. Alsberg had been passing on information from Berlin, but Baldwin thought it was inadequate. As he explained to Emma, he needed affidavits, names, exact identification of places and prisons and of the circumstances of arrest. Otherwise, he told Emma, the material would convince only those temperamentally opposed to the Bolsheviks. He thought it important to persuade liberals, people who would examine the facts. "My hands are tied without the facts," he insisted. Baldwin assured Emma, "My temperature is just as high as yours in regard to political persecutions in Russia, or for that matter anywhere else." But he needed more information before he could persuade others. "None of you fellows interested in the matter have got the goods yet," he complained.[40]

Emma and Sasha, and to some extent Alsberg, insisted that they had got the goods; that the evidence for massive political repression was overwhelming and anyone who denied it was either naive, deluded, or a liar. (Although Berkman met with ACLU chairman Harry Ward and introduced him to other émigrés, he thought the idea that Ward—who did not know Russian and was unfamiliar with conditions there—could secure reliable information was "a first-class joke."[41]) Baldwin's caution outraged Emma. On November 6, 1924, just a week before opening her own campaign in London, she blasted Baldwin with a five-page, single-spaced diatribe, complaining of the cowardice of those in England who refused to "stand out" against the "popular tide" of Bolshevism, and berating Baldwin for his refusal to face "facts."

> Here is the Soviet Government on its knees before the reaction of the world, paying homage to the Fascist Mussolini, recognized by the Catholic Church and the Pope in Rome, accepted by the most capitalistic apologists. Here is Russia, exploiting, robbing and browbeating the workers, filling its prisons, suppressing every breath of life and thought. And yet you people hate like hell to let go of your fetish! How long, dear Roger, are you going to wait? Until all the Russian politicals in the prisons and concentration camps, in Solovetsky and in other such ultra-socialistic burial places are going to die out? Until not one man or woman of ideas will be left in Russia?[42]

Emma charged Baldwin and Alsberg with naïveté for remaining "in utter ignorance of the secret treaty of the Soviet Government to exterminate men, women and children for opinion's sake! I must say I have no patience with such lack of revolutionary experience and training!" "Now listen, dear boy," she continued, "We sent you a list of a thousand names of victims in prisons, concentration camps and exile. This list is only a small part of the many thousands who have been incarcerated, starved, tortured, or even shot. The list was signed by every organization outside of Russia of different political opinions. Yet it seems that this list is not sufficient 'evidence recognized as competent in any court.'"[43]

Clearly something more was at stake here than just differing points of view about Russia. For Goldman, it was a question of her integrity, her reputation as a truth-teller and witness. What enraged her most was that Baldwin did not accept her word, that he should doubt the material sent by people who, "whatever else may be said against them, are known to have been in the revolutionary movement for well nigh a lifetime and have fought for their ideal at the expense of all else." She insisted that the "myth, this terrible superstition that Russia is a workers' experiment and that such things as existed under the Czar cannot possibly be true under the present regime must be exploded. Well, dear boy, you will have to emancipate yourself from that belief." Goldman concluded that the Soviet government had had "a most deteriorating and disintegrating effect both on revolutionary thinking and organization. In fact, it has poisoned the whole social and revolutionary movement. It has inculcated distrust, espionage and cynicism in the ranks of the masses unknown since the days of Jesuitism; it has discredited everything of any value fought for by revolutionary men and women the world over." [44]

Baldwin, however, coolly persisted in his demand for documentation of these claims, especially since the available figures on Russian political prisoners and exiles were considerably lower than Goldman's statements implied, ranging from 1,500 (Harry Ward's estimate) to about 4,500, of whom between 150 and 300 were anarchists.[45] Sometime in the fall of 1924, he decided to authorize Berkman and another Russian anarchist exile in Berlin, Mark Mratchny, to gather detailed information on the prosecution and imprisonment of Russians for opinion's sake, which could be used for a campaign in America.[46] The information, gathered from anarchist, Menshevik, SR, Left SR, and socialist Zionist émigrés in Berlin and Paris, and from prisoners inside Russia, would become the basis of a controversial book, *Letters from Russian Prisons*. In November of 1924, Baldwin and Alsberg also organized, in New York, an International Committee for Political Prisoners, or ICPP, with a membership mainly of distinguished liberals associated with the ACLU, although some anarchists and socialists (no Communists) also belonged.[47]

In the spring of 1925, as the ICPP campaign in New York gathered steam, Roger Baldwin found himself attacked from two sides. On one side, American radicals and liberals, including some members of the ICPP, attacked him as anti-Soviet and anti-Communist, warning that a campaign on behalf of Soviet political prisoners alone could lend itself to conservative purposes in the anti-Communist atmosphere of Coolidge's America.[48] On the other side, Baldwin became the target of Goldman's growing wrath, and of her accusations that he was inexcusably pro-Soviet. What offended Emma most was that Baldwin refused to accept her and Sasha as the final authorities on Russia. "Well, if you think his [Harry Ward's report] is more dependable than the material collected by Berkman and his coworkers you are welcome," Emma wrote him angrily. "I do not think that it is. In fact I insist that reports like Ward's do more harm than good because they contain so many half-truths." When the New York *Nation* devoted most of its March 4, 1925, issue to reports on civil liberties in Russia, she scornfully dismissed the entire edition. Although Ward's lead article was a fair-minded attempt to assess the situation, acknowledging the absence of free speech, press, and assemblage and the vast, vague powers of the GPU, which clearly led to injustices, Goldman considered it "a weak, pale attempt to exonerate the Russian government." In her view, the entire *Nation* was "as false in behalf of Russia as the *New York Times* is false against Russia. Both have played a shameful part in misrepresenting the actual situation and in misleading the A. people."[49]

In Emma's view, the Russians were simply great propagandists—the "Moscow magicians," as she called them. "You people refuse to see the myth that the Bolsheviki are no longer expressive of the Revolution, if they ever were at all," she wrote. Moreover, the Labour party was just like the Bolsheviks, and, she wrote, it was "certain to me that if they will ever be in the position of the Russian rulers they will set up a dictatorship as surely as Russia has." As if competing with the work of Berkman and Baldwin, Emma wanted Roger to help her raise money for an exposé of Bolshevik cruelty to children. It would have greater appeal than the *Letters,* she believed, and would be the best proof against Moscow.[50]

By now, Baldwin too was losing patience. "Dear Emma," he wrote in May, "I have read with deep interest your letter of April 20th and find myself in disagreement with almost every point in your attitude on Russia." He did not think money could be raised for Emma's planned exposé. "I have talked this over with a number of persons who are as much opposed to the Bolshevik dictatorship as you are," he told her, "but who see nothing to be gained by such a procedure. I would not be interested in it myself. I am through with indicting evil in the world merely for the sake of satisfying myself that I have spoken out."[51] Goldman continued to rehearse her old charges that Russia had retarded the social revolution in other countries, that there was little difference between the Fascists in Italy (this was 1925) and the Communists in Russia, and that the destitution of children was the worst possible indictment of the Communists.[52] But by now, neither she nor Baldwin continued the argument with enthusiasm. Though still friendly in tone, their correspondence lagged.

Rather than helping him, Roger Baldwin found that his association with Goldman and with Berkman complicated his work with the ICPP and also his work on *Letters from Russian Prisons.* Although the book was to be issued under the auspices of the committee, in fact Alexander Berkman had done most of the work of collecting information in Berlin, with assistance from other Russian anarchist émigrés in Paris, such as Mollie Steimer and Senya Flechine. Moreover, the vehemently anti-Soviet journalist, Isaac Don Levine, had edited the material and collected many of the letters from prominent intellectuals, which were to be included as testimonials in the book.[53] Baldwin always thought of himself as a friend of the Soviet Union, and insisted that the committee was wholly nonpartisan, that it had "no political bias at all," and that material for the book was gathered at his own direction from "disinterested sources." But Baldwin was reluctant to reveal these disinterested sources, even to members of the committee who worried, like Lewis Gannett of *The Nation,* that failure to identify them would expose the committee "to the charge of deliberate deception."[54] Baldwin himself appeared to recognize that Goldman and Berkman were not disinterested sources, since he decided to omit Berkman's name in the volume. In explaining the reasons to Berkman, Baldwin pointed out, rather disingenuously, that "I personally felt we had to omit your name because it would inevitably arouse widespread criticism at once as a source of partisan propaganda. Very few could understand your dispassionate and scientific approach to the problem. Most would identify you with your own and Emma Goldman's attacks upon the Bolsheviks and your material would suffer thereby." It was essential, he insisted, to attack the policy of repressing dissenters as an issue "separate from the main objectives of the Revolution with which we are in deepest accord."[55]

But in fact, *Letters from Russian Prisons* was a polemical, partisan book, as several members of the ICPP pointed out when they saw it in December of 1925. It consisted mainly of letters and statements by émigrés, (internal) exiles, and political prisoners, with almost no explanations or historical context that might enable the reader to evaluate them. The statements were preceded by twenty-two short letters of endorsement from intellectuals such as H. N. Brailsford, Harold Laski, Bertrand Russell,

Rebecca West, Upton Sinclair, Albert Einstein, and Thomas Mann, criticizing the denial of civil liberties in Russia. A series of legal statutes and regulations concluded the collection. Roger Baldwin and Isaac Don Levine nominally edited the book, but made no attempt to summarize or analyze the information. There were inconsistencies and inaccuracies throughout. All prisoners were identified as prisoners for opinion only, yet a prominent place was given to the case of Maria Spiridonova, the Left Socialist Revolutionary leader who had inspired the assassination of the German ambassador W. von Mirbach in March of 1918 and had helped organize armed revolts against the regime.[56] No information was provided relating to circumstances in which arrests took place, or about the class background of the prisoners, whose political affiliations were also sometimes unclear. Nor were there explanations of the political parties to which they belonged, although this information was crucial for understanding the reasons for imprisonment. The Makhno movement in the Ukraine was not described, yet several of the arrested anarchists were evidently charged with participation in that movement. And there was no attempt to place the Russian situation in a larger international context by comparisons with other countries. That conditions in certain prisons were relatively humane, that the suffering recounted consisted more often of isolation and loneliness than physical brutality, that most of the informants were intellectuals, that in some prisons inmates had considerable rights of self-governance—this information was generally buried in fine print. Not surprisingly, the book was read and reviewed as a wholesale indictment of the Soviet regime, despite Roger Baldwin's protestations to the contrary.

The most telling criticism came from the radical journalist and Latin American correspondent, Carleton Beals, who then lived in Mexico City. In his letter of resignation from the committee, Beals argued that the book was "being used entirely by those who have no love for political and economic freedom in Russia or anywhere else, and who would be the first to clap Roger Baldwin, or Carleton Beals, or Eugene Debs into jail in these United States if they had half a chance." Beals worried that, whatever the veracity of individual statements, the book must be judged "in relation to the great body of information and misinformation about Russia current in the United States; in other words your picture is only part of the picture, and as such, I fear, merely serves to create greater misunderstanding and antagonisms toward Russia."[57]

These criticisms persuaded Baldwin to go to Russia to investigate for himself. He spent much of 1927 traveling, not only in Russia but in other European countries, studying political persecution firsthand. What he saw convinced him that *Letters from Russian Prisons* had been "the truth . . . yet it is only one side of the truth, and only one aspect of oppression in a regime that was marked by many developing liberties."[58] In 1928 he published a sympathetic portrait of the regime, *Liberty Under the Soviets,* in effect a sequel to *Letters,* which dealt with economic as well as political freedoms and attempted to assess the Russian scene in the comparative context of political persecution in other countries, including the denial of civil rights to black Americans. Although Baldwin described the Soviet political structure as a dictatorship by the Communist party, he also asserted that the social and economic system represented the interests of "the overwhelming majority of the population," including the peasants, whose attitude he described as "critically favorable." If the system of internal exile was bad, possibly worse than under the czars, he thought the prison system was better than that of most countries, and that the alleged brutalities of the GPU dated mostly from the years of the Cheka (pre-1922). Baldwin did not minimize the excesses of the GPU or the numbers of political and economic prisoners and exiles—he estimated some twelve thousand to fifteen thousand, three-fourths of whom were members of the old bourgeoisie and not workers or peasants as the anarchists alleged—but he also noted that the international situation was a controlling factor in the administration of the GPU, which grew more repressive in response to perceptions of hostility abroad.[59]

When Baldwin wrote to Emma that his impressions in Russia had been rather more positive than he had expected, she informed him curtly that he had been deceived, that "you saw with the eyes of those whose guest you were and whose interpreters told you exactly what they thought was good for you to know."[60] Emma promised to read his book, though she was certain it would be "fallacious and misleading." In his reply, which was crisper than usual, Baldwin reported that he had had no official interpreters, he had obtained his own. "Some were monarchists, some anarchists, some communists, and several my American friends. I know you can get plenty of evidence against the Soviet regime," he continued, "and out of the mouths of the Bolsheviks themselves. It is a matter of where you put your emphasis, of how you estimate credit and debit."[61] Despite their arguments, Goldman continued to affirm her affection for Baldwin, albeit in her typical double-edged style. "I have undying faith in your honesty and sterling quality," she wrote, "although I frankly admit I have no faith whatever in your judgment." "I feel just the same about you," Baldwin replied. "I don't think you naive, but I think you hopelessly prejudiced."

In one sense, Goldman was correct. Baldwin had been overly optimistic, not so much in his information as in his predictions about "many developing liberties" on the eve of the worst decade of Stalinist repression. Having expected to find Russia a vast undifferentiated prison, he was surprised to discover that "the persecution is a bit different when you see the other sides of the conflicting life that is Russia today." [62] For Emma Goldman there were no other sides. She never questioned her analysis of the "Bolshevik myth." She did, however, occasionally question her choice of tactics. There were moments, in the winter and spring of 1925, when she wondered whether she might have secured better results if her British committee—which existed mostly on paper—had dealt with political prisoners in all countries, not only Russia, as the ICPP had decided to do. [63] Conceivably a broader human rights approach might have prevented her work from becoming an anti-Communist campaign. Moreover, her obsession with the Soviet Union meant she devoted less energy to thinking about anarchism. In a letter to Goldman in the spring of 1925, Max Nettlau astutely questioned whether anti-Soviet activities should be such a high priority for anarchists, or whether more direct efforts toward developing constructive anarchist alternatives might not be preferable. [64]

That Goldman's unrelenting bitterness about Russia owed something to her isolation and loneliness in exile is suggested by a remarkable lecture on China she wrote two years later in Toronto. In this lecture, she acknowledged that, unlike other Western nations, the Soviet Union had been willing to relinquish territorial claims in China. "In that," she wrote, "every liberty-loving man and woman must side with Russia, however critical we are of her dictatorship at home." [65] She never published this lecture, yet it suggested that, in a less alien environment, she was capable of a more balanced view of Russia and a broader vision of international events than was usually evident in her writings. Her essay, with its critical sympathy for both China and Russia, suggests the kind of intellectual work she might have done had she not been so embittered by exile.

In London, however, in 1925, Goldman found little relief from her persistent loneliness. Trapped in a self-defeating cycle, she undercut her efforts on behalf of Soviet political prisoners and human rights with her exaggerated attacks on Russia as a whole. When Havelock Ellis, with whom she had been corresponding for several months, suggested she might be aiding the forces of reaction in England with her anti-Soviet tirades, she replied that she was "grieved" at such a thought, but she could not stop. "I had to speak out," she told him, "no matter the consequences." [66]

The consequences, sadly, were frustration and growing isolation. By the summer of 1925, Goldman was feeling deeply depressed. Her eight months in England had been a "disastrous defeat," she told a friend. She had met hundreds of people, held public meetings, organized a nominal committee, exposed the "fraud" of the Trade Union report. She had published a few articles. But the struggle had led nowhere.[67] She had raised no money to help the politicals. She had made no headway in finding a means of supporting herself in England. The great General Strike in May of 1926, erupting out of a miners' strike, merely underlined her devastating isolation. The defeat of this strike marked a decisive turning point in modern British history and had catastrophic consequences for the entire trade union movement and the Left for years to come. We may imagine that for Emma, this strike, with its massive demonstration of working-class solidarity, would have been a momentous event, an opportunity to take part in an action that she had propagated all her life. Yet she remained completely outside and apart, seeing it mainly in personal terms. Indeed, she left England for a visit to France before the strike had ended. "I could find no one who would help me with a manifesto," she wrote a friend at the time. "I simply could not remain there and be inactive in the face of the strike which I had propagated for 25 years."[68] Characteristically, in her memoirs, Goldman blamed John Turner and other trade union officials for refusing her offers to help, writing that they "feared it would leak out that the anarchist Emma Goldman had some connexion with the general strike."[69]

Emma also felt her life "very empty of friends." "Dearest own Sash," she wrote in November 1925, after returning from lectures in South Wales. "I am awfully tired and so lonely and heartsick. It is a dreadful feeling to come back here from lectures and find not a kindred soul, no one who cares whether one is dead or alive."[70] She insisted that there were "no comrades in London to speak of. And the few are so very English they freeze my blood." With one or two exceptions, the Jewish comrades were "of the kind that I can do nothing with." According to the young British novelist Ethel Mannin, who became a good friend of Emma's in the 1930s, the English found Goldman's bluntness and forthrightness intimidating. Emma in turn found the English self-centered, reserved, cold, and "drab." Even Rebecca West, who had offered her hospitality and introduced Emma to prominent women, such as Lady Rhonnda, publisher of *Time and Tide*, finally struck Goldman as a woman who "radiates light but not warmth"; Emma admitted later that she never felt any closer to West than she did the day they first met.[71] "The English as a race have practiced restraint until they have lost the capacity to express anything, but the Londoners are about the last word in suppression of emotions or feelings," she exclaimed to a comrade in America. "An awful people to live with or to do anything with." Life in London was "a hard proposition for a stranger, I can tell you." [72]

Nor could Emma find consolation in any conviction of the ultimate triumph of anarchism, however distant. Her sense of loss extended to all aspects of her life. "If only I had my old faith," she lamented to Sasha. "But why kid myself, I have no faith left in the people, or the revolution, or our own ideas." [73] In this bereft state, Emma increasingly brooded over the failures of her personal life as well. She felt angry that after all she had done for others in her life, she was really "quite alone," and felt "consumed by longing for love and affection, for some human being of my own." [74]

Long conversations with Eleanor Fitzgerald, who visited London during the summer of 1925, prompted a series of bitter reflections on the "tragedy of the emancipated woman, myself included," particularly the older single woman, who found herself "getting on in age without anything worth while to make life warm and beautiful, without a purpose." Both men and women needed some one person "who really cares," but Emma felt that a woman needed it more "and finds it impossible to meet anyone when she has reached a certain age." Adding to the unmarried woman's difficulty was the fact that people generally disapproved of love affairs between younger men and older women, who were too often considered as unsexual and unattractive. As Emma described it to Sasha, no matter how "modern" she was, as a woman grew older, she was likely to feel more painfully the absence of husband, children, a home, economic security, and companionship; having grown up with traditional expectations, she often found herself feeling cheated—as Emma now felt. In her view, most modern women began to feel "the utter emptiness of their existence, the lack of the man, whom they love and who loves them, the comradeship and companionship that grows out of such a relation, the home, the child." "Ah well," she concluded one of her letters to Sasha, "life is one huge failure to most of us. The only way to endure is to keep a stiff upper lip and drink to the next experience." [75]

Emma's bitterness about "the modern woman" reflected her own feelings of loneliness and loss at a moment when her expectations in England had been disappointed. Her sense of sexual injustice may also have been sharpened by comparisons with Alexander Berkman and his new love in Berlin, Emmy Eckstein, who had helped him make up for the loss of Fitzi in his intimate life (though they remained on friendly terms). Certainly Emma could not help feeling how unequal she and Berkman were in the realm of love—they who had shared so much else in their lives—when he easily formed satisfying, long-term relationships with much younger women while she, the great champion of free love, suffered endlessly from unsatisfied longing and felt keenly the disapproval even among her comrades of her own relationships with younger men. Her letters to Berkman may also have been intended as reproaches for his failure to offer her the companionship she craved and as pleas for solace and reassurance. But for all Emma's dramatizing of the "tragedy" of her situation, her complaints were echoed by many other single working women of her generation who shared her loneliness. Certainly the letters and memoirs of other women such as her friend Rosé Pesotta offer poignant testimony to the difficulties faced by older, unmarried, heterosexual women in a society organized around marriage and motherhood and still dominated by traditional expectations that even the most emancipated women often partly shared.[76]

No doubt Emma's depression kept her from exploring the alternatives actually available to her; for example, working with the anarchist Rose Witcop, the sister of Millie Witcop (Rocker), or with other radical feminists such as Dora Russell in the British birth control movement.[77] Emma described herself as someone "suffering from an incurable disease," trying every doctor and every cure, hoping to "once more throw in my lot with our people who continue in the struggle of liberation."[78] In London, in the summer of 1925, that hope seemed more elusive than ever.

5

Hearts in Unison with Mine

Alternately depressed and hopeful, self-pitying and self-critical, Emma Goldman began reassessing her prospects over the summer of 1925, determined, at the age of fifty-six, to find a way to rebuild her life. "I hate defeat," she explained to Berkman, "and the idea that I have been defeated because I have been torn out of my moorings does not let me rest." [1] Despite her laments about the "modern woman," in her more philosophical moods, she acknowledged realistically that "even the ordinary woman is not sure she will have her children, her man, her home in her old age." [2] The "modern woman" at least could draw on her inner resources in ways unavailable to the others.

Goldman, however, was more likely to seek consolation in outward activities. For the next three years, she experimented with ways to make a living, and with places in which she might "take root." Though she received a monthly allowance from her brother Moishe (Morris) Goldman, a physician in New York, she was determined to find some means of becoming financially independent. She considered a wide variety of alternatives. She would open a beauty parlor to offer anti-dandruff treatments and massage, as she once had in New York; or she would start a combination bookstore, tea room, and gallery where she would exhibit the work of unknown artists and hold lectures and concerts. She tried writing articles for the press but, after her initial articles on Russia, had little success in getting her pieces accepted. Eventually she turned to the anarchist press, which published her work, but could not pay.

She had greater success with drama lectures, which she began offering in the fall and winter of 1925, hiding out in the British Museum Reading Room to prepare. Eventually she turned her lectures into a book-length manuscript, "Russian Dramatists: Their Life and Work," which expanded the discussions of Russian playwrights that she had begun in her 1914 book, *The Social Significance of the Modern Drama.*[3] But despite her active lecturing schedule—she toured Norwich, Manchester, Leeds, Northampton, Bristol, and South Wales, where poverty-stricken coal miners welcomed her enthusiastically—she found herself barely able to cover expenses. The drama book was never published, and the audiences who attended the drama lectures struck her as dull and stolid. "Really Dush," she wrote Berkman in exasperation, "if I had to spend the rest of my life talking to the British middle class, I should prefer to go to a Nunnery. It is awful."[4]

One alternative she seriously considered around this time was that of publishing a magazine, possibly a sequel to *Mother Earth.* This idea had been suggested to Goldman by Max Nettlau, the Viennese anarchist with whom she had been corresponding for many years. The militant activist Emma and the solitary, scholarly Nettlau, author of an immense biography of Bakunin and many essays on anarchist history, had met in London in 1899 and corresponded ever since, sporadically at first, and since the mid-1920s, more regularly. Goldman always treated Nettlau with a certain formality. He was always "Lieber Nettlau," or "Dear Comrade." She admired his erudition and dedication to research, and addressed him with a respect and seriousness that she did not always show toward her American comrades. Nettlau, on the other hand, admired Goldman's energy and activism, and her freedom from organizational ties. For many years hostile to anarcho-syndicalism, which he equated with dictatorship and "anarcho-fascism," Nettlau praised Goldman's status as a free lance. "You were never organized, nor did you wish to organize people," he wrote her approvingly.[5]

Like Emma, Nettlau emphasized the ethical, intellectual, and psychological dimensions of anarchism, the need to create a new "mentality," a transformed moral consciousness or "ethical regeneration," as he put it, that would do away with reliance on authority and cultivate values of tolerance, fairness, mutual concern, and freedom. Like Emma, he was skeptical of the revolutionary spirit of the masses, placing his hopes in an educated liberal minority and urging his comrades to disseminate anarchist ideas among "some of the very best," who might then educate others.[6]

Nettlau placed great value on developing a strong anarchist press, which he saw as an important vehicle for dialogue among anarchists as well as for spreading their ideas. Reminding her of the great importance Kropotkin and other major figures attached to the movement press, he urged Goldman to publish in anarchist papers, where she could write more freely than in the capitalist press. He encouraged her and Berkman to consider starting a paper of their own as a forum for new ideas, especially after the (temporary) demise of the London *Freedom* in 1927, when there was no important English-language anarchist paper outside of the United States.[7]

Emma never rejected this idea, and at various times she tried to persuade Berkman to take on the job of editor of a new paper—a proposition he flatly turned down. Without Berkman's support, she was not interested. He, after all, had edited *Mother Earth* while she had taken charge of financial arrangements, and she may not have felt eager to begin a new job as editor on her own. Moreover, Goldman had essentially subsidized *Mother Earth* through her lectures. It was unclear how sufficient funds could be garnered for an anarchist paper in England or in Canada, where the audiences for her lectures were much smaller. From time to time, Goldman reconsidered a new publication, but in the end, she did not pursue it.

Increasingly Goldman found solace in friendships to which she accorded a growing value. Despite the complaints about her loneliness, she continued to attract the affection and admiration of a remarkable number and variety of people. If some of her friendships ended bitterly, for political reasons, as with Agnes Smedley, or for personal reasons, many more lasted for decades.

The nature and intimacy of these friendships varied, and Goldman herself struck people differently, partly because she played distinct roles with different people. Rebecca West remembered her warmth and charm, and observed that she had "a rollicking sense of fun," although "for the most part she was sad because she had no outlet for her gifts."[8] Despite her admiration for Emma, West found her exhausting, and gradually withdrew. To Ethel Mannin, Emma initially appeared aggressive and forbidding and Mannin was terrified of her.[9] Yet the two women later grew quite close and Emma would remember Mannin as one of the few real friends she had made in London. To Fenner Brockway, who later became head of the Independent Labour party, and worked with Goldman closely during the Spanish civil war, she was a woman single-mindedly devoted to her cause. In his 1942 memoir, *Inside the Left,* he described her as "a stocky figure like a peasant woman, a face of fierce strength like a female pugilist, a harsh voice, a dominating mind, a ruthless will. But I liked Emma too—she would make tea for me in her rooms with a housewifely care which no hostess could exceed; she was simple and sincere in her comradeship and like my Paris friends, she was the absolute revolutionary, living for nothing else, entirely fearless and uncompromising." [10] To Herbert Read, the poet and art critic with whom Emma also developed a friendship, she appeared a woman motivated by essentially maternal sentiments. "The image of her in one's memory," he wrote after her death, "takes the form of an infinitely kind mother to countless lost children, rather than of the political orator and pamphleteer." [11] She could be abrasive, abrupt, gruff in manner, too much the "prima donna," as Fermin Rocker remembered her from his childhood, and given to a sarcasm that often hurt people's feelings. Or she could be tender, warm and gentle, generous both emotionally and financially. She was willing to make large allowances for people whom she liked or sympathized with. She was not distressed by Frank Harris's famous egotism, for example, because she identified with his experience of persecution. As she put it to his wife Nellie, of whom she was also very fond, "because I have been so misunderstood I feel keenly with Frank, he is also being misunderstood and misjudged." In Emma's eyes, his "charming, tender, and beautiful sides" far outweighed his limitations, "and I grow impatient when I hear anybody saying mean things [about him]." [12]

Emma responded strongly and swiftly to people; if she liked them, and especially if they liked her, she would overlook political disagreements. She was "quite smitten," for example, with Paul and Eslanda Robeson, whom she met in the summer of 1925 through Eleanor Fitzgerald. Emma thought Essie Robeson, a laboratory pathologist, "a damn good looker," and Paul Robeson "a beauty. He has the tragedy of the race in his eyes, and when he sings he is sublime," she wrote Berkman. [13] The meeting moved Goldman deeply, and she admitted that she had "never realized the cruelty to the Negro quite so much as I have since I met the Robesons." Robeson told an audience, a few years later, at one of the famous Foyle's Literary Luncheons in London, that Goldman's sympathy and appreciation for his singing, at that critical moment in his life when he was trying to decide on a career, had helped persuade him to pursue music. Goldman gave him a feeling, he said, "I only get otherwise from the novels of Dostoyevsky . . . the feeling that someone exists whose love really embraces all humanity." [14] Although by that time Robeson had grown sympathetic to the Communists, neither of them lost their enthusiasm for the other. During the Spanish civil war, when anarchists and Communists in Spain were fighting each other behind the antifascist lines, Robeson agreed to sing at a benefit concert for Spain organized by Goldman.

As her closest friends understood, beneath the frequently gruff exterior

Goldman craved warmth and affection before everything else, even in epistolary friendships which devoted much time to discussions of politics. One of the closest of these friendships was with a young American writer, Evelyn Scott, whom Emma met sometime in the summer of 1925. Years later, Scott recalled how "Emma was as warm and kind and interested in being helpful as if we had been the oldest friends she had and had known her all our lives." [15] Scott, twenty-four years younger than Goldman, had a romantic past that rivaled Emma's. As a young woman, she had run away from her conservative Tennessee family to live with a lover, an older married man, in Brazil, in circumstances that turned out to be harrowing. Later, she joined the bohemian intelligentsia in Greenwich Village, wrote an experimental autobiographical novel, *Escapade,* which was published to considerable acclaim in 1923, and became part of the expatriate scene in Europe where she continued to write fiction and criticism. [16]

Like Goldman's other young female admirers, Evelyn Scott admired Goldman as a rebel and a great woman, while regarding anarchist ideas with skepticism. Scott had never been politically active, but she traveled among left-wing intellectuals whose commitments she found increasingly alien. According to Scott's biographer, Emma Goldman influenced Scott in adopting a vehemently anti-Communist position that, toward the end of her life, would deepen into a progressive paranoia. [17] Anti-Communism formed a strong bond between the two. For Emma, Scott was an appreciative audience for long tirades about the evils of Communism as "a world-wide menace," and about how Bolshevism gave rise to fascism. [18] Both women waxed eloquent on the dim prospects of the working masses, with Goldman claiming that dictatorship "emanates from the lowest depths" and that "all the modern dictators are either proletarians or peasant stock," and Scott insisting that men were "so terribly stupid that they will probably always be the victim of the cunningly shrewd." [19] It is unlikely Goldman ever praised the Dies Committee as Scott claimed she did, for elsewhere Goldman criticized the committee as "reekingly reactionary" and refused to have anything to do with it. [20] For all their mutual affection, Scott's bizarre political fantasies did not help Emma, who needed accurate assessments of the political scene in America. Instead, Scott reinforced Emma's exaggerated perception of Communist influence in America, adding strange warnings, for example, of the *New Republic* and the Congress of Industrial Organizations (CIO) as the great American menace.

Still, politics did not define the primary attraction between the two women. Scott grew increasingly apolitical, while Emma continued to defend the value of political commitment in an ever more disheartening world. What linked them more deeply was their mutual identification as rebellious women, and as women writers, struggling in a harsh and hostile milieu. They filled their letters with confidences and consolation, and with reflections on the difficulties of writing. Emma found it "a great comfort to know that in faraway America there are a few, you foremost among them, whose hearts beat in unison with mine and that your mind is harmonious with mine without the need of arguments or explanations." And Scott thought Emma's existence "one of my big causes for hope," since "nobody ever lived more honest and brave." For Evelyn, Emma's "great goodness of heart has always meant as much to me as anything . . . she is, in my meaning of the word, a good human being." [21]

Distance, however, often smoothed relationships that, in person, became more problematic. Proximity with others was always difficult for Goldman, as she herself recognized; visits from friends and relatives, even when they were eagerly awaited, often ended in clashes. Those closest to Emma, including Berkman, Stella Ballantine, Ben Reitman, and Eleanor Fitzgerald, complained of her domineering, interfering manner and her tactlessness and insensitivity. Her tendency to misread the emotions of other people, and to project onto them her own anger or jealousy while denying these feelings in herself, caused Emma considerable distress. She was puzzled and hurt at the misunderstandings that frequently arose between herself and others, even with Stella, whom Emma adored and depended on, more than on anyone except Berkman, for emotional and practical support. Although she did not consider herself wholly innocent in quarrels with her intimates, she was nonetheless inclined to blame others while seeing herself as the abused and mistreated party. She was always surprised when people considered her high-handed and self-indulgent since she thought of herself as self-sacrificing and long-suffering.

But despite these traits, Goldman could also be extraordinarily perceptive and empathic. It was as if her psychic hearing were finely attuned only to specific ranges of feeling, so that she was exquisitely sensitive to certain people and to particular kinds of suffering, yet oblivious and intolerant of others. There were people such as Emma's former lover, Ben Reitman, who felt that she had never understood him. There were others, such as the Russian revolutionist Angelica Balabanoff, who felt that no one had ever understood them so well. "To guess what is not put in words—is the greatest and deepest token of solidarity," Balabanoff once wrote to Emma after they both had left Russia. "Emma Goldman was the one who gave it to me." [22]

Friendship, however, did not make up for Goldman's disillusionment in England. By the summer of 1925 she had begun to consider the possibilities of lecturing on the other side of the Atlantic, in Canada, and, she hoped, in the United States. That summer, in order to obtain a British passport, she married a Welsh widower and former coal miner, James Colton, a longtime anarchist who had helped arrange her lectures in South Wales. It was a political arrangement that was common practice among exiles and refugees without recognized citizenship. In October of 1926, with financial help from her Albany admirer, Leon Malmed, Goldman traveled to Canada. She hoped to carve a "field" for herself in the more hospitable climate of Montreal and Toronto, where small but active groups of Jewish immigrant anarchists carried on activities as part of the Workmen's Circle, a fraternal mutual aid society. At first her expectations were fulfilled, as she found herself welcomed enthusiastically, not only by her comrades but also by other members of the Jewish community in Toronto, the largest in Canada after Montreal. "You bet the comrades in T[oronto] are an exceptional bunch of people," she exclaimed to Berkman in February of 1927, four months after her arrival. "In all the years I do not remember having met with so much genuineness, so much sweet hospitality, such fine spirit . . . you'd go wild about them." [23] The Toronto press also championed Goldman, especially the *Toronto Star,* which extolled her "brilliant disquisition on Ibsen" and praised her as "living Ibsenism." [24] The radical Social Gospel minister Salem Bland attended many of her lectures, writing admiringly of her in his column in the *Star.* Goldman was especially pleased since she hoped to reach an English-speaking audience and to organize English-speaking anarchist groups as well. Touring western Canada, she also drew large audiences in Winnipeg and Edmonton. As she had in Montreal, she managed in Winnipeg (which she had last visited in 1908) to organize a group of women—Emma described them as anarchists, Mensheviks, and Zionist-Socialists, suggesting the strength of their European commitments—to continue fund-raising for the Russian politicals. [25]

But by spring of 1927, Goldman had begun to find the Canadian situation depressingly reminiscent of England. "Of course there is no use talking about American, English or Canadian Anarchists," she wrote Berkman from Toronto, "there are no such people . . . the Jews, the older ones, have become alrightniks, and there are no young." [26] She herself was "no longer used to work[ing] with a group. Jewish especially. Every time I attend the group meeting I go home wanting to weep, it is all so petty, so visionless." Her Toronto lectures in the spring of 1927 were poorly attended. And it was "hell" working with people; there were no good workers to help her. Although the comrades in Toronto indicated that they wanted her to stay over the summer, Emma felt lonely and neglected; most of her visitors in the summer of 1927 were family and friends from the United States, including her sister Lena, her brother Moishe, and even Ben Reitman, who had resumed corresponding with her and tried unsuccessfully to renew their affair. But although she had met "a few pleasant people," Emma complained to Berkman that "they are not the kind one can feel intimate with, outside of the work I am doing." She found her comrades friendly but narrow, given to quarrels and long periods of inactivity. "I do not know a thing I have in common with them except propaganda," she lamented.[27]

They, in turn, had mixed feelings about her. The memories of her comrades in Toronto and Montreal capture something of the contradictory impressions that Emma Goldman made on others. For example, Bertha Malmed, the daughter of Rose Bernstein with whom Emma stayed, recalled that the women in the Montreal anarchist group admired Goldman more than they liked her. Her own mother, however, idolized Emma, even though having Goldman as a houseguest kept her constantly busy, cooking, baking, entertaining for all the guests who came to visit. Once, Malmed recalled, in the middle of Goldman's visit, her mother slipped on a scatter rug, falling and hurting her back, so that she was in great pain, though she kept up her work as before. "After a couple of days Emma noticed it and said to her, 'Rose, when I leave, go to the doctor.' Sure enough, when Emma left, she went to the doctor and was immediately operated on. She had broken the tip of her spine. This is Emma Goldman: when I leave, then go to the doctor . . . but my mother idolized her. That kind of incident was part of Emma Goldman. It didn't phase my mother. It phased me."[28]

Others remembered Goldman differently. Millie Desser, then a young student at a commercial high school who acted as her secretary, recalled Emma's patience with her. When she first met Goldman, Desser had been shocked, because "everyone depicted her as a very brusque, brash, highly demanding individual, you know, the way she came across when she spoke." Instead, Desser found her kind and understanding. "She started dictating, and of course I fell far behind. I couldn't keep up with her—she dictated very speedily because her mind worked very fast. And I said, 'Oh

Emma, I'm lost. I can't keep up with you.' She said, 'Don't worry. I'll rephrase, I'll go back to where we started.' And she was so patient with me. And that was really a great surprise to me. She never once lost her temper with me. Not once in all the time I worked with her." [29]

The execution of Sacco and Vanzetti, in August of 1927, deepened Goldman's feeling of loneliness and futility. Although she organized one protest meeting in Toronto, she wanted to join the demonstrations in Boston, to feel herself part of the larger movement whose solidarity might provide some solace in the face of so bitter an injustice. Speaking of the two convicted men, but even more of herself, she wrote Evelyn Scott a few months after the executions that "loneliness, whether in life or in the face of death seems to me to be the most difficult thing to endure." [30]

By the fall of 1927, Emma's enthusiasm for Canada had evaporated. She complained to friends that "there is absolutely no inspiration here, no intellectual companionship whatsoever." Not even a place to get a drink of whisky, which Emma needed each time she lectured to ward off the "freezing sensation" of speaking "in a void." Once again she was determined to leave. "Well, dear old Tolstogub, this year was some rotten proposition," Emma wrote Berkman late in December, "but I am not sorry I faced it here in this unyielding country. Still less sorry am I to kick it out." She attributed her "failure" in Canada partly to the conservatism of the Canadians, the inefficiency and disinterest of comrades, and the opposition of Communists who often heckled her at meetings. Indeed, as Berkman suggested to her, the conservative, antilabor political atmosphere in Canada in the 1920s helped to defeat all labor and left-wing militancy. In Berkman's view, anarchist agitation in this setting was almost impossible, except inside the unions. [31] And even Emma was compelled to admit the ambiguity of conducting an anti-Soviet campaign in the Canada of 1927, since conservatives were eager to jump on the bandwagon for all the wrong reasons, especially after Britain broke relations with Russia in May. As Emma reported to Berkman, "most of the papers here just spit fire about the Communists, one can't just join in the cry at present." [32]

Although Goldman had earlier acknowledged that focusing on the problem of political prisoners in all countries might have had a greater chance of success, she evidently did not consider such a plan in Canada, for reasons that remain unclear. As in England, her insistence on placing the issue of political prisoners within an anti-Soviet, anti-Communist context—instead of a broader human rights context—led her into an impasse since, in the stridently anti-Communist atmosphere of Canada, even she felt reluctant to add her voice. She was left, then, with educational lectures and fund-raising, unconnected to any plan of action. In addition, she frankly saw the groups she organized to raise money for political prisoners as instruments for assisting her return to Canada, an understandable but not inspiring goal.[33] She still hoped to return eventually to the United States. She did not know that Washington had kept her under surveillance ever since her deportation; that American officials approvingly passed around copies of her writings; that diplomatic officers at the U.S. Embassy in London and the U.S. consul in Canada reported her activities to the Bureau of Investigation and the State Department in Washington.[34] When she inquired about returning, she found all doors closed to her, even though Isaac Don Levine, who had helped compile *Letters from Russian Prisons,* wrote a letter to Washington on her behalf, asserting that "she privately states that she no longer believes in revolution as the universal panacea."[35] Levine may have overstated the case, yet Goldman's actual beliefs probably made little difference in the conservative, nativist Coolidge years; her status as an alien, even more than her anarchism, was enough to thwart all efforts to have her readmitted.

Through the fall and winter of 1927, with few avenues for action, Goldman became increasingly depressed. Although Berkman criticized her for being too "individualistic," for dwelling too much on her own personal tragedies when the defeat of anarchism everywhere was a far greater tragedy, she had begun to recognize the extent to which her own well-being depended on that of the movement.[36] For all her independence, she needed an audience, needed a movement and a milieu in order to exercise her abilities. Without the inner resources that Berkman had developed during his long years in prison, she found it more difficult than he to confront the solitude and inactivity of exile. As she wrote to Berkman, she suffered "because I can not find an outlet for my energies, the work I want to give, the service I want to render. And this tragedy is not anything detached from the movement but is right in it, flesh of the flesh and blood of the blood of the movement. It is not a personal question with me (how much personal question was it ever?) it is that the general situation has helped to paralyze me and has made me useless for the work I want to do." Ironically, Berkman's criticism goaded Emma to admit that her efforts in Canada had not wholly failed. "I have done wonders considering that I had very little help," she wrote him, adding that "there is a field if only I did not have to draw my living from the work."[37]

But Goldman did have personal reasons for her growing dissatisfaction. Soon after arriving in Canada, she had fallen in love with Leon Malmed, the anarchist delicatessen owner with whom she had been corresponding ever since she left Russia. Although she had not responded many years earlier, when he had proclaimed his love for her, now he appeared in a new light, as part of her old life that had been stolen from her. He was the man whose love could make good the losses she had suffered. Leon became the symbol of all her hopes for a new life in Canada, the only star on a dark horizon. "I am famished for love and devotion," she wrote him after their first meeting in Montreal, in words echoing her letters to Reitman, "terribly starved for both."[38] Malmed had in fact literally fed her, sending food packages to the Missouri State Penitentiary when she was imprisoned in 1918 and 1919, and later figuratively, through his financial help. At their first meeting in seven years, when he had been warm and eager to see her, Emma found her defenses shattered, her body filled with "my awakened wild heart hunger."[39] She rented a small apartment in Montreal where they could be alone, urging Malmed to return as soon as possible. "Be reckless, Leon, be reckless and live dangerously for once in your life," she urged him pointedly in early November.

Their early meetings fulfilled Emma's fantasies. On Malmed's second visit, in the resort town of Napierville, the two became lovers—"a miracle," Emma later called it, "a child and lover have come to me and life has new meaning." She felt like the biblical Sarah "to whom a son came in old age." This equation of lover and son, which recurred in all of Goldman's sexual relationships, suggests an element of Oedipal fantasy in her love affairs with much younger men. Moreover, mothers could be manipulative and controlling as well as adoring: her lovers were also to be devoted sons.[40] The insistent mother-son imagery suggests that Goldman may have used the mothering role as a defense against tormenting emotions of jealousy, anxiety, anger, and fear that she experienced in spite of herself. But even now, love left her feeling overwhelmingly vulnerable. In a poignant note the day after they consummated the affair, Emma wrote Leon that she was not surprised that she had left her keys in a taxicab that afternoon. "I lost my keys, I lost so much more than that. My head, my heart, my all went with you, why then be surprised at keys?" In almost daily letters those first few weeks, Emma wrote out her longing for

Malmed, proclaiming the ecstasy he gave her, her yearning for the physical closeness that had been absent from her life for so long.[41]

Yet even in these letters there were hints of irritation. What Emma loved in Leon Malmed was less the man himself—in fact he often annoyed her—than his love for her. After many years of knowing him, she was "glad to have found there a reflection of all I have meant to you. It is good to know that one has meant so much in the life of another."[42] Feeling neglected and unappreciated on her arrival in Montreal, Emma placed all her hopes on Malmed, hopes he could not possibly realize, as if he could make up for her other disappointments and give her the validation others denied her. For all her strengths, Goldman needed constant recognition from others to make her feel alive and worthwhile; of all the losses entailed by her exile, the loss of her fame was not the least. "Your E.G. who could reach thousands is now barely able to reach thirty," she wrote bitterly, two days after their first erotic tryst. "Would this make you laugh? But why care? The greatest of the great have been isolated from the rest of mankind, lonely and forsaken, acclaimed only after their death." In any case, she assured him, it did not matter, since she had him, who made her life worth living, who gave her an aim and purpose. "Leon, Leon," she wrote in mid-December. "I cling to this dream as the one brilliant star—I have hitched all my hopes to it—may it come true."[43]

Inevitably, such a heavy weight of expectation was doomed to be disappointed. Emma wanted a savior. Soon the complaints began to mount: Leon did not write; when he did write he burdened her with his family and business worries; he did not visit; when he did come he brought mundane cares from home; his visits were too brief; he was not satisfied with "the dew of the rosebuds" but needed other drink (whiskey) and failed to understand "his maidele. The fountain of life can give her more ecstasy in a few minutes than all the wines and whiskeys in the world and all the champaigns [sic] besides."[44]

By late January 1928, Emma had begun to worry about the fate of their "autumnal love." She urged Leon repeatedly to free himself from his "ugly world" so that he could enter hers, so they could give themselves completely to their passion, "live dangerously, madly, drink in our love, scourged by the lava of our passion." She needed "your devotion, your tenderness and your savagery. I want to be in your arms, your lips pressed to mine. I want you, I want you, lover mine."[45]

It is not clear if Emma really wanted Leon to leave his wife and children to live with her. She was uncomfortable with "the deception we are keeping up," and furious when Malmed's wife accidentally discovered her letters in May of 1927. Still, although their infrequent meetings in the spring and summer usually ended in disappointment, Emma continued to write often, alternating accusations regarding his neglect and insensitivity with professions of "fierce desire." Over the summer of 1927, Malmed suffered some considerable difficulties of his own. On account of his association with Goldman and his support for the defense of Sacco and Vanzetti, he was denied American citizenship, which meant he could not obtain a passport. Emma continued to lecture him on his failings. By September, she felt he had cooled toward her. His letters and visits were becoming infrequent. In a series of letters Emma alluded to sexual difficulties, which she blamed on the brevity of Malmed's visits and his preoccupation with other matters. Indeed, Emma hinted that the wild erotic abandon to which she often alluded was more fantasy than reality. In real life, when he came to see her, harassed and preoccupied, Emma felt "a black wall between us that makes it utterly impossible for the free and beautiful expression of what has come to mean so much to us." She became "so frozen and paralyzed when I see the sinister wall rise up like a monster that I never yet have been able to let myself go." Though her imagination while awaiting him was "aflame with a thousand fancies," Leon's actual presence stifled her desire. "My heart contracts and I have a feeling as if someone would hold me by the throat." For this reason she could not respond "to what my soul craves so violently." Whenever he began "conjuring up Albany," Emma found that "everything in me then turns to ice." At times she was almost apologetic for her lack of physical response. "With you," she wrote, "the physical response is nothing at all when you care for a person. In fact it seems to be easy even if you do not care for the woman much. In my case every little shadow destroys any physical aspect. I feel too sensitive in such matters." [46]

Despite her sexual and financial disappointments with Malmed—she did not hesitate to scold him for failing to ask what she needed or "offering to make my life a little easier, a little more comfortable"—as she prepared to leave Canada in January of 1928, she was suddenly seized with longing for him, as if she still hoped for some final romantic encounter, a repeat of the initial magic of Napierville, that might leave her with memories to cherish. Malmed did travel to Toronto in late January, shortly before her departure for Montreal. The visit disappointed her; he spent all his time with other comrades, she complained, showed no more devotion than if she had never been in his life at all; he did not contribute to her autobiography fund or "even suggest a little parting gift if only in memory of what Napierville meant to you." She kept hoping for one last visit, but Malmed did not come to Montreal, sending instead a bouquet of roses on the day she sailed.[47]

The two comrades continued to correspond. When Emma wrote her autobiography, she omitted their affair, referring only to "my romantic admirer Leon Bass," but making no mention of their relationship in Canada. She had done so, she explained later, because the affair had ended "so disastrously." Still, Emma retained warm feelings for Malmed, who continued to help her financially on occasion, and even arranged a lecture for Goldman in Albany during her 1934 trip to America. He remained part of the wide network of comrades to whom she sent letters and copies of letters. Goldman could be harsh toward Malmed—when he suffered serious financial losses during the Great Depression, she congratulated him, saying that now he would be free of the economic burdens that had previously dominated his attention. Perhaps, like many of Emma's admirers, Malmed accepted her tactlessness as an inevitable part of a complex character. He continued to cherish her as a symbol of freedom in his life, keeping her letters and amassing a considerable archive of anarchist publications. Her legacy to his family was an ambivalent one, however, for she had made demands on Malmed, albeit in the name of an "ideal," which he could satisfy only at heavy cost, financial as well as personal. Trying to make him into an image of her own creation, as she had tried to do with Ben Reitman and Arthur Swenson, she repeatedly ran up against disappointing reality. Each time she chose as lover a man essentially unavailable to her, one whom she tried exhaustingly to change, only to find herself feeling betrayed and abandoned at the inevitable failure.

In the fifteen months of her sojourn in Canada, Emma had experienced a few brief moments of elation, but most of the time her mood had swung between anger and depression. She sought a validation, both political and personal, that neither the conservative Canadian setting nor her distant, married lover could provide. As she prepared to return to the south of France—where she had spent the summer of 1926, and where her friends, including the heiress Peggy Guggenheim, had helped her buy a small villa ("Bon Esprit") in the hills above St. Tropez—she was once again filled with that deep sadness that is so evident in her photographs. Despite the self-pity, there was a wistful poignancy in a letter she wrote a few weeks before she sailed. "Dear Leon," she began, "Don't take this letter in any sense of reproach. It is only that my heart is so heavy. This year I have again had to bury my fondest hopes for love, comradeship, some personal joy and peace. All that came to me like a streak of lightning and died as quickly. My hopes of establishing myself in C.[anada] near enough to A.[merica] also had to be buried. And now I go back as unheralded as I came. I am terribly weary from the hopelessness of it all."[48] There was little that Leon Malmed could say in consolation.

PART TWO

Recoveries

6

Writing a Life

In the early spring of 1929, an enterprising American journalist made his way up the winding Chemin St. Antoine to a small stuccoed villa overlooking the Mediterranean fishing village and bay of St. Tropez. With a tiny vineyard on one side, and a large garden of vegetables, flowering fruit trees, and roses on the other, this retreat on the Côte d'Azur offered an almost monastic seclusion to "the most incorrigible female anarchist the police authorities of the United States ever had, more or less ineffectually, to deal with." She invited the journalist to an exquisite lunch she prepared herself and served outside on the sunny southern terrace. Charmed by her hospitality, the journalist sensed the pent-up physical and mental energy beneath her outward guise of contented housekeeper and expert cook. She impressed him, by turns, as gracious, militant, shrewd, even as "a lost child seeking its mother" as she admitted her longing to return to America and to resume the adventurous life she had lost forever.[1]

That life, Emma Goldman told him, was the subject of an autobiography she was currently writing; she was handling the subject frankly and fully, "without gloves," as she put it. She had begun contemplating an autobiography as early as 1918, while she was imprisoned in the Missouri State Penitentiary, but she never went further than jotting down random notes. As her hopes for creating a "field" for herself in England and Canada faded, she began to take seriously the suggestions of friends that she write her memoirs. The writer Howard Young, brother-in-law of the poet Edna St. Vincent Millay, along with Peggy Guggenheim helped initiate a fund-raising drive to support Goldman through the period of writing. Guggenheim contributed the initial $500. W. S. Van Valkenburgh, editor of *Road to Freedom*, coordinated the effort and acted as a research consultant. Emma herself persuaded friends to return her correspondence, and Ben Reitman brought to Toronto some five hundred of her emotional love letters, especially helpful since she had never been able to keep a diary. A number of prominent figures lent their names to the fund-raising effort, including H. L. Mencken, Edna St. Vincent Millay, the publisher Horace Liveright, the Wisconsin Socialist congressman Victor Berger, Theodore Debs (brother of Eugene), and ACLU founder Roger Baldwin. By the time Goldman sailed from Montreal in February of 1928, the fund had reached $2,500. It was not sufficient to underwrite the project—Emma hoped for $5,000—but with this seed money, she returned to St. Tropez, eager to begin.

Still, she did not write for the pleasure of it. She hoped from the start that income from the memoirs might ease her financial straits. As she told Arthur Ross, the New York lawyer who took over her negotiations with publishers, "My book is my first and last chance in life to get enough material results to secure myself for whatever few years there are left me to live."[2] She hoped too that the autobiography might help secure her eventual return to America by calling attention to the injustice of her deportation and her plight as an exile. She received unexpected encouragement from Theodore Dreiser, who offered to approach publishers on her behalf, and also to work for her readmission to the United States. He had no luck in his efforts to secure an advance for Goldman—evidently he was refused by six publishers. He did later lend his name to efforts to secure her return to America. He also planned to write an admiring portrait of Goldman for his *Gallery of Women,* though nothing came of that project.[3]

Goldman received more concrete help from two other people. One was Alexander Berkman. While Emma was in Toronto, Berkman had begun writing *What Is Communist Anarchism?* (later titled *Now and After*), which proved more difficult than he anticipated. He was suffering a crisis of confidence, and needed Emma's presence and the stimulus of her conversation and suggestions. Her fifty-eighth birthday, which she celebrated in Toronto, prompted several unusually affectionate letters from Sasha, frankly admitting his eagerness for her to return to France—to help with his book as well as to begin her own—and expressing pleasure in their long relationship. Berkman's enthusiasm for her memoirs spurred Goldman's eagerness to begin. She was pleased by his admissions that he needed her and wanted her back in St. Tropez. In Toronto, where she found no intellectual stimulation, she felt exhausted from having to "masturbate my poor brain" for ideas, and "jerk off every lecture" as she put it. Sasha's promise to help with her memoirs reassured her that she would not struggle entirely alone.

Berkman lived in St. Cloud, outside Paris. (He would not move to Nice until 1930.) They were not exactly neighbors, although Emma would spend the winter and spring of 1929 to 1930 staying in a friend's flat in Paris. For day-to-day assistance during the first year of writing, from the summer of 1928 until May of 1929, Goldman relied heavily on "a very impetuous and violent young lady," the young American writer, Emily Holmes Coleman, whom she quickly came to depend upon and adore. Born in Oakland in 1899 to a well-to-do family, Coleman had graduated from Wellesley College in 1920, marrying Loyd Ring Coleman, a friend of Emma's nephew Saxe Commins, the following year. In 1924, Coleman had written Emma a fan letter, and the two had begun to correspond. Later, they met when Emily and her husband moved from Rochester to Paris. Here Emily wrote for the *Chicago Tribune,* published poetry in the avant-garde literary magazine *transition,* and became great friends with Peggy Guggenheim, the writer Djuna Barnes, and other expatriate writers and artists. By all accounts, Coleman possessed a wild, exuberant wit and gift for laughter that made her marvelous company. Later in her life, she returned to America, converted to Catholicism, and spent her last years at the Catholic Worker farm in upstate New York, where she died in 1974. At the time she met Emma Goldman, in the late 1920s, Emily Coleman had begun work on a lyrical, surrealist novel inspired by her experiences in a mental hospital where she had been confined for severe postpartum depression following the birth of a son. Coleman completed *Shutter of Snow* while working for Goldman. It was published in England in 1930. Later she expressed her gratitude to Goldman for her understanding and affection, telling Emma that their year together had "done more for me as a developing person than all the other years put together."[4]

Emma, in turn, found herself enchanted by her irrepressible, larger-than-life literary assistant, who was not phased by her gruffness and gloom. Three weeks after their arrival in St. Tropez, Coleman won Emma's heart by organizing a surprise birthday party, complete with cake and champagne and an expedition to a cafe in the village to dance. Emma loved it, and afterward her letters were full of praise for this "wild woodsprite with a volcanic temper" whom she found to be "tremendously interesting and a damned good companion." Moreover, Coleman's high spirits and sense of humor allowed Emma to give free rein to her sarcasm, without fear of offending. In letters to friends that she dictated to Coleman, Emma reported that Emily was "no good" as an "ordinary typist," that she "not only thinks while I dictate, but she corrects me every time I say anything she doesn't agree with. You can see she follows my train of thought—in fact so much so that she calls me a god-damned liar and yet we have been together only three weeks. But she is such an ass that I don't mind what she says in the least." They had fine arguments "over James Joyce and a lot of other writers who think they are James Joyce," Emma wrote another friend. "This lady is a modern of the moderns. I don't know how she can stomach my writing."[5]

Actually, "Demi," as Emma called her, astutely criticized Goldman's work, pointing out her sometimes heavy-handed humor and lack of distance from her material. "Your whole trouble has been that you have been living this story as well as writing it," Coleman told her once in a letter. She advised Emma first to live it, then to live it detached, as one writes it, though she knew Emma would not agree. Although the extent of Emily Coleman's editorial contribution to *Living My Life* is unclear, Goldman's testimony suggests that she relied heavily on daily conversations and even arguments with Coleman to help her formulate her ideas. After Coleman left for London, in May of 1929, Goldman felt her absence keenly. "Some days I missed you until it hurt," Emma wrote Coleman in December of 1930. "I felt if you were here and I could dictate to you and fight it out I would have the necessary stimuli. . . ." More than anyone else, Emily's faith also helped overcome Emma's painful doubts about her writing. "You helped me more than you can imagine with your understanding and with many other things," Goldman told her years after the memoir was completed. "[You] helped to enrich that year beyond anything I can repay."[6]

A great observer of symbolic dates, Emma Goldman began writing her autobiography on June 27, 1928, her fifty-ninth birthday. She wrote quickly at first, hoping to finish the manuscript by June 1929, "the psychologic moment, as I shall then have covered sixty years in this rotten world, out of which forty have been spent in chasing windmills."[7] During this period, Emma frequently described the autobiography to friends as an obsession that had taken hold of her, like a "disease, a poison in one's blood" that she could not escape. Berkman, who stayed with her for extended periods to help with editing, noted her gloom in his diary, especially toward the end of the project. The atmosphere at St. Tropez was "oppressive even to me, in spite of my good nerves," he wrote once. "One is afraid sometimes to smile or laugh and often we do not exchange a word at meals because E. is in a bad humor generally."[8]

She would write intensely in longhand for three weeks, mostly at night, sometimes for twelve hours at a stretch. Then, for one week she would dictate from her corrected handwritten copy to Emily Coleman, who would type the text. With this method, after five months of writing, she had completed nearly 175,000 words (about 700 typed pages), reaching only to the year 1900. In his diary, Berkman noted late in November of 1928 that Emma was "working hard, now, nights at St. Tr. Sometimes she is worried, not satisfied with her work. But I think it will be OK after a lot of cutting and revising. She thinks I don't understand her struggle in writing and living through the past. Its no use arguing about it though. Our outlook is different. Her attitude to things is very feminine." [9]

Despite the defiant tone in which she asserted her intention to write the book "in my own way, no matter what the cost will be," Emma was nervous about the reactions of others and insecure about her abilities as a writer. Eager for feedback from others, she also tried to preempt criticism by anticipating weaknesses in advance, warning prospective readers such as Arthur Ross not to judge the whole by the parts. She chided those close to her, such as Berkman and Saxe Commins, for giving her insufficient encouragement early in the writing process. If relatives, such as Saxe, offered any criticism, Goldman countered defensively that they had put her on such a high pedestal that they were shocked "to see my humanity and my dominant urge black and white." [10]

Finally Emma did show an early draft to Berkman, in January of 1929, with painful results. "E was hurt at my opinion of her autobiography," Berkman noted in his diary. "Told her all must be reworked. Would take several months at least. Very strained relations. I am sure she thinks I've failed her, but the only way I could help is to take the whole mss and rework it. She was laid in bed the day following our talk about her book." [11] Indeed, Berkman's editing proved a constant source of friction between them. Although Emma trusted his judgment, she argued with him over every change he proposed, almost over every word. Ultimately she appreciated his stringent editing. But she also wanted from him a kind of emotional assurance he could not give her. Her insecurity seems to have surprised Berkman, for he noted in his diary that "I now see she felt very badly that I did not give my opinion more in detail,—before." This was an old story between them: Emma wanting assurances and expressions of appreciation, and Sasha insisting that their responses were so different that talk only exacerbated their difficulties, that "I can't speak orally of my emotional reactions."

In this state of mind, Goldman appreciated the company of Rudolf and Millie Rocker and their son Fermin, who stayed with her in St. Tropez through most of the summer of 1929. In his autobiography, Rocker painted a poignant portrait of Goldman as autobiographer, recalling how she would get up at six each morning, make coffee, write for several hours, clean house, make lunch, spend several more hours writing, make dinner. Afterward they would all sit outside on the terrace drinking coffee and talking. From time to time, Emma would read aloud from a chapter in progress. Sometimes, he recalled, as they sat together under the southern sky, they would suddenly fall silent, giving themselves up to dreams and memories as they gazed out over the lights of the village and the bay and listened to the muffled sounds of fishing boats in the distance. Later, when everyone had gone to sleep, Emma would return to her desk, to write endless letters to America.[12]

In writing her autobiography, Goldman thought of herself partly as a historian, emphasizing her use of "historical data": papers, pamphlets, periodicals, her old letters, and the advice of anarchist historians such as Rudolf Rocker and Max Nettlau. She emphasized to her correspondents that the value of her memoir was partly the "slice of American life I portrayed, and not so much my own private and personal experiences."[13]

But she also thought of herself as an artist attempting an imaginative reconstruction of the past, "infusing life into what is long gone and forgotten, to give it meaning and shape."[14] At moments she saw the value of the book as essentially dramatic and psychological, like a novel. It was "not so much the actual facts" but "the atmosphere and inner state I have tried to recreate," she told Ross. Describing her autobiographical method to Ross, Goldman wrote that she had tried "to transfer myself as far as humanly possible into the particular period described and my reactions at that time to whatever happened to me. That is the way I have attempted to build up my characters from the beginning, until the book will be complete."[15] Though she doubted her writing skills, she did not question her ability to recapture her feelings as she had felt them in the past, or to recall her impressions of other people as they had appeared to her at earlier moments of her life. On occasion she likened writing the memoir to an actor recreating a role—a revealing metaphor suggesting her image of the autobiography as a narration of performances, and the theater as a metaphor for her life as a whole. *Living My Life* is partly about the astonishing succession of roles Goldman played in her life, from factory girl to seamstress, nurse, masseur, and midwife; manager of a troupe of actors, speaker, organizer, and author; birth control campaigner and free speech activist; publisher and prisoner; finally deportee and exile. References to the theater recur often in mentions of performances Goldman attended and descriptions of the actors and impressarios with whom she always got along well. It was no coincidence that Goldman's mentor, the German-American orator and journalist Johann Most, was a frustrated actor who shared Emma's thespian enthusiasm and first recognized, and encouraged, her talent for public speaking.

That Goldman began to write her autobiography at a time when she felt deeply her lack of a public role had important consequences for work she created. Every autobiography is to a great extent a history of the moment in which it is written, a dialogue between the author's present and her memories of the past as they emerge into the present. The "truth" of any autobiography is more the revelation of the author's sense of herself at the moment of writing than the documentation of past events. Rather than re-capturing a previously existing "self," autobiography involves the creation of a self or selves in the act of writing, the invention of an identity or identities that did not exist prior to the written work. Far from recording unmediated experience, an autobiographer imaginatively reshapes experi-ence in ways resembling those of a novelist. She depends not only on the vagaries of memory—itself responsive to the ambiguities of language and narrative—but also on the literary conventions of autobiography. To write an autobiography, then, is to engage not only with one's own past but with the conventions of a genre, and with the limitations of language itself. As Roland Barthes has written, "the one who speaks (in the narrative) is not the one who writes (in real life) and the one who writes is not the one who is." [16]

For a woman, writing an autobiography presents additional dilemmas. While all autobiographies draw on culturally defined models of the self available to the writer, the heroic "self" in Western culture has been over-whelmingly male. That is, the self deemed most worthy of an autobiogra-phy has been, by definition, a masculine self, one engaged in public life, with prominent achievements to display, while the ideal woman has been silent and self-effacing, and therefore without a story to tell. The very no-tion of individuality that has motivated modern autobiography, empha-sizing separateness, independence, and mastery, may well depend on a model of male psychological development that differs from that of female development; the autobiographer who is a woman must negotiate a doubled vision of the self, embodying both male and female cultural ideals. As Sidonie Smith has written, she "must suspend herself between paternal and maternal narratives, those fictions of male and female selfhood that permeate her historical moment." [17]

Living My Life, then, was not a history of Goldman's life as she actually lived it, but a recreation of her life as she saw it at a particular moment, from the summer of 1928 to the spring of 1931. In its massiveness and detail—nearly a thousand pages—it represented an attempt to create something solid and enduring out of what she felt were the ashes of her life. As she told Berkman, what made the autobiography so difficult to write was the renewed sense of loss her memories triggered, "being made aware that I have nothing left in the way of personal relations from all who have been in my life and have torn my heart." [18] As if to counter feelings of loss and defeat, she wanted to present herself as a heroic figure, to demonstrate how the heroic values—strength, perseverance, daring, courage, the ability to stand alone—were enacted in her own life and how they translated into a woman's story. She wished to present herself as a role model for others. As she wrote one friend, "I naturally want to let people see what one can do if imbued with an ideal, what one can endure and how one can overcome all difficulties and suffering in life." [19]

In the early stages of her writing, Goldman began negotiations with publishers in America. Unsure of her literary skill, she felt more confident about the business end of things. She was determined this time to avoid the catastrophes that accompanied the publication of her book on Russia. Early signs were promising, once she had sample chapters to show publishers. The vice president of Horace Liveright told her (having seen part of the manuscript) she had written "the most important, the most fascinating, the greatest autobiography of the century." Still, he offered her only a $1,000 advance, which Emma considered too small considering that he had paid Isadora Duncan—whose memoir she had recently read and admired—$2,500 for hers and, she insisted, "the very material of my work is more universal and more important than Isadora's." [20] Goldman wanted at least as much as Duncan. She was pleased when Alfred Knopf offered her a $7,000 advance for the book, sight unseen, an act without precedent for the firm. Although Saxe Commins acted as her agent, and Arthur Ross as her lawyer, Goldman interested herself in every detail of the contract, including serial and translation rights, the projected price, and advertising and royalties. She especially insisted that the book appear in one large volume, that Knopf agree to extensive advertising, and that the price not exceed $5, since "the people most interested in the story of my life will be intelligent advanced workers and professional people" who could not afford more.[21]

After cables and letters had flown back and forth across the Atlantic for several months, Goldman signed a contract with Knopf on September 30, 1929, granting her an advance of $7,000, with half payable on signing and half on delivery of the completed manuscript, due in March of 1930. She pronounced herself pleased with the contract, and impressed by Knopf. She was amused when Ross told her that she had earned a reputation as a hard-boiled business woman at Knopf. Some people "seem to think and expect that the idealist should live on air and end his life on [a] pauper's field," she told Ross. She instructed him to advise her critics that she had "learned to be hard-boiled from my dealings with some American publishers who botched up my work and cheated me out of all that was due." [22]

Nonetheless, as the March 30, 1930, deadline passed, new difficulties arose. From the beginning of her negotiations with Knopf, Goldman had indicated her intention to bring the autobiography roughly to the present. As late as April 25, 1930, Goldman emphasized the necessity of including a chapter on her two years in Russia and one on her experience in Sweden, because "then the book will end on a high note." [23] But as she approached the end, she found her anxiety mounting and the writing becoming increasingly difficult. Clearly the prospect of calling up her memories of Russia aroused feelings akin to panic. Sometime early in May she decided she could not continue. She was too exhausted to write more, she told a friend, and now wanted to end the book with her entry into Russia.[24] She was "stunned" when Knopf insisted on the importance of bringing the book up to date. The years after her deportation represented "a distinctly separate phase of my life which should not be included here," she explained. To add a superficial account of her post-deportation experience "would detract from the book," she wrote Knopf on May 12, "and what is equally important, it would have an utterly bleak, discouraged and pessimistic ending. I am sure you would not want that, and I am certain that I cannot have it." [25] But Knopf, convinced by Goldman's previous insistence on the importance of including the later material, remained adamant, telling her that they would have to defer publication "until such time as you can bring it up to date because the more people read your manuscript, the more they insist that its interest is cumulative and that as it stands now you have left out entirely what they are most anxious to read about. Everything in it now leads up to your return to Russia and to stop the book there is most obviously to cheat your readers. I may say frankly," Knopf added, "that had you ever said earlier in our negotiations that you intended to close the book with your deportation from this country I should never have agreed to publish it." [26]

To make matters worse, in early March the French government had presented her with an ancient expulsion order, dating from 1901. Goldman had to hire a lawyer (the eminent Henri Torres) and visit numerous offices before it could be rescinded. Two months later, on May 1, Alexander Berkman was deported to Belgium, without identity papers, passport, or money. To get him back to France—with permission to remain—required strenuous, time-consuming efforts that dragged on for a year and a half and eventually involved the International Committee for Political Prisoners in New York, the French Ligue du Droits de l'Homme, and signatures of numerous intellectuals on both sides of the Atlantic—including Thomas Mann, Albert Einstein, Romain Rolland, Bertrand Russell, René Schickele, and others—protesting the persecution that evidently was instigated by Washington. [27]

Knopf remained unmoved by all these difficulties. Furious but resigned, Goldman agreed to write the two additional chapters on Russia and Sweden that she had promised, adding fifty more pages to bring the book up to 1929. But she decided now that her experience with Knopf "has proven to me once more the pitiful and degrading dependence of people who must live by their pen." From now on, she would insist bitterly that publishers were "an awful breed . . . like the State that never allows the individual to question wherefore or why. It only forces him to do or die." What happened with her book became, in Goldman's eyes, another proof of the evils of authority vis-à-vis the individual. [28]

Knopf's most egregious error, in Goldman's mind, was the decision to charge $7.50 for the nearly thousand-page, two-volume work. Even in Saxe Commins's view, that price tag seriously hindered sales in this Depression year of 1931 (the book appeared October 23). Although the contract had specified a price of $5 (and Emma conceded in a letter that if two volumes were necessary, she would accept $6, or whatever price "within reason" Knopf decided upon), her chapter on Russia ran 200 pages; this, plus the short chapter on Sweden and the narrative bringing the book up to date added another 260 pages. When he received the final chapters, Knopf decided the book would indeed have to be published as two volumes, at the price of $7.50. Goldman replied furiously to Saxe Commins that Knopf was violating her contract, that "we never stipulated that I give him two books for the same advance, he forced me to it." Emma saw the high price, and what she considered inadequate advertising—though at first the book was widely advertised, especially in the liberal and radical press—as a deliberate scheme by Knopf to evade their contract and sabotage her book.[29]

As Goldman herself later conceded, the Great Depression had wiped out possibilities for widespread sales. The high price exacerbated the problem, but she herself had been a publisher and must have realized that the immense length of her work would boost the price. Isolated from America, Goldman also overestimated her audience and may have given unrealistic expectations to Knopf and to Arthur Ross—as she would do again when she visited in 1934. "It is bitter to reconcile myself to the fact that this possibility [for success] was deliberately killed by Knopf," she told Sasha.[30]

Goldman's difficulties with Knopf were typical of the problems she often had in her business arrangements. She changed her mind frequently, and then became indignant when others did not agree to the changes. She was also inclined to view disagreement or difference as a conspiracy against herself, and to interpret the motives of others in a slightly paranoid fashion. Still, though capable of driving her colleagues to despair, Emma at moments acknowledged her captiousness with a self-deprecating sense of humor. "Just think," she wrote Arthur Ross in December of 1931, joking about his role as her representative, "[did you know] you have let yourself in for a nag, a brute, a liar and a cheat?" At least she and Ross remained friends.[31]

In *Living My Life*, Emma Goldman set out to write a great American female epic, an anarchist odyssey, showing how, after she committed herself to anarchism at the age of twenty, she remained true to her "ideal" through the vicissitudes of a long, adventurous life. More interested in showing the opportunities opened up to her by the movement than in exploring the origins of her commitment, she began her story with her arrival in New York City in August of 1889. She devoted only a few brief flashbacks to her "ghastly" childhood in Lithuania and East Prussia, and to her troubled adolescence in St. Petersburg. Yet she saw her life as powerfully shaped by her father's anger and bitterness, and by her mother's coldness and detachment. In retrospect, she also saw her unhappy family life as part of a larger landscape of persecution, in which Jews were excluded and taunted, peasants beaten, schoolchildren abused, and women seduced and abandoned. She had grown up, she wrote elsewhere, "largely in revolt" against oppressive authority. Yet she made clear not only that she had rebelled against the world of her childhood but also that she had emulated powerful positive role models, including the famous Russian revolutionary women—Vera Zassulich, Sophia Perovskaya, and Catherine Breshkovskaya for example—who were mythic figures for many daughters of Emma's generation.

America opened to Emma Goldman a wider world than was available to her in Petersburg under the Czars. But it also posed difficult dilemmas. At the center of *Living My Life* is Goldman's uncertainty about her identity—class, cultural, social, sexual, and even political—an issue that agitated her all her life. From her earliest years, she had lived her life crossing borders, not only the national borders she crossed by the age of sixteen, as she moved from Lithuania to East Prussia to Russia to America, but class and cultural ones as well. As a Jew, an immigrant, and an unwanted daughter, later an anarchist, she found herself an outsider in almost every community in which she lived, including her own family. For example, having grown up in precariously petit bourgeois circumstances, she found herself thrust into the ranks of the workers on account of her family's increasing economic difficulties. Her middle-class background and education meant that she brought to the factory floor memories of a better alternative and ideas that helped motivate her turn toward radicalism. With a foot in both camps, she defined her mission as that of awakening workers to the ideals of the radical intellectuals, and awakening the intellectuals to working-class experience.

At the same time, however, her class position involved uncertainty and ambivalence. She did not really think of herself as a worker or identify with other workers, however much she sympathized with them. Two revealing scenes in the autobiography suggest her conflicted class consciousness. In the first scene, the young Emma comes to the aid of a fellow worker, Tanya, who faints at her sewing machine. When the foreman accuses her of shamming, Emma shouts that he is a liar and a brute and takes Tanya off for some fresh air and rest. In the second scene, Emma goes personally to the luxurious office of her boss to ask for a pay raise, since her salary does not cover expenses, much less a book or a theater ticket. "Mr. Garson replied that for a factory girl I had rather extravagant tastes, that all his other 'hands' were well satisfied . . . I, too, would have to manage or find work elsewhere. 'If I raise your wages, I'll have to raise the others' as well and I can't afford that,' he said. I decided to leave

Garson's employ." Goldman narrates this scene without comment. The option of organizing her fellow workers to strike for higher wages does not occur, either to the youthful protagonist or to the adult autobiographer. Although she comes to the rescue of a friend, she does not identify with the other workers as a group, and seeks an individual rather than collective solution to the problem of low wages.[32]

Goldman's doubled class perspective enabled her to speak effectively to audiences of workers and of middle-class intellectuals, yet her ambivalence also distanced her from both, since she felt she belonged fully neither with one nor the other. In a similar vein, the autobiography conveyed the complexity of her multicultural origins, suggesting her uncertainty about her national identity and her conflicting identification with Russia, Germany, and America. Only when she was deported from the United States did she become certain of her "spiritual identity" as an American. The statement of her feelings with regard to men—that she always felt "between two fires" in their presence, simultaneously attracted and repelled—may perhaps be taken as a metaphor for the feelings of conflict that informed her life as a whole. Such conflict, moreover, may help explain the depth of her political passions; lacking roots in any one community, class or culture, anarchism provided the mainstay of her identity, the one stable, definite commitment that lay at the center of her sense of self.

Still, the uncertainty that threads through *Living My Life* may also be seen from another perspective, as a characteristic aspect of many autobiographies by women in public life. In her essay, "Selves in Hiding," Patricia Meyer Spacks has described Goldman's account as "a female variant on the high tradition of spiritual autobiography," similar in kind to the autobiographies of women such as Dorothy Day, Eleanor Roosevelt, and Golda Meir, all public figures whose political involvements have spiritual meaning for them.[33] Drawing on religious metaphors common to anarchist rhetoric—what one critic has called a "displaced religious discourse"—Goldman presented her commitment to anarchism in the language of a religious conversion, and her life as a struggle up the road to Calvary—an image she used often in her letters—during which she must constantly prove her strength and courage.[34] Much of the autobiography traced this struggle, in a detailed, chronological, year-by-year account of campaigns and crusades, arrests and imprisonments across two continents. The climax of this quest—her personal Calvary—was Russia, which she narrated in a two-hundred page "chapter" offering a fuller, more dramatized version of the story presented earlier in *My Disillusionment in Russia*. The book ended with Goldman poised before the next great test, which was the writing of the autobiography itself.

Yet Spacks notes that while spiritual autobiographies characteristically speak of certainty, "drawing energy and conviction from the affirmation of transcendant meaning," the versions by Goldman, Day, Roosevelt, and Meir draw instead on what Spacks calls "a rhetoric of uncertainty: about the self, about the value of womanhood, about the proper balance of commitments." The stories in these women's autobiographies "profoundly contradict themselves; narrating great accomplishments, they express continual doubts; writing of public achievement, they deny ambition." [35] In this sense, Goldman's autobiographical uncertainties may also have been part of the genre as explored by women, a consequence of transgressing the limits set by patriarchal society, not only in life, but also in writing. "Fifty years—thirty of them in the firing line—had they borne fruit or had I merely been repeating Don Quixote's idle chase?" Goldman wrote. "Had my efforts served only to fill my inner void, to find an outlet for the turbulence of my being? Or was it really the ideal that had dictated my conscious course?" [36] Was her life, in short, a triumph of the emancipated woman, or was she an example of the "tragedy of woman's emancipation," that subject about which she had so often lectured? To these questions *Living My Life* offered no reply.

Much of Goldman's autobiography followed the protagonist's effort to integrate her quest for anarchy with her quest for love, that is, to find a way to harmonize her work with more personal, private satisfactions. Anarchism emancipated her from her family and offered her a political identity. But it precipitated major conflicts about her identity as a woman. "I was not hewn of one piece, like Sasha or other heroic figures," she wrote. "I had long realized that I was woven of many skeins, conflicting in shade and texture. To the end of my days I should be torn between the yearning for a personal life and the need of giving all to my ideal." [37] While Goldman situated herself within a tradition of Russian revolutionary women, she acknowledged that tradition as a problematic one on account of its strong ethos of self-sacrifice. She criticized those women "who have no other interests in life but the movement," and insisted on her right to a personal life. Nonetheless she oscillated between portraits of herself as a self-assertive, sexual, liberated woman and as a self-sacrificing, suffering martyr. On the one hand she identified with the biblical Judith cutting off the head of Holofernes to avenge the wrongs of her people; on the other hand she identified also with Dostoyevsky's saintly Sonya, daughter of Marmeladov in *Crime and Punishment,* selling her body to feed her hungry siblings and also acting as Raskolnikov's redeemer. In the end, Goldman presented herself as a revolutionary martyr even while rejecting the ethic of martyrdom.

In tracing the conflict between love and work, Goldman narrated a series of relationships, first with a conventional husband, and later with a series of male lovers, particularly Edward Brady, whose love she found both nurturing and imprisoning. She told how, at the age of thirty-eight, she did finally find a man, the unforgettable Ben Reitman, who "would love the woman in me and yet who would also be able to share my work."

Yet while the relationship with Reitman resolved the conflict between love and work—since he joined her on the road as her "manager"—it also created new difficulties. In the autobiography, Goldman blamed their difficulties on his infidelities—which severely tested her commitment to "free love"—and on the hostility of her immigrant comrades toward this native-born Chicagoan, so alien to their values and traditions. She portrayed Reitman, moreover, as a man whose infantile obsession with his mother interfered with his relations with other women. She only hinted here at the sexual dependence and rich ambivalence of their relationship, which their letters so dramatically expressed.[38] Yet some of this complexity emerged, for example, in the ironic counterpoint between Reitman's mother and Goldman's "Mommy," and the ambivalence about mothering and motherhood that surfaced throughout the book. Goldman frequently drew on metaphors of mothering to describe both her attitude in love and her activism in the movement, a common strategy of women during the Progressive Era to justify a wide range of extrafamilial activities. *Living My Life* also hinted at ways in which she used the role of "Mother Earth"—the name of her magazine—to turn her "children" into "mothers" for herself. While she played the role of "Mommy" to Ben Reitman, she also made him a parental figure, that is, her "manager" who took care of her. Although she used the metaphor of mothering to describe and perhaps legitimize her activity in the movement—"I would find an outlet for my mother-need in the love of all children"—she admitted her ambivalence about becoming a biological mother, and explained her own childlessness in terms of her fears of dependence: of having children dependent upon her, and of becoming dependent herself on account of having children. The "Mother Earth" persona was partly a defense against deeper feelings of vulnerability, and the autobiography suggested ways in which Goldman still saw herself as a motherless child, "a homeless creature" repeatedly locked out of other people's houses, cast out of countries, continually creating alternative "homes" and families of "children" who would also support and "mother" her.[39]

Goldman's writing about sex further illuminated her conflicted sense of identity, and her vision of herself as a transitional woman, "still rooted in the old soil, though our visions are of the future, and our desire is to be free and independent."[40] Although she had long campaigned in public for sexual freedom, especially for women, her own sexual experience had left her ambivalent at best. In her autobiography, however, she wanted to convey the impression of a rich erotic life. She wished, in fact, to rewrite Frank Harris's erotic autobiography, *My Life and Loves,* as a woman's story. She and Harris had discussed at some length the question of writing about sex, and Harris had urged her to write frankly about her own experiences. "We want a woman's view of life and freedom in sex matters, want it badly," he told her. "Your life and mine will be the first chapters in the Bible of Humanity."[41] This was a challenge she could not ignore. Moreover, in her nine-year affair with Reitman, from 1908 to 1917, she had carried on an erotic correspondence inspired by the uninhibited Reitman. By the time she came to writing the memoir, however, over ten years had elapsed since that relationship had ended; this affair, as well as her briefer affairs with Artur Svenssen and Leon Malmed, had ended bitterly, leaving her feeling more abandoned than ever. In this setting, she found it difficult to revive painful memories, and criticized Harris's detailed descriptions as inappropriate to a woman's experience. The "mere physical fact," the "mere physical terms," the "mere physical description" could not convey the tremendous psychological effect of sex, especially for women, she told Harris. She demurred at Harris's suggestion that she write explicitly about herself, insisting that she could not jeopardize the privacy of others. "For me, at any rate," she reported, "it will be utterly impossible to describe the physical side which is, after all, very limited, while the psychological is rich and varied."[42]

Goldman tried to solve the problem by asserting the importance of sexuality in her life while avoiding physical description, and veiling her experience in clichéd language reminiscent of the sentimental novels she had read as an adolescent. She cited her first erotic sensations at the age of six—associated with a peasant servant whose games of "horse" "used to give me a peculiar sensation, fill me with exultation, followed by blissful release." She described her parents' threats about masturbation, her mother's warnings at the onset of menstruation, and an adolescent rape in Petersburg that left her sharply ambivalent about sex, at once attracted and violently repelled.[43] While love-making with Ed Brady had been "profoundly soothing by its music and perfume," with Reitman she was "caught in the torrent of an elemental passion I had never dreamed any man could rouse in me. I responded shamelessly to its primitive call, its naked beauty, its ecstatic joy." Later she acknowledged that "erotically Ben and I were of the same earth," though insisting that culturally they were "separated by centuries of time." She gave full credit to Reitman's sexual power over her. "As lover," she wrote, "he had unleashed elements in me that made all differences between us disappear as so much chaff in a storm."[44]

Such language, with its breathless tone and melodramatic excess, immediately alerts us to a central irony of *Living My Life*. Despite Goldman's radical views of love, the autobiography relied on conventional rhetoric to represent these ideas. Several critics have noted the incongruity between her ideological aspirations and the imaginative forms in which she expressed them, and her reliance on the stock figures and clichés of American popular romance. Like most American political radicals of her generation, Emma had never been a partisan of modernism. The conventional form of her autobiography reflected her relatively conservative aesthetic tastes and desire to appeal to a popular audience. But the discord between her radical values and her conventional style, her inability to portray eroticism convincingly, also reflected the ambivalence of her sexual politics. For all her modern views of love, she nonetheless shared certain ideas more characteristic of the nineteenth-century free lovers than of twentieth-century Freudians. She justified erotic passion by reference to its spiritual and ethical possibilities, its ennobling powers, its capacity to inspire "high thoughts and fine deeds." Her melodramatic style reflected these more traditional ideas, which lurked within her radical politics of love.[45]

Emma Goldman's ambivalence emerged most sharply in her portrayals of the important men in her life—her descriptions of women were generally less angry and ambivalent. Certainly the cruelest portrait in the book was that of Ben Reitman, the man who had aroused her deepest passion, whom she showed as a coward and a buffoon, an infantile, unfaithful, shallow man, at once charming and churlish, dependent on a variety of "Mommies," including Goldman, whom he compulsively seduced and betrayed.

The autobiography itself became an event in both their lives. Goldman and Reitman had resumed their correspondence in 1925, after a hiatus of nearly eight years. Once again they began to exchange letters filled with mutual admiration and recriminations, with warm regards and cold reproaches. They rehashed old grievances. Although suffering periods of ill health, Ben was now a moderately successful physician in Chicago, a lecturer at various medical colleges, and author of a well-received book, *The Second Oldest Profession,* published in 1927. He was eager to see Goldman, for despite his successes, he remained insecure, prey to feelings of worthlessness and self-hatred that his extravagant boasting barely masked. For all their quarrels, Reitman hungered for Goldman's approval, and tried to wring it from her with pleas, threats, and reproaches. He persuaded her to receive him when he visited London in the summer of 1926 and again, in 1927 in Toronto, but both visits ended badly, with ill-feelings on both sides, and flurries of complaints.

Emma's plan to write her memoirs, and Reitman's threat to write his, introduced a new element into their relationship. At stake now, as both of them realized, was a public as well as private image. It was one thing for them to argue old grievances in private letters; Emma now proposed to enshrine her version of Ben L. Reitman in a book for posterity. Worried about the portrait she would paint, he answered her requests for information in a conciliatory tone, assuring her of the greatness of her work. But his ambivalence toward her surfaced repeatedly, and he could not help adding plaintive laments about her cruelty and failure to appreciate him.

When *Living My Life* appeared, in October of 1931, Reitman found his worst fears realized. Although Emma had publicly admitted her addiction to Reitman, describing him as a vivid, exotic character, she presented her passion as humiliating and inexplicable, a painful dependence on a man who was beneath her. In her portrait, he excelled mainly as her promoter and business manager. As a man, she pronounced him a failure: one who stole money from her audience to send to his mother; who slept compulsively with other women and lied about his affairs; who ran away from danger and could not be relied upon; who hobnobbed with police and detectives; who embarrassed Emma before her comrades with his vulgarity and his ignorance. Reitman felt ashamed and betrayed. "Never in my whole life," he wrote, "was I [so] outraged, humiliated, bitter, disappointed and crushed." [46] Emma remained unmoved, and characteristically, Ben continued to beg for her approval, alternating between self-abasing pleas and angry attacks on her brutality and harshness. Far from severing their relationship, *Living My Life* intensified it, so that by 1934, when

Goldman visited America, Reitman offered to manage her lecture tour and begged to visit her in Toronto so he could "re-seduce you beautifully," a proposal she did not accept.

In truth, Goldman omitted much to Reitman's credit in her book, such as his role as "clap doctor" to the poor, his pioneering work in venereal disease prevention, his public health efforts on behalf of Chicago hobos and prostitutes.[47] In her book, Emma called herself a "lovesick fool," "carried away like any ordinary woman of forty by a mad attraction for a younger man . . . an alien to my every thought and feeling, the reverse of the ideal of man I had always cherished." Or she was a long-suffering mother, a patient martyr, a teacher who wanted to inspire and improve. While *Living My Life* hinted at the sado-masochistic patterns of dominance and dependence that characterized this ostensibly "free" relationship, it minimized the periods of despondency which she described in her letters during the affair. While the memoir made clear the conflict she felt as she found herself passionately obsessed with a man whose tastes and habits often repelled her, it did not explore the deeper sources of her attraction, offering as an explanation Reitman's childlike spontaneity, his willingness to love both the woman and her work. To do so she would have had to acknowledge that, for all their differences, she and Reitman had much in common; that qualities she abhorred, like his theatricality and craving for attention, she also shared. Privately, Emma showed considerably more grasp of their relationship than she was willing to admit in print, as this astute 1926 letter revealed. "[I] never could stand uncertainty," she told him. "That was the poignant part in our love. You were the most uncertain quantity I had ever loved."[48]

After the book appeared, Goldman denied any intent to hurt. She hotly took issue with certain reviewers whom she claimed had missed her point. "No one with any intelligence could possibly have gotten the impression, from my portrait of Brady, that he was 'a drunk,' or that Ben R. stole 'from the collections,'" Goldman wrote angrily to Fremont Older, editor of the *San Francisco Bulletin*. "By no manner of means could any sane person interpret his taking money as thievery." She did not say how else it might be interpreted.[49]

Goldman's problematic portrayal of Ben Reitman further illuminates her angle of vision. Like many autobiographies, this one was partly an act of revenge against those who had slighted or hurt Goldman, or for that matter Berkman. Little-known figures in the anarchist movement—particularly men—suffered most in this regard, for they were hardly known except through Goldman's version.[50] But famous individuals were not excepted. Her account of Johann Most was another case in point. The German-American orator and journalist who had been her first mentor in the movement, Most had introduced Goldman into the movement in 1889, yet he had turned against her a year or two later when she rejected him sexually and then joined a rival anarchist group led by his bitter enemy, Joseph Peukert. He had also hurt Goldman deeply in 1892 by attacking both her and Berkman in his paper, *Freiheit,* after Berkman's assassination attempt at Homestead. Indeed, he had angered Goldman so much that, according to her own account, she had horsewhipped him at a public meeting, humiliating him and further splitting and weakening the anarchist ranks, which were already divided over Berkman's act. Thereafter, Most had refused ever again to speak to her. He died in 1906, without a reconciliation.

In her autobiographical portrait of Most, Emma managed both to humanize a man who had been widely satirized as a bomb-throwing fanatic, and to seriously misrepresent his ideas. She described a gifted orator and frustrated actor, a man who repelled others with his imperious intolerance, yet suffered from his isolation and loneliness. At the same time, however, she portrayed him as an unrepentant exponent of violent "propaganda of the deed," and described his criticism of Alexander Berkman's 1892 "attentat" against Henry Clay Frick as a sudden reversal motivated by cowardice and jealousy. Actually, Most had begun to question "propaganda of the deed" years before, as Goldman herself had acknowledged in a sketch published in the *American Mercury* in 1926. Clearly she was aware that in the aftermath of the Haymarket bombing, Most had radically revised his views, concluding that such actions were appropriate only in a milieu in which they would be understood by the workers; that milieu, in his view, did not exist in the United States. Most's repudiation of Berkman, then, did not represent a sudden reversal, but a restatement of views he had formulated several years earlier.[51]

Goldman's deliberate misrepresentation of Most's thinking may have reflected her desire to justify her own act of publicly horsewhipping her former mentor, an act not mentioned in her previous article. She may have wished to punish him posthumously for having cut her out of his life. She may have felt that showing Most abruptly reversing himself made for a more dramatic story. But she may also have been motivated by loyalty to Berkman at the time she was writing. It was Berkman, more than herself, whom Most had attacked, so that clearly she saw herself in the autobiography as avenging Berkman against Most's charges.[52] Her misrepresentation of Most suggests the extent to which the imagined audience of this autobiography was Alexander Berkman; "You will learn something, Sasha dear," she told him, "that you have never known or understood. . . ."[53]

Nonetheless, despite Emma's profuse declarations of admiration and devotion, the portrait of Berkman that emerged in *Living My Life* was a generally unflattering one. Certainly she had powerful reasons for her negative feelings toward Berkman who had, after all, involved her in his own disastrous act in 1892, and after her years of loyal support throughout his imprisonment, had rejected her sexually and taken up with other, younger women even while depending on her financially and emotionally. Yet Goldman found it difficult to acknowledge her mixed feelings toward Berkman, who often complained that she indirectly attacked him in double-edged remarks to other people. In a similar fashion, her anger at him surfaced obliquely here in her emphasis on his youthful "hardness," his fanaticism, his nervousness and dependence on her after his release from prison in 1906, and most of all on his failure to appreciate her great devotion and to sympathize with her affairs of the heart. She downplayed his gifts as an organizer and writer, his sense of humor, and the enormous admiration he enjoyed among the Jewish immigrant workers in America, an admiration that steadily deepened over the years. She cast herself as Berkman's savior, the long-suffering "mother" of her difficult "boy," a martyr who endured his moods and demands on account of her guilt over his long imprisonment for an act in which she had shared. Indeed, although Goldman admitted in the autobiography, for the first time publicly, her part in the assassination attempt of 1892 (that is, testing bombs and raising money for a gun), she defused that admission by stressing her doubts about the ethics of the act and casting the youthful Berkman as something of a fanatic: a portrayal that he hotly disputed.

Berkman's ambivalent presence in the autobiography may become clearer if we consider it in relation to the absence of Emma's younger brother, who died at the age of five or six when she was about seven or eight. This brother had figured prominently in her preliminary notes for the autobiography, where she had associated his death with her fantasy of becoming an avenger like Judith.[54] But she omitted him in the final text. Instead she devoted several pages to a Cinderella-like story of being handed over to her grandmother in Königsberg and turned into a maid by a cruel uncle: an event that evidently occurred around the time of her brother's death and which she may have considered as a kind of punishment. Conceivably Goldman's feelings about Berkman had their origin partly in unconscious guilt over the death of her brother, which she later displaced onto Berkman. If, as her notes for the autobiography suggest, her brother's death was the repressed subtext of her childhood—an event she had been too young to mourn but whose consequences she suffered in the depression, anger, and possibly the blaming reactions of her parents—that death may have helped motivate her powerful response to the deaths of other symbolic "brothers," such as the Haymarket martyrs, and later to Berkman's "living death" in the Western State Penitentiary. Indeed, her brother's childhood death may have contributed to Emma's fierce determination to save Berkman—as she had not been able to save her brother—and to the fantasies of rescue, rivalry, and revenge that surround his portrait in *Living My Life*.[55]

Berkman's central role in the autobiography may also be seen in another light, as the audience to whom the book was addressed. Indeed, not only did Goldman write *Living My Life* partly as an extended love letter to Berkman, she also lived her life partly as a performance for his benefit, as a rivalry with him, and an attempt to win his love and approval, especially after their deportation from America, when he "was all that had been left me from the tornado that had swept over my life." While Goldman was writing the memoir, she and Berkman recapitulated their earlier relationship in the letters they wrote back and forth between St. Tropez and Nice that rehearsed all their old quarrels about the value of Berkman's act, about Leon Czolgosz, about Ben Reitman, even about Russia. In the process they reaffirmed their friendship and renewed their intimacy. Yet the ambivalence remained, memorialized in a text that seemingly gave Emma the last word. In *Living My Life*, she symbolically appropriated Berkman for herself, for her autobiography was his biography as well—at least that was how she intended it—and her powerfully mixed version of him would stand for decades to come.

In the end, *Living My Life* reflected a tension at the heart of Goldman's politics. Though she often thought of herself as standing alone "against the whole world, if need be," it was not by chance that the years of her greatest achievement and happiness, between 1903 and 1917, coincided with the emergence of a broad-based American radicalism, embodied in the Socialist party and the Wobblies as well as the anarchists and radical feminists. Her accomplishments as a lecturer and agitator in America owed much to the existence of this grass-roots radical movement whose aims she helped to dramatize. Moreover, her ability to recruit liberal intellectuals to her support reflected the reform mood of the Progressive Era, whose limits she skillfully demonstrated. In an era when a mass feminist movement was emerging, with women increasingly active in public life, Emma Goldman was simply one of the most visible and controversial figures among many. She was most successful when working in tandem with others, for example in the free speech fights, the birth control campaign, and the movement against World War I and the draft. She worked best, moreover, when she was in love, for her greatest years also coincided with her affair with Ben Reitman. Despite her insistent emphasis on the individual, Emma Goldman was concerned, above all, with individuality, not individualism. She was opposed to conformity, not to collectivity, and she sought all her life to create a community hospitable to the dissenter and the rebel. In her 1904 essay, "The Tragedy of Woman's Emancipation," she discussed the tension of trying "to be one's self and yet in oneness with others, to feel deeply with all human beings and still retain one's own characteristic qualities." [56] *Living My Life* embodied that tension, in ways that even the author did not recognize.

"Hurrah! The baby is born at last," Goldman exclaimed to Agnes Inglis late in February of 1931. "You see my dear," she wrote to Anna Strunsky Walling, "I had to deny myself a child in the flesh. *Living My Life* has taken its place." [57] In late March of 1931 she mailed off the final corrected installment to New York. She felt exhausted, full of pains and aches, with fallen arches and swollen veins. She began having massages and looked forward to several months of rest.

When the first copies arrived in late October, she was "so excited" she "trembled all over," and wished desperately that Sasha were with her to celebrate. She waited eagerly for his response, chiding him for not writing her about it, jokingly reminding him that he had not written the long letter he promised. But Berkman did like it, liked it immensely, thought it "a GREAT WORK, not merely interesting but fascinating, honest, powerful, gripping . . . a true mirror of a goodly part of the American and radical labor movements of those days. In other words," he said, "it is one of the greatest autobiographies I have ever read, and perhaps the greatest a woman has ever written." [58] Comforted by his praise, Emma now waited, in the Parisian flat of a friend, "with longing and dread," for the other reactions to come in, urging all her correspondents, from H. L. Mencken to comrades she had never met, to tell her their impressions, "and whether it has helped you to a better understanding of the ideas to which I and so many others have given our lives."[59]

In fact the reviews were enthusiastic, even glowing. The *New York Times,* the *New Yorker,* and the *Saturday Review of Literature* all recommended it as one of the best nonfiction books of the year. Roger Baldwin praised it in the *New York Herald Tribune* as "a great woman's story of a brave adventure into successive defeats which read like victories." He championed the book as the forthright, fearless intimate revelations of "the most challenging rebel spirit of our times."[60] The liberal Congregational minister, John Haynes Holmes, lectured on the book at his Community Church in New York, praising especially "the perfect frankness of your tale. You spared nobody, least of all yourself." Even Waldo Frank, writing in the *New Republic,* who saw the book as an "elegy for anarchism" and criticized her anti-Soviet views, conceded that "there is something about this woman that is great."[61] If an occasional critic, such as the playwright Lawrence Stallings, excoriated the memoir as "a thousand dull pages of fornication and fanaticism," many more agreed with Freda Kirchwey, editor of the *Nation,* who admired Goldman's capacity for intense emotion, her seeming indifference to external rewards. "She thrives not on success but on opportunities for expression," wrote Kirchwey, "and her vitality is renewed from springs of feeling that never go dry for reasons of outward circumstances." If Goldman's life was one of objective defeat, if she "feels first and thinks later—and less," nonetheless it was also, in Kirchwey's view, a "personal triumph."[62] Emma's nephew, Saxe Commins, who was then an editor at Horace Liveright, went even further, describing it as "the most extraordinary document ever penned by a woman," and one that "certainly ranks with the great autobiographies of the world."[63]

Emma was pleased by this response, though she continued to argue with Berkman, Saxe, and others over the exact nature of her success. She was less pleased with the anarchist response, which tended to be more mixed, and occasionally vituperative. Privately, quite a few of Goldman's comrades were dismayed by what they considered the exaggerated focus on her sex life, her self-serving interpretations of her motives, and her attacks on other anarchists. Some were chagrined at their own portrayals, or absence thereof. The daughter of an American anarchist whom Emma admired was disappointed to find Goldman "such an egomaniac," and doubted that people would be interested in reading "those minute details of her many private affairs," details which implicated others as well as herself.[64] Lucy Parsons, widow of the Haymarket martyr Albert Parsons, thought that "her accounts about herself and Ben Reitman are simply disgusting," speculating primly that "had she left out the sex stuff the book would have appealed to a more thoughtful element. . . . Just why she should have thought it interesting or instructive to list 15 of her 'lovers' is beyond me to understand." [65] The most troubled anarchist response was that of Agnes Inglis, the Ann Arbor friend whom Emma described in the memoir as "the type to whom friendship is a sacrament," someone who had never failed her. Inglis expressed her ambivalence about Goldman most sharply in a letter to Roger Baldwin:

> Her book made such a bad impression on me that it just sent the past into the past and closed the door. I think she is a most remarkable woman—and admire her fearlessness—and the way she always stood out—at the beginning—for the oppressed. But I cannot make gods and heroes out of people. And if I want the battle to go in a certain way I shall be one to help hold up the arms of Moses. But I will not be there for Moses—as Moses. Moseses—when you come to know them—are just Moseses. And without the others to hold up their arms they are nearly like the others. My own opinion of Emma, though, is that she is a great orator and is never dull. . . .[66]

While some critics were motivated by prudishness or personal resentment, they pointed to real limitations in two areas. Although *Living My Life* purported to be partly a history of the anarchist movement, it subtly distorted that history by equating Goldman's activities with those of the movement generally and by placing her at the center of anarchism in America. In fact, beginning around 1903, she had attempted to form what was almost an alternative movement in America, a personal following of middle-class liberals and intellectuals. Anarchism continued primarily as an immigrant working-class movement, whose real strength lay in the small circles of Jewish, Russian, Italian, and Spanish–speaking workers active in the unions, and in various community and cooperative enterprises.[67] Since Goldman was often at odds with others in the movement, her memoir was partly an account of her battles with them and an attempt to justify her own position. Second, her decision to refrain from discussing anarchist ideas tended to reinforce the popular stereotype of anarchism as an essentially emotional ideology. Readers unacquainted with the ideas of anarchism would find little illumination here. Despite her claim, in the memoir and outside it, of devotion to an idea, *Living My Life* undercut that claim by stressing her emotionalism and showing her own attraction to anarchism as visceral and instinctual—and even sexual—rather than intellectual.

In the end, *Living My Life* mythologized Goldman's life, creating a larger-than-life female hero with little of the depression, anxiety, bitterness, jealousy, or loneliness so evident in her letters. It was this figure who increasingly preempted the historical woman in the popular imagination, for *Living My Life* would become the main source of information about Goldman and, for a long time, about anarchism in America. The memoir would ensure Goldman control over her own legend in a way that had eluded her until now, especially since readers hungry for heroes were inclined to downplay its contradictions and confusions. At the same time, her insistence in this memoir on her own sexual interest and experience, especially outside the bonds of marriage and motherhood, constituted a radical challenge to conventions about acceptable female behavior and about the ways in which women could write about their lives. From now on, the invented female hero of *Living My Life* increasingly would merge with the woman, until even she could no longer distinguish between them.

7

My Hungry Heart

Once Emma had mailed Knopf the final typewritten segment of her auto-biography in April of 1931, her old restlessness returned, and she began casting about for something to do. For the next two-and-one-half years, she wandered about Europe in a kind of limbo, half-heartedly offering her services as a lecturer to comrades in various countries, but without any real enthusiasm or conviction, "like a fish out of water, throwing myself around in sheer desperation," as she put it to a friend. Just months after *Living My Life* came out, she felt in "such turmoil of mind and spirit" that she must "get back into the harness to save myself from losing my mind," as she confided to a friend.[1] Over the next two years she lectured spo-radically, in Paris (where she spoke in Yiddish to groups of émigré anar-chists), in Germany, Copenhagen, Holland, and in London, spending summers in St. Tropez.[2] But England remained an alien, unfriendly land-scape, with the old comrades ill or discouraged, she reported to a friend, others unemployed and struggling desperately to survive, and "there are no young people to speak of in our ranks."[3] The Great Depression and growing antiforeign sentiment in France made the position of the émigrés and exiles increasingly precarious. When Hitler was appointed chancellor in March 1933, Goldman's hopes for returning to Germany vanished. The German anarcho-syndicalist movement, along with the rest of the Left in Germany, was crushed, many militants arrested, and some, such as Rudolf Rocker, barely escaped with their lives. Characteristically, Goldman blamed Marxist indoctrination for training the German people in pas-sivity. This "utter lack of resistance" to fascism was not surprising, she wrote a friend. "The people drilled for well-nigh half a century in the Marxian trot, labour disrupted for 15 years by propaganda from Moscow,— how can it be expected to act concertedly and have enough courage to fight back?"[4] She spent the summer of 1933 in St. Tropez in a state of "abject depression," haunted by the feeling that, after forty-four years on the "firing line," with "every minute filled with interest and intensity," she was now "nowhere wanted."[5] Berkman too shared her despair, though his despondency was more political than personal. "The truth is, our movement has accomplished nothing, anywhere," he wrote Mollie Steimer sadly in August of 1933.[6]

Sometime in the summer of 1933, Goldman made the acquaintance of Mrs. Mabel Carver Crouch, a prominent American liberal with wide connections in Washington who was vacationing on the Côte d'Azur. Crouch promised to mobilize support for Emma's admission to the United States. Encouraged by this project, Emma sailed for Montreal in early December. By this time, Crouch had mobilized Roger Baldwin who, with the legal resources of the ACLU, had begun negotiations in Washington for Goldman's return. While Crouch organized a committee of eminent liberals and radicals to sponsor Goldman's visit—the committee included the publishers B. W. Huebsch and Alfred Knopf, writers Sinclair Lewis and Evelyn Scott, John Haynes Holmes and reformers such as Dr. Josephine Baker, Mary Ware Dennett, and John Dewey—Baldwin approached secretary of labor Frances Perkins on Goldman's behalf.

Return of any deported immigrant alien rested with the discretion of the secretary of labor. By mid-November, Baldwin had met with the commissioner of immigration who spoke in this case for Perkins. From these conversations, Baldwin felt optimistic about the prospects. He reported to Emma that several Communists had recently been admitted and "those views are as much, or more, anathema than yours."[7] He assured her a few weeks later that the matter had even gone to the president. "I happen to know that Mr. Roosevelt read your book with great interest," he told Goldman. "He spoke highly of it to a friend of mine."[8] In Canada, Emma waited anxiously. Just knowing her friends wanted her back had already revived her spirits, she wrote Baldwin just before she left Paris, but she was not sanguine about her prospects, and each twist in the negotiations revived her apprehensions. For example, in late December, Washington decided that the list of proposed lecture subjects she had submitted—"Germany's Tragedy," "Hitler, A World Menace," "Dictatorships, Right and Left—A Modern Religious Hysteria"—was unacceptable. She must stick to drama and literature, including her autobiography, without addressing current political issues explicitly. This, Baldwin reported, was the best they could get.[9] Emma was convinced that Washington was trying to prevent her readmission by inventing complications; she was tempted to tell Washington "to go to a hot place," but friends said hers would be a valuable test case for other deportees and she should press ahead.[10] Baldwin explained that the Department of Labor was a liberal administration attempting to stretch reactionary immigration laws; they did not want her to provoke attacks from the Right that might compel them to deport her again, thereby weakening their efforts to liberalize the law. Emma reluctantly consented to the condition, observing wryly that having to observe regulations from Washington was a new experience "for this wild bird who had never been under anyone's control." [11]

As the moment for her return approached, Emma found the "terrible suspense" difficult to bear. On the eve of her departure from Toronto, when the three-month visa was assured, she wrote a moving letter to Berkman about her motives for wanting to return. The "main urge" for years had been "my hungry heart." In Europe she had "nothing. I have you of course. Our friendship is the one redeeming element in the loneliness of the last 15 years. But in an intimate sense I do not even have you." All her ties were in America, "all [the] love I want and crave." Though she was convinced she would "no longer find some one who will respond to my need, my emotional craving," at least she would see her family and friends; for a short time, at least, she would feel needed and wanted.[12]

Once again, as she had on her return to Canada in 1926, Goldman looked forward to her sojourn in the United States as a test of her popularity and of anarchist possibilities. This time her reception exceeded her expectations, as she was given a hero's welcome in New York. Her arrival in New York on February 2, 1934, amid a strike of taxicab drivers, made the front pages of the newspapers. All the major New York papers—including the *Times, Herald Tribune, Sun, World-Telegram,* the *Daily Worker,* and the *Evening Post*—carried notices of her arrival, and forty reporters and cameramen showed up to interview her that day at the Hotel Astor. Roger Baldwin, who accompanied her at her first meeting with the press, recalled later that she had been so uneasy that he had to sit beside her and practically hold her hand.[13]

For the most part the press was sympathetic, even enthusiastic. Predictably the most hostile coverage appeared in the Communist *Daily Worker,* which carried a long article under the headline "Emma Goldman, Here to Make Some Cash, Sneers at U.S.S.R.," accusing Goldman of "complete intellectual affinity with the counter-revolutionary Trotskyites," although Goldman, like almost all anarchists, remained bitterly hostile to the "butcher" of Kronstadt. She consistently found fewer critics among conservatives than among Communists, as a Madison, Wisconsin newspaper noted, praising Goldman for her opposition "to the annihilation of the individual spirit whether the massacre proceed from Mussolini or Marx." [14] She told a St. Louis audience, "When you have lived in a Fascist country . . . and then you come back here, you realize that America still has some freedom. Here you are in this hall listening to me, an anarchist. You and I are not interfered with. You can leave here and know you won't be followed by the police and your homes won't be raided tonight and you won't be sent to concentration camps." In fact Emma was interfered with, for she spoke within strict constraints. Moreover, she was being followed by U.S. government agents, at the behest of J. Edgar Hoover. [15] But the press no longer shared Hoover's paranoia about Goldman. This time journalists treated her with respect, reporting her lectures at great length and more accurately than ever before. [16]

Soon Emma found herself besieged with admirers. Comrades, friends, people outside the movement, all pursued her with invitations and requests for interviews and lectures. Socialist party locals, Jewish unions, Workmen's Circle branches and labor forums asked her to speak. Her publisher Alfred Knopf had a tea in her honor. Editors at *Harpers, Redbook,* the *American Mercury* and the *Nation* requested articles. Three hundred fifty people packed a welcoming banquet at Town Hall, with five hundred more turned away. John Dewey, Roger Baldwin, Henry Alsberg—soon to become head of the Federal Writers' Project—and John Haynes Holmes were among those who spoke in her honor. The audience greeted the exile with tremendous enthusiasm, a mood of almost "religious ardor," reported the *Nation.* A few days later admirers also flocked to Cooper Union, where Emma spoke under the auspices of her comrades. Some two thousand people stormed John Haynes Holmes's liberal Congregational Community Church on Fifth Avenue, hoping to hear Goldman's eulogy of Kropotkin; those outside waited two hours just to catch a glimpse of her. In Rochester she spoke to the largest City Club audience in years, equaled only by the turnout in 1932 for then-governor Franklin Roosevelt when he campaigned for president. Though limited by her agreement with the Labor Department to speak only on literature and the drama, in fact she managed to address current events as well, not only in lectures on "The Drama in Europe" and *Living My Life,* but also on "The German Tragedy" and "The Collapse of German Culture."

Clearly she had lost none of her commanding presence on the podium. A faculty member at a small college in New Jersey wrote to her that her talk was, by unanimous consent, "the finest ever given in the College," and that he had "never seen any person move and stir students as you did." [17] An editorial writer for a Madison, Wisconsin, newspaper wrote that her "intelligence and vitality" had deeply impressed her four hundred listeners in Madison, and added in a personal letter that "as a clear, forceful presenter of facts on important world issues you make all the professors look pallid." [18]

Despite the huge turnout at the early lectures, audiences dwindled once the James Pond lecture bureau took over management of Goldman's appearances on February 13. Although Emma had been eager to hire Pond, who managed such celebrities as Rabindranath Tagore and the American feminist Charlotte Perkins Gilman, the arrangement soon proved a failure. Audiences in cities such as New Haven, Pittsburgh, Columbus, and Toledo were smaller than either she or Pond anticipated. Ill-informed about Goldman, influenced by the inflated predictions of both Emma and of Arthur Ross, Pond had booked huge halls seating several thousand people. He had charged admissions from $.25 to $2.00, and invested heavily in advertising not targeted at any particular audience. Goldman often found herself talking to 250 or 500 people in huge auditoriums seating up to 5,000 people, empty rows staring her in the face. Pond lost money and blamed Emma, not only for promising publicity and assistance she did not deliver, but also for failing to hand over receipts as promised. Emma blamed Pond for unrealistic expectations and bad management, attributing his unsatisfactory performance to his inexperience with "such birds as I am." The hapless Arthur Ross also received a number of single-spaced tirades from Emma enumerating the wrongs done to her. "Pond has completely ruined the magnificent opportunity my re-entry into America has offered," she wrote Arthur Ross. She was beginning to feel that "everything of a commercial nature pertaining to me or my work has a curse on it." [19] In addition, Pond had scheduled her so heavily that she had seen little of the country. After the initial six weeks in New York, she had dashed through a dozen cities, the tour "like a moving picture, everything rushed before my eyes with the same rapidity. AND," she told Sasha, "I got as much out of it all as I usually get from the cinema. Namely nothing." [20]

Emma was also inclined to blame an alleged Communist "boycott" of her appearances for audiences that were smaller than expected. She did not lecture on Russia, but her previous anti-Soviet campaigns had made her a persona non grata to the Communists. Emma herself overestimated the extent of Communist influence in America. "Yes the entire American intelligentsia, American and British, has gone over mit Haut und Haaren [completely] to Communism," she wrote Berkman in August 1934. She was convinced that Communism (and also Fascism) were "the height of fashion," and that people turned to Communism because they could not think for themselves.[21]

Actually, Goldman indirectly praised Communist influence in the United States when she observed approvingly the fighting atmosphere of the unions, "the numerous strikes fought not with kid gloves; the open and outspoken attitude toward revolution."[22] She also praised the "surcharged, electric, and dynamic" spirit of American writers, poets, and dramatists, assuring Berkman that "you'd rub your eyes if you could see some of the plays now given on the American stage. Or the marvelous productions." She was inclined to attribute this militant spirit to the New Deal, insisting that although it was "a failure already," it had "put new life into the workers," and Roosevelt had "unwittingly awakened the whole country to a deeper social awareness and freedom of expression."[23] Actually, the New Deal itself was a response to the militancy of labor and the Communist Left—though party membership remained relatively small, around 30,000 in 1935—rather than the other way around.[24]

As she acknowledged herself, Goldman had little time to develop a deeper grasp of the American political scene, including the role of the American Communist party. She overlooked the extent to which the practical activities of the CP in the labor movement, and the party's fight against unemployment, evictions and racism, helped to attract members. If an idealized vision of the Soviet Union played a part in the romance of American Communism, the concrete efforts of the rank-and-file, at the neighborhood and regional level, were equally as important. In addition, the rise of Mussolini and Hitler added to the party's stature as the most outspoken voice of opposition to fascism.

Racing between lecture engagements, however, Goldman remained focused on more personal issues. She was furious with Pond for his miscalculations. Still, in early April, when her comrades organized her final lectures and banquets in Pittsburgh, Philadelphia, Chicago, and Detroit, big crowds once again showed up to hear her. "Until Chicago I thought that perhaps . . . I had been forgotten and no longer represented [a] drawing force," she confided to one friend. She was greatly relieved to discover that "it was not that I have ceased to draw or no longer count to the

American mind. . . ." Instead, she concluded that "Pond has mismanaged the tour." Could she only be released from Pond and secure an extension to remain in the United States, she was sure she could have a "triumphal tour in every city."[25]

Emma had good reason to be angry at the inappropriate handling of her tour by Pond, but her own exaggerated estimates of her audiences and her unrealistic sense of the tour as a commercial venture had contributed to the financial debacle. In fact, audiences of between 250 and 500 people, accompanied by fair and generous press coverage, were quite impressive. Indeed, when the expatriate writer Gertrude Stein returned to America later the same year for a lecture tour, she had insisted on limiting her audiences to 500 people, and frequently spoke to smaller groups.[26] Only when measured against the huge three- or five-thousand-person halls that Pond had rented did the attendance at Goldman's lectures seem a failure.

But Goldman was welcomed now more as an exile than as an anarchist. The *Nation* suggested that she had become a symbol of a world situation in which growing numbers of people had become refugees from political persecution by fascist regimes. The *Nation* also observed that "it was a middle-aged, middle-class crowd" that had welcomed Goldman reverentially at Town Hall. Goldman was "a pre-war revolutionist," but her present-day admirers were "pre-war liberals." In New York, at least, few young people or workers showed up in the crowd of her welcomers, partly because workers could not afford $1.50 for a banquet, but also because Goldman stood for principles that were alien both to capitalism and to Communism and was a "conscientious objector" in both camps. In that sense, observed the *Nation*, she was "a symbol of the ultimate social cleavage, of differences that cannot be bridged. She is a living and a very acid test of tolerance."[27]

With the expiration of her visa in early May, Goldman returned to Toronto and hoped to secure another U.S. visa later that year. The Roosevelt administration, however, besieged by a growing "anti-Red mania," was unwilling to undertake any action that might fuel controversy prejudicial to their efforts to liberalize the restrictive immigration laws, which several U.S. organizations were trying to stiffen. Even the optimistic Roger Baldwin concluded that Goldman's case was hopeless for the present. Disappointed, Emma nonetheless felt heartened by her visit. "Disgraceful, I know, for a revolutionist and internationalist to be so rooted in one country," she wrote Roger Baldwin.[28] She loved America because it brought out "adventure, innovations, experimental daring, which, except for Russia, no European country does." [29] True, many among the older generation of Jewish immigrant anarchists in America had grown more conservative, closer to the right-wing Socialists they had always disdained. Some were so embittered by events in Russia that they had abandoned any semblance of radicalism, becoming conservative union bureaucrats or New Deal Democrats. [30] But among younger people anarchism in America showed signs of reviving. In 1932, a militant new "Vanguard" group of young Jewish students and workers in New York—many of them children of immigrant anarchists—had begun publishing a paper, the *Vanguard,* one of the best English-language papers in the history of American anarchism. [31] They also organized new anarchist youth groups, and they formed ties with other immigrant anarchist movements such as the Spanish-speaking anarcho-syndicalists grouped around the New York paper *Cultura Proletaria.* [32]

Emma Goldman's contacts with these people awakened her former energies and she was pleased when they came up from New York to see her and consult on movement matters. "Fact is," she confided to Sasha that summer, "I am more inwardly at peace than I have been while tucked away all by myself in Bon Esprit . . . I am not idle and I feel less useless than I have for a long time. That's something to celebrate." [33]

As in 1926 and 1927, Emma and Sasha began during the summer of 1934 another dialogue on anarchism, this time in the growing shadows of fascism and Stalinism. Eight years earlier, with the anarchist movement in "a sort of trance," as Emma put it, she and Berkman had attempted to confront the theoretical and practical limitations of anarchism, which the Russian Revolution had illuminated. [34] Berkman had identified some of these weaknesses, for example the absence of a practical program for the day after the revolution and the disunity endemic among anarchists. He had attempted to address these issues in a book, *What Is Communist Anarchism?,* published in 1929. Yet this essay, in which Goldman had considerable input, dramatized the difficulties the two comrades faced. Although cogently written, it essentially restated the classic communist anarchist alternative to Bolshevism. [35] It contained little that was new and much that ignored economic realities in Russia in the early period of the revolution, for example the inability of worker control to cope with the deepening economic chaos of 1917, or the catastrophic lack of manufactured goods with which to satisfy the demands of the peasantry. [36] It ignored both the role of women in a revolution and questions of strategy and tactics, a perennial anarchist weakness. Despite the optimistic tone of the book,

Berkman often despaired while writing it, acknowledging to Goldman that at moments, he found himself thinking that "the revolution cannot work on anarchist principles. But once the old methods are followed, they'll never lead to anarchism." [37]

Although Goldman had tried to encourage Berkman, she was less interested in working out new revolutionary strategies than in articulating general anarchist principles. She particularly urged him to redefine revolution as "a process of reconstruction rather than what we believed it to be until now, a process of destruction." In other words, the revolution must minimize violence, and destroy as little as possible, "nothing at all in fact except such industries that make for war and disease." [38] Yet she found it difficult to go beyond such general statements, or broad pronouncements such as the need to avoid courts, prisons, and police under all circumstances. [39] She was inclined to wave aside complexities, insisting, for example—despite her own observations of pogrommed villages in the Ukraine—that while rape and robbery may occur during a revolution, they were "isolated cases" and need not happen "so long as everyone is given a chance to participate in the rebuilding of society." She was certain that if only large-scale properties were expropriated during the revolution, leaving smaller properties in private hands, "99 percent of the evils which necessitated the terror in Russia will die a natural death." [40]

In the end, both Goldman and Berkman backed off from the implications of their own best insights. It was as if, having lived through so many storms and upheavals and suffering the insecurity and isolation of exile, neither of them could muster the energy to confront basic theoretical and historical questions. And then neither of them were original thinkers, but rather propagandists, activists whose talents lay more in communicating ideas than in developing new ones. They stopped short of attempting the fundamental revisions of anarchism they both knew were necessary, and at times discouraged those who did, for example Nestor Makhno and Peter Arshinov, who tried to develop an anarchist platform or program. The masses themselves will have to work out a program, Berkman insisted impatiently. In Goldman's eyes, such attempts at a program were tantamount to "Bolshevism." [41]

Emma and Sasha's new dialogue, begun in the summer of 1934, was prompted in part by the invitations Emma had received to write articles for several American magazines and by correspondence with comrades in the United States seeking her views. The articles of 1934 and 1935—"The Tragedy of the Political Exiles" in *The Nation;* "Was My Life Worth Living?" in *Harper's;* "There is No Communism in Russia," in *American*

Mercury—were less revealing, however, than Goldman's private correspondence, which showed her continuing pessimism and ambivalence about the possibilities of any revolution. The strong antidemocratic, elitist strain in her thinking emerged with particular vehemence in the early 1930s. Though she tried to build a theory of revolution around her faith in the individual—and still called herself a revolutionist—her repudiation of the masses led her into an impasse. "For if the masses cannot be relied on since they are so easily swayed by demagogues," wrote Berkman, who would make the revolution? "The FEW exceptional individuals? They can't bring about a social change. Unless they do it as it has been done till now—by violence, political activity, by the state, in short." There would always be exceptional individuals, "but that is not a popular movement for a great social ideal." Without that movement anarchism could not be realized. "In a word, IF the masses are really not to be depended on, then revolution has no sense. . . ." Although during the 1920s Berkman had taken comfort in a long view—redefining the anarchist project as an attempt to infuse coming revolutions with "SOME anarchist spirit and tendency" so that "a series of non-anarchist revolutions will finally end in an Anarchist one"—even he had turned more pessimistic by the early 1930s. Berkman admitted now that he thought anarchism "very far away, and I even doubt that the 'individual' . . . is any good for it." [42]

Goldman continued to insist on her faith in the individual, but her ambivalence toward the masses, whom she believed "will always fall under the sway of unscrupulous spellbinders," reinforced her pessimistic conviction that real social changes would occur only in a distant future. At moments she gave way to bitter elitist tirades, claiming that "it isn't Stalin or Mussolini or Hitler. It is the mob. The mob that loves to be whipped and kisses the hand that smites it." Goldman admitted to Augustine Souchy, the German militant she had met in Moscow, that "more and more I am losing faith in the masses, though not in our ideal. I realize, of course, that tyranny isn't for all time, but will the mob ever awaken to the meaning and beauty of freedom? I used to believe in it implicitly. I am dubious now." She envisioned the mission of anarchism as largely educational, "until our ranks are larger and our ground better prepared." [43] A measure of her pessimism was her tendency, during this period, to blame the failures of anarchism on the lack of "vision" in the masses themselves. In a letter to her friend and comrade, Rose Pesotta, who was then a vice president of the International Ladies Garment Workers' Union, Goldman complained that "if people do not even long for beauty and the things of the spirit, how can they be expected to fight for it?" [44]

Such views were far from the revolutionary optimism of her pre-1917 days, and from any politics that might be called revolutionary. By 1934, both Goldman and Berkman had generally relinquished their faith in revolution, although they continued to think of themselves as revolutionists. But increasingly, they defined their role as that of offering moral support to a younger generation of anarchists, encouraging them to build unity among themselves and to overcome the quarreling endemic to the movement. On concrete questions of strategy and tactics, they had little to offer. Yes, Emma told a young comrade in America who was organizing an anarchist conference, she favored anarchist participation in cooperatives, consumer leagues, and modern schools. Certainly anarchists should join trade unions, trying to infuse them with libertarian methods. Where the IWW still existed, anarchists should join it rather than the unions of the American Federation of Labor (AFL). But then they should also organize anarcho-syndicalist unions as well. In any case, "anarchists must keep close to the workers and take part in their daily struggle thus winning their confidence and their trust." But what role should anarchists play in the unions? Should they try to capture control? Accept union offices? Or should they remain in the rank and file? And what position should anarchists take toward the bitter struggles then raging in unions such as the International Ladies Garment Workers' Union between Communists and anti-Communists? Should anarchists support the movement for unemployment insurance or for an old-age pension law, her correspondent asked? To these concrete questions, Goldman offered no reply.[45]

On one issue Goldman remained adamant: anarchists should never vote in elections. In her view, abstention represented a fundamental anarchist principle, not merely a tactic. She and Berkman had always taken a strong stand against voting, and neither had modified their views.[46] In 1934, voting was not an abstract question, for in the 1931 elections in Spain, the votes of anarcho-syndicalist workers had helped secure the election of a liberal democratic republic. Anarchist abstentionism in the elections of November 1933 had helped the Right regain power, initiating a two-year period of reaction known as the *biennio negro*. Following the October 1934 uprising of Asturian miners—a rehearsal for the revolution of 1936—there would be thirty thousand prisoners in Spanish jails, which only a more liberal regime would release. Goldman maintained her abstentionist position, arguing that if the anarchists were numerous enough to swing elections to the Left, they were also strong enough to rally the workers to a general strike or series of strikes all over Spain—an uncertain proposition at best.[47]

These, however, were old matters. Over the summer of 1934, anarchists also debated the question of cooperation with others on the Left to fight against fascism. The Popular Front period was about to begin, when Soviet foreign policy aimed above all else to secure alliances in the West against Hitler, and when Communist parties, working to form a broad antifascist front, would seek alliances with the social democratic and even liberal parties they had formerly condemned. With Mussolini in Italy, Hitler in Germany, Dollfuss in Austria, and powerful fascist movements elsewhere, antifascism would draw many toward party membership or at least sympathy with the Communists, who seemed to present the strongest force against fascism.

For the anarchists, the rise of fascism posed seemingly insoluble dilemmas. Recalling the destruction of the Russian anarchist movement by the Bolsheviks, most anarchists, including Goldman and Berkman, were loathe to consider any alliances with their traditional enemies.[48] Yet isolation also condemned them to impotence and destruction. Sensitive to this problem, Emma favored cooperation with left-wing, non-Communist workers, presumably socialists. She also favored trying to reach the rank and file of the Communists—not party members but sympathizers "who can be made to see the delusion and snare of party policies." Goldman urged efforts to contact such workers "individually or by means of participating in their demonstrations as independent units and through our literature." If cooperation was necessary, "frankly speaking I should prefer to go with the Socialists, not politically though—but economically; for I feel that even a small amount of liberty is preferable to dictatorship which crushes all liberty."[49]

On the question of Russia, however, Goldman and the anarchists found their views beginning to gain a wider hearing. With Stalin's capture of absolute power in 1928–29, a new era in Soviet history began, which some historians have described as Stalin's revolution from above. It was characterized by a furious campaign against the so-called Right Opposition (the defenders of gradualism), a new commitment to breakneck industrialization, and the forcible collectivization of the peasantry, which had previously consisted of small property owners. The most reliable estimates suggest that between three and four million peasants died in the famine that accompanied this collectivization—a policy that had never been remotely advocated by any of the old Bolsheviks. According to Stephen F. Cohen, these changes constituted "a truly momentous process that radically transformed not only the economic and social foundations of Soviet society but the nature of the political system as well."[50] Soon the war against the peasantry would grow to include a war against the party itself, as was evident in the trials of the Old Bolsheviks who had made the 1917 revolution, and the purges of army officers, the intellectuals, bureaucrats, and many among the professional and technical classes. Although estimates of those arrested, imprisoned, exiled, or killed under Stalin vary widely, the repression was clearly symptomatic of vast social dislocations within a society racing to modernize yet still saddled with the legacy of czarism. Rushing ahead with economic development and socialist transformation, the system became increasingly laden with traditional values of authority, hierarchy, and conservatism, until the Stalinist state acquired quasi-religious trappings that were reminiscent of the Russian Orthodox Church. The repression was symptomatic too of the chaos within a Communist party reacting against a petrifying bureaucracy, yet simultaneously creating new bureaucratic forms. Terror, the police state, and the politics of paranoia spread through the Soviet landscape, leaving a legacy that would endure for decades.[51]

By the mid-1930s Goldman found that her indictment of the Soviet Union had begun to win credibility among American liberals, and even on the Left, particularly since the exiled Trotsky had begun to denounce the betrayal of the revolution by Stalin.[52] But even though she was gratified to see formerly pro-Soviet liberals such as John Haynes Holmes and Eugene Lyons turn more critical, she remained dissatisfied with their analyses. As she had all along, she insisted on tracing the evils of Stalinism back to Leninism, to Bolshevism, and even to Marx. "After all, Stalin is only the exaggerated expression of the Bolshevik ideology and tactics which justify every crime," she wrote John Dewey in early 1938. "It therefore seems to me not quite logical to turn the light on the present ruler of Russia and keep in the shadow the very forces that created Stalin's psychology and conditioned all his actions."[53] As she put it to Rudolf Rocker the following year, "Stalin is after all carrying out the legacy of Marxism."[54] The efforts of her correspondents to make distinctions between the regime of Lenin and that of Stalin, or even between Trotsky and Stalin, only aroused her anger, and provoked her to ever more insistent denials that the Bolsheviks had accomplished anything of any value whatever.[55]

In insisting on the essential continuity between Marxism, Leninism, and Stalinism, Goldman took a position that would become widely shared in the West. The "continuity thesis," as it has been called, would become the basic foundation for Soviet studies in the West, employed for different reasons by those who wished to discredit all forms of socialism by equating it with Stalinist evils, and, to a lesser extent, by those who defended

Stalinism on grounds of inevitability and revolutionary necessity. In arguing the "inevitable" progression from Marxism to Stalinism, Goldman anticipated the basic thesis of the anti-Communist Cold War consensus view of Russia that would prevail especially after World War II.[56]

That Goldman chose to argue about the Russian past rather than exploit agreement about the present suggests the limitations of her strategy in the years 1934 and 1935. Rather than seeking common ground with other anti-Stalinists, she chose to emphasize differences, demanding that those opposed to current Stalinist atrocities condemn the entire socialist system as well. As she wrote to Carlo Tresca, "It is not enough to blame Stalin. It is necessary to expose the entire ideology and jesuitical conception that the end justifies the lowest means." In Goldman's opinion, it did not matter what kind of Marxist one was, it was "the theory itself which tends to annihilate all freedom and initiative."[57] Clearly Emma still felt bitter about what she considered the "betrayal" of the pro-Soviet intellectuals, the "liberal fellow-travellers" whom she considered "more despicable" than the "Communist zealots." Now, when some of these intellectuals were taking a more critical stand toward the Stalin regime, she found new reasons to condemn them.[58]

Despite her pessimistic outlook, Goldman still clung to the notion that a few gifted individuals could conjure up a powerful movement in the United States and Canada. She was more than ever persuaded that if only she or Berkman could be in America, "or did we have but a few well-informed, revolutionary and able individuals, there would be an Anarchist movement of size and quality, there would be a syndicalist movement." The tragedy was that they had no one "either sure of his Anarchist positions or able to make others sure. But that too will come," Emma wrote. "I am convinced of that."[59]

For a few golden weeks in the summer of 1934, Emma believed she had met the man she was looking for. Lecturing in Chicago the previous April, she had met Frank L. Heiner, a thirty-six-year-old former osteopath who, although blind from childhood, was now a graduate student in sociology at the University of Chicago. Heiner had long admired her book, *Anarchism and Other Essays*. When he spoke at a banquet in her honor, he charmed Emma with his eloquence and wit. He was a marvelous speaker, she reported to Sasha soon after, and well-versed in anarchism, though, she added, he was also very shy and lacked faith in himself. She compared Heiner to native American anarchists such as Haymarket martyr

Albert Parsons and also Voltairine de Cleyre. She was sure he would become a "force" in our ranks. "I mean to keep after him," she confided to Berkman.[60]

Heiner pursued Emma on his own, declaring emotionally that he loved her and pleading for a more intimate relationship. Because Emma left Chicago after her lectures there, returning to New York and soon after to Montreal, their love affair unfolded at first through letters that echoed the language of Emma's earlier affair with Ben Reitman. There were further parallels, for Emma had also met Reitman in Chicago, twenty-six years before; he too had symbolized for her the potential of America. "I wanted never to see you again and yet you drew me with magic force," Emma told Heiner early in May. "And now too I am torn between two forces, need of your love and dread of it. The dread of the child that had been burned by the element it did not understand." Still she responded eagerly to Heiner's pursuit, playing the grande dame and telling him that "the test that burned like white heat was that I had to forswear what I longed most for. Passionate response to the wild passion of my body. Love in all its ecstatic forms."[61] This time, though, Emma recognized the barriers between herself and Frank Heiner: she was sixty-five, he was thirty-six; he lived in the United States, where she could not remain; most of all, he was married, with a child and, because he was blind, heavily dependent on his wife, whom he also loved.

For several months after Goldman left Chicago, she and Heiner continued to explore their feelings for each other. Heiner wanted to visit Goldman in Toronto. Goldman, eager for his visit, hesitated. She hated "vulgarity," was loathe to expose her intimate life to the "vulgar smirks and lascivious remarks" of others. "And the world is both vulgar and coarse in its attitude to sex between two unequal ages, especially where the woman is so much older. For after all I will be 65 next month," she wrote, "though my need of love and of passion is as strong and intense as it always had been."[62] Emma worried too that Frank's infatuation for her was conditioned on his inability to see her age and general physical appearance. Not only to Heiner, but also to Sasha and Emmy, back in Nice, she admitted her conflicting feelings: dreading a new attachment fated to end, yet yearning for the love that Heiner was offering her. It was "a comfort to know that I am still able to awaken a beautiful love," she admitted to Emmy, though she was unsure whether she really loved Heiner, or was in love with his love for her.[63] And to Berkman she wrote ironically, that "your Kalamburovna [one of her code names] is an old fool. But as she has never been wise she is not likely to become so now. There is no help for her. Is there?" [64]

In a remarkable letter to Heiner before their meeting in Toronto, Emma suggested how profoundly unwanted she felt, cast out and doomed to loneliness and failure in what she felt as her rivalry for men with other women. In her letter, she described a dream that might have been a metaphor for her life as a whole:

> I dreamed I came to you, to some garret high up, about ten flights that had to be climbed. I came up completely exhausted from the effort. A woman received me who looked like Mary [Heiner's wife] yet was not her. She said I'd have to wait. I waited for two hours. Then you came in, for a brief moment. You had a lesson to give, you told me. And again I waited. Then more women came into the room, all devouring me with their curiosity. I had to escape. And so I walked down all the flights without seeing you again. I woke up with a heavy heart." [65]

Emma had, in fact, written to Mary, partly out of guilt—for Emma had not forgotten her own hurt caused by Ben's many affairs—and an awkward wish to reassure Mary, but perhaps also out of a wish to make claims on Frank, since she managed to boast to Mary of her own "success" with Frank. Because of his blindness, Heiner depended upon his wife to read Emma's letters to him, although he typed his own letters to Emma (which Mary mailed); Mary was therefore privy to Emma's intimacy with Frank while Emma was completely excluded from Frank's intimacy with Mary. That Emma would involve herself in so unpromising a situation, one in which she may have been cast into a private drama being enacted by Frank and Mary Heiner, suggests the measure of her desperate loneliness. Yet the triangular situation also recalled her other love affairs, in which she repeatedly became involved with men who were involved with other women. It was as if she were attempting to undo her father's rejection of her through her own love affairs with men to whom she played a motherly role; yet instead of reversing the original rejection, she reenacted it, confirming her sense of herself as unwanted and undeserving of love. [66] With Reitman, with Swenson, with Malmed, and now with Heiner, she found herself party to a triangle. Even with Berkman Emma was conscious of her position as a third party. Indeed one cannot help feeling that part of the attraction of these love affairs was the opportunity they afforded her to show off to Berkman, to remind him that a man could still love her even if he did not.

Still, the fact remained that a single woman of sixty-four, an exile to boot, had severely limited opportunities in the realm of love. Moreover, Emma had always celebrated love "whether it lasts for one brief moment or for a lifetime." Nor had she ever been a partisan of monogamy, despite her discomfort at Reitman's infidelities. Unwilling to reconcile herself to celibacy, she seized her chance, despite the absurdities to which even she was not wholly blind. When Frank Heiner persisted in his passionate entreaties, her resistance weakened. Finally, in early August, she told him to come.

This time she was not disappointed. For "two fascinating, overpowering, ecstatic weeks," weeks of intimate talk and lovemaking with Heiner, in the privacy of her own apartment (which she had rented partly for this visit), Emma found herself living "a miracle," a "fairy tale one read[s] in one's childhood and which one never believed in one's maturity," a beautiful idyll of "overwhelming bliss." Emma felt she had "never known anyone who combines in himself such tenderness, and strength, such gentleness and determination, above all one who has retained so much romance in the midst of our hard and cruel reality." [67] Snatching a few moments at the typewriter while her "boyfriend" was in the bathroom, Emma confessed to Berkman that "I am infatuated as only old fools can be. His coming into my life seems nothing short of a miracle." Heiner was "the greatest event of the last 17 years," she told Berkman ecstatically. He had all of Ben's "primitiveness," but a tenderness and understanding that Ben lacked. In addition to these qualities, Heiner was also "a born teacher," who spoke beautifully on anarchism to Emma's group of "youngsters." In Frank Heiner, Emma believed she had found "all that I had longed for and dreamed about all my life, and never achieved. Primitiveness, tenderness and complete harmonious blending of intellect, spirit and body. . . ." Until she met Heiner, Emma had in fact doubted whether "I could be awakened any more, or would respond if love, or even a casual sex experience would come my way." [68] From his letters, at least, it seems that Frank Heiner, like Ben Reitman, was an expert lover of women, patient and responsive to the needs of female sexuality. He told Emma he believed a man's pleasure was actually heightened if he stayed inside the woman until she is "released and satisfied and fulfilled," which he understood took longer for a woman than for a man.[69] Erotically and emotionally, Emma found in Frank Heiner what she had always longed for. "Is this not a great wonder at my age?"

Alas, the two weeks passed quickly. "Today is a different Sunday than the last two Sundays when Frank Heiner was here," Emma wrote sadly to Emmy on the ninth of September. "What a world he created for me. Not in my wildest dreams did it come to me that such a creature as he exists, or that one so handicapped as he could possibly live in a world of such beauty. Much less did I expect anything so exquisite would come to me. Well, the miracle actually happened." The depths of feeling that Heiner awakened in her made her question whether she had really lived before. She had discovered unknown emotional depths in herself during the two weeks of Heiner's visit. "Well, I am not the only one who will have to say at the end of my life, 'the more I learn, the more I know how little I know.' " [70]

Filled with her rapturous memories of Heiner, Emma now felt suddenly adrift in the "desert" of Toronto, "like a lost dog roaming about aimlessly. It is a hell of a state for E.G. to be in." In letter after letter to Sasha, Emmy, and Stella, Emma celebrated the wonder of her encounter with Heiner, and mourned the irony that this love should come so late in her life, and in a form that could not last. "Isn't it just like the rotten luck of your Tante that some rare thing should come into her life only to be torn out again?" she lamented to Stella. Yet she felt the event in keeping with the rest of her life. "Always within reach of something very beautiful only to be thrown back to the old yearning and the old loneliness." Still, Emma felt that what Frank had given her was worth the pain she suffered after he left. The two weeks with him had brought "more than years with others. And there is the consciousness that the link between us will remain until my last moment or his. That is already a great deal in this cold, ugly world of ours. . . ." [71]

Goldman also saw in Frank Heiner a potential leader of anarchism in America. He had all the qualities needed—"He is a rebel and he has a perfect mint of wit and humor," she told Sasha, "I met few people so quick in repartee and wit." These were traits that could create something interesting and lively. Yet he would have to have everything read to him, the one serious barrier to his potential for leadership. It is curious that, while Emma was determined to fight so many other obstacles, she regarded blindness as somehow insuperable, though clearly Heiner could act in many capacities. In fact, Emma commented that it had "increased my faith in humanity to find in Frank such an indomitable will to overcome all the terrible difficulties his handicap had put in his way."

A difficulty that could not be overcome, however, was Frank Heiner's marriage, which he evidently had no desire to terminate. He and Emma continued their affair in letters, but while Emma felt "empty, poor, hungry for all your rich nature can give," his erotic letters awakened her desire without offering any means of satisfaction. "Oh, imagine my tongue over your whole body for an eternity," he would write. "You are life, you are eternity, you are all." "My Goddess far above me, my darling, my mother ever close to me, how I worshipped you then and how I worship you at this moment." "When you are torn by your lectures, remember that I know the time of them," he promised; "as the hour approaches and the tension [gets] more painful, I at home will be concentrating on the picture of giving you kisses of encouragement to sustain you. After the lecture, I will be thinking late that night of smoothing you and relaxing you and caressing you." [72]

Time and their continuing separation deepened Emma's dissatisfaction and longing, even though she was busy with lectures and meetings. Heiner evidently made no effort to visit her again in Toronto. By the spring of 1935, she found herself growing desperate. "I tell you, my most precious pal," she wrote self-mockingly to Berkman, "life is cruel. Why in Hell did Frank have to come into my life? Wer hat das gedurft in meinem Alter? [Who should be allowed to do this at my age?] Of all the insane adventures for me to fall madly in love with a youngster at 65. I tell myself every day that it is shere [sic] insanity, or rather senility. But of what avail is our capacity to reason. The heart pfeift darauf [doesn't give a damn]. I [am] simply torn to pieces between my crazy longing to see him again and my feeling that it will only make my departure [from Canada] more painful." [73] In long, poignant soliloquies to Heiner, Emma abandoned herself to her longing, even while suffering (a pain perhaps not unmixed with pleasure) from the knowledge that his wife, Mary, must read them aloud to him. "I stretch out my arms in vain longing," she wrote him, "I dream about you night after night. I live through the two magic weeks with you. In the end to remain desolate [sic] and weary with the heart hunger for your presence and your embrace." She had thirsted for years for "something so complete, such utter fulfillment. And now that it has come I want it terribly, every thought and nerve cries wildly for the blending of our bodies and our spirits. Oh, my Frank, my masterful yet tender lover, I stretch out my arms for you, I want you madly. When will my hunger for you be nourished and my thirst quenched by the fountain [of] you the glorious earth spirit?" [74]

Back in St. Tropez in the summer of 1935, Emma grew frantic. "Oh, my Frank, it was insanity to think I could enjoy life separated from you by thousands of miles," she wrote early in June of 1935. "It was hard enough in Canada. Now it is altogether impossible to endure. What was I thinking about when I decided to sail back here? . . . It was madness, madness to have gone away." [75] "Don't think I do not fight against it," she told Heiner a few weeks later. "I do, every hour. Some days I am furious with myself for ever having permitted you to get hold of my imagination, my every thought, my every nerve. Other days I bless the force that has brought you to me and has rekindled my youth long dead and buried. I am [in] constant conflict with myself, with you, with our love." [76] When Heiner wrote, Emma was ecstatic. "My precious, wonderful lover," she wrote a few months later, "I wonder if you realize the supreme happyness [sic] your three letters have brought me. Just think of it, three letters in less than two weeks. Such joy, such nearness to you, my own Frank. . . . Why Frank, my big tender childlike yet worldly wise sweetheart, I feel richer than if I had won the Irish sweepstakes." She still reveled in his love for her, confiding to him that "no man has ever so completely blended with me, or has anticipated my needs, intellectual and physical, as you." [77] Frank too returned her passion in his letters. "My darling Emma, my sweet, tender precious one, my Goddess, how I long to be with you, to discuss every-thing in Heaven and Earth, to cover you with kisses, to cling to you and hold you and hold you and never let you go. Every memory I have and your every act and move and work make me deeply and ardently and eternally love you." [78]

Still, the distance between them weighed heavily on Emma, who found waiting for Heiner's letters excruciating, particularly when they arrived infrequently. She felt unable to work or to write, couching her complaints in metaphors of pregnancy and birth. "You are the father whose love and passion have impregnated me and no one but you can bring that child to birth," she told him in the summer of 1935. [79] Her growing realization that they would probably never meet again also filled her with despair. She felt increasingly that the "sickening yearning" she suffered was "too steep a price," at her age, for the joy of his infrequent letters. [80] By this time, Emma was in London, once again attempting to expand her "field" as a lecturer. Berkman, in St. Tropez, offered her some sensible advice, perhaps validating her own intentions. "I don't think you have anything to regret, and the experience was surely valuable to both of you," he wrote. "But on the other hand it is a hopeless situation and I think you are right in terminating the correspondence, for it can hold nothing but pain." [81] With her work progressing well in London, and with Berkman's counsel, Emma decided to end the "relationship" that by now had become a matter of infrequent letters.

Emma Goldman and Alexander Berkman in New York, 1917, awaiting trial on charges of opposing the draft during World War I. (UPI/Bettmann Newsphotos)

Right: Flyer for Emma Goldman lecture, London, 1925. (Courtesy International Institute of Social History, Amsterdam) *Below, left:* Mollie Steimer, Paris, ca. 1920s. (Courtesy International Institute of Social History, Amsterdam) *Below, right:* Emma Goldman in St. Tropez, 1929. (Courtesy International Institute of Social History, Amsterdam)

SOUTH PLACE INSTITUTE,

SOUTH PLACE, MOORGATE, E.C.2.

On Thursday, January 29th, 1925,

EMMA GOLDMAN

WILL LECTURE ON

"The Bolshevik Myth and the Condition of the Political Prisoners."

CHAIRMAN: COL. JOSIAH C. WEDGWOOD, M.P.

JOHN TURNER, Member of the TRADE UNION MISSION TO RUSSIA, will also speak.

Doors Open at 7-30 p.m.   Chair taken at 8 p.m.

TICKETS: 3/- 2/- & 1/-. Balcony Free, by TICKET ONLY

From: A. SUGG, 53, Gloucester Road, N.W.1.

And: "FREEDOM" Office, 127, Ossulston Street, N.W.1

Also at DOOR of the HALL on night of Meeting.

Workers Friend, Printers, T.U., 163, Jubilee St., London, E.1.

Above, left: Alexander Berkman and Rudolph Rocker in the south of France, 1930s. (Courtesy International Institute of Social History, Amsterdam)
Above, right: Alexander Berkman and Emmy Eckstein in Nice, 1930s. (Courtesy International Institute of Social History, Amsterdam)
Left: Max Nettlau. (Courtesy International Institute of Social History, Amsterdam)

Opposite: Emma Goldman arriving at Penn Station, New York, where she is greeted by Stella Ballantine, February 1934. (UPI/Bettmann Newsphotos)

Above: Emma Goldman with Stella Ballantine, interviewed in her hotel room in New York, February 1934. (UPI/Bettmann Newsphotos)

Above: Emma Goldman at the City Club, Rochester, New York, April 1934. The woman at the left is Mrs. Samuel Commins, Goldman's sister. (Courtesy Paul Kaplan) *Right:* Emma Goldman's "home" in Toronto, ca. 1934–35. (Courtesy International Institute of Social History, Amsterdam)

Left: Emma Goldman, Senya Flechine, Modest Stein ("Fedya"), and Alexander Berkman at "Bon Esprit," St. Tropez, early 1930s. Flechine, a photographer, set up a timed camera for this portrait in skepticism. (Courtesy International Institute of Social History, Amsterdam)

Below: Emma Goldman with comrades of the CNT-FAI, Albalate de Cinca, Aragon, Spain, October or November 1936. (Courtesy International Institute of Social History, Amsterdam)

Emma Goldman visiting an agricultural collective, Spain, 1936. (Rose Pesotta Papers, Box 44, Rare Books and Manuscripts Division, the New York Public Library, Astor, Lenox and Tilden Foundations)

Anniversary of the Russian Revolution, October 1936, in Barcelona. (Courtesy of the International Institute of Social History, Amsterdam)

It is not clear at what point Emma received a letter from Frank admitting that his attraction to her represented a pattern in his life, that "I had a craving amounting to a physical necessity for women who were physically above the average weight and who could give me definitely maternal responses." [82] It is unclear too how Emma responded to this admission, or to the knowledge, received from Mary early in their affair, that Heiner had had other extramarital relationships prior to the one with her. In fact, Emma learned only after she and Heiner had been corresponding over a year that this had been a time of great difficulty for him. "The past year was a terrible one for me," he told her frankly. He and Mary had separated for a time; the marriage went through a period of great turmoil; he admitted, moreover, that the ending of a previous affair, just prior to his meeting with Emma, had led him to the verge of a nervous breakdown and a period of deep depression, which continued for some months. Though he did not say so explicitly, clearly his relationship with Emma had contributed to the difficulties in his marriage. Not wishing to burden her with his own troubles, Frank had not mentioned these issues in his letters. He now made clear to her, in explicit terms, the impossibility of their ever living together—though he had dreamed of it at times—and advised her not to return to Canada, since he could be with her only for short periods at long intervals. [83]

If the architecture and imagery of Goldman's relationship with Heiner resembled that of her earlier affairs, it differed in one significant regard. With Heiner there was little bitterness in the breakup, and Emma did not feel abused or betrayed, perhaps because this was preeminently an affair of letters. Although she imagined herself "choosing" between love and her ideal, the fact was that Frank Heiner offered her love letters, not love. Characteristically, she transformed the ending of their correspondence into a grand drama of renunciation, an operatic gesture of sacrifice for the cause, yet the truth was that she was merely accepting a reality. What she decided to end was not a real love affair but a fantasy. One of her last letters to Heiner, on December 26, 1935, spelled out her stiffening resolve.

My dearest,

Your cable came yesterday morning. It was the only Christmas greeting I had from anybody. My own Frank, it is not a question of 'changed relationship.' It is that I cannot continue on the rack. More than ever do I need every bit of energy and power of concentration to establish myself in England. The field is large. True, it has been permitted by our comrades to yield nothing for our ideas. Nothing has been done since the war, except during my short visits ten years and three years ago. It will require superhuman strength and determination to clear the ground from all the debris that had accumulated for so long. And unless I put behind me all personal emotions and craving and give myself utterly to the task I will not succeed. AND I MUST SUCCEED, OR MAKE AN END. I CAN NOT FACE THE YEARS LEFT ME GAGGED AND BOUND hand and foot. So, you see my dearest, it is really a question of life and death with me.

The summer has convinced me that my feeling for you completely unfits me for anything else. I am determined therefore not to be as obsessed by that any more. I know myself enough to know that while I will not forget you, or cease to care profoundly, the effort to make Anarchism heard in England and to create a basis for systematic propaganda will fill the void our separation and the long and excruciating intervals of word from you has created. After all, our ideal has always meant more to me than all else. I do not say that I found it easy to choose. But there is no help. . . . Life has taught me that love . . . is not for those who consecrate themselves to an ideal. When you came I quite forgot this truism. Your love swept me off my feet. But last summer forced me to face the fact that I will again have to choose as I have in the past. It's not been easy, believe me my dearest. But it had to be done.

Please understand my Frank, and do not make my task more painful than it is. I embrace you tenderly.[84]

They continued to write for a few more months. But by March of 1936, Emma's determination to end the correspondence had not wavered. Despite the difficulties in England, she wrote, "I have not felt so much at peace in a long while. Just to be on the firing line again, to plead for our ideal . . . has put new energy into me." Active once again, she could separate emotionally from this man whose passionate and sensuous love had, for a brief moment, completely fulfilled her. This time her loss was edged with acceptance. "Goodbye, my dear Frank," she wrote. "Nothing can take away from me or my memory the wonderful two weeks in T. I shall always cherish them and everlastingly thank my good star that has brought you to me. We have deeper ties than the emotional and they will never be broken. I embrace you, my dear, in deepest comradeship."[85]

PART THREE

Beginnings and Endings

8

The Death of
Alexander Berkman

Emma's visit to the United States had renewed her self-confidence. Reassured that she still had "drawing power" and comforted by Frank
Heiner's love, a more relaxed Emma reached out to Berkman's companion, Emmy Eckstein, trying to overcome tensions that had long prevailed
between them. In their letters over the summer, fall, and winter of 1934,
and into the spring of 1935, the two women wrote expansively to one another, sharing confidences, reassurances and even recipes (Emma's for
blintzes). Emma admitted to Emmy the loneliness that had tormented her
in her exile and her doubts about Frank Heiner's love. "If he could see the
reality of his fancy, . . ." she asked Emmy, "do you think he would be so
carried away?"[1] When Emma worried that her comrades would gossip
maliciously about the age difference between them, Emmy rushed to reassure her. "Let them all go to hell. . . . Even today I would be able to
love a man of 90 years . . . WHY NOT?" Sasha was "more interesting to
me than ANY CLEVER AND BEAUTIFUL YOUNG MAN."[2] When Frank Heiner
wrote a letter to Sasha and Emmy full of allusions to "the goddess,"
Emmy reported it humorously. "Emma, it seems that Frank's love for you
made him religious, eh darling? He feels about you as I feel about Sash
and you. We would make a crazy bunch altogether?"[3]

Emmy, in fact, responded eagerly to Emma's affectionate tone with
fantasies of a grand reunion in France and assurances that "you and I
and Sasha are just ONE altogether. Ganz verwirschtelt, wie der Berliner
saght. . . ." (All tangled up together, as the Berliners say).[4] Emmy also
assured Emma that Sasha still needed her. Self-conscious about her limited education, she told Emma that Sasha was "starving" for intellectual
intercourse, that he needed a person "who interests him, who has some-

thing to say, and something to ADD to his knowledge and point of view. THERE IS ONLY YOU, MY DEAR." There was not one interesting person close by, she added. "I am already the most interesting one." [5] For all her jealousy and essentially conservative social values, Emmy Eckstein was a bright, funny, and devoted young woman who confronted with considerable courage her precarious existence with a man much older than herself. In her mish-mash of German and English, she held her own even with Emma, who could be a formidable rival. Everyone agreed that she adored Sasha, even Emma, who at moments wryly admitted her envy. "Some luck that lobster has, to be always so loved by the women in his life," she quipped to a friend.[6]

It had taken many years for Emmy Eckstein to accept the bond between Emma Goldman and Alexander Berkman. She had a lively imagination where other women were concerned, and her jealous outbursts often made Berkman's life difficult. But the bond between Emma and Sasha had grown stronger during their years of exile, despite the fact that they were often separated. Especially after 1930, when Berkman was compelled to give up his work for the Political Prisoners' Relief Committee in order to remain in France, he was the more isolated and financially dependent. After *The Bolshevik Myth,* published in 1925, and his other book, *What is Communist Anarchism?* published in 1929, Berkman worked mostly on translations of Russian and German literature into English (he also translated Eugene O'Neill's *Lazarus Laughed* into Russian for the Moscow Art Theater), a meager source of income at best. He and Emma worked now in separate spheres, partly by choice, but also through necessity. For Berkman had no access to the British passport that enabled Goldman to agitate in English-speaking countries. His residence even in France was precarious. With only a Nansen passport for stateless persons, he was required to renew his visa every few months, a tedious undertaking fraught with anxiety. Even then, he was periodically ordered to leave the country. In such emergencies, he could count on Emma, with her energy and connections, to come to the rescue.

As his own life grew more circumscribed, he also depended on Emma more heavily for contact with a larger world. He admired her unrelenting efforts to build a public life for herself in England, a life that also afforded him a vicarious satisfaction. Their correspondence was punctuated by periodic expressions of mutual admiration and encouragement. In their seemingly endless exchange of letters filled with advice, arguments, complaints, questions, sympathy, jokes, quarrels old and new, grievances,

gossip, declarations of devotion and wistful longing, they wove an inde-
structible fabric of friendship that seemed to surprise even them, at moments when they happened to reflect on their history.

June 12, 1934, Sasha to Emma: "Well, dear, you certainly should
be congratulated, for your spirit is young and indeed you seem younger
now than when I knew you about—well, I'd better not mention how
many years it is back. What's the use? You know, and I know: it's a
good many years, anyhow; and you are still young and full of verve and
energy. . . ."[7]

August 2, 1934, Emma to Sasha: "Dearest own Sasha, my heart yearns
for you until it hursts [sic], especially now when you are so depressed. But
we will have to be patient. Time will pass and we will be together again,
the three of us, more united than ever. Do brace up, my old brave Sash.
Above all do take a real rest as if you had nothing to translate and worry
about."[8]

August 13, 1934, Sasha to Emma: "Yes, dearest sailor girl, it would be
a wonderful thing if you could come over—I long to see you, too, and I
am sure it would do you good to have a change, and we really have many
things to talk over. You know that you always have been a help and inspiration in my work, whatever the work was—I wonder whether you
could manage it."[9]

August 27, 1934, Emma to Sasha: "As to your letter, my own Sashale,
I can't tell you how deeply it moved me. Your wanting to have me come
back now, dearest, you will never know how I longed to rush back when I
got your letter. . . ."[10]

August 30, 1934, Emma to Sasha: "Dearest Sash. This is a red letter
week for me. Two letters from you and two from E. I call that a regular
fortune. . . . Letters are of course no substitute for actual nearness. What
would I not give if I had you and E. close to me, or I were with you. Just to
feel your presence and hear your voice would mean more than words could
express. But since das kann nicht sein [that can not be], letters must take
the place of human contact."[11]

April 14, 1935, Sasha to Emma: "I am damned glad you will soon be
with me. You bet I am looking forward to it. Yes, my dear—no, not only
the blintzes and the gefülte fish—I am sure you will be a great help in my
work, for one needs someone to talk things over, consult, etc. and it will
be much easier when you are with me."[12]

Eagerly anticipating Emma's return to St. Tropez in mid-May of 1935,
Emmy had painted and cleaned Bon Esprit from top to bottom, filling it

with Emma's favorite flowers from the garden. She and Sasha planned to stay there to keep Emma company after her arrival. Sadly, the homecoming proved a painful disappointment to all three. The affectionate intimacy of their letters collided with the strains of actual contact at close quarters. Emma had returned in a melancholy state, depressed about Frank Heiner and wanting to be cared for and consoled almost like a child herself, despite her motherly pose toward her two "children," as if her struggles had entitled her to special consideration. Seeing Sasha and Emmy's intimacy, face to face, deepened her consciousness of her own solitude and loneliness. Instead of reassuring her, their presence seemed to intensify her unhappiness and make her feel unwanted and left out. What was planned as a festive reunion quickly broke down into a strained ménage à trois, with Emma depressed and silent, barely speaking to Sasha or to Emmy, who fled alone after a few weeks back to Nice.

This fiasco led to another flurry of letters over the summer between Nice and St. Tropez, with Emma insisting on Emmy's jealousy, Emmy accusing Emma of hostility and hatred—"your bad eyes," and Sasha desperately trying to make peace all around. Though she denied it to Sasha and to Emmy both, Emma admitted her hatred of Emmy to other friends, confiding to Rudolf Rocker that Emmy's "sickening suspicion that I do not love her, that I do not want her" was "partly right." [13] Emma could in fact be cruel—Emmy complained of her tactlessness and *Stichelein* (taunts or gibes)—as, for example, when she accused Emmy of letting her emotions be ruled by her stomach condition (Emmy suffered from pyloric gastritis and recurrent diverticulitis). "You know yourself," Emma replied harshly to one of Emmy's protestations of affection, "that your nervous state is such that you rise to the heights so often only to come down with a thud. To see black when your stomach bothers you what was white to you when your physical condition was bearable." [14]

With her tendency to attribute to others what was more characteristic of herself, Emma denied that "my Stichelein, or my tactlessness" separated them. "It is something much deeper, something more exclusive of all else. It is your inordinate, almost pathological sense of possessiveness of Sasha. It is this which colors your every thought and action. . . ." Lecturing Emmy about her childishness and "baby talk" (as distinguished from childlikeness, of which Emma approved), Emma revealed inadvertently how deeply excluded she felt from Sasha and Emmy's affectionate camaraderie, telling Emmy that "men of Sasha's intellectual caliber grow tired of such demonstrations of love," and "in the presence of outsiders, it does not sound true or convincing, and it makes us appear foolish in the eyes of those who have to witness or listen to it." [15]

But Emmy knew how to fire off a few rounds of her own. "Listen, darling, it is not fair to reproach me my childishness. Did I ever reproach you your extremely opposite ways? And you tell me that Sasha is getting tired of my DEMONSTRATIVE LOVE??? Emma, darling, if every woman has a lover so tired of her ways as I have one I CONGRATULATE HER!!! It does not seem to me, dearest friend, that you with your 'gravely seriousness' as I call it, could keep the man better than I with my 'childishness.' But you see, I really think that is my and Sasha's own business. . . ." [16]

Despite the charges and countercharges, each had strong motives for desiring reconciliation. There were moments, moreover, when Emma admitted her own part in the summer's fiasco, confiding to "Emmychen" that "it's difficult to be gay when one is not at peace with oneself and ever so many anxieties press on one's head and heart." [17] She acknowledged too that "it is extremely difficult for me to be in close quarters with others. And the more I care for a person the more difficult it is." [18] And again, "I never meant to hurt you in any way, or to be critical." [19] And yet again, "I wish I had suppressed my moods and irritation more than I did. . . . You may believe me I am most unhappy about the end of our summer which had such a promising beginning." [20]

Back of all of Emma's complaints and charges was her persistent feeling that she was not wanted. "I know also that you do not really need me," she wrote to Berkman on the eighteenth of July, "that far from bringing you peace or inspiration, I become a bone of contention and strife. I suffer deeply under it all and yet do not help you in any way." [21] In one of her most poignant letters that summer, Emma admitted to Sasha her painful sense of exclusion.

Dearest Sasha. Today is the 18th. Three months since I came back from my tour. Strange isn't it that in all this time you and I had not a single friendly or intimate talk. Indeed less so than when I was far away. Then you could at least write tender and understanding letters. I suppose distance lends enchantment. Doesn't it dear old scout? Of course I know talk does not signify anything. Still, one does miss closeness, if not in words, at least in deeds with one so interrelated as you and I. We had nothing in all the three months except our past which is a bond I will admit. . . . Yet I know you wanted me back. You certainly made me feel you did. As you made me feel that you really needed me . . . I am not complaining. I only want you to know how terribly I felt the wall that seems to rise between us when we are together. Or if not a wall, something that makes us both tongue tied.[22]

Emma insisted, in another letter, that "I am not the woman who wants the man, whether lover or friend, to slobber over her in a demonstrative way, or to be told so many times a day how much she is cared for. But one does want an occasional kind word, or a tender touch, or the assurance that one really means something in the life of the other." Emma felt that for most of their time together, she had been left to brood in her room, "always alone and to myself." Berkman had not even shown her an occasional affectionate gesture, for fear of Emmy's jealousy. "You are a different human being when we are alone," she remonstrated.[23]

Berkman replied gently but he did not mince words. "Dearest Em," he wrote, "I am very sorry you feel so disappointed with your home-coming this time." He was not given to "emotional expressions," he explained, "particularly not orally. There is no change whatever in my feelings to you, and they cannot change." But the atmosphere in St. Tropez had been "rather heavy." He thought "the real situation is due to your general dissatisfaction with things, which is part of your nature, and to the fact that a 'menage a trois,' as the French call it, is never a success. We have tried it for years now, and surely it does not work. . . . Every person, especially such three very definite natures as we three, must have his or her own atmosphere. If you are put in an atmosphere not your own, you will not fit into it and not be content."

Berkman insisted that Emmy was no longer really jealous of Emma, and that she "was determined to make YOUR stay there happy, as happy as possible. Well, it proved a failure." Defending Emmy's efforts to "make things pleasant for you," Berkman suggested frankly to Emma that "you are not a very easy person to live with."

I think your very best friends will tell you that if they are frank with you. And a person cannot always permit himself to be suppressed and not break out now and then. By suppressed I mean more the atmosphere you create than any words you utter. Do you realize that it came so far that E. was afraid even to laugh or to express her native joy of life because it disturbed you and even was resented by you, as I myself noticed on several occasions. Well, surely people cannot live together under such conditions. And I must tell you, my dear, that I myself was often oppressed by the atmosphere you created. Now, I am not highstrung like E. I can stand a good deal, in every sense. And yet your frequent heavy moods and bad humor were oppressive to me and often I could not even work because of it. . . . All this simply shows that a menage a trois does not work. At least not in this case, though I believe it works in no case. It is unfortunate, but a fact.[24]

Sasha hoped that Emma was not "exaggerating things into tragedies," and insisted again and again on his friendship, which "does not depend on whether I am in St. Tropez or Nice or anywhere else. . . . In fact," he added, "one feels closer at some distance, because in close everyday life there are necessarily frictions, often over little things. And my comradeship and friendship with you has never depended in the past, nor will ever depend in the future, on being in the same house or city." Despite what had happened that summer, from his perspective, there was no change between them, no cause for grief. "What there is, is simply the advisability to live separately. That is all."[25]

What Berkman overlooked, of course, was that while living separately meant for him sharing a household with Emmy, for Emma it meant living alone. Unlike Sasha, she had no private consolation for the loss of her public platform. "Well, not having the one or the other brought me face to face with the fact that I MUST DEVOTE THE REST OF MY LIFE TO SOME FORM OF ACTIVITY," she wrote him in September. "THAT MY PLACE IS MOST ASSUREDLY NOT IN THE HOME. You are too worldly wise not to know that one must have something in life to cling to, a person we love, some creative interest. . . . Well, I cling to my past and my work because I have nothing else, and NO ONE ELSE. NOT YOU EITHER."[26]

If these were pleas for attention from Sasha, they went unanswered. By September, Emma had decided to return to England for yet another attempt to establish herself as a lecturer. She left St. Tropez in November, stopping in Nice and in Paris en route to London. Even before her departure, her relations with Sasha and especially with Emmy had improved markedly. Emma and Emmy were now writing each other affectionately again, with Emma apologizing for her difficult moods—"Don't think it has anything to do with you my dear," she told Emmy. "It has everything to do with my restlessness."[27] And Emmy too, an astute observer both of herself and others, tried to explain why she felt ill at ease in Emma's presence, while also reaffirming her appreciation for Emma's kindness at times of crisis. "I will never forget how you consoled me when our enfant terrible [Berkman] was sent out [i.e. ordered to leave France]," she wrote Emma. "To have you around when one is unhappy—then you are so wonderful. And courageous."[28] Indeed, Emmy reiterated her admiration for

Emma's strength and courage in many letters, almost as if she were trying to absorb some of it for herself. "Emma, dear," she wrote in December of 1935, "how strange life is: there is not a single day that I do not think of you. And we speak of you—always and admiring your energy and sometimes we can't get over how you manage to have this courage at all. . . ." [29]

Over the next months, the three of them would need all the courage they could muster, for Berkman's health had deteriorated, despite all their efforts to deny it. The first hints had come in the summer of 1934, when Emma was still in Toronto, trying to decide whether to permit Frank Heiner to visit her. In July, when Emma pressed Sasha about why she did not hear from him as often as before, he admitted that he had been feeling unusually fatigued and also depressed. His condition was really more mental than physical, he assured her, and nothing to worry about. Emma attributed these changes mainly to the cumulative isolation of exile, the lack of a "fighting atmosphere," and the difficulty and anxiety of attempting to translate Rudolf Rocker's *Nationalism and Culture* (which was eventually translated by someone else). Berkman was inclined to blame advancing years. "I am 64, my dear. And it is THAT that is the matter," he wrote Emma. "I am not as strong as before, get tired easier. But that is not an illness at my age." [30]

Still, Berkman's long letters to Emma during the summer of 1934, describing his unaccustomed tiredness, disturbed her, for she understood that "you are not of the complaining kind. And if you write about a little pain here and there and lassitude I know you are feeling miserable and I can not help worrying." [31] Still, during the next year, while the two were apart, neither one of them pursued the issue. Preoccupied with her own unhappiness on her return to France that summer, Emma did not notice what was happening with Berkman, or perhaps she actively resisted such awareness, for the loss of her beloved comrade was not something she could contemplate without terror. When confronted with unmistakable signs that something was wrong, particularly his difficulty urinating, which began in the spring of 1934, Emma, who was after all a trained nurse, still brushed them off casually as the psychological consequences of exile.

At any rate, it was only when she received a cable from Modest Stein (Berkman's cousin and her youthful lover "Fedya" in her memoirs), who had visited St. Tropez in the summer of 1935, that Emma really paid attention to Sasha's condition. When Stein, in October of 1935, advised her of Berkman's possibly dangerous prostate condition, she wrote Berkman from Paris—where she had stopped en route to England in November of 1935—asking for an explanation, though she was still convinced that "it is your material and often emotional stress which causes most of your trouble." [32] Berkman explained that he had had trouble urinating for some time, and that Stein, that summer, had noticed the problem, since he suffered from similar symptoms, which had been diagnosed as prostate trouble. Emma replied casually. "Oh yes, come to think of it you did mention about your urinal difficulties. But you said it was due to the wine you drank. Well, my dear, it is your old habit of making a conspiracy of the simplest thing. . . ." She hoped that Sasha would see the doctor and get the massage recommended by Modest Stein. [33] However, she was less distressed by Berkman's symptoms than by what she considered his habit of "conspiracy" and tendency to withhold things from her. In a series of letters back and forth in October and November of 1935, the two friends argued the point. Denying that he was keeping anything from her, Berkman wrote pointedly, "I do not believe in carrying my troubles on my sleeve, nor in talking to you or to anyone about every little physical trouble I have. . . . You may call it a habit of 'conspiracy,' but it is nothing of the kind." Talking to Emma would be "worse than useless," he claimed, for she would only misunderstand, and "you would, as usual, have something new to worry about." [34] When Emma replied with several long letters detailing her difficulties in London and complaining of Sasha's unjustness to her, Berkman, with uncharacteristic impatience, urged that they drop the matter. "Dear, its really silly to discuss. I pointed out to you that you use words in the wrong meaning, and you retort by telling me I am always taking part against you. Well, lets talk of other things." [35] Neither one had much heart for continuing the quarrel. "Alright, dear old scout," Emma agreed, "let's not argue anymore. It makes no difference anyhow in my love for you though sometimes you are hard as nails. I am sure you do not realize it yourself. But I know that you never mean to hurt me, or anybody you care about." [36]

Absorbed anew in efforts to organize lectures in London and other British cities, Emma engaged Berkman in discussions of politics. They debated questions such as whether anarchists should ever join a united front with the Communists, and if there were some contingencies—such as the possibility of freeing thirty thousand political prisoners in Spain—that might authorize anarchists to vote in parliamentary elections. But ill health increasingly distracted Sasha. This time it was Emmy whose condition had deteriorated. Emmy suffered considerable pain in the winter of 1935–36, with periods of extreme constipation and severe stomach and intestinal cramps.[37] By early February of 1936, though, Emmy was feeling well enough to write cheerfully to Emma, "Emma, my dear Emma—Hurrah!!!!! I am so much better—so much, that I feel like somebody come back to life after he was dead for a long time. . . . And I am sure—your letters, the affection in it I am craving for—made me better and are the cause of my present condition."[38]

By the time Emmy wrote this letter, though, Sasha's state had worsened alarmingly. "There were some days when I could not piss at all," he admitted to Emma later. When he finally consulted a specialist in Nice, he was told he needed immediate surgery. He entered the Hôpital Pasteur on February 8. The operation took place three days later, on February 11. Emma, in London, learned of the operation and its successful outcome at the same time. The operation could not wait, Sasha explained. Propped up uncomfortably in his bed at the Hôpital Pasteur, Berkman wrote his "Dearest own Sailor Girl" a long, frank, newsy letter describing his own awkward situation and even joking about life on his ward.[39]

Unwell already, Emmy grew exhausted from caring for Berkman, running back and forth from their flat on Cessole Boulevard to the hospital and trying to keep up Berkman's spirits. "It's terrible about the poor kid," Sasha wrote Emma. "She looks all yellow and worn out. . . . But she comes here smiling and has a pleasant word for every patient. Really, they are all waiting for her to come to visit me." Within a week, Emmy too landed in the hospital for tests. Still, Emma was not to worry, Berkman wrote, adding with his typical understatement, "We are OK."[40]

At this point, Emma might have been expected to cancel her remaining lectures in England and return to Nice, but she did not, finding excuses for staying until her lectures were over. If only they had notified her the day before, she wrote Berkman on February 26, she could have canceled her lectures in South Wales. But now, she was obliged to remain. If she left, she would be considered an "unsafe proposition" and would imperil future engagements.[41] At times, Emma seemed almost to resent Sasha and Emmy's suffering as a personal affront to herself. "I am longing for some relief from the bitter struggle, the everpresent anxiety about Sasha and you," she wrote unkindly to Emmy on February 29.[42] Yet Berkman had waited to inform Emma of the operation until after it was over, when he could report a favorable outcome, as if he did not want her to be present. Moreover, it is likely that Emma was deeply frightened by Sasha's condition. Remaining in England, continuing lectures as usual, may have been a way of denying that anything was seriously wrong. Still, even Emma seemed aware of a certain irony in her absence. "Sasha, dearest, it is a god damned shame that I am always away when you need me most." [43]

By early March the situation in Nice had considerably worsened, despite Berkman's efforts to be cheerful about his condition. Sasha was losing all his fine manners, picking his nose and fiddling with his penis, Emmy reported to Emma on March 13. "I really am shocked, and I prepare you Emma darling that this house has gone down in respect to the niveau [level]. . . . So better be prepared." Emmy too was suffering considerable pain, and wanted Emma present in the event that she too would undergo surgery. [44] "And so you have both become demoralized, using spicy language etc.?" Emma wrote back reassuringly. "That's all right dearie, I will stand it. The main thing will be to get you both well and frisky. I'll do my damndest, you bet." [45] Emma's damndest was desperately needed, for now Emmy too was scheduled for surgery. In a rare direct request, Sasha asked Emma to return. "The ONLY important thing now is that you should be here when the operation takes place," Sasha wrote Emma on March 5 from the flat in Nice where he was recuperating. "Emmy feels that she would have so much more courage and faith if you were here at that time. . . ." [46] Sasha hoped Emma could come the first week in April. He was recovering well, he assured Emma. Anxious about Emmy, he made certain to remind Emma that he wanted her too. "With constant thoughts of you, dearest Em, I embrace you lovingly, as ever the same even if non-pissing S." [47]

Perhaps now thoughts of their own mortality inspired both Emma and Sasha to tell how deeply they cared for one another. In the spring of 1936, as medical reports from Nice remained grave, letters traveled back and forth resonant with expressions of affection and admiration. "Dear you have made a heroic struggle—I mean, all your life has been a heroic struggle, but I am referring particularly to the present tour in England," Sasha wrote on March 18. "Our struggle in the U.S. has never had SUCH handicaps as your present struggle in England. And yet I think you have accomplished wonders. . . . Well, dear heart, I can tell you frankly that I don't know anyone else who could have carried through such a struggle against such terrific odds. I know I could never have done it. . . ." [48] "My dearest old chum," Emma replied, "That was a beautiful letter you wrote me the 18th. Not that I did not know how you feel about my struggle and about my work. But a fellow does sometimes long to hear that one's nearest and dearest realizes the struggle and appreciates one's efforts. I don't much give a damn if outsiders, or our comrades, fail to understand, or to care. I do not even care so much about anybody's opinion, as I do about yours . . . I felt it was almost worthwhile to go through the pain and misery of four months to have you say such lovely things about me." [49] And again Berkman: "Hope things are going a bit satisfactory with you, dear heart. You are the greatest revolutionary fighter that ever lived." [50]

By the time she received this handwritten scrawl, however, Berkman had undergone a second prostate operation, which the doctor insisted could not wait until Emma's return. It is unclear at what point a diagnosis of cancer was made, for they did not speak of it in their letters. Berkman's recovery was slower now, made more difficult by his anxiety about Emmy, who continued to suffer pain, though her surgery was postponed. On returning to Nice, early in April, Emma found Sasha more depressed than she had seen him in many years. [51] He remained in the hospital almost two months, until the middle of May, leaving Emma and Emmy to deal with each other without him. Despite the affectionate letters the two women had exchanged while Emma was in England, when Emma returned to Nice her old antagonism toward Emmy surfaced. In letters to comrades, Emma described Emmy harshly and unjustly, accusing her of dwelling on her stomach problems, and of "fixations about me [which] have become more acute with the years and with her growing illness. She actually imagines I want her out of Sasha's life." [52] This was in fact an accurate assessment of Emma's feeling for Emmy, which Emma herself later partly acknowledged. In early June, she went back to St. Tropez, leaving Emmy and Berkman to fend for themselves. "Fact is dear I left Nice because there was nothing I could do to help your recovery," Emma wrote to Sasha on June 11. "But never hesitate to call me if you or Emmy will need me. Nothing matters to me so much as that." [53] Actually, Emma had already begun making plans to sell Bon Esprit and leave France permanently in the autumn. Once before, in 1892, when Berkman was in another frightening situation, facing fourteen years of imprisonment, Emma had also fantasized flight, making plans to leave the United States although in the end, she had not done so. Now too, when Berkman's survival was clearly precarious, she also resorted to fantasies of escape. Still, she remained for the moment in St. Tropez, while Sasha and Emmy stayed in Nice. As they had before, they wrote letters once again, about the practical details of their lives—whether they should save or destroy their letters, for example—and with the usual blend of affection and reproach.

On June 24, Berkman wrote Emma that he would have to postpone his plans to surprise her with a visit on her birthday three days hence. His wound had once again opened, he reported. "This is 6pm," he wrote, "and I have just gotten up from bed to write you that it will take complete rest for several days before I can move about. It is nothing serious, and it has happened several times already . . . I am sorry I can't come, for it was all arranged and I had meant this surprise for you." [54] She must not worry, he added, for the doctor had checked him the day before and found that I am "all OK." Early in the morning on June 27, Berkman sent off an unusually subdued cable of greeting, advising Emma that both he and Emmy were "feeling some better." In the afternoon he telephoned to wish Emma well. Emma had invited their visiting New York comrade, Dr. Michael Cohn, and his family, for lunch. But her mood was somber. "My dear, whom else should I write on this day but you?" she told Berkman. "Only there is nothing to tell. I keep thinking what a long time to live. For whom? For what? But there is no answer. Useless to rake the brain." [55]

At 2:00 A.M. the next morning, Emma received an urgent telephone call from Nice to "come at once." Without a car, she and Cohn were obliged to wait three-and-a-half hours for the first bus that morning, which arrived in Nice an interminable two-and-a-half hours later. According to Emma's later account, they had rushed to the flat on Cessole Boulevard where they found Emmy Eckstein hysterical and distraught, barely able to tell them what had happened. She explained that the night before, Sasha had suffered a severe relapse and agonizing pain. Desperate to find a doctor, Emmy had left the flat in search of a doctor to bring Sasha to the hospital. Alone in the flat and in excruciating pain, Sasha had resorted to the revolver that a friend, knowing his fondness for revolvers, had recently given him as a present. [56] Possibly suicide had been on Berkman's mind for some time, for he had penned a farewell letter to Emma in March, just before his second operation, reflecting that "I have lived my life and I am really of the opinion that when one has neither health nor means and cannot work for his ideas, it is time to clear out." [57]

The shot perforated his stomach and the lower part of his lungs, leaving him conscious but paralyzed below the waist. Because he covered himself with blankets, Emmy remained unaware of what had happened until the doctor who finally arrived toward dawn found the revolver and notified the police. While Sasha was driven in an ambulance to the hospital, Emmy was hauled off to the police station for questioning. Only the testimony of a neighbor who had seen her, barefoot in her nightgown, distractedly pacing the sidewalk in front of the building waiting for the doctor, cleared her of suspicion.

With Cohn and Emmy, Emma raced to the hospital to find Sasha "fully conscious, but in terrific pain, so that he could not speak." He did however recognize them. At some time, Berkman managed to dictate a note, which Emma wrote down. "I testify that I shot myself last night. No one else is responsible. I did it under pressure of great agony." Sasha somehow managed to sign the note. By late afternoon he had lapsed into a coma. Emmy and Emma remained in the room with him. Emmy later told the writer Kay Boyle that Emma had planted herself next to the bed and tried to shunt Emmy aside. Emma remained until 8:30 P.M., when she left Sasha's bedside, planning to return a few hours later. At 10 P.M. she learned that he had died.

Two days later, on June 30, Emma, Emmy, Michael Cohn, and a few other friends and comrades, including the famous Yiddish writer Scholem Asch, whom Berkman had recently met, held a simple farewell ceremony at the Caucade Cemetery in Nice. Emma arranged for a headstone above Sasha's grave. Later, in public letters to the comrades, she told how she had sat with Sasha's body in the mortuary, in silent contemplation of their friendship and shared struggle. For Emma, the memory of that friendship—"the one treasure I have rescued from my long and bitter struggle"—would endure as the touchstone of her remaining years, a memory that gave meaning and direction to her life.[58]

We should not romanticize this friendship, for there were limits to it, disappointments and deep failures of communication that were painful to both of them. That they could not peaceably live together in the same house, or even in the same city for long, remained a source of unhappiness for both of them. Physical separation was the price of their intimacy, which was often most intensely expressed in letters, written in the absence of the other. Neither one ever acknowledged the strong element of competition and rivalry between them or the anger that led Emma to subtly disparage Berkman in her autobiography and in her letters to comrades, and that may have led Berkman, consciously or unconsciously, to fire his fatal shot on the night of Emma's birthday.

Berkman believed their different ways of thinking all came down to gender. "You and I represent ALL the differences that there are between man and woman as a sex," he once told her, emphasizing their conflicting outlooks so often that she felt he enjoyed disagreeing with her.[59] Fearing her propensity to misinterpret, he never felt able to confide his innermost thoughts to her. As he put it once to a comrade, "Enough to say that a house can be divided against itself: differences of temperament, of basic feeling and viewpoint, etc. In short, a lifelong and true friendship, yet always conscious of the sharp line of division which closes the springs of the inner life." [60]

Within these limits, however, they managed to create a relationship of enduring trust, affection, and respect that lost none of its intensity over a period of forty-seven years. Their friendship took the form of an ongoing conversation, interrupted at moments by sharp differences, yet always resumed. For all their arguments—and these were necessary to them too— each one knew the other would be there to help in emergencies, share scarce financial resources, answer letters promptly, offer reassurance or condolences, or just acknowledge shared feelings of despair, which itself helped to ease the loneliness. As the possibilities for anarchism appeared to recede farther into the distance and their own past achievements seemed ever more elusive, each of them felt more strongly how central was this friendship to both their lives. Emma perhaps felt this more deeply than Sasha, for she, despite her adventurousness, was the more emotionally dependent of the two. Yet Sasha too recognized increasingly in the last years of his life how much he needed and depended on her.

During his last months the reserve of a lifetime melted somewhat, and Berkman became more demonstrative, more willing to tell the "Immutable" Emma how deeply he cared for her, for which she was profoundly grateful. In a letter written a few months before he died, he included a moving reflection that might have been an epitaph for both their lives. "It is the 18th," he wrote—that symbolic anniversary of his liberation from prison back in 1906—"but there is not much to congratulate oneself on, is there dear? Except that after all these years, long and hard years and fearful changes in the world, our old friendship has remained unchanged, and indeed stronger and more understanding and intimate than ever. And THAT is a very great deal." [61]

9

Spain and the World

Poetry,
Forgive me for having helped you understand
you're not made of words alone.

—Roque Dalton

In the strange solitude of a world without Berkman, Emma Goldman struggled to come to terms with the most devastating loss of her life. For a while after the funeral she kept busy disposing of Sasha's estate, which consisted mostly of books and papers. But she felt angry, guilty, and confused, convinced one day that Sasha really had wanted to die, certain the next that he had not, that he had taken his desperate step only because he was left alone at a moment of unendurable pain.[1] She blamed herself for not being there to help. And although she tried not to, she also blamed Emmy. "You will see how miserably I have failed Sasha," she wrote Rudolf and Milly Rocker two weeks after Berkman's death. "There is no excuse whatever for my going away to St. Tropez, except my god damned sensitiveness to the unbearable atmosphere of antagonism that had existed in Sasha's place against me." Emmy too blamed herself for having left Sasha alone, so that Emma found herself trying to console an inconsolable Emmy by telling her Sasha would have died even without the gunshot wound (of uremia, she said).[2]

As Sasha had asked that Emma help take care of Emmy in case of his death, Emma honored that last wish. She allotted Emmy a monthly allowance from her own meager earnings and persuaded several comrades to contribute to Emmy's support (the Jewish Anarchist Federation in New York later pledged $10 monthly). Emma also wrote friends and comrades in the United States urging them to push for a U.S. visa for Emmy and even asked Modest Stein if he would marry her in order to bring her to America, where she had a sister.[3]

At the same time, Emma complained endlessly to her correspondents of

Emmy's supposed hypochondria, her jealousy, and her possessiveness—her "sick heredity" which Emma claimed had poisoned Sasha's last years. Emma's hysterical letters to Stella suggest the depth of her jealousy, which she tried desperately to deny. "You MUST help me my Stella," Emma wrote on August 2, "help me by your understanding, by your belief in what I have so often told and written you. I NEVER BEGRUDGE[D] SASHA'S LIFE WITH EMMY. ON THE CONTRARY I DID EVERYTHING IN MY POWER IN EVERY WAY TO SMOOTH THEIR LIFE. TO KEEP IT FREE FROM MATERIAL ANXIETY. I DID EVERYTHING STELLA. PLEASE UNDERSTAND. But of what use was it? The mistrust continues. The gossip about my cruelty goes on."[4]

Whether this gossip was real or imagined is unclear. Sasha's testimony, Emmy's witty letters and the recollections of other friends, such as the American writer Kay Boyle, do not bear out Goldman's spiteful portrayal of the younger woman. Although Emmy Eckstein was jealous of Emma, and even of Sasha's other women friends, Berkman's letters, particularly in the last years of his life, continually praised Emmy's cheerful, uncomplaining devotion to him, especially remarkable since she herself was in pain much of the time.[5] Perhaps Emma was taking out her unacknowledged anger at Sasha on Emmy; almost certainly her rage at Emmy expressed her sense of hurt and exclusion from their intimacy. With Sasha gone, Emmy now received the full blast of Goldman's fury. Emma kept up her barrage of malice in letters to her many correspondents who knew Emmy mainly through herself and Sasha and also in harsh outpourings to Emmy herself. Though Emma constantly accused Emmy of harboring an obsession with needless operations, in fact the young woman's condition was terminal. After a series of unsuccessful operations, she died in 1939, at the age of 39.[6]

Berkman's death seemed to call into question the meaning of Emma's entire life since she had left America, as if all her achievements, her writing, her respected position in the anarchist movement, had suddenly vanished. "Sasha's going has merely accentuated the futility of it all," she wrote Stella early in August. Emma wanted her niece to know "that my life had been empty for years. It was the thought of Sasha, of his health, of his wellbeing, of his work, that gave meaning to my life. That gone, there is really nothing else."[7] At moments in her grief, Goldman was haunted by the idea that both their lives in exile had been futile. She had periodically suffered such doubts and depression. This time, however, her self-reproaches had a sharper edge, for in Berkman she had lost an essential part of her own identity, a crucial link to her life in America, and also her only real tie with Europe. Her sense of homelessness and hopelessness deepened, leaving her feeling completely adrift. "I ask myself all the time why go on?" she wrote the Rockers. "I have lost all that bound me to the past, to our common work and interest. How can I go on living and why? But I suppose I will, in the fool's belief that I can still do good, still serve Sasha's memory and the idea we both held higher than anything else in life." When Mollie Steimer and Senya Flechine arrived in mid-August in St. Tropez, they found Goldman still distraught. Flechine thought she was on the verge of a nervous breakdown. Years later, he recalled his fright at seeing her late at night, walking alone in the garden at Bon Esprit holding a candle, calling out softly, "Sasha, where are you?" Mollie Steimer concurred that this loss was "really something extraordinary and painful." [8]

Still, Sasha had left Emma the legacy of his own faith in her and the memory of their extraordinary friendship. As she had in 1892, when he went to a "living death" in the Western State Penitentiary and she had felt a responsibility to make him come out alive, now too, she felt a special commitment to live up to his expectations, to prove herself worthy of him and continue the ideas for which he had lived.

By late July, Goldman had recovered sufficiently to follow events in Spain, where a social revolution had suddenly blossomed. Spain had proven fertile ground for the growth of anarchism since its introduction in the 1860s by an Italian follower of Bakunin. [9] In part, traditional Spanish regionalism, with strong loyalties to the *patria chica* and hostility to Castilian centralism, meshed with the anarchist emphasis on small-scale organization and the local community. Anarchist conceptions of collectivized agriculture also found precedents in Spanish communal traditions among peasants in rural villages. But most important, desperate landless agricultural laborers on the vast latifundia of Andalusia and Extremadura were attracted to the apocalyptic promises of anarchism, while impoverished textile workers in Barcelona and miners in the northern provinces of Asturias and Oviedo were drawn into the militant trade unions of the anarcho-syndicalist Confederación Nacional del Trabajo, or CNT, organized in 1910. Members of the FAI, the Federación Anarquista Ibérica, founded in 1927, also joined the CNT. The FAI was a smaller, clandestine organization of militants, some of them professional revolutionaries, who provided a powerful anarchist leavening for the CNT, infusing it with antiparliamentary, revolutionary ideas.

Poverty provided the greatest incentive for the growth of anarchism, especially as the most modest efforts at land reform met intransigent opposition from landowners who, allied with a reactionary church hierarchy, conservative industrialists, and the army, thwarted all attempts at change. Anarchists strongly opposed the church and its monopoly on education, calling instead for secular education in "modern schools" that taught science in place of religion. Spanish anarchism had a strong moral and ethical content, and emphasized egalitarian personal relations, at least in theory. Anarchist women, such as Frederica Montseny, were among the few Spanish women who spoke out for equality between the sexes.

Throughout the 1920s, under the dictatorship of Primo de Rivera, of course both the CNT and the FAI had remained clandestine movements, nearly paralyzed by severe repression. When the dictatorship ended in 1930, these organizations sprang to life. Within a short time the CNT and the UGT, the socialist Unión General de Trabajadores, the other powerful labor confederation, had each attracted nearly a million members. The dictatorship had deepened the polarization of Spanish society into two hostile elements, an increasingly intransigent Right, suspicious of democracy and hostile to reform, and a militant revolutionary Left divided between the CNT and the UGT. In cities such as Barcelona, employers and landowners still hired gunmen to assassinate union leaders and militants; the anarchists, who also had their *pistoleros*, retaliated in kind, although the unrestrained *pistolerismo* of the 1920s had waned.

In February 1931, partly with anarchist votes, a Left-liberal republic came into being, proposing moderate reforms at a cautious rate. The Second Republic soon fell afoul of opposition from both Right and Left. Elements of the Right, attracted by Hitler and Mussolini, sabotaged all efforts at a desperately needed land reform. The anarchist Left began a series of "revolutionary gymnastics" or insurrections, to prepare the ground for an approaching revolution. Trapped between two extremes, the government found itself discredited on all sides. The January 1933 anarchist uprising at Casas Viejas dramatized the government's impotence. To the conservatives, Casas Viejas appeared a symbol of the growing violence and chaos of a republic they despised, while the Left was appalled at the government's brutal response, which hardly differed from that of the dictatorship. Thoroughly disgusted, the anarchists abstained from voting in the elections of November 1933. This time the Right won a massive victory, initiating a two-year period of deepening reaction which was known as the *bienio negro*. Within a month, the anarchists fomented another disastrous uprising, centered mainly in Aragon, which was decisively crushed by the new right-wing regime. A more serious revolt among the miners of Asturias in October of 1934 achieved considerable mass support and lasted two weeks before being quelled in a spectacularly savage operation, which resulted in many deaths, widespread torture, and the taking of over thirty thousand political prisoners. By early 1936, the regime had alienated all sectors of the population, with the Left once again temporarily uniting to elect a left-wing popular front government, again partly with anarchist votes. This government, however, still faced bitter opposition from the extreme Left and Right. In July of 1936, the long-anticipated military revolt began. Unexpectedly, this rebellion met spirited resistance, mainly from working-class trade union members, who defeated the revolt in over half of Spain. The uprising also precipitated the beginnings of a dramatic anarchist social revolution, the first the world had ever known.

From St. Tropez, Emma followed these events closely in the press, and found that they helped to ease the pain of mourning. The resistance of the Spanish anarchists and anarcho-syndicalists to the fascist uprising, she told the Welsh writer John Cowper Powys, a long-time admirer, "has kept me from utter despair." [10] She had been slow to recognize the growth of the revolutionary movement in Spain, which Max Nettlau and Rudolf Rocker had celebrated early on. Though she had a long history of contacts with the Spanish immigrant anarchists in the United States, she had been put off by Spanish paternalism toward women. Her negative impressions had been reinforced when she and Henry Alsberg had made a three-week "dash through Spain" in December of 1928. It was hardly long enough to see the country but sufficient to confirm her earlier impression that Spanish men treated their wives and daughters as inferiors, as "mere breeding machines." [11] She was skeptical of the enthusiasm of both Rocker and Nettlau for the Spanish movement, insisting that she had seen no revolutionary spirit there ("But does one ever see it?" replied Nettlau) and wary of investing too much hope in possibilities that could easily vanish. Yet she was quick to admit that she saw all events in light of Russia, and having had one traumatic "plunge" she did not want another. She acknowledged too that her own isolation and sense of exclusion left her "prone to brood and see things through dark glasses." [12] Indeed, Nettlau's enthusiastic reports had piqued her interest sufficiently that in the autumn and winter of 1932 to 1933, she seriously considered returning to Spain for six months to observe developments there, possibly to write a book. She had dropped that plan in favor of America, but not her interest in Spanish developments, which she continued to follow in the press.

Now, when she was confronted with the reality of an actual revolution in Spain, Goldman dropped all her qualms and embraced it without hesitation. Soon after Berkman's death, she began contemplating the possibility of going to Spain. But she knew no Spanish, and considered her ignorance of the language an insuperable barrier to any useful work.

She had not decided what to do when, on August 21, she received a letter from Augustine Souchy, the German anarcho-syndicalist whom she had met in Moscow, and who had been working for some time in Spain. He invited her to take charge of English-language propaganda for the Spanish anarchists, suggesting she go either to Barcelona or to London to open a press bureau for that purpose. She responded instantly and enthusiastically. She would do whatever was needed, go wherever she could be of greatest help. With each day her excitement mounted, especially when Souchy concurred in her proposal that she travel first to Barcelona to observe events firsthand. Despite her regret, reiterated in every letter, that Berkman had not lived to see these great events, she soon began firing off long letters to Souchy outlining ambitious plans for a large-scale propaganda campaign in England—public meetings, canvassing of trade unions, the Independent Labour party and the intelligentsia—and interrogating him on practical details such as office expenses, secretarial help, credentials, and so on. Suddenly Goldman had a purpose in life. She was "what I have always been, the fighter." She felt like herself again. "Darling, darling, I have not felt so enthusiastic in years," she wrote Stella on September 3. "At last I will be on the scene of revolutionary action. I will be able to live up to Sasha's spirit and to my own longing. It seems almost too good to be true." [13]

At dawn on September 17, 1936, Emma Goldman crossed the border at Port Bou. Although the Spanish guards, CNT members, eyed her suspiciously when she presented her British passport, they embraced her as a comrade when she presented her credentials, whisking her off to the local CNT office to introduce her all around. That day, Emma entered revolutionary Barcelona. Crowds of workers jammed the streets, women as well as men dressed in rough overalls or militia uniforms, with pistols stuck in their belts or rifles slung over their shoulders. The bustling restaurants and cafes bore inscriptions announcing their collectivization. Red or red and black flags with the initials of the revolutionary parties and unions draped the buildings—CNT, FAI, UGT, PSUC, POUM.[14] Commandeered cars and trams, buses and taxis, gleamed red and black. Tanks headed for the front sported the letters of the party or trade union to which they belonged. "Waiters and shop-walkers looked you in the face and treated you as an equal," reported George Orwell in *Homage to Catalonia*. "Nobody said 'Señor' or 'Don' or even 'Usted'; everyone called everyone else 'Comrade' and 'Thou' [tú] and said '¡salud!' instead of 'Buenos Días.'" Down the Ramblas, the beautiful central boulevard of the city, people streamed day and night, with revolutionary songs blasting from loudspeakers. Despite the tensions and privations of the war, "there was a belief in the revolution and the future," recalled Orwell, "a feeling of having suddenly emerged into an era of equality and freedom. Human beings were trying to behave as human beings and not as cogs in the capitalist machine." [15]

The revolution that erupted in the Republican zone, especially in parts of Aragon, Catalonia, and the Levante (in the northeast and along the eastern coast of Spain), transformed social life more profoundly in certain respects than even the early stages of the Russian Revolution. Where the fascist uprising was quickly defeated—in about half of Spain—workers organized revolutionary workers' committees and councils to coordinate civilian and military operations. The committees were led by members of the CNT and the UGT, which also directed the collectivization of the principal industries and trades. In Barcelona, where the revolution struck deepest, not only the large, foreign-owned industries and utilities such as textiles, metallurgy, trams, and the telephone exchange were expropriated, but smaller operations—barbershops, taxis, restaurants, hotels—were also taken over by their employees, who proceeded to run them with remarkable efficiency. A system of socialized medicine was introduced by libertarian doctors, dentists, nurses, and other health workers. The trade unions and political parties mobilized militias, which in anarcho-syndicalist Barcelona were organized voluntarily and democratically, without distinctions of rank or pay. Despite widespread terrorism in the early weeks of the revolution, directed mainly against the church and against supporters of the Right, the violence was gradually brought under control; destruction of property was fairly limited. For two months workers in the trade unions virtually controlled Barcelona, the greatest experiment in worker self-management the world had ever seen.

In many parts of the countryside too, collectivization proceeded rapidly, as landless laborers and in some cases small proprietors organized collectives under the leadership of militants from the UGT and the CNT, taking over large and medium-sized estates that were often abandoned by their owners. Scholars have estimated that between one-half and two-thirds of all the cultivated land behind Republican lines was expropriated, collectivization proceeding farthest in Aragon, where perhaps 450 collectives were established. In all, rural collectivization embraced between 400,000 and three million people.[16] The collectives varied greatly, both in the way they were organized, and also in the extent to which they were formed voluntarily, since rural smallholders were far less likely to accept collectivization than the landless braceros who welcomed the process. The results varied too. In some regions, the disorganization that accompanied collectivization lowered production of crucial crops, such as Valencia oranges, disrupting sources of foreign currency.[17] But in many areas, the collectives meant an immediate improvement both in living conditions and in productivity, as new agricultural machinery was introduced, unemployment was eliminated, and members built schools and medical clinics. The collectives distributed resources equally throughout the community, in some cases abolishing money entirely and substituting barter or local vouchers.

For women, especially, both the war and the revolution meant astonishing changes, as women took over men's jobs in the factories and offices, and even joined the militias at the front. Although the male anarcho-syndicalists, and even many women, were not free of the traditional sexual attitudes that pervaded Spanish society generally, and often expected their women to play supportive, subordinate roles, some female militants sought to expand women's roles. In 1936, a group of anarchist university women who published an important magazine, *Mujeres Libres* (emancipated women), formed an organization with the same name, which by 1938 had attracted some twenty thousand members throughout Republican Spain. Dedicated to helping women participate fully within the anarchist movement, Mujeres Libres also worked to foster women's entry into the labor force, to protect the rights of women workers, and to create institutions—such as schools, day care centers, and medical clinics offering free abortion—responsive to women's needs. However incomplete the changes, many women experienced them as an explosion of absolute freedom. According to one militant, "at that time, to be a woman, to be young, was the ultimate."[18]

Long before the outbreak of the war had precipitated the social revolution, however, the growing power of the revolutionary Left in Spain had aroused alarm in statesmen abroad who greatly feared the spread of "Bolshevism," even more than the prospect of a general European war. The events of July 1936 greatly intensified that fear. By the time Emma Goldman arrived in Barcelona, a Non-Intervention Committee had been formed in London, representing all the major European powers. The committee purportedly aimed to guard against outside aid to either side in the war. In reality, Britain and France offered little resistance to massive German and Italian military assistance to the insurgents, while at the same time they rigidly enforced "neutrality" laws that prohibited the sale of arms to the Republic—the legitimately elected government of Spain. Britain's substantial mining and agricultural investments in Spain, as well as its Mediterranean strategic interests, inclined the Tory government to a stance of tacit support for Franco.[19] France, under the Popular Front government of Leon Blum, feared provoking its own powerful right-wing opposition, as well as disrupting relations with Britain. In the United States too, the Roosevelt administration, pressured by isolationist sentiment and by a powerful pro-Franco Catholic lobby, would pass neutrality legislation in January of 1937 that effectively denied all aid to the Republic. Increasingly isolated by Western policies of "malevolent neutrality"—policies that decisively favored Franco—the Republic would soon find itself growing ever more dependent for assistance on the Soviet Union, the only country apart from Mexico that was willing to send arms and advisers.

Soviet aid had not yet begun when Goldman arrived in Barcelona in mid-September, exhilarated by the euphoric atmosphere of the city and by the warmth of her welcome. She quickly installed herself at the foreign propaganda department of the CNT, in a Babel of assorted languages.[20] She felt right at home, even "reborn," as if "walking on air," she wrote later. Never before had she felt so welcomed and appreciated as she did among her Spanish comrades and the other revolutionary exiles working with them. She liked the men with whom she would work—the Spaniard Diego Abad de Santillán, soon to become minister of economy in the Catalan government, in whose home she would stay; the Germans Helmut Rüdiger and Souchy and the Dutch comrade Arthur Lehning, all of whom worked in the foreign propaganda section; the Lithuanian Martin Gudell, her guide and translator; and the Italian militant Camillo Berneri, a former professor at the University of Florence, publisher in Barcelona of a weekly, *Guerra di Classe,* and one of the most outspoken critics of CNT-FAI policy.

Emma threw herself into the work at hand. Between daily visits to see the collectivized industries—railroad, tram, and aviation yards, gas works, textile factories and telephone exchange—she spoke regularly on the radio (English-language broadcasts, which she later learned could not be heard outside Barcelona); she helped prepare the English edition of the weekly *CNT-FAI Information Bulletin;* she took charge of all mail in English. On the radio and at several mass meetings of workers and students that she addressed, she praised the constructive work she had observed everywhere, "nothing destroyed or demolished, not a nail moved in factories, work shops or in the former luxurious houses." Privately, Emma admitted that "excesses" had occurred. But she denied the orgy of atrocities alleged by the press, and emphasized the restraint exercised by workers oppressed during centuries of exploitation.[21]

In October and November, Emma made frequent forays out into the Spanish countryside. She visited the Huesca and the Aragon fronts, where she conferred with the charismatic Buenaventura Durruti; she sat in the trenches in Madrid, within hearing of fascist fire. With Augustine Souchy, she made a longer journey by car, traveling to various agricultural collectives in Catalonia, the Levante, and in Aragon. Goldman found the Spanish peasants more intelligent and attractive than the Russians.[22] She praised a collectivized champagne vineyard, amazed at the good order that prevailed among workers. In the collectivized village of Albalate de Cinca, in the province of Huesca, she admired the tolerance of the peasants who used example, not force, to persuade the "individualists" to join their collective. She especially praised the enthusiasm and knowledge of the young people who wanted to build hospitals, schools, libraries, and museums. "Every youngster without exception was by far better read and better versed in social ideology than many of the young people in the large cities outside of Spain," she reported.[23] The Dutch comrade, Arthur Lehning, who also traveled with Goldman, later recalled their visit to a small collectivized village not far from the city of Valencia where the peasants had abolished money. All exchange was through barter, and goods were distributed on the basis of need. Emma asked, if someone wanted to go to Valencia by bus, how would he manage? The CNT delegate replied that in such cases they had money set aside. "But how do they get the money?" Emma persisted. "There is a committee that decides whether to provide it," was the answer. "Oh," said Emma, only half-joking, "then that is not for me."[24]

Emma was especially anxious to see how the Spanish anarchists dealt with their prisoners. She was eager to see an alternative to the harsh practices she had witnessed in Russia. In an account of his observations in Spain, *Ceux de Barcelone,* the journalist H. E. Kaminski described how he and Goldman, in the autumn of 1936, visited a CNT-FAI prison located in the suburbs of Barcelona in a villa formerly belonging to a marquis. He and Goldman interviewed the police guards who then invited them inside where they talked freely to about twenty prisoners, all evidently supporters of the Right. The men had no complaints and said they were well treated. "Emma Goldman is happy as if after a victorious battle," Kaminski reported, "and we return to the hotel gay like children who have received a present." [25]

Despite her extensive travels, there is little question that Goldman acquired a limited, romantic picture of the Spanish Revolution. Impressed by the efficient workings of individual agricultural collectives and socialized industries, she had little grasp of their relation to the overall economic picture. Dependent mainly upon guides and translators, all of them CNT-FAI members, she had no contacts with critics of the anarchists, and a limited exposure to regions where the anarchists did not predominate. Still, her knowledge of anarchist Spain made her a valuable witness, since so few of those writing about the war had any comprehension of the anarchists whatsoever. [26]

By the beginning of October, Goldman had begun to worry. Several events contributed to her alarm. In the first place, despite the predominance of the unions and the revolutionary committees during the early months of the war, state power had not been crushed, only momentarily disarmed. In a crucial meeting with the president of the Generalitat (the autonomous Catalan government), shortly after the military uprising in Barcelona was defeated, the leading militants of the CNT-FAI had decided not to assume power themselves in Catalonia, tacitly agreeing to the survival of the Catalan government, which had now begun to regain its prerogatives. Invited to participate in this government, in late September several militants of the CNT-FAI accepted positions within it. They defended this decision, which went against the fundamental anarchist commitment to abstention from all governments, as preferable to taking power themselves, which they believed meant exercising an anarchist "dictatorship," and as preferable to remaining outside the centers of decision making. (Goldman, too, consistently defended the anarchists' decision not to assume power.)

A few days later, the Republican government at Madrid decreed the for-

mation of a conventional Popular Army to replace the democratically organized militias that had sprung up in the early days of the rebellion, a move
that further shifted power away from the anarchists and toward the central government. In early November, four CNT-FAI members, including
Frederica Montseny, the "Lenin in skirts," as Emma called her, became
ministers in the central government in Madrid (which immediately moved
to Valencia), a decision marking the effective transfer of power from the
revolutionary committees and councils to the bourgeois Republic.[27]

Goldman watched these developments with mounting apprehension. In
a long letter marked "not for publication" to Mark Mratchny, a Russian
anarchist émigré in New York, now editor of the *Freye Arbeter Stimme*,
she warned that "there are a number of things that seem incongruous and
incompatible with the spirit and the traditions of the CNT, and even more
so of the FAI." All was "not well or reconciliable with what I have
worked for all my life."[28] She confided to Rudolf Rocker, who had replaced Berkman as her closest confidant, that she felt "very puzzled and
grieved at moments" at certain decisions that seemed contrary "to the
marvelous spirit of the comrades and their libertarian determination. Oh, I
wish you were here to help me see as I want to see this tremendous upheaval and how it can be safeguarded from pitfalls."[29]

Most alarming, in Goldman's view, was the behavior of the Socialists
and especially the Communists, who were "already throwing stones between the feet of the CNT-FAI." Emma warned that "the most dangerous
enemy will yet raise his ugly head and that he will not rest until our people
are destroyed."[30] Although she criticized the decision of the CNT-FAI
leaders to enter government ministries, she worried far more about the
growing role of the Communists in Spain, especially since their power was
greatly enhanced by Soviet assistance, which began arriving in mid-
October. With France, Britain, and the United States all adhering to a
nonintervention pact while Germany and Italy rushed weapons and troops
to Franco, Russia, as the only major power willing to help the Republic,
inevitably acquired a tremendous prestige and influence: the small Spanish
Communist party jumped from a few thousand members before the war to
an estimated 200,000 by early 1937.[31]

The arrival of Russian aid initiated sharp changes in the antifascist sectors. The Russians did not want a revolution in Spain, especially not a
revolution led by anarchists. Faced with Hitler's growing power, Stalin
was determined not to alienate his antifascist alliance with France, or to
imperil relations with Britain, which held significant mining and metal-

lurgical interests in Spain. The Communists argued that while London and Paris might support a democratic Spanish Republic, they would never come to the aid of a revolutionary one; it was necessary to postpone any "premature" revolutionary advance that might threaten the possibility of foreign aid. They further argued that to win the war, it was necessary to build the broadest possible antifascist alliance, which meant securing the cooperation of the antifascist bourgeoisie who would fight Franco but in no way support a social revolution.[32] Finally, the Communists insisted that only a unified, disciplined military effort, not the loosely organized militias, could hope to overcome the vast military power of the Nationalists.[33]

These arguments had considerable justification. As the historian Paul Preston has written, many of the policies advocated by Stalin and pursued by the Largo Caballero government were based on a realistic assessment of the attitudes of the great powers. The Communists grasped the decisive nature of the military problem as the anarchists and Socialists had not done.[34] Nor was there any reason to expect that the international labor movement, divided between fiercely anti-Communist Socialists on one side and Stalinists on the other, would mobilize in support of a libertarian revolution in Spain. Indeed, Goldman herself acknowledged early in the war that the international trade union movement was "organized into a veritable fortress against everything the C.N.T.-F.A.I. stands for." Moreover, the anarchists did not dominate loyalist Spain; a determined revolutionary policy risked separating Catalonia and Aragon from the rest of the country and perhaps fatally weakening the Republic from within.[35]

What these arguments overlooked, of course, was the question of morale. The initial successes of the armed workers in defeating the military uprising in July owed much to the enthusiasm born of fighting for a social revolution, for the building of a new world. Many militants, not only anarchists but also members of the dissident Marxist POUM, argued that the revolution could not be separated from the war; only the dedication and élan that the revolution inspired in the Spanish workers could hope to overcome the superior military force of the fascists; it was necessary to advance the social revolution in order to advance the war.[36]

Soviet aid, however, gave the Communists tremendous leverage, rapidly turning them into the arbiters of Republican policy. As they increased their power, they steadily pressed the government of Largo Caballero for a reversal of the dramatic social revolution that had taken place. Sensitive to the charges of the Western democracies about "Bolshevism" in Spain, and anxious to persuade France and Britain to drop their arms embargo, the Communists steadily denied that any revolution had occurred, portraying the struggle as a war of democracy against fascism.[37] Increasingly, the Spanish Communist party became a refuge for nonrevolutionary elements, such as peasant proprietors, bureaucrats, professionals, and shopkeepers, who feared the militance of the workers and landless laborers. In the peculiar circumstances of the Spanish civil war, the Communists came to represent the right wing of the Popular Front coalition, a refuge from revolution. "To save Spain from Marxism, vote Communist," ran a popular slogan.[38]

Goldman worried now, with good reason, that the Spanish Communists, with the backing of the Russians, would annihilate the anarchists in Spain just as the Bolsheviks had in Russia. Despite her great admiration for the freedom that she found in revolutionary Barcelona, she was prepared to accept certain limits. She thought the CNT-FAI in Barcelona were too tolerant of the Communists—"this villainous gang" she called them—who were "sabotaging right and left." She felt that this "sabotage" on the part of the Communists and also Socialists in and out of Spain must be exposed.[39] In mid-October, she included an ominous warning in an address to a mass meeting of FAI youth in Barcelona. Praising their "wonderful achievement," she urged young militants not to ignore the fact that "your enemies are still lurking in the dark. Not only your fascist enemies. There are others. . . . All those who talk of the necessity of new governments, of new rulers, are making ready to forge new chains for your enslavement. They are trying, consciously or unconsciously, to lead your glorious Revolution into channels that will inevitably end in a new form of dictatorship . . . you must make ready," she urged, "to fight on every front that is threatening the Revolution in Spain."[40]

As the days passed, however, and the fighting centered on Madrid, Goldman began to feel helpless, increasingly frustrated by her inability to speak Spanish and her dependence on translators. The growing cooperation of anarchists and Communists felt to her like "a denial of our comrades in Stalin's concentration camps." At moments she felt unhappy in Barcelona, which appeared to her "like all government cities, very difficult to bear, cold and callous."[41] To see huge portraits of Stalin paraded in the streets of Barcelona on the anniversary of the October revolution aroused in her a kind of nausea; she considered that day as one of mourning. As she grew more depressed, her grief over Berkman's death returned; "Just now the wound does not heal," she wrote Stella sadly on December 8.[42]

The prospect of traveling to London chilled Goldman even more. But by December, it was evident that the anarchists could expect little help from the Russians, the only source of weapons from abroad. Soviet arms went mainly to Communist-controlled troops around besieged Madrid while the largely anarchist columns at the Aragon front received almost nothing. Denied weapons, the anarchist militias could not advance, yet they found themselves attacked on all sides as unwilling to fight. Exaggerated stories of anarchist "uncontrollables," of anarchist inefficiency, disorganization, cowardice, and even criminality circulated regularly in the left-wing foreign press, whose correspondents, ignorant of Spanish anarchism, generally denied any legitimacy to the anarchist viewpoint and increasingly ignored the anarchists altogether. A publicity campaign abroad was desperately needed to counter all the lies.

In the third week of December 1936, Goldman returned, exhausted, to London. She moved into a room in the flat of an old comrade, Liza Kodolfsky, and set up an office at 18 Castelton Road, in West Kensington, along with a reading room and library of materials about the CNT-FAI. Within a few weeks, she had also organized a CNT-FAI London Committee, consisting of herself and a handful of comrades, some of them associated with the temporarily defunct monthly, *Freedom*. With a distinguished group of intellectuals and theater people, she also organized a Committee to Aid Homeless Spanish Women and Children, which held several fund-raising concerts and exhibits.[43]

In Britain, as in Spain, she faced a divided political landscape. Following the lead of the Tory government, the London press generally described the Spanish conflict as "rebels" versus "rabble" who were portrayed as marauding, church-burning, atheistic "Reds." According to the editor of the influential leftist journal the *New Statesman and Nation,* the Spanish civil war "was commonly presented in the British press as if the Reds were the Rebels and the Fascists the defenders of legality. . . . Even reputable papers talked as if Franco were the head of a government, and hundreds of thousands of readers were persuaded that the fight in Spain was the result of a Bolshevist uprising."[44] British popular opinion, however, leaned strongly toward the Republic (as did that of the United States, despite the official "neutrality" of the Roosevelt administration). But this sympathy was split in ways that reflected internal divisions within the British Left. Rank and file opinion within the Labour party and the Trade Union Congress strongly favored the Loyalists and called for action against British nonintervention. The more conservative, strongly anti-Communist leadership acted to constrain this sympathy from finding active expression. "The mass feeling pulled in one direction whilst those who grasped the levers of the machine tugged in the other," writes one historian of the period, adding that "the policies of both the National Government and the Labour leadership in relation to Fascism were to a considerable extent determined by their anti-Communism." The Labour leaders were seriously handicapped, "like boxers with one hand tied behind their backs—always their anti-Communist strategy was dominant in their thoughts."[45]

Goldman realized that her best hope for a campaign on behalf of the CNT-FAI lay with the Independent Labour party, the ILP, disaffiliated from the Labour party in 1932, and now vaguely Trotskyist in outlook. By the mid-1930s, the ILP had shrunk to a party made up mostly of intellectuals, cut off from contacts in the trade unions, the heart of Labour strength. It steadily lost ground to the more militant and decisive Communists, whose membership was growing, partly on account of the party's vigorous anti-fascism.[46] Still, the ILP—which Emma considered "the most revolutionary party in England today"—had resources not enjoyed by the British anarchists, including several members in Parliament, a bookshop in central London, and a weekly paper, the *New Leader*. Moreover, cooperation with the ILP did not exclude work with the few active British anarchists who remained, however, isolated and internally divided. And indeed, CNT members urged Emma to work with the ILP in London in the same way they worked in Barcelona with the POUM: "nous collaborons, mais nous ne nous confondons" (we collaborate, but we do not unite).[47]

With Labour dissipating energies in internal quarrels, individual Communists and labor leaders spearheaded the mobilization on behalf of the Spanish Republic, focusing mainly on humanitarian aid. By the time Emma arrived in London, the Spanish aid compaign was well under way, with hundreds of committees all over Britain working to raise money, donate food and clothing, and press for the lifting of the arms embargo.[48] Little, if any, of this aid, however, reached the hands of the CNT-FAI or Catalonia, for that matter. Sent to the Republican government, it went mainly to Madrid, to troops controlled increasingly by the Communists, and to civilian populations in areas where the Communists and Socialists predominated. The largely CNT-FAI troops on the Aragon front received almost nothing, nor did the population in Barcelona, despite the steady flow of hungry, homeless refugees from other areas of Spain into Catalonia. Although anarchist groups in the United States raised money and sent supplies to libertarian Spain, the meager resources of this tiny, fragmented movement constituted a mere trickle of aid. Nor could they compete with the vastly greater resources of the Communists abroad, who channeled much larger amounts of assistance to their Spanish counterparts. Emma Goldman too worked to raise money for her beleaguered comrades. But most of all she wanted to counter the scurrilous portrayals of the Spanish anarchists in the British and American press. By publicizing the revolution, she hoped to awaken the enthusiasm of workers abroad so that they would undertake direct industrial action—strikes and boycotts—against Western policies of nonintervention.

From the start, Emma's position in England as accredited representative of the CNT-FAI was an anomalous one. In the first place, her mission of publicizing the Spanish Revolution ran directly counter to the official press policy of the Republic, which was, after the first few months when news about the revolution did appear in the foreign press, to stress the moderate nature of the Spanish government and to deny that any social revolution had taken place. Goldman argued the reverse. It was almost as if Emma represented an independent state, as "ambassadress for Catalonia" as one wag put it, or rather, for the CNT-FAI, carrying out a foreign press policy distinct from, and opposed to, that of Valencia.[49]

Second, the decision of the Spanish anarchists to enter the Popular Front government had precipitated severe conflict within the movement outside Spain. Instead of finding support from the few militants she could mobilize in England, France, and Holland, Emma found herself confronting a bitterly divided movement. Rather than a center for solidarity with the CNT-FAI, the Paris office of the Syndicalist International (IWMA)—which acted as meeting place for the various national anarchist federations—became the arena for constant wrangling between those who favored collaboration, and those opposed, among whom the Russian émigré anarchists were the most outspoken. Even in London, Goldman was criticized for defending the "reformist" line of the CNT-FAI.

Third, Emma had few contacts within the British labor movement, or with the Left outside the tiny anarchist circles. Her previous anti-Soviet campaign in England had alienated many of the radical intellectuals who, by the mid-1930s, had become increasingly influenced by Marxism. Their sympathies were closer to the Communists who represented the clearest opposition to fascism, in England as well as on the Continent.

The most serious obstacle to Goldman's campaign, however, was the absence of a significant anarchist movement in England, and a powerful

British prejudice against anarchism generally. After the defeat of the 1926 General Strike, perhaps two to three hundred militants remained, scattered in small groups in Norwich, Bristol, South Wales, and Glasgow, with a tiny handful of individuals in London, mostly active in the unemployed movement, and mostly unemployed themselves.[50] Emma tried to start an Anarcho-Syndicalist Union in London, holding weekly meetings and discussions that sometimes drew a fair-sized crowd. But according to her own account, the ASU never attracted more than about twenty actual members, most of them out of work and without connections to the labor movement.[51] Her attitude toward her comrades did not help, for she could be impatient and somewhat imperious, and she approached the campaign in England as if she expected defeat. "Dear comrades," she wrote in an anarchist paper, "here I am in the country where I have always felt completely lost and where I have never succeeded in reaching people."[52] It was not a promising beginning.

Nonetheless, she managed to launch a series of public meetings on Spain in January and February of 1937, which proved amazingly successful, in terms of publicity, attendance, and funds raised. She also spoke outside London, traveling to South Wales, Plymouth, Bristol, and Glasgow in order to create local committees to work for the CNT-FAI. Throughout the war, her meetings attracted large, enthusiastic crowds of seven or eight hundred people. If Emma herself was often dissatisfied, it may have been because she compared this attendance with that of her huge prewar meetings in America. By British standards they were notably successful.[53] By the end of February 1937, she had raised £175—the equivalent of about $5,000 at that time—for women and children evacuated from Madrid (many of whom ended up in Barcelona), with nearly £100 more a few weeks later.[54]

Since it was difficult, and sometimes impossible, to present the anarchist viewpoint in the mainstream press, Goldman attached great importance to *Spain and the World,* a fortnightly anarchist paper launched in November of 1936 by a twenty-two-year-old engineering student. Vernon Richards, publisher and editor of the paper, was the son of an Italian immigrant anarchist and companion of Marie-Louise Berneri, the daughter of Camillo Berneri. Richards proved to be a dedicated publisher and editor, later the author of an influential critique of anarchist policy in Spain and a mainstay of the London anarchist publishing house, the Freedom Press. *Spain and the World,* with a circulation of around 2,000, made available information about anarchist Spain difficult to secure anywhere else in English. Emma herself wrote often for the paper, persuaded the CNT-FAI in Spain to support it financially, and recruited other writers for its pages.

Despite their shared commitment, Richards and Goldman never developed a cordial relationship, although Emma respected his work as an editor. But she found him cold and inhospitable, while he found her vain, intolerant, and dictatorial.[55] She had better relations with people such as Fenner Brockway, the ILP General Secretary, who became one of her most reliable allies and admirers, and especially with Ethel Mannin, whom she persuaded to appear often with her at meetings on Spain, despite Mannin's extreme shyness on stage. Emma also became friendly with the distinguished poet and art critic, Herbert Read, who considered himself a philosophical anarchist. Read aided Goldman in a variety of ways. He helped raise money, contributed funds himself, wrote articles and reviews for *Spain and the World,* and helped recruit other writers as well. She made an enduring impression on him, for he later described her as "one of the most dynamic personalities that I have ever encountered."[56] Emma later told Read that he and Ethel Mannin were the only two "real comrades and friends" she had made during her entire three-year stay in London.[57]

Goldman had barely established herself in London when the anarchist position in Spain dramatically worsened. Over the next few months, the Communists in Spain strengthened their control, even though the Soviet presence in Spain remained relatively small throughout the war: not more than about seven hundred Russians were actually in Spain at any one time; at most, two to three thousand Russians passed through Spain during the war, mainly specialists, tank crews, and fliers, with a few diplomats, all under the supervision of agents of the Russian political police, or NKVD.[58] But the Republic's reliance on Soviet arms gave them a tremendous influence over Republican policy; as historian Douglas Little has observed, the British and American arms embargoes ironically ensured the very thing they were designed to prevent.[59] Moreover, the crack Communist-led Fifth Regiment, and the International Brigades—made up of non-Russian antifascists recruited largely by Communist parties abroad—further enhanced the prestige of the party.

The Russians and the Spanish Communists made no secret of their opposition to anything that might imperil a broad united front of workers and other social strata in Spain or endanger Soviet relations with France and Britain. Nor did they hide their opposition to the anarchists and especially to the POUM, which they falsely denounced as a Trotskyist organization in the service of Franco. As an anti-Stalinist Marxist party with considerable influence in Catalonia, the POUM represented a serious challenge to the Communists, and therefore was especially targeted for destruction. The escalating terror inside Russia, with mass arrests and executions and the big political trials of the Old Bolsheviks beginning in August 1936, further substantiated the fears of both anarchists and the POUM of a bloodbath in Republican Spain.[60]

Mounting tensions finally erupted in the tragic May Days of 1937, triggered by the attempt of the Catalan government to take over the previously CNT-controlled telephone exchange in Barcelona. The move was part of the intensified campaign of the Popular Front government to centralize control under a unified command. When this effort provoked armed resistance, despite efforts of the CNT leaders to stop the fighting, the Valencia government, under pressure from the Communists, launched an all-out attack against the CNT-FAI and the POUM in the streets of Barcelona. Hundreds of militants were killed; over a thousand were arrested and thrown into prison; several leaders, including Camillo Berneri and POUM leader Andreu Nin, were murdered, evidently by Stalinist agents.[61] The left-wing Socialist premier, Largo Caballero, who had increasingly resisted Communist control, was removed. A new government was formed, headed by the pro-Communist Juan Negrín. The four anarchist ministers were also removed from the government (the POUM members had already been expelled) and arrests and repression intensified, aimed not at enemies of the Spanish Republic, but at critics of the Soviet Union and of the Communists, enemies defined, principally, as "Trotskyists" of the POUM and anarchist "uncontrollables." At the same time, Communist-led military divisions were sent into Aragon to break up the agricultural collectives. Collectivized lands were returned to their former owners, local CNT militants and organizers of the collectives were arrested and sometimes shot, although the devastating effect on the harvest compelled officials to halt the assault, at least temporarily, and many collectives reconstituted themselves. But the CNT-FAI, which had once dominated the scene in Catalonia, Aragon, and the Levante, had suffered defeat.[62]

Even before the May Days, Goldman had begun to complain of Communist "sabotage," not only in Spain but also in England. First there was the matter of the Spanish Exhibition Committee. With Fenner Brockway, Ellen Wilkinson, a Labour MP, and others involved with Spanish aid,

Goldman had helped organize a traveling exhibition of photographs documenting the war and the revolution in Catalonia. Part of the proceeds would go to the CNT-FAI. Although the exhibit was highly praised in London and in the provinces where it later toured, Emma soon began to complain to Stella Ballantine of the "rotten undercurrent of antagonism against me and the CNT-FAI" in the committee, which she blamed on the "Moscow gang." She said she had to "hold on to myself with iron will not to tell the outfit to go to hell."[63] In letters to friends, Goldman began to portray her struggle less as a battle against fascism than against the Communists, not only in Spain but also in England, since they controlled most of the Spanish aid committees and solidly opposed the CNT-FAI.[64] Even the ILP, staunchly anti-Stalinist, were "Marxians, after all." She did not trust them. As for the Labour party and the Trades Union Congress, they too opposed the CNT-FAI. According to Emma, none of the press, not even the liberal *Manchester Guardian* or the *Daily Herald,* would discuss the anarchists fairly. The anarchists in Spain were terribly naïve, "simply children" in their estimate of the European Left.[65]

After the May Days, her dilemmas deepened. Grieved and outraged, Emma now fought to get a reasonably accurate account of the Barcelona events into British and American newspapers. The liberal press, however, balked at publishing information critical of the Republican government, both from ignorance and from considerations of strategy. George Orwell, who had witnessed the May Days, later observed that "the accounts of the Barcelona riots in May . . . beat everything I have ever seen for lying."[66] Influenced by official Republican propaganda, which was carefully censored, British and American newspapers, especially the liberal and Left press, generally portrayed the May Days as a "revolt" by anarchist "uncontrollables" and the "Trotskyite" POUM who had instigated the uprising, fomenting disunity and disarray behind Republican lines in ways which, whether deliberate or not, played into fascist hands.[67]

Journalists who suggested a different interpretation of events, for example George Orwell and Josephine Herbst, found that their reports were rejected. Much of the Left press appeared to follow the lead of Louis Fischer, the *Nation*'s correspondent in Spain who got his information direct from the Russian ambassador and later, from Juan Negrín, the premier whom he admired as much as he scorned the anarchists. It was Fischer who first reported many of the charges that became part of the antianarchist, anti-Catalonian litany: that the anarchists ran away from battle, hoarded weapons in Barcelona, withheld munitions from Madrid, and were infiltrated with fascists.[68]

Pro-Loyalist editors, of course, reacted against the pro-Franco, anti-Communist position of much of the British and American press. They believed that emphasis on the repulsive sides of the Republican government would only strengthen support for the British and American arms embargo. In this war, all press coverage inevitably functioned as propaganda for one side or the other, and those who favored the Loyalists feared adding ammunition to the well-supplied fascists.[69] The result, however, was reporting that was unusually distorted. As Goldman put it, almost all the liberal and Left papers, not only a party organ like *Daily Worker,* but the London *Daily Herald* and the *News Chronicle,* not to mention conservative papers like the *New York Times* and the *Times* of London were "full of lies about our people." A few dissenting voices on the Left presented more truthful accounts. Liston Oak in the *New Statesman and Nation* and Bertram Wolfe in the *Nation,* George Orwell in the *New Leader, Time and Tide,* and the *New English Weekly,* all criticized the conventional view of the May Days. They offered a more complex picture of Spanish events, though they were not always favorable to the anarchists.[70] These voices, however, remained relatively isolated.

Goldman now began directing her assaults ever more sharply against "the murderous Stalin gang" in England as well as in Spain. In January of 1937, she had published an article in *Spanish Revolution* claiming that while fascism was bad, "the enemy within" was "worse by far." In her view, the United Front in Spain was "daily proving a graver danger than Fascism itself."[71] Her next assault was an article on "The Soviet Political Machine" for the June 4 issue of *Spain and the World.* In this article, her most outspoken attack to date, she compared Russia under Lenin—when "there was still a semblance of fair play"—to Russia under Stalin, a man "determined to exterminate everybody who has looked into his cards." The May events in Spain had proven "that the Soviet political grinding machine does not only do its deadly work in Russia, but in all other countries as well." She painted a grim picture of a Republican Spain where some two thousand "Communists" were allegedly arriving each week, and where the Soviets were arming Spanish Communists for eventual takeover of the country, though Goldman still predicted an eventual anarchist triumph. Other readers might well have drawn different conclusions.[72]

These articles, with their misleading insinuation of a vast Soviet presence in Spain, implied that a Republican victory would simply install Stalinism: a conclusion even Goldman rejected. But by now, her anger seems to have extended almost indiscriminately to all parties to the Spanish conflict, including the anarchists inside and outside of Spain. She was dismayed by the conciliatory position, during the May Days, taken by the Spanish anarchist leaders in Barcelona—who had urged their fellow militants to put down their arms rather than risk a bloodbath in an effort at resistance. She was also angry at critics of the CNT-FAI within the international anarchist movement, whom she felt failed to comprehend the actual dangers of the war. The Russian émigré anarchists in Paris and others associated with the IWMA had long kept up a barrage of criticism against the CNT-FAI for its policy of collaborating with the Republican government. Their attacks in the movement press were especially painful for Goldman because many of the most outspoken critics were close friends, such as Mollie Steimer and Senya Flechine, the Russian exile Voline, and the IWMA secretary Alexander Shapiro, who had fled Russia with Goldman and Berkman in 1921. In addition, antimilitarist anarchists in Holland condemned the use of arms by the Spaniards, though they also provided humanitarian aid, and some American comrades threatened also to open a campaign against "betrayals" by the CNT-FAI leaders. To make things worse, Emma's longtime correspondent Max Nettlau had become a 100 percent partisan of the CNT-FAI, bitterly attacking the anarchist critics—"the sandfleas who produce little papers in Holland or who produce nothing at all in Toronto."[73] Nettlau also criticized Emma herself for expressing any reservations at all about CNT-FAI strategy.

Goldman might well have ignored such "loving" criticism, saving her energies for more constructive work, as her comrades in Barcelona advised. Yet, coming from close friends such as Mollie Steimer, she found it difficult to ignore, especially since she partially agreed with it.[74] In answering Steimer and other critics, Goldman attempted to work out her own position with regard to CNT-FAI policies that she really opposed. In the end, she based her arguments on a strong sense of emotional solidarity with her Spanish comrades, despite her tactical disagreement with them. "Well, I still hold that the [Spanish] comrades made the blunder of their lives to go into the united front," she wrote Steimer. "But here is the difference. . . . You are now sitting in judgment on our people who are daily facing danger, and who are surrounded by enemies on every side." To her great credit, Goldman did not lose sight—at least not for long—of the constructive achievements of the Spanish anarchist movement. The Spaniards, she told Steimer, were "a different breed. . . . Anarchism to them was never a cold and grey theory for a lot of misfits who come to us in every country. . . . Besides, lets not deceive ourselves, we have no movement worthy of the name in any other country . . . Spain alone has built up a magnificent movement, Spain alone has brought about the Social Revolution. Spain alone is making a magnificent constructive effort. I do not care what the comrades think of the wrong steps the CNT-FAI have made . . . deplorable as they are, they are yet insignificant [compared with] the scope and grandeur of the work they are doing and of the example they are setting the whole world." [75]

To quell her own doubts, Goldman was eager to return to Spain. [76] In late September 1937, she arrived in Barcelona, where she remained for two months. Once again she found herself swept up by the grandeur of the Spanish epic. "The more I see and hear the more amazing I find my comrades," she wrote Ethel Mannin, "their frailties and their strength. An amazing people these Spanish are, they completely baffle me and fill me with awe and wonder." [77] The revolution, she found, was "far from lost." Despite government efforts to dismantle the collectives in Aragon and part of Catalonia, she had found them "keeping up as if no harm had come to them"; they were "in better-organized condition and in better working order" than before. [78] She affirmed repeatedly that, despite the military assault on the Aragon collectives, many were still functioning. [79] She was relieved to find that even if the "Moscow gangsters" had gained the upper hand, they had little popular support, and were, in her view, "hated more intensely than the Fascists." [80] She was convinced more than ever that only the arms embargo on Republican Spain had compelled the Spanish comrades to make compromises with the government; had the anti-Franco forces been able to purchase arms abroad, Stalin would never have gained the upper hand in Spain.

But Goldman was disturbed by the escalating persecutions within antifascist Spain, especially as the trials of the Old Bolsheviks had begun in Moscow. Over the summer of 1937, a political police, the Servicio de Investigación Militar, was established in Spain. Ostensibly created to ferret out Fifth Column Francoist activity, the SIM increasingly came under the control of Russian advisers and the Spanish Communist party, which used it to eliminate enemies of the Communist party rather than the Spanish Republic. Members of the POUM were victims of the most savage repression, but many anarchists, including organizers of the rural collectives, were also arrested and imprisoned. Some were shot or "disappeared." Goldman estimated later that there were some 2,500 antifascist prisoners in Republican jails, whose "crimes" no one could quite explain. [81]

Emma found her own position increasingly difficult. She relied for advice on Rudolf Rocker, whom she had elevated to the position of her most trusted confidant after the death of Alexander Berkman, and who shared her stance of critical solidarity. Rocker was probably instrumental in keeping her from pushing her criticism too far. But he was far away in the United States, and not so prompt a correspondent as Berkman. It was a measure of Emma's isolation in London, and of the anarchists' isolation outside of Spain, that Emma now felt herself so deeply alone, as if the burden of defending the CNT-FAI fell entirely on her shoulders. Without the ongoing dialogue with Berkman, she felt increasingly uncertain about how to respond to new developments in Spain. She pursued a confused and contradictory course, now ardently defending the Spanish comrades, now criticizing their "naïveté" (even in the *New York Times,* which needed no convincing), now minimizing the evils of the Republic in comparison with the potential catastrophe of a Nationalist victory, now denouncing the Republic as a Stalinist dictatorship. At one moment she argued that "democracy" was only another name for fascism, at another moment she insisted that fascism was much the worse, that one could at least "breathe" in a democratic republic. She would concede the necessity of common action with the Communists, and then denounce cooperation with Communists as a betrayal. To those who criticized CNT-FAI strategy, she offered a passionate defense; to those who defended them, she offered criticism. She lurched from crisis to crisis, ever on the verge of resigning as representative of the CNT-FAI, yet more than ever committed by ties of loyalty and solidarity. In Spain, close to the bombs and the barricades, the urgency of the struggle against fascism overwhelmed all other considerations. In London or in Paris, she was swayed by the criticisms of the purists.

At moments Emma began to doubt again whether there could be an anarchist revolution. "By its very violent nature Revolution denies everything Anarchism stands for," she wrote a friend. "The individual ceases to exist, all his rights and liberties go under. In fact life itself becomes cheap and dehumanized . . . Spain has again proven that nothing remains of Anarchism when one is forced to make concessions that undermine the ideal one has struggled for all one's life. You see my dear I do not feel very happy in my shoes." [82]

Toward the end of 1937, Goldman's conflicting loyalties came to the test. Mariano Vázquez, the young Secretary-General of the CNT-FAI, asked Goldman to attend a December meeting in Paris of the IWMA, in order to defend the position of the CNT-FAI to the critical comrades outside Spain. Goldman felt deeply unhappy at the prospect, knowing that the meeting would be bitter and hating to become involved in movement "squabbles." Her apprehensions were well-founded, particularly since the Spanish comrades also chose that moment to ask that the IWMA call on their longtime enemies—the Socialist Second International and the Communist Third International, both hostile to anarchism—for a common stand against fascism.[83]

In her plea to the IWMA to support the CNT-FAI, Goldman acknowledged the legitimacy of arguments raised by the critics. She noted also the extent to which these critics—many of them émigré Russian anarchists—had been so deeply traumatized by their experience with the Bolsheviks that they could not think beyond it. Those who had most strongly defended the Bolsheviks in 1917–21, Emma noted, "who had explained every step of the dictatorship as 'revolutionary necessity' are now the most unyielding opponents of the CNT-FAI." Having learned their "lesson" from Russia, they were determined not to repeat it. As Goldman suggested, however, the experience in Russia had also blinded them to the differences in the Spanish situation. Even more than the Russian Bolsheviks, the Spanish anarchists had found themselves completely isolated, abandoned even by the international proletariat, which had given some support to the Russian Revolution. There was no organized anarchist movement anywhere in the world except in Spain and, to a much smaller degree, in Sweden. The Spaniards found themselves facing, not just Spanish fascists, but Germans and Italians equipped with modern weaponry, planes, and tanks. These could not be met with bare hands and untrained militias which, in the face of such assault, "proved very inadequate indeed." This was Goldman's first admission that the anarchist militias had been less than satisfactory. "My contact with our comrades at the various fronts during my first visit in 1936 convinced me that some training was certainly needed if our militias were not to be sacrificed like newborn children on the altar of war." Goldman argued too that "once we realised that it would be impossible to meet hordes of Fascists armed to the very teeth, we could not escape the next step, which was militarisation." These actions, like so many others of the CNT "were not of their making or choosing. They were imposed upon them by the development of the struggle. . . ."[84]

Finally, however, these considerations were secondary to the fundamental political problem of how to "awaken the international proletariat to come to the rescue of the anti-fascist struggle in Spain; and unless we can create unity among ourselves, I do not see how we can call upon the workers of the world to unite in their efforts to conquer Fascism and to rescue the Spanish revolution." Emphasizing the constructive achievements of the Spanish comrades, the fact that they were "the first, not only in Spain but in the whole world, to repulse Fascism," stressing her conviction that they will eventually "return to first principles" if fascism could be conquered, Goldman ended with an emotional plea. "Comrades, the CNT-FAI are in a burning house; the flames are shooting up through every crevice, coming nearer and nearer to scorch our comrades. At this crucial moment, and with but few people trying to help save our people from the consuming flame, it seems to me a breach of solidarity to pour the acid of your criticism on their burned flesh. As for myself, I cannot join you in this."[85]

Despite her eloquent appeal, Emma returned to London depressed. She was not sure she had convinced the "critics." She had not even convinced herself, for her talk had drawn heavily on Vázquez's arguments and even on his language, which she had often disputed.[86] In letters to Stella Ballantine, Rudolf Rocker, and others, she complained that her Spanish comrades had "become insane with the obsession that they, more than anybody else, must hang on to the anti-Fascist front even if their so-called allies are doing everything in their power to smash it, have in fact smashed it." The price, she felt, was already too great.

In fact, Emma Goldman and the CNT-FAI were close to a break, not over anarchist concessions to the Republican government, but over how far she could go in publicly criticizing the Communists. Even before she went to Paris, she had published another outspoken article in the December 10 issue of *Spain and the World* on "Political Persecution in Republican Spain." In this article, Emma described her discovery of "thousands of our comrades" in the prisons of Barcelona and Valencia—1,500 in Valencia's Model Prison alone—with no charges against them, in most cases, except "the idiotic charge of 'Trotskism' [sic]." "I soon discovered the same situation repeated in every town and village I visited. Thousands of comrades and other genuine revolutionaries were filling the prisons under the Negrin-Prieto and Stalinist regime." Goldman ended her indictment with a call to prominent European intellectuals "who would surely protest if made aware of the political persecutions rampant under the Negrín, Prieto and Communist regime."[87]

The articles immediately provoked a pointed response from Barcelona, from Mariano Vázquez, and from Pedro Herrera, on behalf of the Peninsular Committee of the FAI, asking that she tone down her public criticism of the Republican government and the Communists. It was "not appropriate or convenient" to speak a great deal abroad about these persecutions, they warned, since such talk discouraged support from abroad and "is very damaging for us. The international proletariat asks: 'Why should we aid anti-fascist Spain if its government undertakes innumerable persecutions and its actions are much worse than that of any other bourgeois government?' "

> We believe, dear comrade, that you must reflect on this question. We believe also that it is not necessary to speak constantly of the repression exercised by our government and of many events which are occurring in Spain. One may say something, but from time to time. You must recall that surrounding the war in Spain are many interests and intervening powers who follow their own point of view. For this reason it is necessary to reflect deeply and examine the pro and the con before saying something which could be damaging for our cause. . . . It is above all in England where we are obliged to make our propaganda with a great deal of tact.[88]

Tact, however, had never been Goldman's strong point, and she showed little signs of developing it now. But she was hurt by this letter, so much so that she had to draft her reply three times before she was able to send it. Written just a few weeks after her speech at the meeting of the IWMA in Paris, it presented a far more pessimistic picture of her findings in Spain on her second visit, stressing the destruction wrought by the Negrín regime on the Spanish Revolution, and pointing out that the anti-Stalinist Left abroad had already begun to criticize the repressive role of the Communists in Spain.

Emma insisted that "the only way to rekindle the enthusiasm of the workers in every land for your struggle and your aims is to unmask the lying face of Stalin and his followers and to let the world see it in all its hideous nakedness. Whether you agree with it or not, it's being done by many people outside of our own ranks. It is really impossible to escape the growing indignation in revolutionary ranks against the undermining effect of Soviet rule."[89]

Actually, the repression of revolutionaries was not well-known outside Spain due to Republican censorship and self-censorship by the Left press abroad, which feared damaging the Loyalist cause. Although Goldman complained repeatedly in her letters from London that she was constantly confronted with questions about Communist persecution in Republican Spain, there is evidence that such questions may often have come from the Right, and that Goldman did not always distinguish between fascist and communist hecklers. In his memoir, Albert Meltzer, then a young member of the movement, told of inviting Goldman to address a meeting in South London. Suddenly she faced hostile shrieks from someone in the audience shouting that she should go back to Russia.

> "So," she cried. "This is typical Stalinist perfidy. When a Russian is prepared to bow down to Stalin, he is worshipped. But when a Russian is against Stalin, they cry out, down with the Russians, send them back to Russia! And why do they want Emma Goldman in Russia? Because when they get her there they will kill her!" This was a most effective reply, wires crossed or not, which silenced the lot (except Ethel Mannin, who was in the chair, and whispered across frantically, "He's a Fascist, not a Communist," as if it mattered.[90]

Emma continued her work for the CNT-FAI in London in the early months of 1938, renting new offices at 21 Frith Street, off Shaftsbury Avenue, in central London this time. She mounted exhibitions of Catalan children's drawings and of lace work by refugee women. She organized a second "musical evening," which turned out a "flop," according to Emma, yielding only £40 (20 percent of which went to the ILP) after three months of work.[91] She made certain the anarchists were represented at the annual May Day celebrations in Hyde Park, and spoke herself at Speakers' Corner. Emma and Rose Pesotta, who was visiting her and planned to travel to Spain herself, now came up with a new proposal to foster direct contacts between the Spanish revolutionary workers and rank and file trade unionists in England. If only British workers could actually see for themselves the collectivized industries and villages, they might overcome their hostility to anarchism and be moved to some form of direct action for Spain. But this plan, which might have been useful in the early months of the war, came too late to put into practice. With few contacts in the labor movement, Emma was limited to mailing circulars to trade union branches and locals, explaining the structure of the CNT-FAI and offering to provide further information. She received a few encouraging responses, but nothing came of the plan.[92]

Emma also tried, without much success, to organize a British branch of a new "apolitical" organization, Solidaridad Internacional Anti-Fascista, or SIA, which had been started in Spain by Frederica Montseny to raise funds for humanitarian relief, especially for Catalonia. Goldman managed to put together yet another distinguished roster for the letterhead of SIA, including George Orwell (who was surprised to learn of his inclusion), Havelock Ellis, Rebecca West, Laurence Housman, and John Cowper Powys. But these were mostly supporters on paper. Apart from Ralph Barr, a hard-working militant who was one of the mainstays of the CNT-FAI office, only Ethel Mannin really became active. Mannin agreed to serve as the treasurer (Goldman was secretary) and worked hard in this position, evidently succeeding in efforts to place fund-raising appeals in the British press where Goldman had failed.

By the spring of 1938, the eyes of the world were turning east toward Germany. Hitler occupied Austria in March, and began his move toward Czechoslovakia, whose dismemberment British Prime Minister Neville Chamberlain officially accepted at Munich in September. The war against the Jews escalated, as a new spate of anti-Semitic laws were enacted. With the approach of another European war, international interest in Spain began to decline. In the summer of 1938, Russian shipments of weapons fell off as the Soviet Union gradually withdrew support for the Republic. Now, in letter after letter, Emma Goldman complained of the failure of her efforts in England. Though she attended the Emergency Conference on Spain in April of 1938, at which all the major Spanish aid groups in Britain were represented, she came away with the sense that the majority of delegates were merely using Spain as a device for advancing the Popular Front at home.[93] And then the news from Spain was "so crushing I don't remember one thing from another," she wrote Rudolf Rocker in early April. "I am at the very pitch of nervous excitement and it is only sheer force of will that I keep going at all."[94]

Adding to Emma's distress was the news from New York that her beloved Stella had been hospitalized for severe depression. Relations between these two women were sometimes difficult, and Stella often suffered from the feeling of being overshadowed by her famous family—first as niece of a famous aunt, then as sister of a distinguished editor, Saxe Commins, later as mother of a noted son, the publisher Ian Ballantine. Her husband too, E. J. Ballantine, was a respected actor. In Emma's presence Stella sometimes felt prey to an "inferiority complex," as she put it, and even to the feeling that Emma did not love her, a feeling that may have been a sign of her developing illness. But if Emma could be insensitive to her niece's vulnerabilities, and often made heavy demands on her, she did love Stella and depend on her emotionally, as well as in practical ways. Stella's illness distressed her deeply, for she spoke of it in almost all her letters to close friends and took an active interest in her niece's treatment. Although Emma regarded Stella as her "child," in fact Stella had also played a caretaking role toward Emma; her illness meant that Emma lost yet another of her emotional supports just when she most needed them.

In this setting of political and personal crisis, Emma Goldman tried hard to restrain the anarchist critics who kept up their barrage of attacks on the CNT-FAI, but she herself chafed at having to hold back her criticisms, not so much of the CNT-FAI, but of the Soviet and Communist role in Spain. "It is exactly the same as when Sasha and I began to expose the doings in Russia," she complained. "Then too some of our comrades . . . charged me with injuring the Russian Revolution. Our Spanish comrades are now doing the same." She was willing to go a long way with them, she continued. "But being gagged as far as the dreadful Stalin regime is concerned and all the truly harrowing things the Communists have and are doing in Spain. No, I cannot submit to that."[95]

By the summer of 1938, Emma was desperate to leave England, "this dreadful country" that was "more fascist than the fascists." She began planning her return to Canada, to agitate for Spain in a country where she was better known. But first she wanted to go back to Spain, to confront her comrades there directly, before deciding her own course of action. In late August of 1938, she departed for Barcelona, where she remained seven weeks. Nationalist troops had already reached the Mediterranean, cutting off Catalonia from the rest of Republican Spain. The battle of the Ebro was in full swing, temporarily delaying Franco's victory by a few weeks. Emma found herself buoyed once again by the revitalizing Spanish atmosphere. The revolution, she reported, was far from vanquished.

But now the Spanish Libertarian Movement (encompassing the CNT-FAI and also the Libertarian Youth) appeared close to a split. Goldman attended a stormy National Plenary of Regional Committees of the Spanish Libertarian Movement, held in Barcelona October 16–30. At these meetings, conflicts between "collaborationists" and "abstentionists" burst into the open. On one side, Mariano Vázquez of the CNT defended the cooperation of the CNT-FAI with the Popular Front government as a tactical necessity. He argued further in favor of continued resistance even against overwhelming military odds, on the grounds that a prolonged war might merge with the outbreak of a general European war in which the democracies would be compelled to intervene against Franco. On the other side, Pedro Herrera and others of the FAI demanded a return to classic anarchist principles of abstaining from any cooperation with the state, accusing Vázquez and other CNT militants of opportunism and abandoning basic principles.

Emma Goldman's sympathies clearly were with those of the FAI who demanded a return to classic principles, but her attitude was tempered by a fear of the growing threat to Catalonia.[96] In any event, the position of the National Committee of the CNT, defending the policy of collaboration, was supported by almost all the attending delegations, precipitating divisions that were to continue within the Spanish anarchist movement even in exile. On this occasion, Emma did not speak out, although privately she evidently expressed her agreement with the FAI. For all the outrage in her letters regarding anarchist relations with the Communists, she hesitated to give advice on internal matters; even when asked, she often declined to give an opinion, feeling that "now is not the time."[97]

The question of political persecution continued, however, to preoccupy her, especially after she attended the trial that month in Barcelona of POUM leaders accused of collaboration with the fascists on the basis of blatantly manufactured "evidence." Emma held no brief for the POUM. She regarded them as essentially similar to other Communists, despite their anti-Stalinist position. She claimed that during the May Days the POUM tried to use the CNT to seize government power; if successful they would have annihilated the CNT-FAI just as Trotsky destroyed the Russian anarchists.[98] But now she, like CNT-FAI members such as Frederica Montseny, defended the innocence of the accused POUM members, who were eventually acquitted.

Emma continued to protest to Vázquez about anti-Fascist prisoners in Republican jails, but neither he nor the usually reassuring Martin Gudell wished to pursue the issue as Fascist troops approached Barcelona. Returning wearily to London at the end of October 1938, she resumed her work, but with renewed fear of what lay ahead. The lease on the Frith Street office was due for renewal; Emma herself reported to her Spanish comrades that she did not think her achievement in London merited keeping the office. She had suspected ever since her conflicts with Mariano Vázquez had erupted early in 1938 that he wanted to withdraw her mandate as representative of the CNT-FAI in London, although Martin

Gudell and others assured her that this was not the case. In December of 1938, however, Gudell informed Goldman that the CNT-FAI had decided to close the London office. Since Emma herself had recommended this course, it is unlikely that the decision signified an effort to dissociate her from the organizations.[99]

On December 27, just a few days after Franco launched his final offensive against Catalonia, Goldman traveled to Amsterdam. She went to organize the papers of Alexander Berkman, which she had given to the International Institute for Social History. Intending to spend two weeks, she spent four, arranging and sorting the letters, diaries, and manuscripts, in preparation for her departure for Canada. That Goldman chose this moment, when the fall of Barcelona was almost certain, to immerse herself in private affairs, suggests a capacity for distance and detachment that her emotional rhetoric seemed to belie. But it is possible also that her flight to Amsterdam expressed an effort to assert control over her life in the only realm where it was possible to do so, at a moment when everything else was so out of control. Sorting out the papers of Berkman's life was a way of trying to bring order into what must have seemed the chaos of her own. Also, in light of the approaching general European war and the fact that she was nearing seventy, she must have known that she would never return to Europe. It was as if the death of the Spanish Revolution and the imminent defeat of the Republic turned her thoughts once again toward her most cherished friend, whose loss she had never ceased to mourn. Her sojourn in Amsterdam—for here she read many of his letters and diaries for the first time—was a last ritual of farewell to her beloved Berkman, and to an era of her life that was gone forever.

By the time Emma Goldman returned to London, Barcelona had surrendered. Though she had insisted in her letters that Barcelona, like Madrid, would achieve a miracle and manage to resist, Nationalist troops marched into the city almost unopposed while thousands of militants fled across the border to France. There is little question, as Goldman herself would argue, that the demoralization caused by the sabotage of the social revolution as well as the exhaustion of nearly three years of war, and the lack of food and water during the final days, contributed to the collapse. Yet ultimately, it was the overwhelming superiority of Nationalist manpower and arms which determined the final outcome.[100]

Now, from the bare, filthy, freezing concentration camps at the French border, Emma received heart-wrenching reports. Here Spanish refugees seeking asylum were herded behind barbed wire, as if they were escaped felons rather than fighters for freedom. Mariano Vázquez of the CNT, Lucía Sánchez Saornil of the SIA, Pedro Herrera, and others wrote from Paris describing the Catalonian collapse, and the desperate conditions on both sides of the border. Diego Abad de Santillán, to whom Emma had been especially close, sent her a bitter analysis of events, which she essentially adopted as her own. "Catalonia was not conquered, but betrayed, sold!" he wrote. "There was no contact with the enemy—therefore one cannot talk of a military defeat, but of a political debacle. . . . The people had grown weary of a war that was not their war." [101]

The Spanish defeat gave renewed urgency to Emma's plan to leave for Canada where she might work to gain asylum for the Spanish exiles and raise money to help them settle in new lands. She spent her last months in England trying to persuade Ethel Mannin, who had suddenly turned pacifist, to take over as head of the London SIA in order to continue fundraising efforts. As she prepared to sail for Canada, carrying credentials both from the IWMA and from the SIA for her work, she became involved in a bitter dialogue with Mariano Vázquez. Even as the Spanish militants poured over the border into France, she and Vázquez exchanged angry letters about the causes of the Catalonian collapse. Goldman was convinced the Communists were to blame. She wanted Vázquez to tell her "of the real forces that compelled you and the other comrades of the CNT-FAI to give up the defense of Barcelona . . . I fear that it was the Negrín Communist allies of yours who have played you false." Goldman's letter could hardly have been comforting to Vázquez, since it tacitly blamed the defeat on the anarchists themselves. "You once told Martin [Gudell] that I was always suspicious or afraid of your allies," she wrote. "Already when I was in Barcelona last [autumn] I had a feeling that in the crucial moment you of the CNT will be betrayed and left to your own devices." She continued: "I fear it was your own sterling honesty and your childlike belief in the need of working with the government which brought about the final debacle. Please do not take offense. It is my deep interest and my abiding faith in you which makes me tell you frankly that you were duped by the miserable Negrín and Communist gang who hated the CNT-FAI as much as the Fascists." [102]

Vázquez, of course, did not agree. Writing from Paris on February 21, he spelled out what was essentially the Popular Front position, insisting that "once again I must repeat what I have told you before: that here nobody has betrayed anybody. What has happened all along is that circumstances imposed what every time was contrary to our wishes. The circumstances, my dear friend, were the lack of arms brought about by the attitude of the Democracies. The fact is that one country alone cannot fight against the whole world. . . ." Vázquez insisted that the war had not been lost because of "those compromises to which you and some other comrades always refer. It was rather the opposite. We did not compromise enough but were too revolutionary, thereby frightening world capitalism." Revolutions, he continued, could never take place in countries like Spain "while there does not exist a world-wide proletarian solidarity and a revolutionary consciousness capable of preventing the enemy from swallowing us." [103] If Spain had concentrated on a Republic instead of a revolution, the democracies might have come to their aid. "Precisely what was needed was not to make the revolution before winning the war." Vázquez emphasized now the importance of outside help from the international proletariat if a revolution is to be won. "You recognize that I am right in my assertion that the Revolution cannot triumph in any country," he wrote, "if it is not backed by the solidarity of the proletariat. That is precisely the whole point and towards this end it is necessary to devise a way whereby no more isolated revolutions are attempted so that we may avoid sterile sacrifices. We must be capable of preparing conditions so that at least it will break out in two or three countries at once." [104]

Both Goldman and Vázquez, in different ways, took a partial view of the war. Goldman tended to view events from a Catalonian perspective, seeing the war as it appeared in Barcelona: a battle between Communists and anarchists behind Republican lines. From this vantage point she blamed the defeat mainly on the Communists' political machinations and their efforts to reverse the revolution. She tended to ignore and distort the international context, and the military situation outside of Catalonia. Mariano Vázquez blamed the Western democracies, whose failure to aid the Republic had made the Soviet Union into an arbiter of Spanish policy, and imposed what he felt were unavoidable limits on the anarchists. Vázquez overlooked the devastating lowering of morale—the greatest resource of the Spanish revolutionaries—caused by the rolling back of the revolution and by the tactics of the Communists. [105]

In the end, Goldman's own anti-Communism prevented her from recognizing the extent to which anti-Communism had contributed to the abandonment of the Spanish Republic by the democracies, and had hindered efforts in Britain, France, and the United States to channel a widely felt sympathy into effective action. A deep dread of left-wing revolution, whether anarchist or Communist, weighed heavily in the shaping of Western policy in Spain.[106] Moreover, far from alienating workers or leftists abroad, as Goldman claimed, Stalin's role in Spain, however inadequate and self-interested, and even sordid, had aroused enthusiasm for Russia abroad and delayed the disillusionment with Moscow that the purges and trials were beginning to engender in the Left. As Ethel Mannin pointed out, it was simply not true, as Emma claimed, that the workers and intellectuals had been apathetic toward the Spanish war, for this war had inspired a massive, grass roots international aid campaign; it would remain an emotional focal point for the Left for years to come.[107]

In this connection it is worth recalling the words of George Orwell in "Looking Back on the Spanish War," published in 1943. Writing just a few years after *Homage to Catalonia,* Orwell now saw the Communists and the Spanish Republic in a larger context. "The broad picture of the war which the Spanish Government presented to the world was not untruthful," he wrote. "The main issues were what it said they were. But as for the Fascists and their backers, how could they come even as near to the truth as that? . . . Their version of the war was pure fantasy. . . ." For all his criticisms of the Republican side, Orwell left no doubt about his sympathies. "In essence it was a class war," he wrote. "If it had been won, the cause of the common people everywhere would have been strengthened. It was lost, and the dividend-drawers all over the world rubbed their hands. That was the real issue; all else was froth on its surface."[108]

In the tremendously complex circumstances of the Spanish civil war, Emma Goldman never developed a clear strategy on behalf of the Spanish anarchists nor an analysis of Spanish events. Whereas earlier she had celebrated the mass, leaderless aspect of the Spanish Revolution, she now saw this as its greatest weakness. As she put it to Milly Rocker in April of 1939, "In a measure we are paying for our belief that the masses as such can bring about fundamental change. There never was a more proletarian revolution than the Spanish one, but there was a terrible poverty in great minds and strength of character. That was the real tragedy of Spain."[109] She planned to write a book on Spain mainly to expose the "dastardly acts" of the Communists and the "truly Judas part Stalin has played."

But Goldman's limitations as a propagandist and analyst were not hers alone. They were also those of the anarchist movement, and it is clear that nothing Goldman could have done would have changed the outcome in Spain, or modified British foreign policy. Nothing could have overcome the international isolation of the Spanish anarchists, which was due to the absence of any comparable movement abroad and the international hostility toward the anarchists, within the labor movement and the Left. Spain had dramatized the tensions between ethical and political aims which lay at the heart of the anarchist project, illuminating its great creative strengths and also the weaknesses of an anti-political movement suddenly confronted with the possibilities of power.[110]

Emma Goldman's solidarity finally counted more for the Spanish anarchists than her liabilities. She had never before worked within a mass organization nor occupied a position in which she was carrying out policy formulated by others. Although she always insisted she was following a discipline she imposed on herself, she found that discipline very difficult. In the Spanish campaign, she worked against internal, psychological resistances as well as political obstacles. That she was able to cooperate for so long with the CNT-FAI was testimony to the depth of her commitment. She never ceased defending the Spanish revolutionaries who had shown the practical, constructive possibilities of anarchism, and in her view, had given "the first example in history how Revolutions should be made."[111]

Emma Goldman said later that the Spanish Revolution and civil war had influenced her more profoundly even than her experience in Russia. Seeing anarchism as a living reality all around her, she felt her entire life vindicated. And then she had been made to feel wanted in ways she had never known before. "In all my life I have not met with such warm hospitality, comradeship and solidarity," she wrote of her Spanish comrades. "I know no other people who beat them."[112] On her seventieth birthday, Mariano Vázquez, with whom she had had so many bitter arguments, sent her a cable from Paris, on behalf of the Spanish Libertarian Movement, expressing their appreciation of her struggle on their behalf. "You have understood us and our aim as few who came to our shores have understood us," he wrote. "For this, among many other reasons, you have become part of us, never to be forgotten." He declared Emma "our spiritual mother," a guide and inspiration for the future.[113]

Goldman was deeply moved by this tribute—"the most beautiful tribute I have ever received"—and sent copies to all her friends. "Call it vanity if you will," she wrote one comrade who thought her gesture boastful. "I call it ordinary human longing for kindred spirits, for kindness to one whose whole life has been damned little glory but lots of misunderstanding and disappointment."[114] With all the bitter tragedy of this war, Spain had helped to heal a wound within her, not only the loss of Berkman, the loss of faith she experienced in Russia, or even the losses entailed by her deportation, but a deeper loss, the long loneliness that had haunted her all her life. She would still complain of feeling isolated, cut off and out of place, still suffered "under deep depressions." But gradually a new equanimity entered her letters. Physically she felt better than she had in years.

Even in defeat, the Spanish anarchists gave to Emma Goldman what she had been seeking for so long—a vision of heroism, a sense of belonging. In Spain, for a brief transcendent moment, she knew at last what it meant to come home.[115]

10

Last Exile

In March of 1939, Goldman prepared to depart for Montreal. She arranged for Ethel Mannin to take over the SIA. Late in March she traveled to Paris, where she found "sickening disintegration among the comrades." Not only was "everybody against the other to the extent of threatening their lives, but the hatred, jealousies and greed rampant among the refugees smells to the heavens. . . ."[1] After ten days in Paris, she was relieved to sail. On April 8, she boarded the *Alaunia* at Le Havre, en route to Montreal. Exhausted and grieving, Goldman found the trip exhilarating, as if, for a few days at least, she could throw off the weight of history. She had found a "remarkable first novel" in the ship's library and spent all day out on deck reading. The novel was *Gone with the Wind*.[2]

Goldman arrived quietly in Montreal, somewhat disappointed by the absence of fanfare. In Toronto, however, comrades and admirers as well as the press and photographers turned out to greet her. She immediately arranged to give a few lectures in English and in Yiddish on the subject of Spain. After years of feeling "choked up" when speaking before British audiences, unable to free herself from the fear "that I would be treading on people's toes," Emma found she was finally able to relax "and my voice rang out free and strong as in the olden days. You cannot imagine my liberated sensation."[3]

Pleased by the warmth of her reception and by offers from several comrades for her to live with them, Goldman opted for her own small apartment in the home of two Dutch comrades—"the main thing is the feeling of freedom and independence," she admitted. Later another comrade, Dorothy Rogers, also joined the household. Soon friends were receiving the familiar Emma Goldman letterhead stationery, this time with her new address at 295 Vaughan Road, on a quiet, shaded street in Toronto. She enjoyed visits with her family, who came up from New York. June 27, her

seventieth birthday, brought an avalanche of cards and cables—forty-five
cables and wires from France, Holland, Sweden, and every important
town in America, she reported proudly, like a child showing off her presents. Not only her "immediate comrades," but many Jewish labor organizations and friends had sent greetings. Her friend Esther Laddon had a
garden party for her, while the Italian, Jewish, and English anarchist
groups in Toronto had arranged a special dinner. Friends told her she
looked better than she had five years before. By a tragic irony, late on the
afternoon of her birthday, Goldman received a cable that Mariano Vázquez was dead. After surviving the battles of the civil war, he had drowned
while swimming in a river near Paris on an outing with friends.[4]

Still, over the summer of 1939, Emma grew more detached from the
Spanish situation. She used her other "birthday"—August 15, the date
when she entered the movement fifty years earlier—to organize a series of
dinners to create an Emma Goldman Spanish Refugee Rescue Fund. She
planned a six-week lecture tour through western Canada for November,
that attracted reasonably large audiences and was successful, she re-
marked "from a moral point of view." She felt that there was indeed "a
field" for her. She approached Benjamin Huebsch of Viking Press about
the possibility of a book about Spain. She corresponded with her former
lover, Ben Reitman, continuing to rehash old quarrels and grievances.

Over all these activities, in the summer of 1939, the approaching European war cast long shadows. Goldman was not, and had never been, a
pacifist. In 1938 and early 1939, she argued with British and Dutch pacifists and antimilitarists, insisting on the necessity for armed resistance in
Spain, underlining the differences between democracy and fascism, even
allowing that Kropotkin may have been correct in opposing Germany during World War I.[5] She responded vehemently when Ethel Mannin turned
pacifist and claimed no difference between fascism and capitalism. "Dearest you keep saying the Spanish struggle has become a mere struggle for
anti-Fascism," she wrote Ethel in January of 1939. "Even if it were true,
which I have already stated it is not, there would be nothing wrong in
it. . . . Anti-Fascism to the Spanish people means the chance to continue
their revolutionary constructive work. They have never lost sight of that.
For well they know that while under democracy they will also have enemies to fight it will still be possible to do it. Under Fascism all chances
will be lost for many years to come."[6]

Still, it is doubtful that Goldman ever really contemplated supporting
the Allies in the approaching war against Hitler. Mannin's pacifist argu-

ments alarmed her because she feared Ethel would withdraw from the SIA, and she wanted Mannin to remain as its British head. Two weeks later Goldman wrote an American friend, Lillian Mendelsohn, in quite a different vein, insisting that "war has never settled anything. It is only if the people within a country rise to their stature and break their chains that war can be at all justified, but never an imperialist war—of that I am certain, and I am definitely decided to stand out against it no matter what the consequences."[7] Goldman maintained this position until the end of her life. Even to Ethel, in March of 1939, Emma reported that "much as I loathe Hitler, Mussolini, Stalin and Franco I would not support a war against them and for the democracies which, in the last analysis, are only Fascist in disguise. If I have supported civil war in Spain it was only because the social revolution was at stake. . . ."[8]

It is likely that Goldman's bitterness at the defeat of Loyalist Spain strengthened her antiwar position at this time. The failure of England and France to aid Spain's struggle against fascism undoubtedly made her less sympathetic to them now that they faced the same threat. The Stalin-Hitler Pact in August of 1939 added to her disgust, though she could not help admitting a certain *schadenfreude* in seeing the two dictatorships allied (which she had evidently predicted nearly six years earlier).[9] In her letters of October and November of 1939, Goldman continued to insist that another war would not end Hitlerism, and that wars settled nothing.[10] She assured Herbert Read, in early October of 1939, that "my attitude in re the war is exactly the same as it was in 1917." Certainly she opposed Nazism; but the impetus to oppose Hitler "must come from within Germany and by the German people themselves. War, whoever will be victorious or vanquished, will only create a new form of madness in the world." Similarly, Goldman felt that the power of Stalin would be broken only from within Russia, "by the people themselves," not from outside. Britain would only be changed by a revolution in British colonial possessions. "In other words, it must come from the bottom up and not from the top down." But although she still opposed all dictatorships and demanded help for refugees, Goldman now expressed an uncharacteristic fatalism, compounded no doubt by her fear of being deported back to England should she engage in active opposition to British policies or any kind of civil disobedience. "Alas, neither you nor I can have a deciding effect one way or the other," she told Read.[11]

Emma Goldman found her antiwar position more difficult to maintain in 1939 than it had been in 1917. For one thing, the Jewish immigrant anarchists in Toronto and in the United States nearly all supported a war against Hitler.[12] Even those who considered themselves pacifists, like Ahrne Thorne, a Polish immigrant who was part of the Yiddish anarchist group in Toronto, felt that "this was my war," and prepared to join the army. According to Thorne, Emma felt torn between her sense of identity as a Jew and her anarchist conviction that national wars were capitalist rivalries between essentially similar states. "There was a very deep conflict in her," Thorne recalled. "It tormented her. Here again she saw a conflict where reality was so contrary to the ideas that she held all her life—always oppose every war." [13] She still believed, as she told a reporter for an American Jewish newspaper in 1934, "the final emancipation of the Jew lies only in an international movement such as anarchism, in which the Jewish proletariat and intelligentsia of every land link up their work with similar groups throughout the world. And finally achieve freedom for all. Nationalism of any kind is not the answer to the Jewish question." [14] Emma had never been a Zionist, and felt that a Jewish state would recreate the evils of all other states. She regarded the revival of interest in Yiddish culture among the Jewish communities in Montreal and Toronto in the 1930s as "a form of retrogression." [15] Despite her encounter with pogrommed villages in the Ukraine in 1920, she seems to have watched the emerging anti-Semitism under Hitler after 1933 with a certain detachment. She argued that Hitlerism must be abolished from within Germany, not by "external forces" from abroad. "Jews should be proud to have been singled out for persecution by the Nazis," a newspaper quoted her as saying in 1934. "The Jew contributed so much to the magnificent culture which the Nazis hate that they, in their determination to return to the past and throw that culture aside, ended by hating the Jews." [16]

Goldman was just as ready to criticize the Jews for failing to organize to fight Hitler and Mussolini. In a January 1939 letter, she claimed the Jews "have never lifted a finger to prevent the advent of Hitler in Germany or have shown the least resistance in any country. Please do not think that I feel they are getting what they deserve—no, but I cannot close my eyes to the fact that the Jews have failed miserably to defend their own grounds. I insist further that if Hitler had only persecuted the Polish Jews he would have had 90 percent of the German Jews on his side, just as Mussolini had nearly all the Jews in Italy on his side. . . ." [17]

It was true that the generally middle-class, assimilated German Jews tended to look down on the *ostjuden*—the poorer East European Jews— and that in the 1930s a number of Jews, Hannah Arendt among them, sharply criticized Jewish leaders in Germany and in France for failing to mount an outspoken resistance to mounting anti-Semitism. Yet the reasons for this relative lack of resistance were complex, compounded of fears of violent retaliation that tended to follow such protests, unwillingness to believe that an actual war against the Jews was underway, persistent hope that the worst was over, the extreme vulnerability of the relatively aged German Jewish population, and, in 1939, hesitancy to provoke Britain, which, while it restricted entry of refugees into Palestine (a British mandate) and into England, was also committed to fight against Nazi Germany.

Still, Goldman took a strong position defending Jewish rights of asylum. She strongly criticized Britain and other countries for their refusal to accept Jewish refugees, and challenged a member of the ILP, Reginald Reynolds (Ethel Mannin's husband), when he opposed Jewish rights of asylum in Palestine (in 1938) and upheld the right of other countries to deny entry to Jewish refugees; Goldman argued that Jews must have the same rights of asylum as other persecuted peoples, in Palestine and everywhere else. Reynolds's position, she argued, was simply anti-Semitic. Asylum in Palestine was necessary "for those from places where the Jew cannot breathe." [18]

But Emma Goldman remained more detached about the war against the Jews than she had about the war in Spain. Perhaps after a war that left over half a million dead and two million in prison or cast into exile, the Jews seemed one more group among the many victims of fascist brutality. Her remarks as late as 1939 show that, like many Jews, she vastly underestimated the nature of German anti-Semitism, just as she had been slow, by her own admission, to acknowledge the depth of Ukrainian anti-Semitism in the years prior to the Russian Revolution.

Goldman never changed her mind about the war, nor altered her harsh judgments about the Jews in Germany. Instead she threw herself into a campaign to prevent the deportation of four young Italian immigrant anarchists who, in early October, had come afoul of the Canadian War Measures Act by virtue of possessing antifascist "subversive literature." One of them, Arturo Bortolotti, was also found to possess a revolver, which further complicated his case. Bortolotti had long been active in antifascist work in Toronto, and Goldman saw his case as an attempt of local fascists to secure his deportation, the equivalent clearly of a death sentence. Emma considered Bortolotti as of the same caliber of Sacco and Vanzetti, and frequently compared him with Alexander Berkman, using his initials, A.B., to emphasize the connection. Soon after his arrest on October 4,

Goldman threw herself into a campaign, forming a Save Arthur Bortolotti Committee, hiring a defense lawyer, and undertaking an energetic and far-ranging fund-raising campaign on both sides of the Canadian border.

Emma herself recognized the psychological importance of this campaign. In a candid note to Milly Rocker on October 14, she admitted that she welcomed just such a task. "I was wondering what to do this winter," she wrote. "I am no longer in doubt since the arrest of our people. Heaven only knows how long their defense will last and there is no one else to take over the job. I have to do it." [19]

Still collecting funds for the Emma Goldman Spanish Refugee Fund, Goldman devoted most of her time to efforts on behalf of Bortolotti and another comrade. Friends of Emma's in New York and elsewhere now received the familiar torrent of urgent appeals, cajoling, demanding, pleading, and scolding in an effort to scare up support and funds. Emma expected comrades in the United States to come through for her. She was disgusted when the Italian comrades proved to be too divided by quarrels to unite in an effort for Bortolotti, or when others were too committed to helping potential deportees closer to home. By contrast, she was thrilled when Spanish comrades of the SIA in the United States voted to send $219 of their own meager funds to aid the fight of the Italians in Canada.

The campaign lasted through the winter, keeping Goldman busy and focused. By early February, the two Italians were still awaiting possible deportation. Bortolotti had caught a bad flu while in prison. Released on bail, he returned to his room in the boarding house, where Emma visited him daily, tenderly nursing him back to health. Eventually, through her efforts, all the arrested anarchists, including Bortolotti, were released. Years later, Bortolotti remembered Goldman's generosity with a pang of guilt, wondering if the work she devoted to his case might not have weakened her own condition. In fact, her own testimony suggests the reverse—for Goldman thrived on struggle and welcomed the chance to be active and useful.

Saturday, February 17, 1940, Emma felt particularly cheerful. She worked all day dictating letters to Millie Desser, who was acting as her secretary. At about five o'clock, Desser left the house on Vaughan Road. That evening, recalled Arturo Bortolotti, the Toronto Libertarian group that Emma had organized planned to gather at her place as they did every Friday or Saturday night for discussions. The subject for that week was Giordano Bruno. [20] Around five, as Millie Desser was leaving Emma's house, Bortolotti set out in his old car to pick up three couples to bring them to Emma's place. When he arrived at the third house, the telephone rang for him. Dorothy Rogers' voice came over the wire. "Come quick," she said. "Emma had a stroke." Emma had been sitting with two friends and herself, Dorothy told him, laughing and talking, when suddenly she collapsed in her chair without a word.[21] "I don't know how I drove without causing accidents," Bortolotti recalled later, "because I was out of my mind. And I arrived on Vaughan Road there, and saw Emma, moaning—she couldn't talk any more. Just to think that here was Emma, the greatest orator in America, unable to utter one word."[22]

Bortolotti telephoned Ahrne Thorne, who took the trolley car out to the house. By the time he arrived, Thorne remembered, the ambulance had come, and they were taking her out on a stretcher. At that moment, with her good hand, she pulled down the hem of her skirt, over her knee. "And I don't know why I remember this gesture—I remember it all the time," he added. "When somebody writes about her fairly young years and her sexual adventures, I remember that chaste, innocent gesture. At that time, about 15–20 minutes after a stroke, taken away on a stretcher to the hospital, she remembered to cover her naked knee."[23]

Goldman had suffered a massive cerebral hemorrhage. At the Toronto General Hospital, where she spent the next six weeks, she was also diagnosed with diabetes. She was completely paralyzed on her right side, unable to speak, although she understood everything said to her and could say a few words, with great difficulty. A nurse remained with her round-the-clock, and a physiotherapist came twice a week to massage her immobilized arm and leg. She appeared to gain strength, and the paralysis on her right side began to diminish, although she suffered from insomnia, and when she could not sleep, she was very unhappy. Stella Ballantine reported that Emma "weeps a great deal."

In late March, Emma was brought back to her apartment on Vaughan Road, where she continued to improve. She was able to see visitors, and Bortolotti remembered how she had struggled to point out her address book when informed that a friend was about to travel to Mexico; she wanted to give him the address of people who might help him. Emma's illness had prompted Stella to organize a Friends of Emma Goldman Committee to help raise money for her care and pressure Washington to allow her to return to the United States. John Haynes Holmes, the publisher B. W. Huebsch, playwright George S. Kaufman, Roger Baldwin, John Dewey, Freda Kirchwey, Norman Thomas and others made up the committee. But by early May the prognosis was not good. Goldman suffered another slight stroke and by May 8, she had begun to withdraw. "We cannot rouse her to take an interest in anything but the most personal contacts," wrote Dorothy Rogers to a friend. "Even her brother's name does not bring much response." [24]

Emma Goldman died on May 14, 1940. Her body was taken to the Labor Lyceum in Toronto, where she had spoken many times. Her longtime admirer, the Reverend Salem Bland, delivered a eulogy. Denied entry into the United States for so many years, she was now permitted, in death, to cross the border to the land she always considered her home. In Chicago, scene of the Haymarket tragedy that had marked Goldman's political awakening, her body rested in state at a funeral home, where many people passed her bier to pay their final respects. Her coffin was draped with banners of the SIA-FAI. Flowers from friends, comrades, and organizations all over the country were heaped about. As she was carried from the hall, people lined the streets in silence, watching as the procession approached Waldheim Cemetery, and chimes from the chapel rang out a requiem. Beside the grave, a comrade read the lines from the gravedigger's scene in *Hamlet*. Rose Pesotta recalled later the sunshine, the flowers, and the birds singing, as Emma Goldman was laid to rest. Pesotta and Stella Ballantine placed bouquets on the neighboring grave of Emma's friend Voltairine de Cleyre. Ben Reitman placed red roses in the arms of the statue commemorating the Haymarket martyrs. Rose and Stella each selected a bouquet which they placed on Emma's coffin.

In New York, at Town Hall on May 31, Pesotta, Rudolf Rocker, Norman Thomas, Roger Baldwin, Carlo Tresca, John Haynes Holmes, Martin Gudell, and several longtime comrades honored Emma Goldman in a last memorial meeting on the stage where Emma herself had spoken six years earlier. They paid tribute to the courage and tenacity of this lifelong fighter for freedom and justice. Yet in death, as in life, Goldman continued to evoke complicated feelings in her admirers. "The memorial meeting conveyed one idea to me," recalled one comrade, "and perhaps to many others: what a fighter E. had been, how courageous she was, and how untiring. I am glad I could feel that way. I like this to be the after-taste." Another friend put it more bluntly. "She had many faults, but she was a mensch." [25]

In the eulogies, obituaries, and even editorials that followed her death, Goldman's admirers and critics sought to recruit her for particular causes of their own. Jacob Siegal, editor of the Socialist *Forward* observed approvingly that Goldman had come out of Russia "an entirely different woman, and much more conservative." He was certain that if she were alive today, she would be aiding the fight against Hitler.[26] For much of the capitalist press, her repudiation of the Bolsheviks constituted a kind of repentance. In their hands, Goldman became a cudgel with which to beat Communists, her life a fable about the virtues of American capitalism, which they defined as "freedom." "She had a quality rare among the devotes of economic dogma," editorialized the *New York Times*. "She was honest. She who had had such aureate visions of revolution saw in the Soviet regime only a new form of tyranny."[27] "To her credit it must be said that she was equally violent in her denunciations of the Stalin Soviets," wrote the *Brooklyn Eagle*.[28] The *New York Herald Tribune* noted that "Emma Goldman became a patriot the hard way."[29] The *New York Post* observed that it was only after she went to Russia that she discovered, in America, the land "that at least approximated what she had been seeking so long."[30]

The newspapers were wrong, yet they suggest the difficulty of situating Goldman politically and historically. In truth, she found the realization of her dream, not in capitalist New York, but in anarcho-syndicalist Barcelona, and among the peasants of Catalonia and Aragon. For all her disillusionments, she remained an anarchist all her life. But anarchism itself was a Protean politics, capable of accommodating a wide range of visions. Anarchists were not necessarily revolutionaries. After her sojourn in Russia, she vacillated in her views, at times insisting that fundamental change could only emerge through a social revolution, at other times arguing in favor of gradual change by a process of educating the "individual." She worried more about making the wrong kind of revolution than about not making one at all. She warned of serious limitations in the Russian version of socialism, yet in rejecting one Bolshevik myth, she helped articulate another myth which, especially in the United States, has been far more adverse in its effects. As her admirer, Roger Baldwin once put it, "Anti-Communism in its effect on civil liberties became much more of a menace than Communism. Communism never affected our civil liberties very much but anti-Communism did . . . I think anti-Communism was a menace."[31]

In the end, the anarchists, and Goldman herself, suffered most from their obsessive anti-Communism and anti-Marxism, for it drained their energies from more constructive anarchist efforts and prevented them from addressing the problems within anarchism, which Berkman had sharply delineated as far back as 1921. Though Goldman too recognized the need for a new anarchist literature to address contemporary issues, she never attempted such a project. Instead she dissipated her energies in thousands of letters that repeated over and over the same litanies, yet did not advance the cause of anarchism. Tragically, she herself became a victim of the feeling she had helped to foster, for it was partly that hysterical Red scare mentality that prevented her return to the United States.

In the post-1917 era, Goldman's narrow focus on the Soviet Union and the United States tended to exclude the rest of the world, especially the developing world, where issues of revolution and reaction were posed far more starkly—in India and Nicaragua and Cuba, for example. It was significant that when she directed her attention to China, her arguments even about Russia changed. Although she occasionally offered ironic asides about British "democracy" as practiced in India and Egypt, she rarely followed up the logic of her criticisms; anticolonialism never captured her imagination. She castigated American liberals and radicals for condoning in the Soviet Union the human rights abuses they condemned in the West, but she had little to say about other massive rights abuses in the Third World. Domination was always Emma Goldman's great theme, but in exile the broad scope of her criticism narrowed to focus increasingly on the evils of the Communist state.

For all the bitterness of her rejection of Marxism, it is possible to exaggerate the differences between her vision of anarchism and the socialism of her Marxist contemporaries—for example, Rosa Luxemburg, whose emphasis on the importance of mass spontaneity and free initiative from below foreshadowed her own. Indeed, the lives of these two women suggest comparisons, for they were both East European Jewish women, born within two years of each other, of essentially petit-bourgeois origins, who became leading figures in revolutionary movements in the West. Both struggled to combine a commitment to radical politics with personal, private satisfactions. Both remained deeply committed to an internationalist outlook, trenchantly criticizing the limits of bourgeois nationalism. Both opened new public spaces for women through the power of their own example. Goldman went further than Luxemburg in exploring the psychological conflicts of women, in capitalist societies as well as within radical movements aiming to transform them. Even more than Luxemburg, she dramatized the dilemmas of the single "emancipated" woman whose intellectual and political commitments often conflicted with emotional needs she could not wholly accept.

Born in the shadows of the Franco-Prussian War, Emma Goldman died as Hitler's tanks smashed into Belgium. It was fitting that her life should be framed by two major wars, for she herself was "quite a warlike person," as one admirer put it, and for all her commitment to peace and justice, felt most like herself in the midst of combat. "I belong on the firing line," she would say.[32] Fitting, too, that her years in exile should be framed by two great revolutions that dramatized the strengths and weaknesses of anarchism. A libertarian with an authoritarian manner, Goldman often contradicted, in her dealings with others, the ideals she espoused on the platform. Yet she moved people as few other women of her time had done, not only in her powerful oratory but privately, too. A measure of her capacity to touch people was a tender letter from a prison mate of twenty years earlier that she received on her deathbed in Toronto. "My beloved comrade," wrote Ella Antolini, who had been a young girl imprisoned with Emma at the Missouri State Penitentiary. "Your illness caused me much grief and I am wishing with all my heart that you may be well . . . I am still the little person you knew—tho sadder and a bit wiser, and your wonderful personality stands out very clearly in my memory."[33]

It is ironic that Goldman has often been praised for her shortcomings and criticized for her virtues: honored for her tendentious attacks on Soviet Russia and Marxism, and criticized for her defense of the Spanish anarcho-syndicalists, with their tragic compromises and concessions during the civil war. Yet a more accurate reading of her life might be the reverse. Criticisms of Bolshevik authoritarianism and hierarchy were made earlier, and more trenchantly, by Marxists such as Rosa Luxemburg and Alexandra Kollontai.[34] Trotsky and other dissident Communists offered more far-reaching critiques of Stalinism. But few outside of Spain itself, even among the anarchists, grasped as fully as Goldman the significance of that revolution that burst forth in July 1936. She was quick to recognize in the Spanish agricultural collectives, the self-managed factories, the schools, hospitals, and city services run by and for working men and women, a creative anarchist achievement of lasting importance. Approaching seventy, still mourning the death of her lifelong comrade Alexander Berkman, accustomed all her life to her role as a "free lance," she gave herself up to this last great battle, revealing the depths of solidarity and generosity that transcended all her doubts and confusion.

That stern face, frowning into the future, reminds us of her sorrows and her failures, the dreams defeated but not destroyed. She drew on her lifelong sense of exile to fight for a new world in which all people might feel at home, a world without boundaries or borders, where no one would be deported for dissident opinions and all would share freely in the wealth of the earth. She kept aloft the ideas of the great anarchists, Bakunin and Kropotkin, that means influence ends, that the form of the revolutionary movement influences its content, that freedom can only be created by freedom. She went far beyond her mentors in denouncing the limited freedom of women, inside the anarchist movement as well as outside it, and she offered herself as a militant example of revolt against conventions and taboos.

On her seventieth birthday, an admirer tried to assess her significance. "It was not what you did or said that helped me, but what you were," he wrote in June of 1939, "the mere fact of the existence of your spirit which never gives in and fights on no matter how thick is the darkness in the world and in our own little worlds." [35] But Goldman herself may have written her own most powerful epitaph. In a lecture on a woman she considered her precursor, the great eighteenth-century feminist writer Mary Wollstonecraft, she also inscribed her own face. "In conflict with every institution of their time since they will not compromise," Goldman wrote, "it is inevitable that the advance guards should become aliens to the very ones they wish to serve; that they should be isolated, shunned, and repudiated by the nearest and dearest of kin. Yet the tragedy every pioneer must experience is not the lack of understanding—it arises from the fact that having seen new possibilities for human advancement, the pioneers can not take root in the old, and with the new still far off they become outcast roamers of the earth, restless seekers for the things they will never find." [36]

Abbreviations

EG refers to Emma Goldman, AB to Alexander Berkman.

The following abbreviations are used throughout the notes:

IISH: International Institute for Social History Amsterdam

NYPL: The New York Public Library

Schlesinger Library: Arthur and Elizabeth Schlesinger Library on the History of American Women, Radcliffe College

Tamiment Library: Tamiment Library, New York University

ICPP: International Committee for Political Prisoners

UIC: Library, University of Chicago at Illinois.

LML: Living My Life (New York: Knopf, 1931).

MDIR: My Disillusionment in Russia (1925; reprint New York: Thomas Crowell, 1970).

BM: The Bolshevik Myth (New York: Boni & Liveright, 1925).

NAH: Nowhere at Home: The Letters from Exile of Emma Goldman and Alexander Berkman, ed. Richard Drinnon and Anna Maria Drinnon (New York: Shocken, 1975)

VOF: Vision on Fire: Emma Goldman on the Spanish Revolution, ed. David Porter (New Paltz, N.Y.: Commonground Press, 1983).

Notes

Introduction

1. Plays include Lynn Rogoff's *Love Ben, Love Emma,* Howard Zinn's *Emma!,* Michael Dixon's *Live Tonight: Emma Goldman,* Stephanie Auerbach's *A Woman of Valor,* and a musical, *Red Emma,* by Carol Bolt. Leonard Lehrman has written an opera based on Goldman's life.

2. Eric Hobsbawm, *The Age of Empire, 1875–1914* (New York: Pantheon, 1987), p. 331.

3. Walter Lippmann and Charles Merz, "A Test of the News," *New Republic,* 4 August 1920, p. 3.

4. Individualist anarchists, a much smaller group within anarchism, accepted private property and capitalism; precursors of the present-day Libertarian party in the United States, they opposed all forms of government control but did not advocate the socialization of property.

1 The Sailing of the *Buford*

1. Eleven of the 249 were being deported for criminal acts or illegal entry into the country. See Richard Powers, *Secrecy and Power: The Life of J. Edgar Hoover* (New York: Free Press, 1987), p. 51.

2. *New York American,* 19 December 1919.

3. EG to Eleanor Fitzgerald, 18 December 1919, XVI-9, EG Archive, IISH.

4. See EG, *LML,* pp. 711–25; also *New York World, New York Times, New York American, New York Call, New York Globe and Commercial Advertiser,* 19–22 December 1919.

5. EG to Frank Harris, 27 December 1919, EG Archive, IISH.

6. *New York World,* 22 December 1919; *New York Times,* 22 December 1919.

7. *Washington Post,* 22 December 1919.

8. Powers, *Secrecy and Power,* p. 73; see also John Higham, *Strangers in the Land* (New York: Atheneum, 1965), pp. 229–33; also William Preston, Jr., *Aliens and Dissenters: Federal Suppression of Radicals, 1903–1933* (New York: Harper & Row, 1963).

9. At this time black Americans were also a particular target of investigation

for the Justice Department, which feared "Bolshevik subversion" among them. Goldman and Berkman did not note this fact, and they dismissed the idea that racism and nativism were significant as sources of the Red Scare, writing that "the United States has fortunately always been free from the vicious spirit of race hatred and persecution of the foreigner. The native negro excepted, this country has known no race question" (*Deportation: Its Meaning and Menace* [New York: Stella Comyn, 1919], p. 13). Goldman would later change her views when she met the black singer, Paul Robeson, in London, but in general racial and religious persecution, including anti-Semitism, concerned her far less than political persecution.

10. For descriptions of conditions aboard the *Buford,* see *LML,* pp. 717–25; AB, "The Log of the Transport *Buford,"* the *Liberator,* 4 April 1920, reprinted in AB, *BM,* pp. 13–27; see also EG to Frank Harris, 27 December 1919, XVI-9, EG Archive, IISH; EG to Frank Harris, 16 January 1920, 504–108, Record Group 59, National Archives; "Ellis Island: A Protest," *Pearson's,* May 1920, pp. 890–903; also the series of letters Goldman wrote to Stella Ballantine from the *Buford,* contained in XVI-9, EG Archive, IISH.

11. AB, "Bolshevik Myth," MS p. 17, EG Papers, NYPL.

12. EG to Stella Ballantine, 8 January 1920, XVI-8, EG Archive, IISH.

13. See Alice Wexler, *Emma Goldman in America* (Boston: Beacon, 1984), p. 259.

14. EG to Stella Ballantine, 5 January 1920, XVI-6, EG Archive, IISH.

15. EG to Stella Ballantine, 4 January 1920, XVI-6, EG Archive, IISH.

16. EG to Stella Ballantine, 14 January 1919, XVI-6, EG Archive, IISH.

17. EG to Stella Ballantine, 13 January 1920, XVI-6, EG Archive, IISH.

18. Zorin was secretary of the Petrograd Committee of the Communist party, and editor of the daily *Krasnaya Gazetta.*

19. *London Daily Express,* 20 January 1920, 21 January 1920.

20. *London Daily Herald,* 20 January 1920, 22 January 1920.

21. EG to Frank Harris, 29 January 1920, XVI-8, EG Archive, IISH. What appeared to her at the time as a "wonderfully impressive" event seemed in retrospect menacing and sinister. In *My Disillusionment in Russia,* Goldman described the "dark hall filled to suffocation," and the women in black nun's attire, "their faces ghastly in the yellow light." EG, *MDIR,* pp. 3–4.

2 Stranger in a Strange Land

1. Most of the other deportees from America were housed in the Smolny Institute, a former school for daughters of the aristocracy that had been converted into a central office of the revolution.

2. Moshe Lewin, *The Making of the Soviet System* (New York: Pantheon,

1985), p. 296; see also Paul Avrich, *Kronstadt 1921* (New York: Norton, 1970), p. 8; William Henry Chamberlin, *The Russian Revolution, 1917–1921* (New York: Macmillan, 1935), p. 342.

3. EG to Frank Harris in EG, "Ellis Island: A Protest," *Pearson's,* May 1920, p. 903; EG to Ben Reitman, 8 March 1920, original accession, f. 19, Ben Reitman Papers, UIC.

4. See Sheila Fitzpatrick, *The Commissariat of Enlightenment* (Cambridge: Cambridge University Press, 1970); also John Willett, *Art and Politics in the Weimar Period* (New York: Pantheon, 1978), pp. 34–43.

5. See *LML,* p. 740; also Victor Serge, *Memoirs of a Revolutionary,* trans. Peter Sedgwick (London: Writers & Readers, 1984), pp. 99–100.

6. EG to Stella Ballantine, 28 January 1920, Record Group 59, Office of the Counselor, 504–108, National Archives.

7. AB to Eleanor Fitzgerald, 28 February 1920, XIV-8, EG Archive, IISH.

8. EG to Stella Ballantine, 28 February 1920, XVI-8, EG Archive, IISH.

9. See Beatrice Farnsworth, *Alexandra Kollontai: Socialism, Feminism, and the Russian Revolution* (Stanford: Stanford University Press, 1980); also Richard Stites, "Alexandra Kollontai and the Russian Revolution," in *European Women on the Left,* ed. Jane Slaughter and Robert Kern (Westport, Conn.: Greenwood, 1981), pp. 101–124; Bernice Glatzer Rosenthal, "Love on the Tractor: Women in the Russian Revolution and After," in *Becoming Visible: Women in European History,* ed. Renate Bridenthal and Claudia Koonz (Boston: Houghton Mifflin, 1977), pp. 378–81.

10. *MDIR,* p. 170; see also *LML,* pp. 756–57.

11. *New York World,* 31 March 1922.

12. *MDIR,* pp. 17–19, 32–33.

13. Angelica Balabanoff, *My Life* (New York: Harper & Bros., 1938), pp. 253–54; *LML,* p. 761.

14. *MDIR,* p. 34; *LML,* p. 765.

15. EG to Stella Ballantine, 25 May 1920, EG Papers, Schlesinger Library.

16. Shatov organized the defense of Petrograd against the counterrevolutionary army of General Yudenich, and served as Minister of War and as Minister of Railways in the Far Eastern Republic. Later he directed the building of the Trans-Siberian Railroad. On Russian anarchism see Harold Joel Goldberg, "The Anarchists View the Bolshevik Regime" (Ph.D. diss., University of Wisconsin, 1973), pp. 135–49; Paul Avrich, *The Russian Anarchists* (Princeton: Princeton University Press, 1967), pp. 69, 172; Voline, *The Unknown Revolution, 1917–1921,* trans. Holley Cantine and Fredy Perlman (Detroit: Black & Red, 1974), pp. 267–69, 577; S. A. Smith, *Red Petrograd* (Cambridge: Cambridge University Press, 1983), pp. 142–45.

17. See Avrich, *The Russian Anarchists,* pp. 179–89; also Goldberg, "Anarchists," pp. 149–54.

18. See *Road to Freedom,* 15 July 1926 and March 1928; also Roger Baldwin, "The Anarchists in Russia," MS, Roger Baldwin Papers, Princeton University Library.

19. See Peter Arshinov, *History of the Makhnovist Movement,* trans. Lorraine Perlman and Fredy Perlman (Detroit: Black & Red, 1974), pp. 242–43; also Goldberg, "Anarchists," pp. 78–106; Voline, *The Unknown Revolution,* pp. 541–686; also Paul Avrich, *Anarchist Portraits* (Princeton: Princeton University Press, 1988), pp. 111–24.

20. EG to Stella Ballantine, 4 November 1920, EG Papers, Schlesinger Library.

21. AB diary, 12 April 1920, XXV, AB Archive, quoted in Nicolas Walter, "Alexander Berkman's Russian Diary," *The Raven,* November 1987, pp. 286–87. Years later, Emma judged the Russians harshly. "The Russian anarchists, what were they but a handful of refugees from other lands, and exiles from prison, unorganized and at each other's throats. No wonder they played such an insignificant part." EG to Harry Weinberger [1938], EG Papers, NYPL.

22. EG, *MDIR,* p. 36. George Lansbury, *My Life* (London: Constable, 1928), pp. 229–30. Lansbury wrote that Goldman and Berkman had "refused to see or hear anything but evil spoken about the Bolshevik regime."

23. EG to Stella Ballantine, 25 February 1921, XVI-8, EG Archive, IISH.

24. See Edward Hallett Carr, *The Bolshevik Revolution, 1917–1923* (1952; reprint, New York: Norton, 1980), pp. 211–17; Isaac Deutscher, *The Prophet Armed* (1954; reprint, New York: Vintage, 1965), pp. 493–95.

25. EG to Stella Ballantine, 25 May 1920, EG Papers, Schlesinger Library.

26. See J. Edgar Hoover to William Hurley, 14 January 1921, RG 59, Office of the Counselor, 861.0-1007, National Archives; Candace Falk, *Love, Anarchy and Emma Goldman* (New York: Holt, Rinehart & Winston, 1984), p. 316.

27. AB Coxe to William Hurley, 16 April 1920, RG 59, Decimal F.861.0-645, National Archives; AB, *BM,* pp. 87–88; AB to Eleanor Fitzgerald, 28 Feburary 1920, in *NAH,* p. 21. In his autobiography, Bertrand Russell, who met Harrison at about the same time in Russia, also identifies her as a spy. Bertrand Russell, *Autobiography of Bertrand Russell,* vol. 2, 1914–1944 (Boston: Little, Brown, 1968), p. 151.

28. Marguerite Harrison, *Marooned in Moscow* (New York: Doran, 1921), pp. 141–44.

29. Ibid.

30. See letters from J. Edgar Hoover, then special assistant to the attorney general, to W. L. Hurley at the State Department. A letter of 14 January 1921 reported learning from a "confidential source" that Emma contemplated marriage to a Russian correspondent for the *New York World* in order to acquire American citizenship and return to the United States (Record Group 59, Office of the Counselor, f. 851.0-1007); another letter of 22 March 1920 from "confidential informant H"—possibly Marguerite Harrison—reported Berkman's alleged intention

to organize a group of terrorists in Russia to be sent into other countries (Record Group 59, Office of the Counselor, 861.721, National Archives).

31. See Hoover to Hurley, 11 October 1928, RG59, Office of the Counselor, 851.0-1046, National Archives.

32. AB to Eleanor Fitzgerald, 21 May 1920, Record Group 59, Office of the Counselor, National Archives.

33. EG to Stella Ballantine, 25 May 1920, 8 June 1920, XVI-8, EG Archive, IISH.

34. Wm. Hurley to F. Burke of Bureau of Investigation, 22 January 1920, (Record Group 59, Office of the Counselor, 861.0-655, National Archives); EG to Stella Ballantine, 25 May 1920, EG Papers, Schlesinger Library.

35. *Chicago Tribune,* 18 June 1920.

36. *New York Times,* 19 June 1920; see, for example, "Emma Goldman Homesick," 8 May 1920, p. 2; editorial, 10 May 1920; "Emma Goldman sees Tyranny in Russia," 18 June 1920; "Homesick in Heaven" (editorial), 19 June 1920; "Emma Goldman on Bolshevism," 9 October 1920; "Deportees to Russia Want to Come Back," 9 October 1920; "Confirms Discontent of Emma Goldman," 23 October 1920; see also EG to Stella Ballantine, 3 November 1920, EG Papers, Schlesinger Library.

37. EG to Stella Ballantine, 4 November 1920, XVI-8, EG Archive, IISH.

38. *The Nation,* 8 December 1920, p. 632; *LML,* p. 852.

39. EG to Stella Ballantine, 25 May 1920, EG Papers, Schlesinger Library.

40. EG to Stella Ballantine, 3 November 1920, EG Papers, Schlesinger Library.

41. On Alsberg, see Monty Noam Penkower, *The Federal Writers' Project* (Urbana: University of Illinois Press, 1977); also Jerre Mangione, *The Dream and the Deal: The Federal Writers' Project, 1935–1943* (Boston: Little, Brown, 1972).

42. See Henry Alsberg, "Russia: Rose-Tint vs. Smoked Glass," *The Nation,* 15 June 1921, pp. 844–46.

43. See, for example, "Will Russia Drive the British from Asia?" 14 August 1920; "Russian Impressions," 21 August 1920; "The Soviet Domestic Program," 28 August 1920; "Tyranny by Prophets," 4 September 1920; "Russia's Industrial Problem," 11 September 1920.

44. *MDIR,* pp. 119, 147.

45. EG to Stella Ballantine, 3 November 1920, XVI-8, EG Archive, IISH; *MDIR,* p. 164. In a letter to Max Nettlau, Goldman criticized the Russian romanticization of the peasantry. "Look at the idealistic peasants of Turgeniev and Tolstoy, and the tramps of Gorky," she wrote. "I searched for them all up and down Russia, but did not find any like them. I have concluded that no such types exist. . . . " EG to Max Nettlau, 9 March 1929, Nettlau Archive, IISH.

46. *MDIR,* pp. 126, 140.

47. EG to Stella Ballantine, 3 November 1920, XVI-8, EG Archive, IISH; also EG to Charney Vladeck, 12 February 1935, XIX, EG Archive.

48. EG to Stella Ballantine, 3 November 1920, XVI-8, EG Archive, IISH.

49. EG to Max Nettlau, 24 March 1924, Nettlau Archive, IISH: "There is one thing [in Ricarda Huch's biography of Bakunin] that disturbs me very much. Ricarda Huch claims Bakunin hated, or rather keenly disliked the Jews. And that a contributory element to his dislike of Marx was Bakunin's dislike for the Jews. Now what is there about it?" "Please remember dear comrade, I have no pronounced racial feeling. I can very well understand Bakunin criticizing the commercial Jews without being anti-Semitic. Huch, however, emphasizes dislike which is quite another matter. I wish you would enlighten me on that."

50. Voline, *The Unknown Revolution*, pp. 265–68.

51. EG to Stella Ballantine, 28 November 1920, XVI-8, EG Archive, IISH.

52. AB to Eleanor Fitzgerald, 23 October 1920, 6 November 1920, XVI-8, EG Archive, IISH. EG to Stella Ballantine, 25 February 1921, XVI-8, EG Archive, IISH.

53. EG, *MDIR*, pp. 178–83.

54. Serge, *Memoirs of a Revolutionary*, p. 116.

55. Chamberlin, *The Russian Revolution*, vol. 2, pp. 264, 356.

56. EG to Stella Ballantine, 4 November 1920, 28 November 1920, 2 March 1921, 28 November 1920, XVI-8, EG Archive, IISH.

57. Henry Alsberg, *New York Post*, 29 March 1924, p. 629. Victor Serge made a similar observation in his *Memoirs*, noting that "the American background of Emma Goldman and Alexander Berkman estranged them from the Russians, and turned them into representatives of an idealistic generation that had completely vanished in Russia" (pp. 153–54).

58. EG to Stella Ballantine, 4 November 1920, XVI-8, EG Archive, IISH.

59. EG to Stella Ballantine, 28 November 1920, XVI-8, EG Archive, IISH.

60. EG to Stella Ballantine, 10 April 1921, 28 November 1920, XVI-8, EG Archive, IISH.

61. EG to Stella Ballantine, 10 April 1921, 25 February 1921, 28 November 1920, 19 May 1921, XVI-8, EG Archive, IISH.

62. Avrich, *Kronstadt*, p. 37.

63. *LML*, pp. 882–83.

64. Serge, *Memoirs*, pp. 128–29.

65. Avrich, *Kronstadt*, p. 132.

66. Ibid., p. 6.

67. Ibid., p. 211; Emma later gave varying figures for those slain, from "tens of thousands" to eighteen thousand, implying that most of those killed were sailors; Henry Alsberg's estimate of eight hundred in his June 1921 article in the *Nation* suggests that more accurate estimates were available even at the time; see also *LML*, p. 886.

68. AB diary, 12 April 1920, XXV, AB Archive, IISH, quoted in Walter, "Berkman's Diary," p. 287.

69. AB diary, 2 March 1921, XXV, AB Archive, IISH, quoted in Walter, "Berkman's Diary," pp. 287–88.

70. EG to Stella Ballantine, 21 April 1921, 19 May 1921, XXVII, EG Archive, IISH.

71. EG to Stella Ballantine, 21 April 1921, XVI-8, EG Archive, IISH.

72. Rudolf Rocker, *Revolución y Reacción,* trans. Diego Abad de Santillán (Buenos Aires: Editorial Tupac, 1952), pp. 629 ff.

73. EG to Stella Ballantine, 12 July 1921, XVI-8, EG Archive, IISH; *LML,* p. 888.

74. On NEP see Stephen F. Cohen, *Bukharin and the Bolshevik Revolution* (Princeton: Princeton University Press, 1980), especially pp. 123–59.

75. Ibid., p. 125.

76. See *LML,* pp. 871–72; *BM,* p. 290.

77. *Le Libertaire,* 7–14 January 1921; Daniel Guerin, *Anarchism,* trans. Mary Klopper (New York: Monthly Review Press, 1970), pp. 106–7; Rudolf Rocker, *Die Bankrotte des russischen Staatskommunismus* (Berlin: Der Syndikalist, 1921). See also Goldberg, "Anarchists," pp. 190 ff.

78. Serge notes their influence in his *Memoirs,* writing that "what with Kronstadt, these tragedies [executions and deportations of anarchists] and the influence of Emma Goldman and Alexander Berkman on the working-class movement in the Old World and the New, an unbridgeable gap was now to open between Marxists and libertarians" (pp. 153–54). See also Branko Lazitch and Milorad Drachovitch, *Lenin and the Comintern,* vol. 1 (Stanford: Hoover, 1972), p. 314.

79. Rocker reported that delegates with whom he spoke in Berlin in late 1920 expressed a critical attitude toward what they saw as a suffocating atmosphere of despotism, with labor forbidden to strike, police espionage rampant, censorship, and mounting restrictions on individual liberty. See Rocker, *Die Bankrotte*; for the reaction of a Spanish delegate, see Angel Pestaña, *Setenta Días en Russia: Lo que yo ví* (Barcelona: Tipografia Cosmos, 1924), and *Setenta Días en Russia: Lo que yo pienso* (Barcelona: Antonio Lopez, 1924).

80. EG to Stella Ballantine, 17 October 1921, XVI-8, EG Archive, IISH; *LML,* p. 138.

81. Agnes Smedley to EG, n.d., in *NAH,* p. 135. Smedley explained to Emma, "I spent years in China and the only ones who offer any hope for the Chinese workers and peasants are the Communists. Also, I saw the colossal gains of the Russian workers, their unwavering enthusiasm and their keen minds. I met all kinds of them everywhere, and I believe they are on the only possible road." Agnes Smedley to EG, 24 September 1934, XVI-1-4, EG Archive, IISH.

82. See Carr, *The Bolshevik Revolution,* vol. 1, pp. 185–86, vol. 2, pp. 283–87.

83. EG to Stella Ballantine, 1 October 1921, 17 October 1921, XVI-8, EG Archive, IISH.

84. *LML,* pp. 900–1.

85. See Goldberg, "Anarchists," p. 199. Goldberg notes that Cherny was either shot or died during an interrogation.

86. EG to Stella Ballantine, 17 October 1921, XVI-8, EG Archive, IISH.

87. AB diary, 22 November 1921, Record Group 59, State Department Decimal File 311.6124K47/10, National Archives.

88. EG to Stella Ballantine, 21 November 1921, XVI-8, EG Archive, IISH.

89. Balabanoff, *My Life,* pp. 250–51.

90. EG to Stella Ballantine, 21 November 1921, XVI-8, EG Archive, IISH.

91. EG to Agnes Inglis, 17 August 1921, XVI-8, EG Archive, IISH.

92. EG to Stella Ballantine, 20 December 1921, XVI-8, EG Archive, IISH.

3 Russia as (M)other

1. AB diary, 5 December 1921, f. 311.6124K47/10, United States Army, Military Intelligence Division.

2. Evan Young to Secretary of State, 9 December 1921, 31 December 1921, Record Group 59, State Department Decimal File 311.6124K47, National Archives.

3. Evan Young to Secretary of State, 10 December 1921, 16 December 1921, 22 December 1921, Record Group 59, State Department Decimal File 311.6124-K47/4, National Archives; [J. Edgar Hoover] to Richard Pennoyer, 23 December 1921, American Embassy, Berlin, State Department Decimal File 861.0-1007, National Archives; U.S. Embassy, Berlin to William Hurley, 18 January 1922, State Department Decimal File 861.0-668, National Archives; Assistant Commissioner General, Department of Labor to William Hurley, 3 March 1922, State Department Decimal File 861.0-669, National Archives; Secretary of U.S. Embassy, Berlin to William Hurley, 20 February 1922, State Department Decimal File 861.0-669, National Archives.

4. EG to Harry Weinberger, 9 December 1921, Weinberger Papers, Yale University Library; Goldman apparently did consider marriage to Harry Kelly, but decided against it. See EG to Stella Ballantine, 23 January 1922, XVI-8, EG Archive, IISH.

5. EG to Stella Ballantine, 23 January 1922, XVI-8, EG Archive, IISH; Rocker, *Revolución,* pp. 245–47.

6. EG to "My Darling" [Stella Ballantine], 31 December 1921, f. 0110-154, U.S. Army, Military Intelligence Division.

7. *LML,* p. 933.

8. Evan Young to Secretary of State, 31 December 1921, Record Group 59, State Department Decimal File 311.6124K47/10, National Archives.

9. Henry Alsberg, *The Nation,* 15 June 1921, p. 846; EG to Stella Ballantine, 23 January 1922, XVI-8, EG Archive, IISH; see also *LML,* pp. 921–24.

10. American Consul General to Secretary of State, Memorandum: "Movements of Emma Goldman," 26 July 1922, Record Group 59, State Department Decimal File 311.6124, National Archives; see also EG to Bertrand Russell, 8 July 1922, in *The Autobiography of Bertrand Russell, 1914–1944*, pp. 173–74.

11. EG to Max Nettlau, 16 February 1922, Nettlau Archive, IISH.

12. *LML*, p. 939.

13. *The Russian Tragedy*, *The Russian Revolution and the Communist Party*, and *The Kronstadt Rebellion*, republished as a book by Cienfuegos Press, Orkney (1976); and by Phoenix Press, London, (1986).

14. Maximalists were a wing of the SRs; Universalists were a formerly pro-Bolshevik branch of the anarchists.

15. *Freedom*, January and February 1922.

16. EG to "Comrade" [Max Nettlau], 17 February 1922, Ramus Papers, F. 41, IISH: "Frankly, I am not interested in reaching the foreign elements in A. so much as I am in the Americans. I do not mean to say that the other work should not be done, but it is certain that without the American masses emancipated, there is no hope of anything vital for America."

17. Walter Lippman, "A Test of the News," *New Republic*, 4 August 1920.

18. EG to Stella Ballantine, 11 February 1922, XVI-8, EG Archive, IISH.

19. EG to Stella Ballantine, 23 January 1922, XVI-8, EG Archive, IISH.

20. Joe Spivak, secretary of International Anarchist Aid Federation, 6 March 1922, EGXVI-1, EG Archive, IISH.

21. EG to International Anarchist Aid Federation, 25 March 1922, XVI-1, EG Archive, IISH.

22. The London *Freedom* issued them as a pamphlet, *The Crushing of the Russian Revolution;* the conservative Yiddish New York paper, *Der Tog*, and the Berlin weekly *Der Syndikalist*, also ran them; see A. W. Murray to "Monsieur," 22 August 1924, EG Archive, IISH, for granting of the *World* credential to Goldman under her married name, Mrs. E. G. Kershner. She also accepted a credential as special correspondent for the *World*, apparently to facilitate the extension of her visa in France, before she left for England and possibly also to assist her work in Britain.

23. *New York World*, 24 March 1922, 26 March 1922.

24. See Alexandra Kollontai, *The Workers' Opposition*, Solidarity pamphlet 7, (London, 1921). On Rosa Luxemburg's critique of the Russian Revolution see Peter Nettl, *Rosa Luxemburg* (New York: Oxford, 1969), pp. 430–36; also *Rosa Luxemburg Speaks* (New York: Pathfinder, 1970), pp. 365–95.

25. *New York World*, 26 March 1922.

26. *New York World*, 27 March 1922.

27. *New York World*, 30 March 1922.

28. *New York World*, 4 April 1922.

29. *New York World*, 27 March 1922. See EG to Stella Ballantine, 3 Novem-

ber 1920, EGV-8, IISH. Also EG to Israel Zangwill, 11 December 1924, EG Papers, Tamiment Library, NYU.

30. EG to Max Nettlau, 4 March 1922, 13 March 1922, 24 March 1922, 7 April 1922, 22 April 1922, 11 May 1922, Nettlau Archive, IISH.

31. EG to "Carl," 6 August 1922, XVI-8, EG Archive, IISH.

32. EG to Max Nettlau, 23 September 1922, F. 41, Ramus Archive, IISH. The New York *Daily Worker,* which called Goldman " a sister to Denikin," paid her a backhanded compliment by claiming she had betrayed the American workers "to whom she was a kind of god." *Daily Worker,* 1 April 1922.

33. Arthur Swenson to EG, 10 May 1922, XVII-C, EG Archive, IISH.

34. EG to Arthur, n.d., XVIII-C, EG Archive, IISH.

35. EG to Arthur, n.d., XVII-C, EG Archive, IISH.

36. Goldman reported to her niece that the flat cost under $16 a month, or 30,000 marks, which was a lot for Germans, but it was nearly impossible to find anything for much less. EG to Stella Ballantine, 28 September 1922, XVI-8, EG Archive, IISH. According to Robert C. Williams, *Culture in Exile: Russian Emigres in Germany, 1881–1941* (Ithaca: Cornell University Press), p. 111, there were nearly 500,000 Russian émigrés in Berlin in 1922–23.

37. EG to Max Nettlau, 22 October 1922, Nettlau Archive, IISH.

38. EG to Stella Ballantine, 6 December 1922, 19 December 1922, XVI-8, EG Archive, IISH.

39. Clinton Brainard to EG, 4 April 1923, Weinberger Papers, Sterling Library, Yale University.

40. EG to Stella Ballantine, 14 November 1923, XVI-8, EG Archive, IISH. The reasons for the error remain obscure. Berkman believed that Brainard had probably never received the second installment of the manuscript mailed from Berlin. Or, if he had, he neglected to deliver it to Doubleday and Page, who simply published what they received. An outraged Goldman concluded that, whether through "stupid neglect or intent," the president of Harper and Brothers was certainly "a crook" who had failed to abide by his contract with her and now was responsible for "mutilating" her manuscript. In her sense of helplessness and outrage, Emma struck out harshly even at Harry Weinberger, blaming him for not checking proofs and charging him with negligence in allowing such a crime to occur, charges for which she later apologized, admitting that her distress had caused her to feel "as if everybody had conspired to make a mess of my work." EG to Harry Weinberger, 23 December 1923, 26 December 1923, Weinberger Papers, Yale University Library.

41. EG to Harry Weinberger, 14 May 1924, Weinberger Papers, Yale University Library.

42. *MDIR,* p. xlviii.

43. *Le Libertaire,* 7–14 January, 11–18 November 1921; Guerin, *Anarchism,* pp. 106–7; Rocker, *Die Bankrotte;* Groupe des Anarchistes Russes Exiles en Allemagne, *Repression de l'Anarchisme en Russie Sovietique,* trans. Voline (1922;

Paris: Editiones de la Libraire Sociale, 1923); also *The Russian Revolution and the Communist Party,* the pamphlet by a group of Moscow anarchists, which Berkman translated; see *The Russian Tragedy* (1922; reprint, London: Phoenix Press, n.d.). By early 1922, all of the major anarcho-syndicalist federations—in Italy, Spain, France, Germany and the United States (the IWW)—had rejected affiliation with the Comintern and the Red Trade Union International. Goldberg, "Anarchists," pp. 107–134.

44. EG to Max Nettlau, 6 December 1922, XVI-8, EG Archive.

45. EG to Max Nettlau, 7 August 1922, Nettlau Archive, IISH.

46. *MDIR,* p. 251.

47. On Makhno, see *MDIR,* p. 110. Privately, Goldman was even more critical of Makhno. See EG to AB, 6 October 1924, XII, EG Archive, IISH; EG to AB, 15 March 1927, XIX, AB Archive, IISH.

48. See Avrich, *Kronstadt,* p. 28, also S. A. Smith, *Red Petrograd,* p. 242.

49. See G. Maximov, *The Guillotine at Work* (Chicago, Alexander Berkman Fund 1940), p. 368. Maximov wrote that at the beginning of 1920, the bakers' union was the only anarcho-syndicalist union in Moscow. See also Carr, *The Bolshevik Revolution,* vol. 2, p. 214; Diane Koenker, *Moscow Workers and the 1917 Revolution* (Princeton: Princeton University Press, 1981), pp. 259–60.

50. *MDIR,* p. 124.

51. Years later, Goldman would insist that the "revolution" had benefited women while the "regime" had done nothing. See EG to Ethel Mannin, 16 July 1937, XVII, EG Archive, IISH.

52. Fitzpatrick, *The Commissariat of Enlightenment,* pp. 73–74; also Cohen, *Bukharin,* pp. 20–276. Only 3 percent of the country's teachers were party members, and in 1929, less than 12 percent of all state employees; of official press personnel in 1925, perhaps one-third were non-Communist.

53. *MDIR,* pp. 221–32.

54. See Carr, *The Bolshevik Revolution,* vol. 2, pp. 211–27; Avrich, *Kronstadt,* pp. 26–31; Goldman later said that "out of the whole Russian debacle, only the peasants have gained a single thing. They have the land. . . ." This admission contradicts Goldman's earlier claims of failure, since the peasants constituted some 80 percent of the Russian population in the late 1920s. See W. S. Van Valkenburgh, "Emma Goldman Speaks Again," *Road to Freedom,* December 1926. See also Cohen, *Bukharin,* p. 274: "In short-term gains, the peasant had emerged as the chief beneficiary of the upheaval."

55. Cohen, *Bukharin,* p. 125.

56. *MDIR,* p. 233; *LML,* p. 900.

57. *MDIR,* pp. 257, 250, 258. There are no references to writings by either Marx or Lenin anywhere in the book, and it is unclear how familiar either Goldman or Berkman were with Marxism. See William Nowlin, "The Political Thought of Alexander Berkman" (Ph.D. diss., Tufts University, 1980).

58. See Cohen, *Bukharin,* p. 53; also Smith, *Red Petrograd,* pp. 149–50.

59. Michael Bakunin, "Statism and Anarchy," in *Bakunin on Anarchy*, ed. Sam Dolgoff (New York: Vintage, 1971), p. 332.

60. EG to Max Nettlau, 12 December 1922, Nettlau Archive, IISH.

61. EG to AB, 17 December 1927, in *NAH*, p. 81. In an unpublished lecture, "Constructive Revolution," Goldman would argue later that Bakunin had been wrong to assert that the spirit of destruction was also the spirit of construction, except in the sense that cultural change cannot occur unless old conceptions and values are eradicated. The failures in Russia were due not only to the Bolsheviks and the backwardness of the masses, but to their lack of constructive preparation for self-organization. More than anything else, that preparation was needed if a truly libertarian revolution were one day to be achieved (EG Archive, IISH).

62. Irving Howe, *World of Our Fathers* (New York: Harcourt, Brace, Jovanovich, 1976) p. 329; also Leonard I. Krimmerman and Lewis Perry, eds., *Patterns of Anarchy* (New York: Doubleday, 1966), p. 98.

63. For example, EG to John Haynes Holmes, 27 January 1940, 17 February 1940, John Haynes Papers, Library of Congress. See also Guerin, *Anarchism*, p. 108; Murray Bookchin, "Listen, Marxist!" in *Post-Scarcity Anarchism* (Berkeley: Ramparts Press, 1971), pp. 204–8; Noam Chomsky, "The Soviet Union and Socialism," *The Radical Papers*, ed. Dimitrios Roussopoulos (Montreal: Black Rose, 1987), pp. 50–51. For an analysis of the "continuity" thesis, see Stephen F. Cohen, *Rethinking the Soviet Experience* (New York: Oxford, 1985), pp. 38–62: "Stalin's new policies of 1929–1933, the 'great change' as they became known, were a radical departure from Bolshevik programmatic thinking."

64. Cohen, *Bukharin*, pp. 272–73. Fitzpatrick, *The Commissariat of Enlightenment*, pp. 288 ff.

65. See Robert V. Daniels, *The Conscience of the Revolution*, (Cambridge, Mass.: Harvard University Press, 1960), pp. 3–4; Cohen, *Rethinking the Soviet Experience*, pp. 50–53; Lewin, *Making of the Soviet System*, pp. 191–92, 262–64.

66. H. L. Mencken, *American Mercury*, May 1924, p. 122.

67. *New York Times*, 27 January 1924, III, p. 13, 1 February 1925, III, p. 10.

68. *Springfield Republican*, 10 January 1924.

69. *Times Literary Supplement* (London), 5 March 1925, p. 159. See also *Spectator*, 21 February 1925, p. 288.

70. *The Nation*, 12 April 1922, p. 413; *New Republic*, 15 July 1925.

71. Henry Alsberg, *New York Post*, 29 March 1924, p. 629.

72. Henry Alsberg, *New York Herald Tribune*, 26 April 1925, V, p. 5.

73. *The Nation*, 18 February 1925.

74. See Harvey Klehr, *The Heyday of American Communism* (New York: Basic, 1984), p. 4. Even at the peak of its popularity, the American Communist party never exceeded 100,000 members, many of whom belonged for relatively short periods. See Klehr, pp. 365–66, 413.

75. *The Nation,* 18 February 1925.

76. *New York Times,* 16 March 1919, VIII, p. 3, quoted in Peter G. Filene, *Americans and the Soviet Experiment, 1917–1933* (Cambridge, Mass.: Harvard University Press, 1967), p. 59.

77. Marguerite Harrison, *There's Always Tomorrow* (New York: Farrar & Rinehart, 1935), pp. 427, 434–36; see also complaints from a woman member of the National Civil Federation about Harrison's "pro-Bolshevik" talks before women's clubs (22 April 1922, Record Group 59, State Department Decimal File 861.645, National Archives).

78. Goldman took pains to distinguish her anti-Bolshevik arguments, which favored the revolutions of 1917, from those of the Mensheviks and other social democrats such as Karl Kautsky, who argued that Russian industrial backwardness precluded the possibility of a genuine socialist revolution in Russia in 1917. In Goldman's view, such arguments failed to consider "the psychology of the masses at a given period," which in Russia, was ready for revolution. *MDIR,* p. 243.

79. See Albert Lindemann, *The 'Red Years': European Socialism versus Bolshevism, 1919–1921* (Berkeley: University of California Press, 1974), p. 222: "In most countries less than half of the prewar membership [of socialist organizations] converted to the communist cause in the 'red years' of 1919–1921." See also Stephen White, *Britain and the Bolshevik Revolution* (London: Macmillan, 1979), pp. 204–233.

80. David Caute, *The Fellow Travelers* (London: Weidenfeld and Nicolson, 1973), p. 82.

81. E. Malcolm Carroll, *Soviet Communism and Western Opinion, 1919–1921* (Chapel Hill: University of North Carolina Press, 1965), pp. 15, 19.

82. Filene, *Americans and the Soviet Experience,* p. 148.

83. 16 April 1924, 15 May 1924, Record Group 59, State Department Decimal File 861.0-668. See also "Emma Goldman's Blue Days in Red Russia," *Literary Digest,* 15 December 1923, *Illustrated London News,* 22 November 1924; *New York Herald Tribune,* 21 December 1924; *London Sunday Chronicle,* December 1924.

84. The reviews of Berkman's 1925 book, *The Bolshevik Myth,* emphasized this point: "There is nothing new in the volume. The world had either known or guessed all that Berkman tells" (*Literary Review,* 26 September 1925); "His recital of official idiocies, graft, murder, is vivid, but hardly new" (*New York World,* 12 April 1925); "Bears out the impression entertained by most of us" (*Outlook,* 15 July 1925); "Adds many interesting details to the picture of Communist inefficiency, corruption and brutal autocracy with which the world is already familiar" (*New York Times,* 26 April 1925).

85. "Emma Goldman Weary of Bolshevism," *New York Times,* 7 December 1924, IX, p. 5.

86. EG to Stella Ballantine, 20 December 1921, XVI-8, EG Archive, IISH.

87. On the Abrams case, see Richard Polenberg, *Fighting Faiths: The Abrams Case, the Supreme Court, and Free Speech* (New York: Viking, 1987); on Mollie Steimer, see Avrich, *Anarchist Portraits,* pp. 214–26.

88. EG to "Darlin' little Mollie," n.d. [1920s], B-G, Flechine Archive, IISH.

89. Ilya Ehrenburg, *Memoirs: 1921–1941* (New York: World, 1963), p. 16. See also John Willett, *Art and Politics in the Weimar Period* (New York: Pantheon, 1978), pp. 67 ff.

90. EG to Frank Harris, 9 March 1924, VI, EG Archive, IISH.

91. EG to Stella Ballantine, 7 December 1923, VII-B, EG Archive, IISH; AB to Dr. Michael Cohn, 10 October 1922, in *NAH,* p. 24. In his diary, Berkman claimed to have written the entire last chapter, the "Afterword," in *My Disillusionment*. If he did, Goldman never acknowledged his contribution. See AB "Diary," 22 May 1930, XXI, AB Archive, IISH.

92. Kay Boyle, "Alexander Berkman," *The Phoenix* (Summer and Fall 1977): 158–71. Also Kay Boyle, interview, San Francisco, 22 July 1979. Boyle knew both Berkman and Goldman in the 1930s in the south of France, where she became close to Emmy Eckstein; Eckstein lived with Boyle briefly in 1938, after Berkman's death.

93. EG to Leon Malmed, 21 September [1923], EG Papers, Schlesinger Library.

94. The IWMA was also referred to by its French and Spanish initials (AIT) and German (IAA).

95. Fermin Rocker, interview, London, July 1986; also Rudolf Rocker, *Revolución,* pp. 252 ff.

96. Fermin Rocker, interview, London, July 1986.

97. EG to AB, 18 March 1932, XVIII-C, AB Archive, IISH.

98. Berkman edited a *Bulletin* for the Joint Committee for the Defense of Revolutionists Imprisoned in Russia, a group made up of émigré Mensheviks, SRs, and Left SRs as well as anarchists. Later he would also serve as a secretary of the International Working Men's Association (IWMA) Relief Fund for Anarchists and Anarcho-Syndicalists Imprisoned or Exiled in Russia.

99. EG to Frank Harris, XVI-1, EG Archive, IISH.

100. Frank Harris, "Emma Goldman," *Contemporary Portraits,* 4th series (London: Grant Richards, 1924).

101. EG to Frank Harris, 9 March 1922, VI-1, EG Archive, IISH.

102. Frank Harris to EG, 15 March 1924, VI-1, EG Archive, IISH.

103. EG to Frank Harris, 2 June 1924, Frank Harris Papers, Harry Ransom Humanities Research Center, University of Texas at Austin.

104. AB to EG, 25 August 1924, XII-B, #8702, EG Archive, IISH.

105. EG to AB, 20 August 1924, XII-B, EG Archive, IISH.

4 Anti-Soviet Campaigns

1. *LML,* p. 966.

2. Stephen Graubard, *British Labour and the Russian Revolution, 1917–1924* (Cambridge: Harvard University Press, 1956), p. 291; also White, *Britain and the Bolshevik Revolution,* pp. 232–33.

3. William J. Fishman, *East End Jewish Radicals, 1875–1914* (London: Duckworth, 1975), p. 308.

4. EG to AB, 2 October [1924], XII-B, EG Archive, IISH.

5. See John Quail, *The Slow-Burning Fuse* (London: Granada, 1978), pp. 305–6.

6. Russell, *Autobiography,* vol. 2, pp. 173–74.

7. EG to AB, 20 December 1924, *NAH,* p. 32.

8. EG to AB, 22 December 1924, *NAH,* p. 35.

9. EG to Roger Baldwin, 5 January 1925, EG Papers, NYPL.

10. Harold Laski to EG, 29 December 1924, Nettlau Archive, IISH.

11. Russell, *Autobiography,* p. 172.

12. Bertrand Russell to Henry Alsberg, 29 August 1923, ICPP, Box 5, Folder: Protest Letter to Soviet Russia, NYPL.

13. Harold Laski to EG, 29 December 1924, Nettlau Archive, IISH.

14. EG to Bertrand Russell, 9 February 1925, EG Papers, Tamiment, NYU; also Nettlau Archive, IISH.

15. Bertrand Russell to EG, 14 February 1925, EG Papers, Tamiment Library; in her autobiography, his wife, the feminist Dora Russell, wrote that neither she nor her husband felt they could support Goldman's campaign, "so great already was the hostility to the Bolsheviks in the West." Dora Russell, *The Tamarisk Tree* (London: Elek Books, 1975), p. 97.

16. EG to Roger Baldwin, 5 January 1925, EG Papers, NYPL.

17. See, for example, *U.S. Senate Hearings,* vol. 65, pt. 7, April 24, 1924, for a discussion of this point during Senate debates over recognition of Russia; also Harry Ward to Roger Baldwin, 20 September 1924, ICPP Papers, Box 7, Folder: Ward, NYPL.

18. EG to Harold Laski, 9 January 1925, *NAH,* p. 38; EG to Havelock Ellis, 15 January 1925, EG Papers, Box 2, #12, Tamiment, NYU.

19. EG to AB, 24 February 1925, Nettlau Archive, IISH.

20. Martin Durham, "British Revolutionaries and the Suppression of the Left in Lenin's Russia, 1918–1924," *Journal of Contemporary History* 20, no. 2 (April 1985):219–20.

21. See Fenner Brockway's account of his effort to persuade the Political Prisoners Committee of the Second International that there were political prisoners in

Italy, Spain, India, and other countries apart from Russia. Fenner Brockway, *Inside the Left*, (London: Allen & Unwin, 1947), pp. 166 ff.

22. EG to Havelock Ellis, 26 February 1925, EG Papers, Tamiment Library.

23. Preface to second volume of the American edition of *MDIR*, p. liii.

24. EG, "There is No Communism in Russia," *American Mercury*, April 1935, p. 397; Serge, *Memoirs*, p. xv; EG to AB, 2 October [1924], XII-B, #8706, EG Archive, IISH.

25. *Westminster Gazette*, 7 April 1925; *Illustrated London News*, 22 November 1924; *New York Times*, 13 November 1924, 22 November 1924, 7 December 1924, IX, 30 January 1925, 5 April 1925; *The Times* (London), 13 November 1924, 23 November 1924, 30 November 1924, 7 December 1924, 31 January 1925; *London Daily Express*, 10 November 1924; *American Mercury*, June 1926.

26. *Times* (London), 31 January 1925; *New York Times*, 30 January 1925.

27. *Russia. The Official Report of the British Trades Union Delegation to Russia and Caucasia, November and December 1924* (London: Trade Union Congress General Council, 1925), p. 17. See also *Nation*, 1 April 1925, and *The Times* (London), 28 February 1925, for summaries.

28. EG to Roger Baldwin, 20 April 1925, EG Papers, NYPL.

29. EG to Roger Baldwin, 5 January 1925, EG Papers, NYPL.

30. *Russia*, p. 95.

31. EG to Harold Laski, 9 January 1925, in *NAH*, p. 39.

32. EG to Odette Keun, 21 May 1925, Nettlau Archive, IISH.

33. John Turner to EG, 29 December 1924, Nettlau Archive, IISH.

34. "Russia and Her Investigators," typescript, EG Archive, IISH; see also "Emma Goldman Denounces Rule of Soviet," *New York Times*, 5 April 1925.

35. EG to AB, February and March 1925, XIX, AB Archive, IISH. Goldman's accuracy was a subject of dispute between her and Berkman, who criticized her penchant for misinterpretation and insinuation. "You yourself often tell me I am not accurate in facts," Emma wrote him, a charge she attributed to his antifeminism. See EG to AB, 2 October [1924], XVI-B, #8706, EG Archive, IISH. One example suggests Goldman's careless use of evidence. The British trade union report, she noted, gave the following figures for 1924 elementary schools and enrollments: 63,713 first grade schools with 4,683,000 pupils. Goldman compared these figures from the report with those of Lunacharsky, allegedly quoted in *Pravda* for October 19, 1924. Lunacharsky's figures were considerably lower, showing a decline from the prewar period: 49,000 elementary schools, with 3,700,000 pupils. "I wonder who is more misled," asked Goldman, "the Commissar of Education or the Trade Union Delegation?" (EG, "Russia and Her Investigators," p. 6, EG Archive, IISH.) But Goldman's figures were actually for October 1923, the period of lowest enrollment (for in fact the NEP, by reducing state expenditures, drastically cut the resources available for education). School enrollment began to climb again in late 1923, so that by the fall of 1924,

when the British delegation visited Russia, it was considerably higher. The citation from *Pravda* used by Goldman referred to a 1924 speech of Lunacharsky that cited 1923 figures. See Sheila Fitzpatrick, *Commissariat,* p. 285.

36. The report's statement blurs the important distinction between state support and party control; the ruling party did not dominate many areas, including the press, the universities, the schools, or even state bureaucracies, during the 1920s. Nor does Goldman note the predominance of private economic enterprise. According to Stephen Cohen, during the 1920s, "most citizens, particularly the immense peasant majority which still constituted over 80% of the population, lived and worked remote from party or state control" (see *Bukharin,* p. 271).

37. Alsberg, "Russia: Smoked-Glass vs. Rose-Tint," pp. 844–47.

38. Bertrand Russell to Alexander Shapiro, 6 October 1923, ICPP Papers, Box 5, Folder: Protest Letter to Soviet Government, NYPL.

39. Henry Alsberg to Roger Baldwin, 17 May 1924, ICPP Papers, Box 5, Folder: Alsberg, NYPL.

40. Roger Baldwin to EG, 15 September 1924, EG Papers, NYPL; Roger Baldwin to AB, 8 September 1924, ICPP Papers, Box 5, Folder: Soviet Russia, NYPL.

41. AB to Roger Baldwin, 11 August 1924, ICPP, Box 5, Folder: Soviet Russia—Alexander Berkman, NYPL.

42. EG to Roger Baldwin, 6 November 1924, EG Papers, NYPL.

43. EG to Roger Baldwin, 6 November 1924, EG Papers, NYPL.

44. EG to Roger Baldwin, 6 November 1924, EG Papers, NYPL.

45. Harry Ward estimated, from figures he secured from émigrés and from sources inside Russia, that there were about 1,500 political prisoners and internal exiles, mostly of the old intelligentsia—doctors, lawyers, engineers, professors—and/or members of the old non-Communist revolutionary groups, such as Mensheviks, Socialist Revolutionaries and anarchists. See the *Nation,* 4 March 1925, p. 234; also "Memorandum Regarding Political Prisoners in Russia, ICPP Papers, Box 7, Folder: Ward, NYPL. Ward's figures were challenged by others who argued that many prisoners considered as criminals were really political prisoners—that is, aristocrats, university students, and priests. See F. A. MacKenzie to *The Nation,* 4 March 1925, pp. 293–94. Louis Fischer, *The Nation's* pro-Soviet correspondent, estimated a total of 4,500: 1,500 exiles and 3,000 in jail. For comparative purposes, Fischer pointed out that Germany in 1924 had about 7,000 political prisoners. Other figures for 1924 and 1925 include between 6,000 and 17,000 in Poland, 10,000 in Bulgaria, and over 25,000 in India. See Louis Fischer, "Political Prisoners Under Bolshevism," *The Nation,* 4 March 1925, pp. 237–38; also Louis Fischer to the editors, *The Nation,* 20 May 1925, p. 573; Ludwig Lore to *The Nation,* 4 March 1925, p. 294; Henri Barbusse, "Jailing Workers in Poland," *The Nation,* 11 March 1925; Roger Baldwin, "Political Prisoners," *The Nation,* 21 January 1925, p. 70. By November of 1924, Berkman in

Berlin had compiled a list of 1,000 prisoners and exiles, which included Mensheviks, SRs, Left SRs, Anarchists, and Zionist-Socialists. See Berkman to Baldwin, 30 May 1924, ICPP Papers, Box 5, Folder: Soviet Russia, NYPL. Anarchist prisoners and exiles, according to anarchist sources inside and outside Russia, numbered between 150 to 300. See *Bulletin of the Joint Committee for the Defense of Revolutionists Imprisoned in Russia* (Berlin), *Bulletin of the Relief Fund of the IWMA,* and the *Bulletin of the Anarchist Red Cross,* 1924–28.

46. Baldwin made this decision on his own account, securing money for expenses from Charles Garland's Personal Service Fund, of which he was a trustee. Roger Baldwin, "To Whom it May Concern," 28 November 1924, ICPP Papers, Box 5, Folder: Soviet Russia, Miscellaneous, NYPL.

47. Members included socialists such as Charney Vladeck, manager of the bitterly anti-Soviet *Jewish Daily Forward,* Norman Thomas, Sidney Hillman, and Morris Hillquit; anarchists Harry Kelly, Carlo Tresca, Pedro Esteve, Rose Bernstein; *Nation* editor Freda Kirchwey, historian Samuel Eliot Morrison, former Wobbly Elizabeth Gurley Flynn, Oswald Harrison Villard of pro-Soviet *New Republic;* black sociologist and leader W. E. B. DuBois, radical journalist Carleton Beals, and attorneys Clarence Darrow and Felix Frankfurter.

48. See Eleonore von Eltz, "Report to Temporary Executive Committee," 20 May 1925, ICPP Papers, NYPL.

49. EG to Roger Baldwin, 20 April 1925, EG Papers, NYPL. *The Nation* urged liberals to focus on specific abuses, and not let themselves be carried away "into general denunciation of the Russian Government and its leaders" (p. 232). On *The Nation,* see Sara Alpern, *Freda Kirchwey* (Cambridge, Mass.: Harvard University Press, 1987).

50. EG to Roger Baldwin, 20 April 1925, EG Papers, IISH.

51. Roger Baldwin to EG, 15 May 1925, Roger Baldwin Papers, Princeton University Library.

52. EG to Roger Baldwin, 23 October 1925, EG Papers, Harry Ransom Humanities Research Center, University of Texas, Austin.

53. Minutes, ICPP, 20 May 1925, ICPP Papers, Box 6, NYPL.

54. Lewis Gannett to Roger Baldwin, 1 October 1925, ICPP Papers, Box 5, Folder: Soviet Union, NYPL: "Unless we are perfectly frank about the names and affiliations of these people we expose ourselves to the charge of deliberate deception." (In fact, Baldwin had gone ahead with the book without even informing all committee members of its contents; several, including Freda Kirchwey and Jerome Davis, demanded their names be removed from the list of sponsors; others, including W. E. B. DuBois, Carleton Beals, and Upton Sinclair, resigned from the committee.) See Freda Kirchwey to Roger Baldwin, 16 October 1925, Carleton Beals to Roger Baldwin, 10 December 1925, Upton Sinclair to Roger Baldwin, 16 December 1925, "Memorandum #2" from Kenneth Durant (Tass), ICPP Papers, NYPL.

55. Roger Baldwin to Alexander Berkman, 3 October 1925, ICPP Papers, Box 5, Folder: Soviet Union, NYPL.

56. See Carr, *The Bolshevik Revolution,* vol. 1, pp. 172-73.

57. Carleton Beals to Roger Baldwin, 10 December 1925, ICPP Papers, Box 5, Folder: Letters from Russian Prisons, NYPL.

58. Roger Baldwin to MEB, 18 October 1927, Roger Baldwin Papers, Princeton University Library; see also Roger Baldwin's account to the ICPP of two months' travel in the Soviet Union: "To Our Friends," 23 September 1927 (no. 6), in ICPP Papers, Box 5, NYPL.

59. "I have talked with many ex-prisoners in Russia and abroad, and have read also all the published accounts of the prison experiences of others, and from all of them I gathered that police brutality such as we know it in America is now rare in Russia. To Americans it should be said that the brutality appears to be insignificant compared with the routine cruelties of the third degree practiced daily by every sizeable police department in the United States." Roger Baldwin, *Liberty Under the Soviets* (New York: Vanguard, 1928), p. 186.

60. EG to Roger Baldwin, 3 May 1928, Roger Baldwin Papers, Princeton University Library.

61. Roger Baldwin to EG, 1 June 1928, Roger Baldwin Papers, Princeton University Library.

62. Roger Baldwin to MEB, 18 October 1927, Roger Baldwin Papers, Princeton University Library.

63. EG to AB, 25 February 1925, XIX, AB Archive, IISH. Soon after the publication of the *Letters,* Baldwin also authorized Berkman to begin collecting data on political repression in Poland. Later the committee would publish useful information on political repression in Cuba, Venezuela, Italy, and Peru while amassing information on many other countries, raising money for relief and organizing letter-writing campaigns. As a forerunner of Amnesty International, the committee did useful work once it adopted a broader focus.

64. Max Nettlau to EG, 6 March 1925, XVIII, EG Archive, IISH.

65. EG, "Chinese Revolution," EG Papers, Tamiment Library.

66. EG to Havelock Ellis, 26 February 1925, EG Papers, Box 2, Tamiment Library.

67. EG to AB, 5 December 1924; EG to "dear friend," (probably Frank Harris), n.d., XVIII-B, EG Archive; EG to Senya, 22 August 1925, Flechine Archive, B-G, IISH.

68. EG to Leon Malmed, 24 May 1926, EG Papers, Schlesinger Library.

69. *LML,* p. 984.

70. EG to AB, 23 November 1925, ABXIX, IISH.

71. EG to AB, 6 October 1924, XII-B, EG Archive, IISH; EG to Ethel Mannin, 8 September 1933, #17322, EG Archive, IISH; see also Victoria Glendinning, *Rebecca West* (London: Weidenfeld & Nicolson, 1987), pp. 99-101.

72. EG to Joseph Ishill, 24 November 1925, Joseph Ishill Papers, Harvard University; EG to Senya Flechine, 22 August 1925, Flechine Archive, IISH.

73. EG to AB, 6 June 1925, XIX, AB Archive, IISH.

74. EG to AB, 28 May 1925, *NAH*, p. 128.

75. EG to AB, 4 September 1925, *NAH*, p. 133.

76. Elaine Leeder, "The Gentle Warrior: Rose Pesotta, Anarchist and Labor Organizer" (Ph.D. diss., Cornell University, 1985).

77. See Nicolas Walter, "Guy Aldred," *The Raven* 1 (no. 1), pp. 87–88; Dora Russell, *The Tamarisk Tree,* pp. 169, 174.

78. EG to AB, 18 November 1931, *NAH,* p. 50.

5 Hearts in Unison with Mine

1. EG to AB, 7 July 1925, XIX, AB Archive, IISH.

2. EG to AB, 10 September 1925, *NAH,* p. 134; EG to AB, 6 September 1925, XIX, AB Archive, IISH.

3. Like her earlier book, "Russian Dramatists" largely followed the ethical approach of Kropotkin in his 1905 study, *Ideals and Realities in Russian Literature,* demonstrating the social criticism implicit in the works of the great Russian dramatists. But while calling for an art to awaken the masses to "higher conceptions of thought and life," Goldman took pains to distinguish her vision of popular art from that of pro-Soviet artists such as the director Vsevelod Meyerhold: "higher conceptions of thought and life" evidently did not include Marxist conceptions, which were "propaganda." Ironically, Goldman's lectures on American theater were fresher and less tendentious, judging from her fragmentary notes on Eugene O'Neill, on the feminist playwright Susan Glaspell, and on the little theater movement in America, which Emma herself had helped inspire. "Foremost Russian Dramatists," XXIX-C, #22428, EG Archive, IISH.

4. EG to AB, 9 November 1925, XIX, AB Archive, IISH.

5. Max Nettlau to EG, 19 March 1929, XVIII, EG Archive, IISH.

6. Max Nettlau to EG, 22 December 1923; 9 August 1925, 30 March 1927, XVIII, EG Archive, IISH.

7. Max Nettlau to EG, 16 March 1928, XVIII; EG Archive, Nettlau to EG, 21 December 1929, XVIII, EG Archive, IISH.

8. Glendinning, *Rebecca West,* p. 100.

9. Ethel Mannin, *Privileged Spectator* (London: Jarrolds, 1939), p. 62.

10. Brockway, *Inside the Left,* p. 298.

11. Herbert Read, EG Papers, Tamiment Library.

12. EG to Nellie Harris, 29 July 1925, Humanities Research Center, University of Texas, Austin. At this time Harris's third volume of his autobiography, *My Life and Loves,* had been seized by American authorities.

13. EG to AB, 20 August 1925, XIX; AB Archive, EG to AB, 23 August 1925, XIX; AB Archive, EG to AB, XIX, 23 August 1925, AB Archive, IISH. Fitzgerald was secretary of the Provincetown Playhouse, which was putting on a performance in London of Eugene O'Neill's play, *The Emperor Jones,* with Robeson in the lead role.

14. EG to Frank Harris, 6 September 1925, EG Archive, XVIII-B; Paul Robeson mss, 1 March 1933, II-6, EG Archive, IISH.

15. Evelyn Scott to Stella Ballantine, 1 March 1940, courtesy of Federico Arcos.

16. See D. A. Callard, *Pretty Good for a Woman: The Enigmas of Evelyn Scott* (London: Jonathan Cape, 1985), pp. 191, 164.

17. See Callard, *Woman,* pp. 191, 164.

18. EG to Evelyn Scott, 22 November 1938, EG Papers, Tamiment Library; EG to Evelyn Scott, 9 February 1939, courtesy Eva Langbord.

19. EG to Evelyn Scott, 9 February 1939, courtesy Eva Langbord; Evelyn Scott to EG, 4 November 1939, courtesy Federico Arcos.

20. "Yes, you are good to say it, Emma dear—there is some satisfaction in having the Dies Committee expose a little of the truth." Evelyn Scott to EG, 4 November 1939, courtesy Federico Arcos; EG to Bill Ryan, 19 December 1939, *VOF,* pp. 197–98.

21. EG to Evelyn Scott, 9 February 1939, courtesy Eva Langbord; Evelyn Scott to EG, 4 November 1939, courtesy Federico Arcos; Evelyn Scott to SB, 1 March 1940, courtesy Federico Arcos.

22. Angelica Balabanoff to EG, Monday, 8 February (n.y.), XVIII-C, AB Archive, IISH.

23. EG to AB, 26 February 1927, XIX, AB Archive, IISH.

24. *Toronto Star,* 30 November 1926; see also interview with Frederick Griffin, *Toronto Star,* 31 December 1926.

25. EG to AB 15 March 1927, XIX, AB Archive, IISH. EG to AB, 26 February, 1927, XIX, AB Archive; Goldman added that "the Jewish press in America would make you vomit."

26. EG to AB, 15 March 1927, XIX, AB Archive, IISH.

27. EG to AB, 2 May 1927, XIX, AB Archive, IISH.

28. Interview with Bertha Malmed, Rochester, New York, May 1983.

29. Paul Kennedy, "Emma Goldman: A Life of Anarchy," (Canadian Broadcasting Corporation, 1983), p. 28.

30. EG to Evelyn Scott, 17 October 1927, *NAH,* p. 199.

31. AB to EG, 7 December 1929, *NAH,* p. 79.

32. EG to AB, 6 June 1927, XIX, AB Archive, IISH.

33. EG to Esther Laddon, 15 February 1928, Esther Laddon Papers, Schlesinger Library.

34. Norman Arthur to William J. Burns, 16 April 1924, State Department

Decimal File 861.668, Record Group 59, National Archives. 21 October 1926, Record Group 59, State Department Decimal File 311.6124, National Archives.

35. Isaac Don Levine, 8 November 1926, State Department Decimal File 861.668, Record Group 59, National Archives.

36. AB to EG, 7 December 1927, *NAH,* p. 78.

37. EG to AB, 23 December 1927, EG Papers, Tamiment Library.

38. EG to Leon Malmed, 2 November 1926, EG Papers, Schlesinger Library.

39. EG to Leon Malmed, 2 November 1926, EG Papers, Schlesinger Library.

40. EG to Leon Malmed, 17 November 1926, 19 November 1926, EG Papers, Schlesinger Library. See also Falk, *Love, Anarchy and Emma Goldman,* pp. 74–77.

41. EG to Leon Malmed, 17 November 1926, EG Papers, Schlesinger Library.

42. EG to Leon Malmed, 21 November 1926, EG Papers, Schlesinger Library.

43. EG to Leon Malmed, 18 November 1926, 12 December 1926, 13 December 1926, EG Papers, Schlesinger Library.

44. EG to Leon Malmed, 29 December 1926, EG Papers, Schlesinger Library.

45. EG to Leon Malmed, 5 February 1927, 21 February 1927, EG Papers, Schlesinger Library. See Karen Rosenberg, "The 'autumnal love' of Red Emma," *Harvard Magazine* (January–February 1984), pp. 52–56.

46. EG to Leon Malmed, 10 July 1927, 14 July 1927, 29 September 1927, EG Papers, Schlesinger Library.

47. EG to Leon Malmed, 3 February 1927, EG Papers, Schlesinger Library.

48. EG to Leon Malmed, 7 January 1928, EG Papers, Schlesinger Library.

6 Writing a Life

1. Frederic A. Steele, typescript, Emma Goldman Papers, Tamiment Library.

2. EG to Arthur Ross, 2 September 1929, V, EG Archive, IISH.

3. EG to Frank Harris, 29 June 1927, XVIIIB, EG Archive, IISH. Writing her for information about "pivotal incidents" in her early life in America, Dreiser told her that he thought his portrait would help publicize her autobiography, and that it "would result in your return to this country. I think I might be even more able to justify you to society than you yourself would," he wrote, "because I have always felt that I knew, not exactly why you are as you are mentally and chemically, but being what you were, why you did as you did." He promised her that on an imminent trip to Washington, he would use his influence to "have the ban on you lifted. You really belong on Thirteenth Street, near Fourth Avenue." (Theodore Dreiser to EG, 15 December [1928], IISH.) Unfortunately Goldman was too busy with her autobiography to offer Dreiser much assistance, and the portrait remained unwritten. Yet corresponding with Dreiser may have awakened

Goldman's memories of *Sister Carrie*, for the opening paragraphs of *Living My Life* strongly echo those of Dreiser's novel.

4. Emily Coleman to EG [1930], XVIII-C, EG Archive, IISH.

5. EG to AB, 29 June 1928, EG Archive, IISH; EG to Evelyn Scott, 26 June 1928, *NAH*, p. 84; EG to Ben Capes, 4 July 1928, Esther Laddon Papers, Schlesinger Library.

6. Emily Coleman to EG, n.d., EG Archive, XVII-C, IISH; EG to Demi Coleman, 6 December 1930, XVII-C, EG Archive, IISH; EG to Demi Coleman, 24 February 1939, EG Papers, Schlesinger Library.

7. EG to Arthur Ross, 25 June 1928, V, EG Archive, IISH.

8. AB diary, 29 September 1930, XXI, EG Archive, IISH.

9. AB diary, 30 November 1928, XXI, AB Archive, IISH.

10. EG to Saxe Commins, 27 January 1929, EG Archive, IISH.

11. AB diary, 19 January 1929, XXI, AB Archive, IISH.

12. Rocker, *Revolución y Regresión,* pp. 679 ff.

13. EG to John Haynes Holmes, n.d., EG Papers, NYPL.

14. EG to W. S. Van Valkenburgh, 7 June 1927, EG Archive, XV-A, IISH.

15. EG to Arthur Ross, 10 October 1929, EG Papers, Tamiment Library.

16. Quoted in John Paul Eakin, *Fictions in Autobiography: Studies in the Art of Self-Invention* (Princeton: Princeton University Press, 1985), p. 25; see also Kenneth Barkin, "Autobiography," *Societas* 6, no. 2 (Spring 1976): 83–108.

17. Sidonie Smith, *A Poetics of Women's Autobiography* (Bloomington: Indiana University Press, 1987), p. 19.

18. EG to AB, 20 February 1929, in *NOAH,* p. 145.

19. EG to Van Valkenburgh, n.d., EG Archive, IX-12, IISH.

20. Maurice Hanline to EG, 5 June 1929, EG Papers, Tamiment Library; EG to Horace Liveright, 17 July 1929, XVII, EG Archive, IISH.

21. EG to Arthur Ross, 8 April 1929, EG Papers, Box I, Tamiment Library; EG to Arthur Ross, 24 August 1929, V, EG Archive, IISH.

22. EG to Karin Michaelis, 11 October 1929, EG Archive, XVII-A, IISH; EG to Saxe Commins, 14 October 1929, EG Archive, XVII-A, IISH.

23. EG to Arthur Ross, 10 October 1929, EG Papers, Box 1, Tamiment Library; EG to Arthur Ross, 23 April 1930, XV-B, EG Archive, IISH.

24. EG to Harry Kelly, 6 May 1930, X-8, EG Archive, IISH.

25. EG to Arthur Ross, 10 May 1930, XV-B, EG Archive, IISH; EG to Alfred Knopf, 12 May 1930, V, EG Archive, IISH.

26. Alfred Knopf to EG, 3 June 1930, V-B, EG Archive, IISH.

27. EG to Arthur Ross, 23 November 1930, EG Papers, 72 M1:55, Tamiment Library. See also Richard Drinnon, *Rebel in Paradise,* pp. 292–93.

28. Goldman was also furious when Knopf sold the Yiddish translation rights for her autobiography to the Socialist *Forward,* insisting that it belonged in the

anarchist *Fraye Arbeter Stimme,* although earlier she had opposed having it appear in the anarchist paper because of its small circulation. She also hated the *Forward*'s translation, which she thought "common" and unliterary. See EG to Arthur Ross, 18 June 1930, V, EG Archive, IISH; EG to Mendel Oscherovitch, 1 December 1931, Yivo Institute.

29. EG to Ross, 10 September 1929, V, EG Archive, IISH; EG to Saxe Commins, 8 October 1931, XVIII-A, EG Archive, IISH.

30. EG to AB, 14 December 1931, XIII-A, EG Archive, IISH; EG to AB, 16 December 1931, XIII-A, EG Archive, IISH.

31. EG to Ross, 21 December 1931, EG Papers, Tamiment Library.

32. *LML,* pp. 16–17; Carolyn Ashbaugh makes this point in *Lucy Parsons: American Revolutionary* (Chicago: Charles Kerr, 1976), p. 181.

33. Patricia Meyer Spacks, "Selves in Hiding," in *Women's Autobiography: Essays in Criticism,* ed. Estelle C. Jelinek (Bloomington: Indiana University Press, 1980), p. 134.

34. On the anarchists' use of religious imagery see Blaine McKinley, " 'A Religion of the New Time': Anarchist Memorials to the Haymarket Martyrs, 1888–1917," *Labor History* (Summer 1987): 386–400; see also Peter Conn, *The Divided Mind: Ideology and Imagination in America, 1898–1917* (Cambridge: Cambridge University Press, 1983), pp. 292–314.

35. Spacks, "Selves in Hiding," pp. 131–32.

36. *LML,* p. 686.

37. *LML,* p. 153.

38. See Wexler, *Emma Goldman in America,* pp. 139–161; Falk, *Love, Anarchy and Emma Goldman.*

39. According to the memoir, Goldman was told by doctors that she suffered from an inverted womb, a catch-all gynecological condition that was not known, however, to cause infertility. She was also told that surgery could correct the condition, but she chose not to have the operation. In reality, she seems to have suffered from endometriosis, which may have caused both her severe menstrual cramps and her infertility. See Falk, *Love, Anarchy and Emma Goldman,* pp. 30, 147–48.

40. EG to AB, 4 September 1925, *NAH,* p. 133.

41. Frank Harris to EG, 23 January 1925, *NAH,* p. 125.

42. EG to Harris, 7 August 1925, *NAH,* pp. 129–30.

43. *LML,* pp. 20–23; EG to Ethel Mannin, 15 May 1933, EG Papers, NYPL.

44. *LML,* pp. 420, 433–44, 695.

45. Richard Poirier to author, 15 September 1981. Conn, *The Divided Mind,* pp. 292–315); also Mari Jo Buhle, "Emma Goldman," *In These Times,* 23–29 January 1985, pp. 10–11; see also Rachel Blau DuPlessis, *Writing Beyond the Ending: Narrative Strategies of Twentieth-Century Women Writers* (Bloomington: Indiana University Press, 1985), pp. 40 ff.; That Goldman had been reading books

such as Isadora Duncan's *My Life,* and Marie Jenney Howe's romantic biography, *George Sand: The Search for Love,* may have had some influence in this respect.

46. Ben Reitman to EG, 6 December 1931, EG Archive, IISH, quoted in Falk, *Love, Anarchy and Emma Goldman,* p. 399.

47. Roger Bruns, *The Damndest Radical: The Life and Work of Ben Reitman* (Urbana: University of Illinois Press, 1987).

48. EG to Ben Reitman, 9 March 1926, quoted in Suzanne Poirier, "Emma Goldman, Ben Reitman, and Reitman's Wives: A Study in Relationships," *Women's Studies* 14 (February 1988): 277–97.

49. EG to Fremont Older, 19 December 1931, Bancroft Library, University of California, Berkeley.

50. For example, she showed her first husband as impotent and suicidal; her lover Ed Brady as driven to drink and suicide by frustrated longing for her; another anarchist lover, the Greenwich Village denizen Hippolyte Havel, as a petulant, if talented, drunk. She portrayed the German-American anarchist Carl Nold engaged in an ugly fight with his wife who resented having to yield the one bed in their tiny flat to Emma, while she and her husband slept on the floor. She showed the American anarchist Voltairine deCleyre as mean-spirited and ungenerous; the Yiddish anarchists of the Lower East Side as timid and provincial. She unfairly implied that Abraham Isaak, the editor of a Chicago anarchist weekly, *Free Society,* had inadvertently inspired the assassination of President McKinley by placing a spy warning about Leon Czolgosz in his paper and implicitly accused Isaak of implicating her in the assassination by telling a reporter she had introduced Leon Czolgosz to them.

51. I am grateful to Heiner Becker for making this point clear to me. In her *American Mercury* article, Emma had placed Most's attack on Berkman and herself within the context of his previously awakened doubts about the value of the *attentat* and had emphasized that his repudiation of Berkman had only seemed to her then a betrayal of his principles. *LML,* p. 105; Max Nettlau to EG, 23 December 1931, XVII, EG Archive, IISH. See Heiner Becker, "Johann Most," *Haymarket Scrapbook,* ed. Dave Roediger and Franklin Rosemont (Chicago: Charles Kerr, 1986), pp. 137–39; also Heiner Becker, *John Most* (Muntzen: Büchse der Pandora, 1985); Rocker, *Johann Most,* pp. 199 ff.

52. In his 1912 account, *Prison Memoirs of an Anarchist,* Berkman had implied that Most suddenly reversed himself in 1892 and suggested that he may have been motivated by fear of being held responsible for Berkman's act and risking yet another imprisonment: an understandable hypothesis from one who had been the victim of Most's harsh criticism and was only recently released from prison himself. But Goldman, writing in 1928, knew that Berkman's 1912 account had erred, yet she essentially repeated his analysis, which cast a more favorable light on Berkman as well as on herself than the analysis she had presented in 1926.

53. EG to AB, 29 June 1928, XVIII-C, EG Archive, IISH.

54. See Wexler, *Emma Goldman in America,* p. 13; also "The Early Life of Emma Goldman," *The Psychohistory Review* 8, no. 4 (Spring 1980): 11 ff.

55. I am grateful to Dr. Alan Z. Skolnikoff for insights suggested to me in a letter, 5 October 1980.

56. Emma Goldman, *Anarchism and Other Essays* (1911; reprint New York: Dover, 1969), pp. 213–14.

57. EG to Agnes Inglis, 22 February 1931, Labadie Collection, University of Michigan, Ann Arbor; EG to Ann Strunsky Walling, 3 October 1931, IV-A, EG Archive, IISH.

58. AB to Minna Lowensohn, 2 December 1931, XIV-B, AB Archive, IISH.

59. EG to Eunice Schuster, 18 November 1931, EG Archive, IISH.

60. *New York Herald Tribune,* 25 October 1931.

61. John Haynes Holmes to EG [1932], EG Papers, 72M1:196, Tamiment Library.

62. *The Nation,* 2 December 1931, 612–14; see also Sara Alpern, *Freda Kirchwey: A Woman of the Nation* (Cambridge, Mass.: Harvard University Press, 1987), pp. 96–97. Goldman liked Kirchwey's review, which she thought "the most penetrating and understanding," as she told Kirchwey a few years later. EG to Freda Kirchwey, 14 July 1934, VI-2, EG Archive.

63. Saxe Commins to EG, 13 June 1931, EG Archive, IISH.

64. Jennie Austin to Carl Nold, 13 March 1932, EG Papers, Labadie Collection, University of Michigan.

65. Lucy Parsons to Carl Nold, 30 May 1932, Labadie Collection, University of Michigan.

66. Agnes Inglis to Roger Baldwin, 11 July 1935, Labadie. EG to Ann Lord, 22 July 1935, EG Papers, Labadie Collection, University of Michigan.

67. See Paul Buhle, "Anarchism and American Labor," *International Labor and Workingclass History,* 23 (Spring 1983): 21–34; Dorothy Gallagher, *All the Right Enemies: The Life and Murder of Carlo Tresca* (New Brunswick: Rutgers University Press, 1988).

7 My Hungry Heart

1. EG to Arthur Ross, 7 August 1932, EG Papers, 72M:103, Tamiment Library; EG to Van Valkenburgh, 4 Jan. 1932, XV-A, EG Archive, IISH.

2. Goldman avoided French anarchist groups that were "constantly watched" and stayed away from anarchist meetings in Paris that were always "full of spies." EG to AB, 15 November 1925, AB Archive, XIX, IISH.

3. EG to Joseph Ishill, 29 March 1933, Houghton Library, Harvard University.

4. EG to Joseph Ishill, 29 March 1933, Joseph Ishill Papers, Houghton Library, Harvard University.

5. EG to H. Tilton, 21 October 1933, #12,251, EG Archive, IISH.

6. AB to Mollie Steimer, 16 August 1933, Berkman File, Flechine Archive, IISH.

7. Roger Baldwin to EG, 16 November 1933, ACLU Papers, vol. 609, p. 63, Princeton University Library.

8. Roger Baldwin to EG, 27 December 1933, ACLU Papers, vol. 609, p. 63, Princeton University Library.

9. Roger Baldwin to EG, 2 January 1934, ACLU Papers, vol. 690, Princeton University Library.

10. EG to Angelica Balabanoff, 7 January 1934, XVI-2, EG Archive, IISH.

11. EG to Ross, 16 January 1934, XVIII-B, AB Archive, IISH.

12. EG to AB, 21 January 1934, ABXVIII-B, AB Archive, IISH.

13. Roger Baldwin, interview by Peggy Lamson, transcript, p. 51, Roger Baldwin Papers, Princeton University Library.

14. *Daily Worker,* 7 February 1934; Madison *Times,* 29 March 1934. See also *New York Herald Tribune,* 3 February 1934; *New York Sun,* 8 February 1934; *New York World-Telegram,* 1 February 1934; *New York Times,* 10 January 1934, 12 February 1934.

15. See Drinnon, *Rebel in Paradise,* pp. 278–79.

16. EG to AB, 19 February 1934, XVIII-C, AB Archive, IISH.

17. Edward H. Zabriski to EG, 29 April 1934, Harry Weinberger Papers, 29-9, Yale University Library.

18. Ernest L. Meyer to EG, 22 May 1934, Weinberger Papers, 29-9, Yale University Library.

19. EG to Arthur Ross, 5 April 1934, EG Papers, Tamiment Library, NYU.

20. EG to AB, 14 March 1934, XVIII-B, AB Archive, IISH.

21. EG to AB, 19 February 1934, XVIII-C, AB Archive, IISH. See Klehr, *The Heyday of American Communism,* p. 153 ff; Mark Naison, *Communists in Harlem during the Depression* (Urbana: University of Illinois Press, 1983); Eric Foner, "Why is there no Socialism in the United States?" *History Workshop* (Spring 1984), p. 72. Foner estimates the CP had "under 100,000" at its peak. EG to Ben and Idea Capes, 16 February 1934, EG Papers, Schlesinger Library.

22. EG to AB, 27 May 1934, *NAH,* p. 235.

23. EG to AB, 27 May 1934, *NAH,* p. 235.

24. Klehr, *Heyday of American Communism,* pp. 165–66.

25. EG to C.V.[Cook], 2 April 1934, XVIII-B, AB Archive, IISH, EG to AB, 2 April 1934, XVIII-A, AB Archive, IISH.

26. James R. Mellow, *Charmed Circle. Gertrude Stein and Company* (New York: Praeger, 1974), pp. 382–84.

27. "Emma Goldman," *The Nation,* 21 March 1934, p. 320.

28. EG to Roger Baldwin, 20 December 1934, ACLU Archives, Princeton University Library.

29. EG to AB, 27 May 1934, *NAH,* p. 234; EG to Roger Baldwin, 19 June 1935, X-8, EG Archive, IISH.

30. See Joseph Cohen, "The Jewish Anarchists," trans. Esther Dolgoff, type-script, chap. 52; also Dolgoff, *Fragments,* pp. 19, 24–28; also Paul Buhle, interview with Morris Nadelman, 8 April 1980, Oral History of the American Left, Series IV, Filmmaker Tapes and Transcripts: "Anarchism in America" [Pacific Street Films], Tamiment Library.

31. Interview with Sam Dolgoff, New York, 13 May 1983; see also Dolgoff, *Fragments,* pp. 11–17.

32. Dolgoff, *Fragments,* pp. 75–78.

33. EG to HB [June or July 1934], XVIII-A, AB Archive, IISH.

34. EG to Joseph Ishill, 29 December 1927, Joseph Ishill Papers, Houghton Library, Harvard University.

35. The book was reissued in 1936 under the title *Now and After: The ABC of Communist Anarchism;* Freedom Press in London issued an abridged version, *ABC of Anarchism,* in 1964.

36. See Smith, *Red Petrograd,* pp. 246–48, 259–60.

37. AB to EG, 25 June 1928, *NAH,* p. 84.

38. EG to AB, 29 June 1928, 3 July 1928, *NAH,* pp. 87–89.

39. Occasionally Goldman tried to be more concrete, arguing against expropriation, for example, and extolling peasant cooperatives and the goal of economic autonomy for nations. See EG to AB, 6 June 1927, XIX, AB Archive, IISH.

40. In fact, many of the small properties initially expropriated after the October revolution were returned to private ownership under the NEP. See Cohen, *Bukharin,* pp. 123–24; also Carr, *Russian Revolution,* vol. 2, pp. 337, 339.

41. AB to Max Nettlau, 28 June 1927, I-a, AB Archive, IISH. Also AB to Abe Coleman, 14 April 1934: "We had no practical method of systematic propaganda among the working masses; nor did we have any practical program to be applied on the day after the Revolution." XIV-A, AB Archive, IISH. EG to AB, 6 June 1927: "One thing I fervently hope, that you do not allow yourself to be carried away by the stupid programmes, the idea of party, etc. . . . As you say yourself, it is Bolshevism only it lacks the ability and vision of the leading Bolsheviks." XIX, AB Archive, IISH.

42. "The Tragedy of the Political Exiles," *Nation,* 10 October 1934; "Was My Life Worth Living," *Harpers,* December 1934; "There is No Communism in Russia," *American Mercury,* April 1935; AB to EG, 21 June 1934, VIII-B, AB Archive, IISH; AB to Mollie Steimer, 10 June n.d. (pre–1930): "Real progress, in the direction of OUR ideas, is very slow, yet it exists, nevertheless. One revolu-

tion does not change a world, even if it were a successful one. . . . Our own work is therefore clear—to break down the old belief in the State and political parties, and to prepare the people to rely on and exercise their own powers in their revolutionary activities—now and in the revolution." II, Flechine Archive, IISH. AB to EG, 12 May 1934, XVIII-A, AB Archive, AB to EG 4 February 1935, XVIII-B, AB Archive, IISH.

43. EG to Augustine Souchy, 20 January 1935, XVI-7, EG Archive, IISH; EG to "comrade," 27 May 1935, EG Papers, Schlesinger Library.

44. EG to Rose Pesotta, 17 December 1935, EG Papers, NYPL.

45. Joe Goldman to EG, 11 June 1934, Lindner Archive, IISH; EG to Joe Goldman, 31 July 1934, EG Papers, Tamiment Library.

46. EG to AB, 16 June 1934, XVIII-C, AB Archive, IISH.

47. EG, "Anarchists and Elections," *Vanguard,* June–July 1936. *Vanguard* editors disagreed, arguing that criticism of Spanish anarchist tactics should be based on an analysis of the concrete situation, not abstract principle.

48. EG to AB, 16 June 1934, XVIII-C, AB Archive, IISH; AB to EG, 1 July 1934, XVIII-A, AB Archive, IISH.

49. EG to Joe Goldman, 31 July 1934, EG Papers, Tamiment Library.

50. Stephen Cohen, *Bukharin,* pp. 337–39.

51. See Arch Getty, *Origins of the Great Purges: The Soviet Communist Party Reconsidered, 1933–1938* (Cambridge: Cambridge University Press, 1985), pp. 4–9, 201–6; Moshe Lewin, *The Making of the Soviet System,* pp. 286–314; Stephen G. Wheatcroft, "New Demographic Evidence on Excess Collectivization Deaths," *Slavic Review* 44, no. 3 (Fall 1986): 505–8.

52. As she reported to Berkman, it was interesting to hear John Haynes Holmes tell her "Well EG, you and Berkman are coming into your own. You were the first to disclose the butcheries in Russia. Now we all know and have to admit it." EG to AB, 24 January 1934, AB Archive, IISH, quoted in Drinnon, *Rebel in Paradise,* pp. 283–84.

53. EG to John Dewey, 10 January 1938, Harry Weinberger Papers, 29-10, Yale University Library.

54. EG to Rudolf Rocker, 19 October 1939, Rocker Archive, 107, IISH.

55. EG to Eugene Lyons, 7 September 1938, courtesy of Charles Glasser.

56. Drinnon, *Rebel in Paradise,* pp. 304, 332; Drinnon, ed., *Living My Life* (New York: NAL, 1977), p. 733; Stephen Cohen, *Rethinking Soviet Realities,* pp. 40–56.

57. EG to Ethel Mannin, 18 November 1937, *VOF,* p. 301.

58. See for example EG to John Haynes Holmes, 27 January 1940, 17 February 1940, John Haynes Holmes Papers, Library of Congress.

59. EG to AB, 30 June 1934, XVIII-A, AB Archive, IISH.

60. EG to AB, 9 April 1934, EG to AB, 21 May 1934, XVIII-A, AB Archive, IISH.

61. EG to Frank Heiner, 6 May 1934, XIV, EG Archive, IISH.

62. Ibid.

63. EG to Emmy Eckstein, 3 July 1934, XVIII-A, EG Archive, IISH; EG to Emmy Eckstein, 30 July 1934, *NAH*, p. 181.

64. EG to AB, 12 July 1934, XVIII-A, AB Archive, IISH.

65. EG to Frank Heiner, 25 June 1934, XIV, EG Archive, IISH.

66. Alice Wexler, "Emma Goldman in Love," *Raritan* 1, no. 4 (Spring 1982): 131–32; Falk, *Love, Anarchy and Emma Goldman,* pp. 428–29.

67. EG to Stella Ballantine, 9 September 1934, XVII-A, EG Archive, IISH. EG to Emmy Eckstein, 28 August 1934, XVIII-A, AB Archive, IISH.

68. EG to AB, 30 August 1934, XVIII-A, AB Archive, IISH; EG to Stella Ballantine, 31 August 1934, 9 September 1934, XVII-A, EG Archive, IISH.

69. Frank Heiner to EG, n.d., XIV, EG Archive, IISH.

70. EG to Emmy Eckstein, 9 September 1934, XVIII-A, AB Archive, IISH; EG to AB, 1 October 1934, XVIII-A, AB Archive, IISH.

71. EG to Emmy Eckstein, 9 September 1934, XVIII-C, AB Archive, IISH; EG to Stella Ballantine, 31 August 1934, XVII-A, EG Archive, IISH; EG to Emmy Eckstein, 9 September 1934, XVIII-A, AB Archive, IISH.

72. Frank Heiner to EG, n.d., XIV, EG Archive, IISH, quoted in Falk, *Love, Anarchy and Emma Goldman,* p. 433.

73. EG to AB, 4 March 1935, XVIII-C, AB Archive, IISH.

74. EG to Frank Heiner, 26 April 1935, XIV, EG Archive, IISH.

75. EG to Frank Heiner, 12 June 1935, XIV, EG Archive, IISH.

76. EG to Frank Heiner, 7 July 1935, XIV, EG Archive, IISH.

77. EG to Frank Heiner, 20 September 1935, XIV, EG Archive, IISH.

78. Frank Heiner to EG, n.d., XIV, EG Archive, IISH.

79. EG to Frank Heiner, 7 July 1935, XIV, EG Archive, IISH.

80. EG to Frank Heiner, 5 December 1935, XIV, EG Archive, IISH.

81. AB to EG, 9 December 1935, XVIII-A, AB Archive, IISH.

82. Frank Heiner to EG, n.d., XIV, EG Archive, IISH.

83. Frank Heiner to EG, n.d., XIV, EG Archive, IISH, quoted in Falk, *Love, Anarchy and Emma Goldman,* p. 464.

84. EG to Frank Heiner, 26 December 1935, XIV, EG Archive, IISH.

85. EG to Frank Heiner, 2 March 1936, XIV, EG Archive, IISH.

8 The Death of Alexander Berkman

1. EG to Emmy Eckstein, 3 July 1934, XVIII-A, AB Archive, IISH; EG to Emmy Eckstein, 20 October 1934, VIII, EG Archive, IISH.

2. Emmy Eckstein to EG [1935], XVIII-A, AB Archive, IISH.

3. Emmy Eckstein to EG, n.d., XVIII-A, AB Archive, IISH.

4. Emmy Eckstein to EG, 19 December 1934, XVIII-A, AB Archive, IISH.

5. Emmy Eckstein to EG, 1 January 1935, XVIII-A, AB Archive, IISH.

6. EG to Henry Alsberg, 27 June 1930, *NAH,* p. 162.

7. AB to EG, 12 June 1934, XVIII-A, AB Archive, IISH.

8. EG to AB, 2 August 1934, XVII-A, EG Archive, IISH.

9. AB to EG, 13 August 1934, XVIII-A, AB Archive, IISH.

10. EG to AB, 27 August 1934, XVIII-A, AB Archive, IISH.

11. EG to AB, 30 August 1934, XVIII-A, AB Archive, IISH.

12. AB to EG, 14 April 1935, XVIII-C, AB Archive, IISH.

13. EG to Rudolf Rocker, 23 July 1936, f. 107, Rocker Archive, IISH.

14. Falk, *Love, Anarchy and Emma Goldman,* p. 459; EG to Emmy Eckstein, 1 August 1935, XXVIII-C, AB Archive, IISH.

15. EG to Emmy Eckstein, 1 August 1935, XVIII-C, AB Archive, IISH.

16. Emmy Eckstein to EG [1935], XVIII-A, AB Archive, IISH.

17. EG to Emmy Eckstein, 12 August 1935, XVIII-A, AB Archive, IISH.

18. EG to Emmy Eckstein, 16 August 1935, XVIII-A, AB Archive, IISH.

19. EG to Emmy Eckstein, 4 September 1935, XVIII-A, AB Archive, IISH.

20. EG to Emmy Eckstein [August 1935], XVIII-A, AB Archive, IISH.

21. EG to AB, 18 July 1935, XVIII-A, AB Archive, IISH.

22. EG to AB, 18 August 1935, XVIII-A, AB Archive, IISH.

23. EG to AB, 4 September 1935, 23 August 1935, XVIII-A, AB Archive, IISH.

24. AB to EG, 20 August 1935, XVIII-C, AB Archive, IISH.

25. AB to EG, 1 September 1935, XVIII-A, AB Archive, IISH.

26. EG to AB, 4 September 1935, XVIII-A, AB Archive, IISH.

27. EG to Emmy Eckstein, 12 August 1935, XVIII-A, AB Archive, IISH.

28. Emmy Eckstein to EG, Nice, Friday, XVIII-C, AB Archive, IISH.

29. Emmy Eckstein to EG, 30 December 1935, XVIII-C, AB Archive, IISH.

30. AB to EG, 6 September 1934, XVIII-A, AB Archive, IISH.

31. EG to AB, 15 August 1934, XVIII-B, AB Archive, IISH.

32. EG to AB, 21 October 1935, XVIII-C, AB Archive, IISH.

33. EG to AB, 25 October 1935, XVIII-B, AB Archive, IISH.

34. AB to EG, 28 October 1935, XVIII-C, AB Archive, IISH.

35. AB to EG, 3 November 1935, XVIII-B, AB Archive, IISH.

36. EG to AB, 6 November 1935, XVIII-B, AB Archive, IISH.

37. Emmy Eckstein to EG, n.d., XVIII-A, AB Archive, IISH.

38. Emmy Eckstein to EG, 2 February 1936, XVIII-C, AB Archive, IISH.

39. AB to EG, 17 February 1936, XVIII-C, AB Archive, IISH.

40. AB to EG, 23 February 1936, XVIII-C, AB Archive, IISH.

41. EG to AB, 26 February 1936, 7 March 1936, XVIII-B, AB Archive, IISH.

42. EG to Emmy Eckstein, 29 February 1936, XVIII-C, AB Archive, IISH.

43. EG to AB, 7 March 1936, XVIII-B, AB Archive, IISH.

44. Emmy Eckstein to EG, 13 March 1936, XVIII-C, AB Archive, IISH; Emmy Eckstein to EG, n.d., XVIII-C, AB Archive, IISH.

45. EG to Emmy Eckstein, 14 March 1936, XVIII-C, AB Archive, IISH.

46. AB to EG, 5 March 1936, XVIII-C, AB Archive, IISH.

47. AB to EG, 5 March 1936, XVIII-C, AB Archive, IISH.

48. AB to EG, 18 March 1936, XVIII-C, AB Archive, IISH.

49. EG to AB, 22 March 1936, *NAH*, pp. 254–55.

50. AB to EG, 21 March 1936, XVIII-C, AB Archive, IISH.

51. EG to Rudolf and Milly Rocker, 12 April 1936, f. 107, IISH.

52. EG to Rudolf and Milly Rocker, 13 May 1936, f. 107, Rocker Archive, IISH.

53. EG to AB, 11 June 1936, XVIII-B, AB Archive, IISH.

54. AB to EG, 24 June 1936, XVIII-C, AB Archive, IISH.

55. EG to AB, 27 June 1936, *NAH*, p. 259.

56. AB to EG, 16 January [1927], XIX, AB Archive, IISH.

57. AB to EG, 23 March 1936, *NAH*, pp. 257–58.

58. EG to "comrades," 12 July 1936, *NAH*, pp. 265–68.

59. AB to EG, 20 May 1929, *NAH*, p. 152.

60. AB to Michael Cohn, 10 October 1922, *NAH*, p. 24.

61. AB to EG, 18 March 1936, *NAH*, p. 253.

9 Spain and the World

1. EG to Stella Ballantine, 6 July 1936, EG to Stella Ballantine, 19 July 1936, EG Papers, NYPL.

2. EG to Rudolf and Milly Rocker, 13 July 1936, f. 107, Rocker Archive, IISH.

3. Among Sasha's papers, Emma had found a note: "I don't want to continue to live a sick man and dependent. Forgive me, darling Emmy and you too Emma. Help Emmy. Love to all, Sasha." Courtesy of Charles Glass. EG to Stella Ballantine, 19 July 1936, f. 10, Rocker Archive, IISH.

4. EG to Stella Ballantine, 2 August 1936, EG Papers, NYPL.

5. Interview with Kay Boyle, San Francisco, 20 July 1979.

6. Reporting Emmy's death to Eleanor Fitzgerald, Emma wrote, "If ever there was a human being who deliberately marched into the arms of death it was Emmy. And yet no human being I have ever met clung to life, so as she, and was so mortally afraid of death. She knew operations would kill her, yet she went under the knife with the greatest of ease. She was the strangest critter I have ever met. . . . As to what she did to Sasha and to me. It is all over so there is no use to write about it. Except this, that while she hated me with deadly hatred and dragged me through the mire, I could never cast her off completely. . . . Poor E's

whole life consisted of deception and such self-centeredness as I have never met before." EG to Eleanor Fitzgerald, 30 June 1939, EG Papers, Tamiment Library.

7. EG to Stella Ballantine, n.d., EG Papers, NYPL.

8. EG to Stella Ballantine, 4 August 1936, EG Papers, NYPL; EG to Rockers, 13 July 1936, Rocker Archive, 107, IISH; Mollie Steimer and Senya Flechine, interview, July 1980, Oral History of the American Left, Series IV, Filmmakers' Tapes and Transcripts: *Anarchism in America* [Pacific Street Films], Tamiment Library.

9. On Spanish anarchism see Murray Bookchin, *The Spanish Anarchists: The Heroic Years, 1868–1936* (New York: Harper & Row, 1977), and Gerald Brenan, *The Spanish Labyrinth* (1943; reprint Cambridge, Mass.: Cambridge University Press, 1985), pp. 131–202.

10. EG to John Cowper Powys, 31 July 1936, EG Archive, IISH.

11. EG to Max Nettlau, 8 February 1935, *NAH*, p. 185. In the 1890s, Emma had participated in protests against the tortures of political prisoners at the infamous Montjuich Prison in Barcelona; she had worked with immigrant anarchists such as Pedro Esteve, editor of the influential paper, *Cultura Obrera;* and she had been instrumental in publicizing the ideas of the Spanish libertarian educator Francisco Ferrer, who had spearheaded the Modern School movement in Spain. See "An Unexpected Dash Through Spain," *Road to Freedom,* April 1929.

12. EG to Nettlau, 13 May 1931, Nettlau to EG, 20 July 1931, 19 September 1932, Nettlau Archive, IISH.

13. EG to Stella Ballantine, 11 September 1936, 3 September 1936, EG Papers, NYPL.

14. PSUC, Partit Socialista Unificat de Catalunya, effectively the Catalonian Communist party; POUM, Partido Obrero de Unificación Marxista, dissident, anti-Stalinist communist party.

15. George Orwell, *Homage to Catalonia and Looking Back on the Spanish War* (London: Penguin, 1966), p. 10.

16. See Burnett Bolloten, *The Spanish Revolution* (Chapel Hill: University of North Carolina Press, 1979), p. 67; Gaston Leval, *Collectives in the Spanish Revolution,* trans. Vernon Richards (London: Freedom Press, 1975), pp. 14–15; Pierre Broué and Emile Témime, *The Revolution and Civil War in Spain* (London: Faber & Faber, 1972), p. 157. Sam Dolgoff, in *The Anarchist Collectives* (New York: Free Life Editions, 1974), p. 71, cites estimates varying between 1,265 and 1,865 collectives.

17. See Paul Preston, *The Spanish Civil War, 1936–1939* (London: Weidenfeld & Nicolson, 1986), pp. 128–29.

18. See Liz Willis, *Women in the Spanish Revolution* (London: Solidarity, 15 October 1975, pamphlet no. 58); Temma Kaplan, "Other Scenarios: Women and Spanish Anarchism," in *Becoming Visible: Women in European History,* ed. Renate Bridenthal and Claudia Koonz (Boston: Houghton Mifflin, 1977), pp. 400–

421; Martha Ackelsberg, "'Separate and Equal'? Mujeres Libres and Anarchist Strategy for Women's Emancipation," *Feminist Studies* 12, no. 1 (Spring 1985): 63–83; also "Mujeres Libres: Individuality and Community; Organizing Women during the Spanish Civil War," *Radical America* 18, no. 4 (1984): 8–19; quote from Teresa Pamies, "The Spanish Civil War," Granada Television.

19. Douglas Little, *Malevolent Neutrality: The United States, Great Britain, and the Origins of the Spanish Civil War* (Ithaca: Cornell University Press, 1985), pp. 221, 247–65.

20. José Peirats, *Emma Goldman: Anarquista de Ambos Mundos* (Madrid: Campo Abierto Ediciones, 1978), p. 196 ff.

21. EG to Tom Bell, 4 October 1936, EG Papers, Schlesinger Library.

22. "I never thought such intelligence among peasants possible," she wrote to the Rockers. EG to Rudolf and Milly Rocker, 1 October 1936, EG Papers, NYPL.

23. EG to Stella Ballantine, 18 November 1936, EG Papers, NYPL; "Albalate de Cinca," *Spain and the World,* 5 March 1937. See also *VOF,* p. 66.

24. Arthur Lehning, interview, Amsterdam, 23 July 1986.

25. H. E. Kaminski, *Ceux de Barcelone* (Paris: Denoël, 1937), pp. 223–40.

26. EG to Rose Pesotta, 12 July 1938, Rose Pesotta Papers, NYPL. Most correspondents were headquartered in Madrid and got their information from official government sources or even from the Russians.

27. After the war, several anarchist writers criticized the leadership of the CNT-FAI—the "influential militants" of the Central Committee—for having imposed the decision to enter the ministries on the mass membership, without adequate consultation. See Vernon Richards, *Lessons of the Spanish Revolution* (1953; reprint London: Freedom Press, 1983), pp. 68–80; José Peirats, *Anarchists in the Spanish Revolution* (Detroit: Black & Red, 1977), pp. 184–89. It is significant that Goldman, who opposed that decision, nonetheless reported in the summer of 1939 that all the comrades she had met in Spain had favored entering the government; that as late as September 1937, when she had "made the rounds" between Barcelona and Madrid, she had heard no criticism of Mariano Vázquez (the CNT general secretary) or of the generally conciliatory policy of the CNT-FAI toward the Republican government. See EG to Rudolf Rocker, 31 August 1939, 107, Rocker Archive, IISH. See Sam Dolgoff's discussion of this controversy in *Fragments: A Memoir* (Cambridge, Mass.: Refract Publications, 1986), pp. 120–27.

28. EG to Mark Mratchny, 3 October 1936, XVI-7, EG Archive, IISH.

29. EG to Rudolf Rocker, 1 October 1936, 107, Rocker Archive, IISH; also EG Papers, NYPL.

30. EG to Rudolf and Milly Rocker, 1 October 1936, 3 October 1936, f. 107, Rocker Archive, IISH.

31. Brenan, *The Spanish Labyrinth,* p. 306; Bolloten, *The Spanish Revolution,* p. 124, gives higher figures.

32. An alternative to the policy of the Communists might have been an alliance, in the early days of the war, between the CNT, the UGT and the POUM, a working-class unity that would have strengthened the revolutionary forces and made them less vulnerable to manipulation by Russia and by the Communists. See Richards, *Lessons*, pp. 55–57; also see Orwell, *Homage to Catalonia*, pp. 61–62: "If the Anarchists, the P.O.U.M., and the Left wing of the Socialists had had the sense to combine at the start and press a realistic policy, the history of the war might have been different."

33. See Broué and Témime, *The Revolution and Civil War in Spain*, pp. 190–95. See Paul Preston, "The Tactics of Amnesia," the *New Statesman*, 8 August 1980, pp. 16–17: "Neither the criminality of Stalinist methods nor the erosion of popular morale can obscure the extent to which many aspects of Communist policy were both realistic and inevitable. Rejected by the democracies, loyalist Spain faced certain defeat in the winter of 1936 until the Soviet Union intervened. Thereafter, the Communists showed that they understood the decisive nature of the military problem as the anarchists and left-wing Socialists had not done. This is not to excuse the dictatorial nature of Communist policy in Spain. It is, however, to say that to pass judgment on that policy without recalling that a war against fascism was going on is . . . unhistorical. . . ."

34. Preston, *Spanish Civil War*, pp. 78–80, 119–138; see also Paul Preston, "The Tactics of Amnesia," the *New Statesman*, 8 August 1980, pp. 16–17. On the other hand, Bolloten argues that no curbing of the revolution could have persuaded Britain or France to alter their policies. See Bolloten, *Spanish Revolution*, p. 173.

35. See Senex, "Anarchist Tactics in Spain," *Vanguard*, February 1938. Also "Emma Goldman on the United Front in Spain," *Spanish Revolution*, 8 January 1937.

36. This position was articulated most trenchantly by Camillo Berneri in his influential paper *Guerra di Classe*. Berneri argued that "the dilemma 'War or Revolution' has no longer any meaning. The only dilemma is this: either victory over Franco, thanks to the Revolutionary War, or Defeat." Berneri predicted early that neither France nor England would aid the Republic, and that halting the revolution in hopes of securing their aid was futile. Instead he proposed a strategy of intensified guerilla warfare behind fascist lines, agitation for Moroccan independence, and pushing forward the social revolution. See Camillo Berneri, "Letter to Frederica Montseny," *Spain and the World*, 4 June 1937; the letter was originally published in *Guerra di Classe*, 14 April 1937; see Noam Chomsky's discussion of Berneri in "Objectivity and Liberal Scholarship," *American Power and the New Mandarins* (New York: Random House, 1967), pp. 109–116, 139.

37. See, for example, the *New York Times*, 7 September 1936.

38. Broué and Témime, *The Revolution and Civil War in Spain*, p. 211; also Brenan, *The Spanish Labyrinth*, p. 325.

39. EG to Mark Mratchny, 3 October 1936, XVI-7, #12326, EG Archive, IISH.

40. "Address at the Mass-Meeting of the Youth of the FAI, 18 October 1936, *Bulletin of Information, CNT-AIT-FAI*, English ed. October 1936, courtesy of Federico Arcos.

41. EG to Stella Ballantine, 14 November 1936, EG Papers, NYPL; EG to Rudolf Rocker, 3 November 1936, EG Papers, NYPL.

42. EG to Stella Ballantine, 8 December 1936, EG Papers, NYPL.

43. Stella Churchill served as the treasurer; sponsors included Dame Sybil Thorndike, novelists Ethel Mannin, Rebecca West, and John Cowper Powys; Havelock Ellis, Sir Barry Jackson, and the actor John Gielgud.

44. See Kingsley Martin, *Editor, "New Statesman" Years, 1931–1945* (Chicago: Henry Regnery, 1968), p. 212.

45. K. W. Watkins, *Britain Divided: The Effect of the Spanish Civil War on British Public Opinion* (London: Thomas Nelson & Sons, 1963), p. 181; see also Little, *Malevolent Neutrality*. In January of 1937, the Roosevelt administration passed an arms embargo outlawing the sale of arms to either side in Spain—a move particularly detrimental to the Republic, since the Nationalists secured weaponry from Germany and Italy.

46. See Robert E. Dowse, *Left in the Centre: The Independent Labour Party* (Evanston, Ill.: Northwestern University Press, 1966). Between 1932 and 1935, the ILP declined from over 16,000 members to a little more than 4,000 (Dowse, p. 193); between 1931 and 1939, the CP grew from 2,500 to 18,000 members. The ILP had a strong regional, decentralist, provincial orientation, and by the 1930s, was strongest in Scotland and Lancashire.

47. Martin Gudell to EG, 11 March 1937, XVIII-D, EG Archive, IISH.

48. Jim Fyrth, *The Signal Was Spain: The Spanish Aid Movement in Britain, 1936–1939* (London: Lawrence & Wishart, 1986), p. 21; see also Martin, *Editor,* p. 214.

49. Alfred Meltzer, a young British anarchist, calls Emma "ambassadress" in his brief memoir, *The Anarchists in London, 1935–1955* (1976; reprint, London: Black Flag, n.d.), p. 14.

50. George Woodcock in Paul Kennedy, "Emma Goldman," p. 25; Quail, *The Slow-Burning Fuse,* emphasizes that the movement had something of a resurgence in 1936; see pp. 306 ff.

51. EG to Martin Gudell, 29 March 1938, XXVIII-B, EG Archive, IISH. In his memoir, Albert Meltzer writes that the membership of the ASU increased very rapidly, though "the unemployed movement, in which we had many supporters, still remained the field of success rather than the factory floor" (p. 16). The nature of the "success" remains unexplained.

52. "Emma Goldman Appeals for Understanding and Support of the CNT-FAI," *Spain and the World,* 5 February 1937.

53. Vernon Richards, interview, London, 29 July 1986.

54. EG to Jeanne Levy, 24 February 1937, XVI-7, EG Archive, IISH; EG to Helmut Rüdiger, 9 March 1937, XXVIII-D, EG Archive, IISH.

55. Vero Richards to EG [8 August 1939], EG to Vero Richards, 29 August 1939; courtesy of Heiner Becker.

56. Herbert Read to EG, 8 August 1939, XXXI, EG Archive; EG to Herbert Read, 1 July 1939, XXXI, EG Archive, IISH; EG to Herbert Read, 7 October 1939, EG Papers, Tamiment, NYU.

57. EG to Herbert Read, 5 June 1939, Tamiment Library, NYU. Another of her admirers and frequent correspondents was the Welsh writer John Cowper Powys, whom she had met in New York.

58. Hugh Thomas, *The Spanish Civil War,* 3d ed. (London: Hamish Hamilton, 1965), p. 984; see also Bolloten, *The Spanish Revolution,* p. 520, n. 98.

59. Little, *Malevolent Neutrality,* p. 248. Goldman later claimed that the Russians had sent old, worn-out weapons. According to Hugh Thomas, "Russian equipment was better qualitatively than anything to be found outside Britain or the U.S. Indeed, the Russian tanks and aircraft were as effective as, if not better than, anything in the world." See Thomas, *The Spanish Civil War,* p. 441.

60. An apocryphal editorial attributed to *Pravda,* 17 December 1936, was widely circulated in the anarchist press in Spain in December of 1936: "So far as Catalonia is concerned, the cleaning up of Trotskyist and Anarcho-Syndicalist elements there has already begun, and it will be carried out there with the same energy as in the U.S.S.R." See, for example, Rudolf Rocker, *The Tragedy of Spain* (1937; reprint, London: ASP, 1986), p. 29.

61. Bolloten considers the possibility that Berneri may have been assassinated by Francoist agents working for Mussolini's secret police in Spain; see *The Spanish Revolution,* p. 430.

62. For accounts of the destruction of the collectives, see Leval, *Collectives,* pp. 329–38; Ronald Fraser, *Blood of Spain: An Oral History of the Spanish Civil War* (New York: Pantheon, 1986), pp. 390–94; Bolloten, *The Spanish Revolution,* pp. 461–63.

63. See Fyrth, *The Signal Was Spain,* p. 217; EG to Ballantine, 26 January 1937, EG Papers, NYPL.

64. EG to Fenner Brockway, 7 April 1937, XXVIII-D, EG Archive, IISH; EG to Jeanne Levey, 24 February 1937, XXVIII-D, EG Archive, IISH. See also EG to Fenner Brockway, 7 April 1937, XVIII-D, EG Archive, IISH.

65. EG to Harry Kelly, 5 April 1937, EG Papers, NYPL; EG to "Comrades," 11 March 1937, XXVIII-D, EG Archive, IISH.

66. George Orwell to Geoffrey Gorer, 16 August 1937, in *The Collected Essays, Journalism and Letters of George Orwell* (London: Secker & Warburg, 1968), p. 285.

67. See, for example, the *New Statesman and Nation,* 22 May 1937, pp. 837–

939; the *Nation*, 15 May 1937; *Daily Worker*, 11 May 1937. The *Nation*'s editorial provoked a sharp response from Bertram Wolfe, who sought to refute it in a long letter, published June 5, 1937. The editors in turn stated their disagreement.

68. See Kingsley Martin's reasons for rejecting the articles in *Editor*, p. 215; George Orwell, *Collected Essays*, pp. 276, 285; Bernard Crick, *George Orwell* (London: Secker & Warburg, 1980). See also George Orwell, "Spilling the Spanish Beans," *New English Weekly*, 29 July 1937, 2 September 1937; also Elinor Langer, *Josephine Herbst* (New York: Warner, 1983), pp. 251–52. Besides establishing editorial policy for the *Nation*, Louis Fischer may also have influenced the editor of the *New Statesman and Nation*, Kingsley Martin, whom he once guided around Spain, and who essentially shared his pro-Communist, antianarchist views. A *Nation* editorial in June 1937 affirmed that the magazine "has steadily depended upon Mr. Fischer's personal experience and continuing contact with developments in Spain to supplement the material available in the press." The previous autumn, 1936, Emma Goldman almost met Fischer in Barcelona. In his 1941 autobiography, *Men and Politics* (New York: Duell, Sloan & Pierce, 1941), Fischer described how he had fled from Moscow to Spain in the fall of 1936, at the beginning of the trials, hoping to find evidence of the "good" Russia which he had now begun to doubt. Familiar with Russian from his years in Moscow (but knowing no Spanish), Fischer was in the habit of consulting daily with the Soviet ambassador to Spain, Marcel Rosenberg, whose interpretations of events clearly shaped his own. Eager to hear the anarchist viewpoint, Fischer was told by Rosenberg that he should consult Emma Goldman in Barcelona. Subsequently Rosenberg informed him, erroneously, that Goldman had become ill and left Spain (p. 371). Fischer doubted "whether I could have achieved very much, for the trouble [between the anarchists and the Communists] ran very deep" (p. 371). Still, in light of the important role of the *Nation* in influencing American left-wing opinion, one cannot help regretting that Fischer and Goldman did not meet, though the chance of any real dialogue was remote. See Kirchwey's editorial in the *Nation*, 5 June 1937.

69. Douglas Little notes that the lone Foreign Office critic of Britain's policy of neutrality was Sir Laurence Collier, who pointed out how Germany and Italy used British fears of Communism to pursue their own aggressive ends, which were more dangerous to Britain than Communism. See Little, *Malevolent Neutrality*, p. 255.

70. Orwell, "Spilling the Spanish Beans," *New English Weekly*, 29 July 1937 and 2 September 1937. Bernard Crick claims that the ideas in *Homage to Catalonia* were "common stock among the free left." Crick, *George Orwell*, pp. 437–38.

71. "Emma Goldman on the United Front," *Spanish Revolution*, 8 January 1937.

72. Paul Preston states that 59,380 brigadiers fought in Spain, not all of them Communists, though many were; see Preston, *The Spanish Civil War*, p. 160; Broué and Témime estimate 50,000, *The Revolution and Civil War in Spain*,

p. 377; Thomas, *The Spanish Civil War,* p. 982, estimates 35,000. The Brigades included two thousand Britons, mostly workers, about half Communists. See Watkins, *Britain Divided,* p. 168. Orwell noted that a staple of Fascist propaganda was the charge that a Russian army occupied Spain. See *Looking Back on the Spanish War,* in *Homage to Catalonia,* pp. 234-35.

73. Max Nettlau to EG, 20 March 1937, XVIII, EG Archive, IISH.

74. Mollie Steimer to EG, 14 January 1937, #20091, EG Archive, IISH.

75. EG to "Mollitchka," 19 January 1937, #20094, EG Archive, IISH.

76. EG to Rudolf Rocker, 14 May 1937, f. 107, Rocker Archive, IISH.

77. EG to Ethel Mannin, 19 September 1937, EG Papers, NYPL.

78. "Address to the International Workingmen's Association, December 1937, in *Red Emma Speaks: Selected Writings and Speeches by Emma Goldman,* ed. Alix Kates Shulman (New York: Vintage, 1972), p. 377.

79. EG to "Comrades," 11 November 1937, Lindner Archive, IISH. In fact, after extensive destruction carried out by the Communists, many collectives were allowed to reform—in order to avoid further damage to the harvest—and continued in existence until the end of the war.

80. EG to "Comrades," 11 November 1937, Lindner Archive, IISH.

81. See "Political Persecution in Republican Spain," *Spain and the World,* 10 December 1937. Pierre Besnard, a secretary of the IWMA, estimated 2,000 prisoners in late 1937; George Orwell thought there were 3,000 prisoners in February of 1938. See George Orwell to Raymond Mortimer, 9 February 1938, *Collected Essays.* Bertram Wolfe suggested 10,000 prisoners in December of 1937, almost certainly an inflated figure, while POUM leader Julian Gorkin agreed with Goldman's estimate of 1,500 in the Modelo Prison of Valencia in late 1937. See Wolfe, *Civil War in Spain,* p. 88; *Spanish Revolution,* 6 December 1937. See also E. H. Carr, *The Comintern and the Spanish Civil War* (New York: Pantheon, 1984), pp. 44-46.

82. EG to Mark Crevans, 4 March 1938, EG Papers, [NYPL].

83. See Peirats, *Emma Goldman,* pp. 252-56.

84. "Address to the International Working Men's Association," in *Red Emma Speaks,* p. 383.

85. *Ibid.,* p. 385.

86. Peirats, *Emma Goldman,* p. 256.

87. Although she was permitted to visit the Modelo prison and also the women's prison in Barcelona—both of which impressed her for their relatively humane conditions—she was denied permission to visit at least one of the prisons in Valencia. It is unclear from the article how she determined the numbers of prisoners, if foreigners were not allowed entry into many prisons. "Political Persecution in Republican Spain," *Spain and the World,* 10 December 1937. On Stalinist persecutions, see Peirats, *Anarchists,* pp. 225-34; Bolloten, *The Spanish Revolution,* pp. 208-9; Thomas, *The Spanish Civil War,* pp. 777-808.

88. Pedro Herrera and Mariano Vázquez to EG, 11 January 1938, XXVIIIB, #19187, EG Archive, IISH.

89. EG to "Dear Comrades," 20 January 1938, XXVIII, #19240, EG Archive, IISH.

90. Meltzer, *The Anarchists in London*, p. 15.

91. EG to Rose Pesotta, 24 May 1938, XVII-A, EG Archive, IISH.

92. EG to Ethel Mannin, 9 May 1938, X, EG Archive, IISH.

93. EG to Harry Kelly, 28 April 1938, EG Papers, NYPL.

94. EG to Rudolf Rocker, 5 April 1938, f. 107, Rocker Archive, IISH.

95. EG to Stella Ballantine, 19 January 1938, XXVII-C, EG Archive, IISH.

96. See Peirats, *Emma Goldman*, pp. 286–87; also *Anarchists,* pp. 295–301; also *Anarquistas en la Revolución Española* (Toulouse: Ediciones CNT, 1953), vol. 3, p. 303.

97. See, for example, EG to Mariano Vázquez, 15 May 1938, XXVIII-B, EG Archive, IISH; EG to Helmut Rüdiger, 2 June 1938, XXVIII-A, EG Archive, IISH. Also José Peirats to author, 12 August 1986.

98. EG to Ethel Mannin, 4 January 1938, XI, EG Archive, IISH.

99. I have found no evidence to support Robert Kern's claim that the CNT withdrew her credential. See "Anarchist Principles and Spanish Reality: Emma Goldman as a Participant in the Civil War 1936–39," *Journal of Contemporary History* 11, no. 293 (July 1976): 247.

100. See Preston, *The Spanish Civil War,* p. 149.

101. Diego Abad de Santillán to EG, 14 March 1939, f. 107, Rocker Archive, IISH.

102. EG to Vázquez, 16 February 1939, XXVII-E, #20411, EG Archive, IISH.

103. Mariano Vázquez to EG, 21 February 1939, f. 107, Rocker Archive, IISH.

104. Mariano Vázquez to EG, 5 March 1939, f. 107, Rocker Archive, IISH.

105. EG to Mariano Vázquez, 27 February 1939, f. 107, Rocker Archive, IISH.

106. See David J. Valaik, "Catholics, Neutrality, and the Spanish Embargo, 1937–1939," *Journal of American History,* 54, no. 1 (1967), pp. 73–85; Little, *Malevolent Neutrality,* pp. 246 ff, 265; also Little, "Red Scare, 1936: Anti-Bolshevism and the Origins of British Non-Intervention in the Spanish Civil War," *Journal of Contemporary History,* 23, no. 2 (April 1988): 291–312.

107. Ethel Mannin to EG, 22 November 1938, X, EG Archive, IISH.

108. Orwell, *Homage to Catalonia and Looking Back on the Spanish War,* pp. 234, 240.

109. EG to Roger Baldwin, 30 November 1936, EG Papers, NYPL; EG to Milly Rocker, 24 April 1939, f. 107, Rocker Archive, IISH.

110. See Nico Berti, "Anarchism: Towards an Historical Balance Sheet," *Volontá* 37, n. 3 (1984).

111. EG to Roger Baldwin, 30 November 1936, EG to Rudolf Rocker, August 26, 1936, quoted in Porter, *VOF,* pp. 57, 56.

112. EG to Maximilian Olay, 18 November 1939, courtesy of Federico Arcos.

113. Mariano Vázquez to EG, 12 June 1939, EG Archive, IISH; copy in Ben Reitman Papers, II, file 130, University of Illinois, Chicago.

114. EG to Vero Richards, 29 August 1939, courtesy of Heiner Becker.

115. See EG to Wim. Jong, 10 February 1937, EG Papers, NYPL. Goldman wrote that going to Spain was "like coming home after a lifetime of pilgrimage from land to land."

10 Last Exile

1. EG to Rudolf Rocker, 31 March 1939, f. 107, Rocker Archive, IISH.

2. Goldman to "Liza," 29 April 1939, EG Papers, NYPL.

3. Emma to Liza, 29 April 1939, EG Papers, NYPL.

4. EG to Rockers, 27 June 1937, f. 107, Rocker Archive, IISH.

5. Goldman wrote to Wim. Jong, (10 February 1937, EG Papers, NYPL): "I have always maintained that armed counter-revolutionary attack cannot be met in any other way except by an armed revolutionary defence." Passive resistance in Spain, she added, would be "suicidal." See also EG to Edward Dahlberg, 19 July 1938, XXVIII-C, EG Archive, IISH.

6. EG to Ethel Mannin, 24 January 1939, XXVI, EG Archive, IISH.

7. EG to Lillian Mendelsohn, 17 February 1939, courtesy William Mendelsohn.

8. EG to Ethel Mannin, 5 March 1939, XXVI, EG Archive, IISH.

9. EG to Herbert Read, 7 October 1939, Tamiment Library, NYU.

10. EG to Pauline Turkel, 6 November 1939, courtesy of Federico Arcos.

11. EG to Herbert Read, 7 October 1939, EG Papers, Tamiment Library.

12. See Dolgoff, *Fragments,* pp. 112–13.

13. Kennedy, "Emma Goldman," p. 33.

14. *Jewish Standard,* 1934, Emma Goldman Scrapbook, NYPL.

15. *Jewish Standard,* 29 June 1934.

16. *St. Louis Star,* 1934, ACLU Papers, Princeton University Library.

17. EG to Mark Mratchny, 30 January 1939, EG Papers, NYPL.

18. "Palestine and Socialist Policy," *Spain and the World,* 26 August 1938.

19. EG to Milly Rocker, 14 October 1939, f. 107, Rocker Archive, IISH.

20. An Italian philosopher who was burned to death in Rome in 1600 for espousing the heretical ideas of Copernicus.

21. Dorothy Rogers to Sadie and C. V. Cook, 24 March 1940, courtesy of Federico Arcos.

22. Kennedy, "Emma Goldman," p. 34; Arturo Bortolotti, interview, Venice, September 1984.

23. Kennedy, "Emma Goldman," p. 34; also Ahrne Thorne, interview, New York, July 1984.

24. Dorothy Rogers to John Cowper Powys, 8 May 1940, courtesy of Federico Arcos.

25. Johanna Clevans to Agnes Inglis, 4 June 1940, Labadie Collection; "Rose" [ex-wife of Ben Reitman] to Ben Reitman, n.d., XVII-C, EG Archive, IISH.

26. *Chicago Daily News,* 17 May 1940.

27. *New York Times,* 15 May 1940.

28. *Brooklyn Eagle,* 17 May 1940.

29. *New York Herald Tribune,* 15 May 1940.

30. *New York Post,* 14 May 1940.

31. Peggy Lamson, interview with Roger Baldwin, p. 140, Roger Baldwin Papers, Princeton University Library.

32. Leonard Abbott to Agnes Inglis, 20 February 1943, Labadie Collection, University of Michigan Library.

33. Ella Antolini [Pomilio] to EG, 27 March 1940, courtesy of Federico Arcos.

34. See especially Rosa Luxemburg, "The Russian Revolution," in *Rosa Luxemburg Speaks,* ed. Mary-Alice Waters (New York: Pathfinder, 1970), pp. 365-95; Elzbieta Ettinger, *Rosa Luxemburg* (Boston: Beacon, 1986), pp. 224-27.

35. William Zuckerman to EG, 27 June 1939, EG Papers, Timiment Library.

36. Alice Wexler, "Emma Goldman on Mary Wollstonecraft," *Feminist Studies,* 7, no. 1 (Spring 1981): 114.

Index

Abrams free-speech case, 86
All-Russian Committee for Aid to the
  Hungry, 53
Alsberg, Henry, 37, 44, 60, 96, 97,
  200; on EG's *My Disillusionment*,
  81–82; and EG's return to United
  States, 160; and Russian political
  prisoners, 102–5
American Civil Liberties Union
  (ACLU), 103, 104, 105, 132, 158
American Federation of Labor (AFL),
  84, 167
American Mercury, 150, 160, 165–66
American Relief Administration, 53
Anarchism/anarchists, 3–4; British,
  93–94; Canadian, 120–21; Ger-
  man, 85–86; Goldman and, 10–11,
  78–79, 97–98, 115–16, 164–68,
  189; Russian, 29–32, 42, 74;
  Spanish, 198–213 passim; U.S.,
  155–56, 163–64
Anarcho-syndicalists, 51–52, 61,
  68, 115
Anarcho-Syndicalist Union (ASU),
  213
Andreyev, Leonid, 23
Andreyeva, Madame (Mrs. Maxim
  Gorki), 19
Anti-Communism: Roger Baldwin on,
  242; in Canada, 122–23; EG's
  contributions to, 2–3, 92–110,
118, 161–62, 212, 242–43; in
  England, 92–110, 217; in Spain,
  230–31; in United States, 3,
  83–84, 217
Anti-Semitism: under Hitler, 237–38;
  Ukrainian, 39, 40–42, 74, 238
Antolini, Ella, 244
Arbeter Fraint (Worker's Friend), 86
Arendt, Hannah, 237
Arshinov, Peter, 31, 165
Arts: EG's *My Disillusionment* on,
  76–77; flourishing of, in Petrograd,
  23–24
Asch, Scholem, 194
Avrich, Paul, 47–48

Baker, Josephine, 158
Bakunin, Michael, 3, 4, 41, 79, 198,
  245; Nettlau's biography of, 115
Balabanoff, Angelica, 27–28, 54, 55,
  119–20; *My Life as a Rebel*, 28
Baldwin, Roger, 94, 97, 101, 132,
  240; on anti-Communism, 242; attacks on, 105–7; and death of EG,
  241; and EG's autobiography, 154,
  155; and EG's return to America,
  158–59, 160, 163; and *Letters from
  Russian Prisons*, 107, 108–9; *Liberty under the Soviets*, 109–10; and
  Russian political prisoners, 103–5
Ballantine, Ian, 25, 69, 225

Ballantine, J. Edward, 225
Ballantine, Stella, 17, 28, 49, 64, 71,
94; her criticism of EG, 119; and
death of EG, 241; depression suffered by, 225–26; and EG's articles
in *New York World,* 65; and EG's
cerebral hemorrhage, 240; EG's
correspondence with, 18, 24–46,
35, 36, 40, 41, 43, 44–45, 49, 52,
53–54, 55, 60, 174, 197, 201, 209,
222; eye ailment of, 85; and Spanish civil war, 216, 222; visits to EG
in Germany of, 69, 85
Barnes, Djuna, 133
Baron, Fanya, 54
Barr, Ralph, 225
Barry, Griffin, 20, 28
Barthes, Roland, 137
Bass, Leon, 127. *See also* Malmed,
Leon
Beals, Carleton, 108
Beatty, Warren, *Reds,* 1
Berger, Victor, 132
Berkman, Alexander (Sasha): and anarchist exiles in Berlin, 102, 103;
anarchist views of, 164–65, 167,
168, 170, 243; in Archangel, 42;
his assassination attempt on Frick,
11, 150, 151; *The Bolshevik Myth,*
87, 182; and Arturo Bortolotti,
238; his correspondence with EG,
91, 94–95, 111, 112, 113, 115,
120–24, 159, 161–62, 166, 171–
72, 174, 175, 182–95 passim;
his correspondence with Eleanor
Fitzgerald, 26, 34–35; death of,
193–94, 196, 197, 209, 220, 244;
*Deportation: Its Meaning and Men-
ace* (with EG), 15–16; deportation
of, from America, 9, 12–13, 15–
18; deportation of, from France,
140; despondency of, 158; deterio-

rating health of, 188–93; diary of,
60, 71, 87, 134, 135; his editing of
Mother Earth, 12, 116; and EG's
articles in *New York World,* 63, 64;
and EG's autobiography, 132–33,
134–35, 138, 151–52, 153, 154;
and EG's move to England, 91; and
EG's relationship with Frank Heiner,
173, 175, 176; entry of, into Soviet
Russia, 19–20; in Germany, 68,
69, 89; and Marguerite Harrison,
33–34, 83; imprisonment of, 11,
12; his interview with Lenin, 27;
and Kronstadt conflict, 46–49; in
Latvia, 56, 58–60; and *Letters from
Russian Prisons,* 107; in Moscow,
50, 54; Most's repudiation of, 150–
51; papers of, organized by EG,
228; in Petrograd, 21, 26, 28–29,
31–32, 33, 42, 43, 45–50; and
Red Trade Union International, 51–
52; his relationship with Emmy
Eckstein, 87–88, 112, 181–82; his
relationship with EG, 4, 11, 12, 44,
87, 88, 91, 119, 151–52, 172,
194–95; in Sweden, 61, 67; in the
Ukraine, 37–38, 40, 42; *What Is
Communist Anarchism?* (later *Now
and After*), 79, 132, 164–65, 182;
his work with Petrograd Museum of
the Revolution, 36–43, 50, 54, 55;
his writings about Russia, 62, 72;
younger women of, 12, 70, 113,
151
Berneri, Camillo, 204, 213, 215
Berneri, Marie-Louise, 213
Bernstein, Ethel, 14, 16–17
Bernstein, Rose, 121
Bialik, Hayyim Nahman, 40
Birth control movement, 113, 153
Black Guards, 30, 74
Blackwell's Island Penitentiary, 11

Bland, Salem, 120, 241
Blok, Alexander, 21
Bloor, Ella Reeves, 52
Blum, Leon, 204
Boni, Albert, 71
Bortolotti, Arturo, 238–40
Boyle, Kay, 194, 197
Brady, Edward, his relationship with
EG, 145, 147, 149
Brailsford, H. N., 107
Brainard, Clinton, 71–72
Branting, Karl, 67
Breshkovskaya, Catherine, 63, 142
Brest-Litovsk, Treaty of, 21–22,
29, 39
Brewster, Dorothy, 83
British Committee for the Defense of
Political Prisoners in Russia, 100
British Museum, 89, 114
British Trade Union Delegation (Mis-
sion), 28, 95, 100; report of,
100–102, 111
Brockway, Fenner, 116, 214, 215; In-
side the Left, 116–17
Brooklyn Eagle, 242
Bruno, Giordano, 239
Buford, 73; sailing of, 14–19
Bureau of Investigation, 13, 60, 123

Call, 64, 69, 83
Caminetti, Anthony, 13
Carpenter, Edward, 94
Chaliapin, Feodor, 23
Chamberlain, Neville, 225
Cheka (secret police), 23, 29, 33, 48,
66, 109; executions by, 24; "Red
Terror" of, 65, siege of Black
Guards by, 30; and strikes, 45–46.
See also GPU
Cherny, Lev, 54
Chicago Tribune, 19, 35, 84, 133
Citizenship Act (1922), 88

Clayton, John, 19, 20, 33, 35–36
Cleyre, Voltairine de, 171, 241
CNT-FAI, and Spanish civil war,
204–32 passim
CNT-FAI Information Bulletin, 205
CNT-FAI London Committee, 210
Cohen, Stephen, 81, 168–69
Cohn, Michael, 72, 193, 194
Coleman, Emily Holmes (Demi),
133–34, 135; Shutter of Snow, 133
Coleman, Loyd Ring, 133
Colton, James, 120
Commins, Saxe, 133, 225; and EG's
autobiography, 135, 138, 140–41,
154
Committee to Aid Homeless Spanish
Women and Children, 210
Communism. See Anti-Communism
Communist party, 30; American,
64–65, 83, 162; British, 84,
92–93, 98; conflicts between Rus-
sians and Ukrainians in, 38; Ger-
man, 68; Spanish, 207–209,
214–15, 219; Zhenotdel of, 26, 76
Confederación Nacional del Trabajo
(CNT), 198, 199, 201, 202, 204.
See also CNT-FAI
Congress of Industrial Organizations
(CIO), 118
Conn, Peter, 147
Coolidge, Calvin, 105, 123
Crouch, Mabel Carver, 158
Cultura Proletaria, 164
Czolgosz, Leon, 152

Daily Express, 99
Daily Forward, 83
Daily Worker, 159–60, 217
Dalton, Roque, 196
Day, Dorothy, 143, 144
Debs, Eugene, 108, 132
Debs, Theodore, 132

Denikin, A. I., 39
Dennett, Mary Ware, 158
Der Syndikalist, 62, 68
Desser, Millie, 121–22, 239
Dewey, John, 158, 160, 169, 240
Die Freiheit, 10
Dies Committee, 118
Doctorow, E. L., Ragtime, 1
Dollfuss, Engelbert, 168
Dostoyevsky, Fyodor, Crime and Pun-
    ishment, 145
Doubleday and Page, 71–72
Dreadnaught, 98
Dreiser, Theodore, 132
Duncan, Isadora, 138
Durruti, Buenaventura, 205

Eckstein, Emmy, 112, 171; her corre-
    spondence with EG, 174, 181–82,
    187–88; death, 197; and death of
    Berkman, 193–94, 196; health
    problems of, 184, 189–90, 191,
    192; her relationship with Berkman,
    87–88; her relationship with EG,
    183–88, 192, 196–97
Ehrenburg, Ilya, 87
Einstein, Albert, 108, 140
Ellis, Havelock, 94, 99, 110, 225
Ellis Island, 9, 12–14, 15–16
Emergency Conference on Spain, 225
Emerson, Ralph Waldo, 16

Family Code (1918), 22, 76
Federación Anarquista Ibérica (FAI),
    198, 199, 202. See also CNT-FAI
Federal Writers' Project, 37, 160
First International, 3
Fischer, Louis, 216
Fitzgerald, Eleanor (Fitzi), 42, 45, 69,
    112–13, 117; Berkman's letters to,
    26, 34–35; her criticism of EG,
    119; EG's letters to, 13, 44

Flechine, Senya, 86–87, 107, 198,
    218
Flynn, William J., 13
Forward, 242
Franco, Francisco, 236; and Spanish
    civil war, 204, 207, 208, 210, 215,
    226–27, 228
Frank, Waldo, 154
Frauenbund, 89
Fraye Arbeter Stimme, 207
Freedom, 62, 93–94, 116, 210
Freedom Press, 213
Freeman, 64
Freie Arbeiter Union Deutschlands
    (FAUD), 68, 86, 89
Freiheit, 150
Frick, Henry Clay, 11, 150
Friends of Emma Goldman Commit-
    tee, 240–41

Gannett, Lewis, 107
General Strike (1926), 111, 213
Gilman, Charlotte Perkins, 161
Goldman, Emma: in America, 127,
    159–63, 171, 181; anarchist views
    of, 4, 164–70; her anger toward
    Russia, 57–58; anti-Soviet cam-
    paign of, 92, 94–110 passim,
    122–23, 161–62, 212; antiwar
    position of, 236–37; in Archangel,
    42–43; articles for American maga-
    zines requested of, 160, 165–66;
    and Berkman's deteriorating health,
    188–93; and Arturo Bortolotti,
    238–40; in Canada, 110, 120–28,
    132, 158–59, 163, 171, 174, 175,
    234–41; and John Clayton, 35–
    36; death of, 241; and death of
    Berkman, 193–94, 196, 197–98,
    209, 220, 244; death of her half-
    sister, 35; death of her mother, 85;
    deportation of, 9, 10, 12–18, 44;

depressions suffered by, 44–45, 57, 111–13, 157–58, 197–98, 223; and Emmy Eckstein, 181–88, 192, 196–97; in England, 91, 92–102, 110–20, 187, 190–91, 210–19, 227, 228; entry of, into Soviet Russia, 19–20; and famine (1921), 53–54, 77–78; in France, 91, 131–36, 157–58, 175–76, 183–87, 192, 220–22; friendships of, 116–20; in Germany, 67–71, 85–90; and Frank Harris, 89–91; and Marguerite Harrison, 33–34, 83; image of, 1–5; on Jews under Hitler, 237–38; and Kronstadt conflict, 46–49, 77; and Kropotkin, 10, 32–33; in Latvia, 56, 58–60; lecture tours of, 10, 114–15, 157, 158, 160–61, 162–63, 190–91, 235; legacy of, 241–45; marriages of, 10, 12, 59, 120; on modern woman, 113–14, 115; in Moscow, 50–55; in the Netherlands, 228; in Petrograd, 21, 23–36, 42, 43–50; prison terms served by, 11, 12, 44, 124, 131, 244; and Red Trade Union International, 51–53; her relationship with Alexander Berkman, 4, 11, 12, 44, 87, 88, 91, 119, 151–52, 172, 194–95; her relationship with Edward Brady, 145, 147, 149; her relationship with Frank Heiner, 170–78, 181; her relationship with Leon Malmed, 124–28, 146, 172; her relationship with Ben L. Reitman, 11–12, 69, 119, 127, 145, 146, 147–49, 153, 155, 171, 172; her relationship with Arthur Swenson, 61–62, 69–70, 127, 146, 172; sexual radicalism of, 4, 10, 146–47, 156; and Agnes Smedley, 53; in Spain, 201, 204–10, 219–20, 226–27; and Spanish civil war, 198, 200–233; strokes suffered by, 240–41; in Sweden, 61–62, 64, 67; in the Ukraine, 37–42, 74, 75; U.S. surveillance of, 58–59, 123; her wish to return to United States, 59; her work with Petrograd Museum of the Revolution, 36–43, 50, 54, 55, 77

Goldman, Emma, works of:
—*Anarchism and Other Essays*, 11, 170
—articles of, in *New York World*, 65–67, 69, 72, 75, 78
—*Deportation: Its Meaning and Menace* (with A. Berkman), 15–16
—*Living My Life* (autobiography), 11, 36, 38, 70, 78, 92, 127, 131–33, 160; Emily Coleman's assistance with, 133–34, 135; discussion of, 141–53, negotiations with Alfred Knopf over, 138–41, 157; reactions to, 153–56; writing of, 134–38
—*Mother Earth* (monthly magazine), 11, 12, 52, 86, 115, 116, 145
—*My Disillusionment in Russia*, 40, 71–72, 73–82, 84–85, 99–100, 144
—*My Further Disillusionment in Russia*, 72
—*The Social Significance of the Modern Drama*, 11, 27, 114–15
—"The Tragedy of Woman's Emancipation," 153

Goldman, Lena (sister), 121
Goldman, Moishe (Morris, brother), 114, 121
Gompers, Samuel, 84
Gorki, Maxim, 19, 23, 27
GPU, 66, 101, 102, 106, 109
Great Depression, 127, 141, 157
Gudell, Martin, 204, 227–28, 229, 241

Guerra di Classe, 204
Guggenheim, Peggy, 131, 133

Harding, Warren, 83
Harper and Brothers, 71
Harpers, 160, 165
Harris, Frank, 87, 89–91, 117; *Contemporary Portraits,* 90; *My Life and Loves,* 90, 146
Harris, Nellie, 117
Harrison, Marguerite, 33, 83; *Marooned in Moscow,* 33–34
Haywood, Big Bill, 52
Heiner, Frank L., 184, 188; his relationship with EG, 170–78, 181
Heiner, Mary, 172, 175, 177
Herbst, Josephine, 216
Herrera, Pedro, 223, 227, 229
Hitler, Adolf, 41, 162, 166, 168, 199, 242; appointment of, as chancellor, 157; EG's lecture on, 158; EG on, 235–37; growing power of, 207; occupation of Austria and Czechoslovakia by, 225; occupation of Belgium by, 244
Hobsbawn, Eric, 2
Holmes, John Haynes, 154, 158, 160, 169, 240, 241
Homestead Steel strike (1892), 11
Hoover, J. Edgar, 14, 15, 34, 160
Housman, Laurence, 225
Huebsch, B. W., 158, 235, 240

Ibsen, Henrik, 25, 120
Illustrated London News, 99
Immigration Act (1918), 9, 12
Independent Labour party (British, ILP), 93, 116, 201, 211, 216, 224, 238
Industrial Workers of the World (IWW, Wobblies), 10, 52, 167
Inglis, Agnes, 56, 153, 155

International Anarchist Aid Federation, 64
International Committee for Political Prisoners (ICPP), 37, 105, 107, 110, 140
International Congress of Communist Women, 52–53
International Institute for Social History, 228
International Ladies Garment Workers' Union, 166, 167
International Workingmen's Association (IWMA). *See* Syndicalist International
Ionovna, Zlata Lilina, 27, 28

Jefferson, Thomas, 16
Jensen, Albert, 60
Jewish Anarchist Federation, 196
Jews: in Britain, 93; in Canada, 120; Goldman and, 74, 120; in Russia, 39–42, 74
Journeys from Berlin/1971 (film), 1–2
Joyce, James, 134; *Portrait of the Artist,* 1
Justice Department, 13, 15, 34, 58, 85

Kamerny Theater, 77
Kaminski, H. E., *Ceux de Barcelone,* 206
Kaufman, George S., 240
Keel, Thomas, 94
Keller, Helen, 45
Kelly, Harry, 64
Kersner, Jacob, 10, 12, 59
Kirchwey, Freda, 154, 240
Knopf, Alfred, 138–41, 157, 158, 160
Kodolfsky, Liza, 210
Kolchak, A. V., 17
Kollontai, Alexandra, 26–27, 28, 76,

244; *The Social Basis of the Woman Question,* 27; "The Workers' Opposition," 66
Korolenko, Vladimir, 40
Kronstadt tragedy, 46–49, 52, 77
Kropotkin, Peter, 4, 50, 72, 78–79, 115, 245; his critique of Bolsheviks, 66; death of, 32–33; EG's article on, 65; EG's eulogy of, 160; EG's meetings with, 32; *Ethics,* 32; his influence on EG, 10; museum dedicated to, 31; his opposition to Germany in World War I, 235
Kropotkin, Sophie, 32
Kulturliga, 41

Labor, Department of, 9, 58, 60, 159, 160
Labour party (British), 84, 90, 92–93, 94, 210–11, 216
Laddon, Esther, 235
Lansbury, George, 32, 90
Largo Caballero, Francisco, 208, 215
Laski, Harold, 94–95, 96, 97, 101, 107
Left Socialist Revolutionaries, 23, 30, 46, 53, 108; outlawing of, 50, 65
Lehning, Arthur, 204, 205
Lenin, Nikolai, 27, 28, 32, 50, 169; EG's article on, 217; *State and Revolution,* 29; on state capitalism, 50, 65
Leninism, 66, 169
LeSueur, Meridel, 2
Letters from Russian Prisons, 96, 105, 106, 107–9, 123
Leval, Gaston, 51–52, 72
Levine, Isaac Don, 107, 108, 123
Lewin, Moshe, 22
Lewis, Sinclair, 158
Liberator, 36, 53
Libertarian Youth, 226

Ligue du Droits de l'Homme, 140
Lincoln, Abraham, 16
Lipkin, Dora, 14, 16–17
Lippman, Walter, 2, 62–63
Little, Douglas, 214
Liveright, Horace, 132, 138, 154
London Daily Herald, 28, 32, 37, 90, 216, 217
London School of Economics, 94
Lunacharsky, Anatoly, 23, 27, 28
Luxemburg, Rosa, 9, 66, 243, 244
Lyons, Eugene, 169

McKinley, William, 11
Makhno, Galina, 42
Makhno, Nestor, 31, 39, 42, 74, 108, 165
Malatesta, Errico, 64, 72
Malmed, Bertha, 121
Malmed, Leon, 88, 120; his relationship with EG, 124–28, 146, 172
Malmed, Mrs. Leon, 125–26
Manchester Guardian, 216
Mann, Thomas, 108, 140
Mannin, Ethel, 214, 219, 224, 231, 238; her friendship with EG, 111, 116; pacifism of, 229, 235–36; and Solidaridad Internacional Anti-Fascista, 225, 229, 234, 236
Marx, Karl, 3, 79, 169
Marxism, 3–4, 66, 78, 169–70, 243, 244
May Days, 2, 215–18, 224
Medvedev, Roy, 169
Meir, Golda, 143, 144
Meltzer, Albert, 224
Mencken, H. L., 81, 132, 153
Mendelsohn, Lillian, 236
Mensheviks, 46, 50
Meyerhold, Vsevolod, 23, 77
Millay, Edna St. Vincent, 131, 132
Minor, Robert, 52

Mirbach, W. von, 108
Missouri State Penitentiary, 11, 44, 124, 131, 244
Montseny, Frederica, 199, 207, 225, 227
Moscow Art Theater, 23, 77, 182
Most, Johann, 10, 86, 137, 150–51
Mother Earth, 11, 52, 86, 115, 145; Berkman's editing of, 12, 116
Mratchny, Mark, 105, 207
Mujeres Libres, 203
Mujeres Libres, 203
Mussolini, Benito, 162, 166, 168, 199, 236, 237

Nabat Confederation, 42
Narodniks, 29, 30
Nation, 36, 64, 65, 69, 81; and Henry Alsberg, 37, 96; on Bolshevism, 83, 102–3; on civil liberties in Russia, 106; EG's articles in, 165; on EG's autobiography, 154; and EG's return to U.S., 160, 163; and Spanish civil war, 216, 217
Nazism, 42, 236
Negrín, Juan, 215, 216, 223, 229
Nettlau, Max, 64, 71, 115–16, 200, 218; his biography of Bakunin, 115; and EG's autobiography, 136; EG's correspondence with, 69, 73, 79, 110, 115
New Deal, 162
New Economic Policy (NEP), 51, 67, 77, 80–81, 99, 100; introduction of, 49–50
New English Weekly, 217
New Leader, 211, 217
New Republic, 64, 65, 81, 107, 118, 154
News Chronicle, 217
New Statesman and Nation, 210, 217
New York American, 14

New Yorker, 154
New York Evening Post, 159
New York Herald Tribune, 84, 154, 159, 242
New York Post, 81, 242
New York Sun, 159
New York Times, 36, 62, 81, 84, 106, 242; on Bolshevism, 83, 85; on EG's anti-Soviet campaign, 99, 100; on EG's autobiography, 154; and EG's return to United States, 159; on Spanish civil war, 217, 220
New York World, 37, 63, 64, 71; EG's articles on Russia in, 65–67, 69, 72, 75, 78
New York World-Telegram, 159
Nin, Andreu, 215
Ninth Party Congress, 33
No-Conscription League, 12
Non-Intervention Committee, 204

Oak, Liston, 217
Older, Fremont, 149
O'Neill, Eugene, *Lazarus Laughed*, 182
Orwell, George, 216, 217, 225; *Homage to Catalonia*, 202, 231; "Looking Back on the Spanish War," 231
Owen, W. C., 94

Pankhurst, Sylvia, 98
Parsons, Albert, 155, 171
Parsons, Lucy, 155
Pearson's, 90
Perkins, Frances, 158
Perovskaya, Sophia, 142
Pesotta, Rose, 113, 166, 224, 241
Petlura, S., 31, 39
Petrograd Museum of the Revolution, 36–37, 40, 50, 54, 55, 77
Peukhert, Joseph, 150

Political Prisoners' Relief Committee, 182

Pond, James, 161, 162–63

Popova, Lyubov, 23

Post Office Department, 60

POUM, and Spanish civil war, 202, 208, 211, 215, 216, 219, 227

Powys, John Cowper, 200, 225

Pravda, 101, 102

Preston, Paul, 208

Proletkult, 24, 77

PSUC, 202

Pulitzer, Joseph, 63

Rainer, Yvonne, *Journeys from Berlin/1971*, 1–2

Rapallo, Treaty of (1922), 68

Read, Herbert, 117, 214, 236

Red Army, 30, 31, 33, 39

Redbook, 160

Reds (film), 1

Red Scare, 1, 44, 65, 83, 93, 243

Red Trade Union International (Profintern), 48, 51–53

Reitman, Ben L., 18, 88, 121, 124, 152; anti-Semitic remarks of, 41; and death of EG, 241; EG's correspondence with, 131–32, 147–48, 235; infidelities of, 11, 148, 172, 173; his relationship with EG, 11–12, 69, 119, 127, 145, 146, 147–49, 153, 155, 171, 172; *The Second Oldest Profession*, 148

Reynolds, Reginald, 238

Rhonnda, Lady, 111

Richards Vernon, 213–14

Rivera, Primo de, 199

Road to Freedom, 131

Robeson, Essie, 117

Robeson, Paul, 117

Robins, Raymond, 30

Rocker, Fermin, 89, 117, 136

Rocker, Millie Witcop, 68, 86, 89, 113, 136, 196; and Spanish civil war, 231

Rocker, Rudolf, 59, 64, 68, 72, 89, 169; *The Bankruptcy of State Communism*, 51; and death of Berkman, 196; and death of EG, 241; and EG's autobiography, 136; EG's friendship with, 85–86; and EG's relationship with Emmy Eckstein, 184; *Nationalism and Culture*, 188; and Spanish civil war, 200, 207, 220, 222, 225

Rodchenko, Alexander, 23

Rogers, Dorothy, 234, 240, 241

Rolland, Romain, 140

Roosevelt, Eleanor, 143, 144

Roosevelt, Franklin D., 158, 160, 162, 204, 210

Ross, Arthur, 161; and EG's autobiography, 132, 135, 136, 138–39, 141

Rüdiger, Helmut, 204

Russell, Bertrand, 61, 94, 95–97, 103, 140; *Autobiography*, 94; and *Letters from Russian Prisons*, 96, 107; *The Practice and Theory of Bolshevism*, 96

Russell, Dora, 113

Russian Friends of American Freedom, 28

Sacco, Nicola, 122, 126, 238

San Francisco Bulletin, 149

Santillán, Diego Abad de, 204, 229

Saornil, Lucía Sánchez, 229

Sartre, Jean-Paul, 3

Saturday Review, 90, 154

Saxonia, 15

Schickele, René, 140

Scott, Evelyn, 118–19, 122, 158; *Escapade*, 118

Selective Service Act (1917), 12

Serge, Victor, 46, 99; *Memoirs of a Revolutionary,* 43, 47, 52
Servicio de Investigación Militar (SIM), 219
Shakol, Alexandra, 37
Shapiro, Alexander, 54, 218; and EG's articles in *New York World,* 63, 64; in Germany, 68; in Latvia, 56, 58–61; in Sweden, 61, 67
Shatov, William, 29, 32
Shaw, Bernard, 90
Shop Assistants Union, 100
Siegal, Jacob, 242
Sinclair, Upton, 108
Slocombe, George, 90
Smedley, Agnes, 53, 116
Smith, Sidonie, 138
Socialist Second International, 51, 98, 221
Solidaridad Internacional Anti-Fascista (SIA), 225, 229, 234, 236, 239
Souchy, Augustine, 52, 166, 201, 204, 205
Spacks, Patricia Meyer, "Selves in Hiding," 143–44
Spain and the World, 213–14, 217, 222
Spanish Exhibition Committee, 215–16
Spanish Libertarian Movement, 226, 232
Spanish Refugee Rescue Fund, Emma Goldman, 235, 239
Spanish Revolution, 217
Spectator, 84
Spiridonova, Maria, 53, 65, 108
Springfield Republican, 81
Stalin, Joseph, 80, 166, 170, 207–8, 236; characterization of era of, 168–69; concentration camps of, 209; EG's article on, 217; political terror of, 169; and Spanish civil war, 208, 219, 223, 226, 231
Stalinism, 81, 99, 164, 169–70, 244
Stallings, Lawrence, 154
Stanislavsky, Konstantin, 23, 77
State Department, U.S., 34, 35, 58, 60, 85, 123
Steimer, Mollie, 86–87, 107, 158, 198, 218
Stein, Gertrude, 163
Stein, Modest, 188–89, 196
Strikes, Soviet 45–46
Svensson, Artur (Arthur Swenson), his relationship with EG, 61–62, 69–70, 127, 146, 172
Swope, Clifton, 71
Syndicalist International (International Workingmen's Association, IWMA), 88, 212, 218, 220–22, 223, 229

Tairov, A., 77
Tatlin, Vladimir, 23
Tenth Party Congress, 50
Third International (Comintern), 25, 27, 28, 51, 221
Thomas, Norman, 240, 241
Thoreau, Henry David, 16
Thorne, Ahrne, 237, 240
Time and Tide, 99, 111, 217
Times (London), 84, 99, 100, 217
Times Literary Supplement (London), 81
Toronto General Hospital, 240
Toronto Star, 120
Torres, Henri, 140
Trade Union Congress, 93, 100, 210–11, 216
Transition, 133
Tresca, Carlo, 170, 241
Trotsky, Leon, 33, 169, 227, 244
Turner, John, 100, 101, 111

Unión General de Trabajadores (UGT), 199, 202
Union of Russian Workers, 9
United States Military Intelligence, 33

Vanguard, 164
Van Valkenburg, W. S., 131
Vanzetti, Bartolomeo, 122, 126, 238
Vázquez, Mariano, 220, 222, 223, 226–27, 229–30; death of, 235; his tribute to EG, 232
Viking Press, 235
Voline (pen name of V. M. Eikhenbaum), 72, 218
Vorse, Mary Heaton, 52

Walling, Anna Strunsky, 153
War Communism, 22–23, 45, 66, 75, 77, 80
Ward, Harry, 103, 104, 105, 106
War Measures Act, 238
Webb, Beatice, 84
Webb, Sidney, 84
Wedgwood, Josiah, 94, 100
Weinberger, Harry, 59, 72, 88
Wells, H. G., 94
West, Rebecca, 94, 99–100, 108, 111, 116, 225

Westminster Gazette, 99
White Guards, 46
Wilde, Oscar, 90
Wilkinson, Ellen, 215
Wilson, Woodrow, 16
Witcop, Millie. *See* Rocker, Millie Witcop
Witcop, Rose, 113
Wolfe, Bertram, 217
Wollstonccraft, Mary, 245
Wood, Leonard, 10
Workers' Opposition, 50, 62, 67, 98
Workmen's Circle, 120, 160
World War I, 9, 12, 21–22, 153, 235
World War II, 235–38, 244
Wrangel, P. N., 31, 33

Young, Howard, 131
Yudenich, N. N., 21, 42

Zangwill, Israel, 94
Zapata, Emiliano, 31
Zassulich, Vera, 142
Zinoviev, G. E., 25, 27, 46–47
Zinoviev letter, 93
Zionism, 41
Zorin, S., 19, 21, 25–26, 28